CHEMICAL WARFARE

CHEMICAL WARFARE

Edward M. Spiers

University of Illinois Press
Urbana and Chicago

Published in the United States of America by
University of Illinois Press, Urbana and Chicago
Published simultaneously in Great Britain by
The Macmillan Press, Ltd
Manufactured in Hong Kong

Library of Congress Cataloging in Publication Data
Spiers, Edward M.
   Chemical warfare.

   Bibliography: p.
   1. Chemical warfare.   2. Disarmament.   3. Deterrence
(Strategy)   I. Title.
UG447.S64   1985   358'.34   85–14157
ISBN 0–252–01273–9
ISBN 0–333–34659–9 (UK edition, Macmillan)

Contents

Preface

In writing this book I have sought to focus upon the two approaches of disarmament and deterrence as means by which a recurrence of chemical warfare could be avoided. I shall try to place the contemporary debate on these issues within a broad historical and strategic context, and shall hope, thereby, to re-examine the tactical utility of poison gas, the chequered history of attempts to control its usage, and the problems which beset NATO in the maintenance of a credible deterrent. In choosing this theme I have not assumed that deterrence and disarmament are contradictory policies. On the contrary, I believe that progress towards disarmament will depend largely upon the confidence which states have in their own security, and in the likelihood of that security enduring, while any attempts to bolster the chemical deterrent of a democratic state, or an alliance of democracies, will require public confidence that disarmament remains a diplomatic priority. Arguably the link could be even stronger, that is, if opposing deterrents were perceived by either side as credible, this could reduce the expected utility of poison gas and serve as an incentive to abolishing the development, production, stockpiling and transfer of chemical weapons. I would argue, too, that this topic now warrants serious examination since the use of mustard gas and tabun, a nerve gas, has been confirmed in the Gulf War and has exposed both the deficiencies of the Geneva Protocol and the risks of an inadequate deterrent.

I should like to acknowledge my indebtedness to the many individuals and institutions who have assisted me in my research. Professor John Erickson of Edinburgh University proffered invaluable guidance and support when I began my endeavours. Julian Perry Robinson of the Science Policy Research Unit, Sussex University, replied to my numerous inquiries with kindness and consideration, never failing to supply the requisite materials or to answer specific questions. Professor David Dilks of Leeds University and Professor Geoffrey Best always responded favourably whenever I sought their support for my grant applications. I am also especially grateful for the advice and guidance of Dr F. R. Bridge, Leeds University; Gary B. Crocker, United States Mission, Geneva; Stuart J. D. Schwartzstein, National Strategy Information Center; Mrs Joan Link, Foreign and Commonwealth Office; J. François Gordon, UK Delegation to the Conference on Disarmament; and Mark C. Storella, the Institute for Foreign Policy Analysis. I am particularly indebted to Colonel James E. Leonard, Bureau of Politico-Military Affairs, Department of State, who was immensely generous in his support of my research and who kindly agreed to read my manuscript. Any remaining blemishes, mistakes, and errors of omission or commission are entirely my own responsibility.

In conducting my research I received several very useful briefings from Ms Blair Murray, Department of State; General Gerald G. Watson; General Horace Russell; Joseph D. Douglass; Brad Roberts; Ivo Spalatin, House Foreign Affairs Committee; Donald Campbell, House Armed Services Committee; Robert Bell, Senate Foreign Relations Committee; Doug Graham, Senate Armed Services Committee; Captain James Bush; Richard K. Betts; Sohrab Kheradi, UN Center for Disarmament; Michael Deane, Ilana Kass and Andrew G. Roth, Advanced International Studies Institute; and Professor Matthew Meselson. I also profited from several visits to the Chemical Defence Establishment, Porton Down, for which I am extremely grateful to the present Director, Dr G. S. Pearson, his predecessor, Dr R. G. H. Watson and the various members of staff who were so generous with their time and advice. I must express my gratitude, too, to Colonel D. G. McCord for permitting me to visit the Defence (NBC) Centre, Winterbourne Gunner, where Wing Commander G. J. Wilson and his staff answered my many and various questions.

I am grateful to many other people who assisted me with my research inquiries or visits, namely Peter Jenner and Hector Verykios, NATO headquarters, Brussels; W. A. Morrison, Counsellor and Military Adviser, Permanent Mission of Canada to the United Nations; Major C. Trull; Robert A. Mosher, Office of the Assistant Secretary of Defense; Miss Anthea Buckeridge, Embassy of the United States; Joyce L. Sulahian and Ingrid Lehmann, United Nations Department for Disarmament Affairs; and Mary Derr, Bureau of Educational and Cultural Affairs. I would also like to thank several librarians and archivists for their assistance and co-operation, especially Mr Philip Reed, Deputy to the Keeper, Department of Documents, the Imperial War Museum; Mr C. A. Potts, Ministry of Defence Library; Mr Sven Welander, Chief, League of Nations

Archive and Historical Collections Unit; Miss Marion M. Stewart, Churchill College, Cambridge; and the staffs of the Library of Congress, Public Record Office, National Library of Scotland and the inter-library loan services of Leeds University.

I am obliged to several individuals and institutions for access to unpublished manuscripts of which they own the copyright: Earl Haig of Bemersyde, the Liddell Hart Centre for Military Archives, King's College, University of London, Dr J. E. Hodgkin, Mr E. Douglas Kingsley, the Trustees of the Imperial War Museum for access to the papers of Field Marshal Sir John French, and the Controller of Her Majesty's Stationery Office for permission to refer to Crown Copyright records in the Public Record Office.

I am profoundly indebted to the British Academy for a grant from the Small Grants Research Fund in the Humanities and to the United States Information Service for another grant to facilitate my research.

I am particularly grateful to Mrs Elizabeth Seaward for her patience and diligence in typing and retyping the drafts of this manuscript. I am also indebted to Fiona, my wife, for enduring the preparation of this work and for her scholarly advice and criticism of the final text.

EDWARD M. SPIERS

1 Introduction

Chemical weapons still arouse a remarkable degree of ire and passion. This reaction is understandable; it reflects the stigma with which these weapons are viewed, the frustration aroused by the failure to ban them, and the difficulty of assessing their current importance. Although chemical weapons have occasionally been promoted as intrinsically no more heinous than conventional weapons,[1] they have generally been viewed as particularly odious. Characterised as weapons of mass destruction, they are largely invisible, indiscriminate in their effects, and tend to undermine the body from within. Using chemicals designed for the benefit of man against man, they seem to pervert the true course of science. Such condemnation has been enshrined in the Geneva Protocol of 1925, which many now interpret as part of customary international law and as thereby proscribing the first use of poison gas or germ warfare. Nevertheless, chemical weapons have been used in subsequent wars; more potent weapons have been devised; and large stocks of these munitions are still retained.

Uncertainties beset any assessment of chemical weapons either as instruments of war or as a means of deterrence. In the first place, chemical arsenals are usually shrouded in considerable secrecy. There is little information openly admitted or reliably confirmed about the size and composition of the various stocks. As governments are forced to rely upon intelligence gleaned by national intelligence means, defectors' reports and covert agencies, their estimates of the enemy 'threat' can vary widely. Harold Brown, the former American Secretary of Defense, once admitted that 'there is no decent estimate' of the Soviet chemical inventory.[2] Secondly, whenever suspicions are voiced about the possible use of toxic weapons it is immensely difficult to confirm the allegations. Military operations involving the use of gas are rarely announced or independently observed, and any evidence requires careful scientific scrutiny. Thirdly, such scrutiny is rendered indispensable because allegations of chemical warfare have been a traditional ploy of propagandists. As they can also be used to justify

1

chemical rearmament or retaliation in kind, they require serious assessment.

Theoretically toxic chemicals, which are extremely versatile, may be used to accomplish a wide variety of military missions. Some are lethal while others are merely incapacitating. Some incapacitate or kill; others merely irritate. Some are transient in their effects; others can contaminate areas over periods of hours, days or many weeks. Capable of inflicting casualties over large areas, chemical weapons can envelop formations which had dispersed to avoid nuclear attack or small targets whose precise location is unknown. They are also 'search weapons', able to penetrate shelters, buildings, trenches, and other types of fortification. Clouds of nerve gas, unlike explosives, can surprise an enemy by an off-target attack (i.e. by letting the agent drift downwind). If delivered on-target, salvoes of chemical munitions may build up a cloud over the target in fifteen to thirty seconds. Casualties will accrue, especially if the enemy is not alert, as men seek cover from the fragmentation effects while trying to don their masks, or among men who adjust their masks improperly.[3] Persistent agents, too, may be employed as weapons of area denial, contaminating large tracts of territory, foreclosing avenues of movement and resupply, and containing an enemy within smaller zones which are more easily attacked. Chemicals offer the prospect of killing or incapacitating an enemy without damaging vital economic or military objectives, such as bridges, factories, ports, railways and airfields. Above all, chemical weapons inspire more fear than conventional munitions; they could terrorise civilian populations and demoralise ill-trained or poorly protected combat units.

Chemical and not biological (bacteriological) weapons will comprise the main focus of this study. Although pathogens, as living organisms, are much more potent than chemical agents on a weight-for-weight basis, and can inflict casualties over a much wider area, they have always posed problems of storage and delivery. Dissemination is particularly difficult as the agents are generally highly susceptible to ultraviolet light, temperature, and other environmental factors. Once disseminated, a biological agent could retain its viability (ability to live and multiply) while losing its virulence (ability to produce disease and injury). Its effectiveness could not be easily predicted since the factors which promote or retard the spread of disease are only partially understood. Local standards of public health and sanitation will affect the contagiousness of certain diseases, while an epidemic, once started, could persist unexpectedly or spread in unexpected directions, even proving a hazard to an attacker whose base was close to the target area. Biological agents also require a lengthy incubation period, varying from one to several days, and so are hardly suited to the requirements of a fast-moving battle.[4] But these difficulties may not always persist; recent advances in genetic engineering, by which genes can be split and recombined, could produce highly toxic or disease-producing biological agents which are stable and militarily useful.[5]

The chemicals which could be used militarily are either anti-personnel or anti-plant agents. As this work is primarily concerned with the potential significance of chemical weapons in the European theatre, it will only refer to anti-personnel weapons. Although various agents were used as herbicides and defoliants in the Vietnam War, they would have merely a marginal utility in a major European conflict. The physiological effects of chemical agents, whether lethal, incapacitating or irritating, will provide the basis for their classification. Each class of agents may be subdivided according to their pathological symptoms, persistence, and dosage required to produce incapacitating or lethal effects. To avoid undue complication, the agents will be generally described in the introduction and their properties summarised in the three appendices.

The irritating or harassing agents, often disseminated as smokes, are characterised by their immediate action, non-persistence and effects which are comparatively brief in duration. Only lethal in extremely high concentrations, they produce a wide array of irritating sensations. Some are particularly irritating to the eyes (lachrymators), some provoke fits of sneezing and coughing (sternutators), some cause severe itching or stinging sensations (orticants) and some, if swallowed, will induce bouts of violent vomiting. The main irritants will provoke all these sensations to a greater or lesser extent.[6] CN (Chloroacetophenone) is the classical tear gas. Developed at the end of the First World War, it has been used in military training and as a riot control agent. Adamsite (DM), also developed in 1918, acts more slowly than CN but is more vigorous, causing not merely intense lachrymation and coughing but also severe headaches, nausea, sneezing and vomiting. Even more effective is 2-chlorobenzalmalononitrile (CS), which was developed at Porton Down in the 1950s. Its effects occur almost instantly and, depending on dosage, range from a slight prickling sensation in the eyes and nose to a gripping pain in the chest, a copious flow of tears, salivation, streaming nose and coughing, retching and sometimes vomiting. Few people will voluntarily endure the symptoms produced by concentrations higher than 2 milligrams per cubic metre, although after repeated exposures, tolerance can develop to concentrations below about 10 mg/m^3.[7] Harassing agents were employed extensively in the Vietnam War, but none, with the possible exception of CS, are likely to be employed in a major war between well-trained and highly motivated forces, equipped with modern respirators.

Incapaciting agents are to act on the mind and body of their victim, causing disorientation, mental disturbance, sleepiness and a lack of concentration. Their effects are unpredictable but could last for hours or days after exposure. Of these agents, BZ was once standardised as an American CW agent. It is a solid which can be dispersed in aerosol form. It takes effect within half an hour, with hallucinations, loss of concentration and unpredictable behaviour reaching a peak in four to eight hours, and taking up to four days to pass. Although the effects of BZ are normally temporary, they are not predictable. Victims, receiving a similar dosage, may not respond in identical fashion; some may behave in a random, even maniacal, manner before gradually returning to normal.[8] As unpredictable behaviour on the part of the enemy is hardly desirable from a military point of view, this has led to a 'de-emphasis' of incapacitatory agents.

For military purposes, lethal agents remain the most important. Choking and vesicant agents, the classical gases of chemical warfare, were used extensively in the First World War. Chlorine and the more toxic phosgene are both lung irritants; they act by inflaming the lung tissues, so allowing increasing quantities of fluid to enter the lungs from the bloodstream. In severe cases the victims die from asphyxiation, drowning in the plasma of their own blood. These agents are unlikely to be employed in a modern war because their toxicity is low by contemporary standards, and their smell warns of their presence, so enabling gas masks to be donned before a lethal dosage is inhaled.

Vesicants are more effective as casualty-producing agents. Capable of injuring any body tissue, they mainly attack the eyes and skin, producing burns, blisters and even temporary blindness, which may last a week or more. As they are not particularly volatile, they can persist in the field for long periods, retaining their effectiveness for days or weeks after dissemination. In sufficiently high concentrations, they are lethal if absorbed through the skin and, if made sufficiently airborne, they can be lethal by inhalation. There are two main categories of vesicant – the arsenicals (lewisite and the dichloroarsines) and the mustards. Lewisite is slightly more toxic by inhalation than distilled mustard (HD) and acts as a systemic poison if absorbed in the tissues. But the arsenicals exude distinctive odours and cause immediate eye pain, which warns of their presence. They also hydrolyse rapidly and so lose effectiveness and persistence in wet or humid conditions. Mustards emit less smell, especially those produced by processes developed during the Second World War, are slow to dissolve in water, and can penetrate leather, clothing, plastic and other materials, readily. As a general cell poison, they act insidiously as a liquid or vapour hazard, with the victim experiencing his first symptoms four to six hours after exposure. Although pure mustard freezes at 57° Fahrenheit, it can be combined with other vesicants, including lewisite and agent T, to facilitate its dissemination in cold weather. Having proven itself as a weapon of area denial in 1917–18, mustard gas was the most widely stockpiled agent of the Second World War. Nitrogen mustard (HN-3) and the compounds T and Q are less volatile than HD but all are persistent and useful in denying terrain.[9] Substantial stocks of mustard are still held in the arsenals of the superpowers.

Another legacy from the First World War are the blood gases, hydrogen cyanide and cyanogen chloride. Stockpiled during the Second World War, they are still retained partly because they are difficult to filter efficiently from air and partly because they act very rapidly. Once inhaled and absorbed in the bloodstream, they block the oxygen circulation within the body and cause death extremely quickly. Unlike hydrogen cyanide, cyanogen chloride can inflict casualties in small sublethal dosages, and, in high concentrations, can penetrate gas mask canisters more readily than most other agents. Yet its military attraction is greatly diluted by its choking, lachrymatory and highly irritating effects which warn of its presence. The only warning of hydrogen cyanide is the onset of its symptoms.[10] It is highly volatile and disperses quickly after deployment. If disseminated prior to a mass attack, hydrogen cyanide could force defenders to protect themselves and so reduce their combat efficiency, while enabling their adversaries to advance without similar protection.

Neither mustard nor hydrogen cyanide compare in effectiveness with the organophosphorus compounds, known as nerve gases. The first such compound, tabun, was discovered in December 1936 by Dr Gerhard Schrader, a German scientist, in the course of research on new insecticides. As tabun was much more toxic than phosgene, and was only barely perceptible to the human senses, its military potential was quickly recognised. The German government authorised large scale production in April 1942 at Dyhernfurth, near Breslau. By April

1945, some 12 000 tons of tabun had been made and concealed from the Allies. The Germans had also begun research on two more potent nerve gases: sarin and soman. Known as the G agents, these gases are stored as liquids. Depending on their respective volatility, they can be discharged as a cloud of vapour or as a spray of liquid droplets. Practically odourless and colourless, they can penetrate the body by inhalation or by absorption through the skin. The agents react with several enzymes in the body but principally with acetylcholinesterase, an enzyme responsible for destroying acetylcholine after it has performed its function of transmitting nerve impulses. By inhibiting the enzyme, control over the affected part of the nervous system is lost and acetylcholine, a powerful poison, rapidly accumulates. Very low dosages will cause a running nose, tightness of chest, dimming of vision and contraction of the eye pupils. At higher dosages, the symptoms will progress more rapidly through difficulty in breathing, nausea and vomiting, involuntary defecation and urination, tremors, headache, convulsions and finally death (usually in the wake of respiratory failure). A lethal dosage, if inhaled, will kill within fifteen minutes but, if absorbed through the skin, may not prove fatal for one or two hours. Victims of a sublethal exposure will probably recover completely within a few days, although some who suffered prolonged convulsions may suffer irreversible brain damage.[11]

Even more toxic than the G agents are the V agents which were discovered in Britain in the 1950s. VX has been stockpiled as a military weapon. It can be dispersed in sprays as a direct contact hazard, especially on exposed skin, or as a persistent indirect hazard since its volatility is akin to that of heavy motor oil and it will contaminate the ground and other surfaces. If applied directly to the skin, VX can incapacitate or kill in minute quantities (about 5 mg-min/m^3 and 15 mg/man respectively). It can also kill by permeating ordinary summer combat clothing and boots (some 100 mg/man). If disseminated at about 300 kilograms per square kilometre, VX could persist as a lethal hazard over several days or weeks, depending on the weather.[12]

The high toxicity of nerve agents is their most important feature. It means that fairly small amounts of an agent can inflict substantial casualties, especially if an adversary has failed to take defensive precautions. It also facilitates the contamination of large areas with a comparatively small expenditure of ammunition. Should persistent agents be used, sizeable tracts of terrain could be contaminated for several days or weeks. The standard American nerve gases are sarin and VX, while the Soviets are thought to retain four nerve agents,[13] particularly soman, whose volatility is similar to that of sarin, and a more persistent agent, VR-55, which may be soman thickened with synthetic polymers.

Several toxins (highly poisonous substances, usually produced by living (biological) organisms) are even more potent than nerve agents. Among those once considered as military agents are staphylococcal enterotoxin B (which produces staphylococcal food poisoning), saxitoxin (paralytic shellfish poisoning) and botulinal toxin A (one of the most virulent poisons known to man). As the development, production and stockpiling of such agents are proscribed under the Biological and Toxin Weapons Convention (and their use banned under the Geneva Protocol), the allegations of toxin usage, even of the comparatively less potent, trichothecene mycotoxin, in Afghanistan and South-East Asia aroused considerable controversy. The substance of these charges will be examined in Chapter 5 but their mere presentation simply underlines the potential array of agents which can still be used in chemical warfare.

Chemical munitions are rendered even more attractive because they do not require extraordinary methods of delivery (although they normally demand strict safety procedures in their storage, transportation and handling). They can be adapted for delivery by mines, mortars, artillery, rockets, missiles and aircraft. The chosen mode will depend upon the tactical mission and the operational requirements. Of the artillery systems, the multibarrelled rocket launcher is peculiarly suited to the launching of chemical attacks. The Soviet BM-21 fires forty rounds in twenty seconds over a maximum range of 20.5 kilometres. A battalion of these launchers could fire 720 rounds in under thirty seconds to amass a lethal concentration over one square kilometre.[14] Of the longer range systems, ground attack aircraft are still immensely versatile. Unlike missiles they may be intercepted, but they can deliver huge payloads over considerable distances and are more accurate and flexible in their method of attack. In favourable weather, they need not overfly their target but can release the agent upwind, letting it drift down to its target. Four thousand kilograms of sarin, if sprayed across wind over 6 kilometres, could wreak havoc upon an enemy 5 kilometres downwind. If the latter donned their respirators when they felt the first symptoms, and used efficient medical countermeasures, they could expect 20 to 30 per cent fatal casualties and 70 to 80 per cent light casualties. Should the counter-measures prove ineffective, the figures could be 80 and 20 per cent respectively.[15] Alternatively, aircraft could bomb their targets with persistent or non-persistent agent or drop cluster bombs to create a uniform spread of persistent agent.

Chemical weapons depend more than any other armament upon atmospheric and topographical factors. Once toxic agent is released, it will mix with the air to form a toxic cloud whose effectiveness depends on its concentration and the length of time it takes to pass by a man.[16] The distance travelled by the cloud will depend upon the wind velocity (high winds will dissipate the cloud), and the evaporation rate of the chemical which will vary with changes in the ground and air temperature. A significant risk could exist as far as 100 kilometres downwind. The hazard would be maximised in a highly stable atmosphere (virtually no air movements) when the cloud is propelled by gentle winds (7 km/hour) for a sufficiently long period of time (about fourteen hours for a sarin attack of 500 kg/km). Stable conditions are likely to exist in combination at the end of a sunny day, when a temperature inversion occurs (that is, when the ground begins to cool a layer of cooler air may be formed beneath a mass of hot light air and the cooler air, because of its greater density, does not rise so leaving the atmosphere in stable equilibrium). Temperature inversions are likely to persist throughout the night, disappearing shortly after sunrise. They may last for several days in winter or in overcast weather and often occur in valleys or plains surrounded by high peaks. Whereas high temperatures will accelerate evaporation and the danger of a vapour hazard, snow will inhibit evaporation and increase the persistence of ground contamination. Light rain will disperse and spread the chemical agent, so spreading the surface for evaporation. Heavy rain will dilute and displace the agent, facilitating its ground penetration and accelerating the destruction of water-sensitive compounds (e.g. lewisite).[17]

Topographical factors, such as uneven terrain, vegetation and man-made structures, will compound the atmospheric turbulence. Under stable atmospheric conditions, gas clouds will move steadily over flat and even countryside. But clouds will divide to avoid high ground, follow valleys and ravines, and accumulate in hollows, so breaking up and reducing the concentration of the contaminant. The persistence of the agent will be affected by the texture and porosity of the soil and by the presence or absence of vegetation. Chemical contaminants, though slow to penetrate the canopy of forests or woods, will persist for much longer in woods than in open terrain. Similarly they will persist longer in urban areas than over open ground. Despite the higher surface temperature of built-up areas, the building materials are frequently porous and will absorb and retain liquid chemical agents, while the factors which will tend to reduce persistence in open country (sunshine, wind over ground, etc) are of less significance in a city. Climate and terrain are so important in determining the persistence of contamination that the same agent may persist for periods ranging from several days to weeks, or even months, depending on local circumstances (see Appendix 3). As a consequence, 'the *a priori* classification of chemical agents as persistent or non-persistent, solely on the basis of different degrees of volatility, is somewhat arbitrary'.[18]

The effectiveness of chemical weapons depends not only upon local conditions but also upon the adequacy of an opponent's anti-chemical defences. The degree of protection can be comprehensive and extremely effective. It requires initially some means of detection to warn of the movement of a toxic cloud upwind of the target, so enabling the defensive forces to don their protective clothing. Since mustard gases and nerve agents of low or intermediate volatility may penetrate unbroken skin, even through normal clothing, additional clothing covering the whole body surface must be worn as well as a gas mask, with a filter and absorption system, often in canister form. Modern gas masks, if properly fitted and worn correctly, can protect against all known chemical agents. Anti-chemical clothing, when worn with a respirator, gloves and overboots, also provides excellent protection, although the degree of protection will depend on whether the fabric is rubber-coated and so impermeable to liquid agents, or chemically treated to permit the passage of air and moisture but not toxic vapours. Impermeable clothing provides the greatest degree of protection but it becomes highly debilitating if worn continuously, especially in warm environments. Even permeable clothing, as examined more fully in Chapter 7, will impair a whole range of physical activities.

To minimise dependence on such equipment, collective protection is a prerequisite. Toxic-free areas can be established by means of a filtered air supply and the maintenance of internal over-pressure in all enclosures, whether buildings in fixed installations like command posts and air bases, or in military vehicles including tanks and armoured personnel carriers, or in modern naval vessels by internal citadels or in improvised field shelters. Decontamination of personnel and equipment will provide further relief from the dangers of chemical agents. It is a labour-intensive process, involving a copious supply of water, the appropriate choice of decontaminants and the availability of suitable equipment (portable dispensers, scrubbers, pressurised sprayers etc). In the event of protective defences proving fallible, especially if damaged in combat or if donned too late, medical defences are available. Compact auto-injectors, carrying a nerve agent antidote, are issued to each serviceman; they can be self-administered whenever the symptoms of nerve gas poisoning begin to be felt. They have to be administered promptly and will only save the lives of those who have received slightly more than the median lethal dose of nerve gas.[19] Artificial respiration by specially designed positive pressure resuscitators may also be necessary to counter the effects of more severe poisoning. In all these defences the objective need not be 100 per cent protection: the defence may aim at ensuring that sufficient personnel will be able to survive a chemical attack and to operate as effectively as possible in contaminated conditions. Attaining this state of readiness, which will involve intensive training and the investment of substantial resources to protect service and supporting civilian personnel, may contribute to deterring a chemical attack, along with credible offensive countermeasures.

In these circumstances, chemical weapons might now seem somewhat old fashioned. Renowned for their impact during the First World War, they have now been overshadowed by the advent of nuclear weapons. They can be offset by protective and, to a lesser extent, by medical means. Yet they have now acquired a fresh salience, reflecting recent developments in arms control, military conflicts, and contemporary strategy. In the first place, the Arab–Israeli War of October 1973 confirmed a relative disparity between the chemical equipment of the Soviet Union and the United States. Captured nuclear, biological and chemical (NBC) defensive/protective equipment, which the Soviets had supplied to Egypt and Syria, 'confirmed that Soviet and Warsaw Pact forces are the most highly trained and best equipped in the world to operate in an NBC environment'.[20] When coupled with intelligence reports of a continuing Soviet programme to develop and stockpile chemical munitions, and compared with the relative decline of the American NBC defence posture in the 1970s, this alarmed senior military and political advisers in the Pentagon.

Secondly progress towards the control of chemical weapons has been extremely slow. Under United Nations auspices various committees, based in Geneva, originally the Eighteen Nation Committee on Disarmament now the Conference on Disarmament, have been engaged in seeking a chemical weapons convention since 1968. Having separated chemical and biological weapons, a Biological Weapons Convention was signed in 1972. But doubts about the effectiveness of that convention, which lacks any verification provisions, have been matched by the disappointment over the failure of the bilateral US–Soviet working group (1976–80) to conclude a CW agreement. Apart from the intrinsic difficulty of reaching such an agreement, especially over the ability to verify any convention, the discussions have been overshadowed by the Strategic Arms Limitation Talks (SALT). The failure of the latter, following the invasion of Afghanistan in December 1979, and the consequent demise of detente, have compounded the difficulties of negotiating over chemical weapons.

These prospects have been further complicated by the allegations that the Soviet Union has violated the BW Convention and has used chemical weapons in Afghanistan. An outbreak of anthrax near Sverdlovsk in April 1979 raised fears that the Soviets were still developing biological weapons. These suspicions were compounded by subsequent charges that the Soviets have employed chemical weapons in Afghanistan and have supplied such weapons for use in South-East Asia. Although Western governments remain committed to seeking a treaty which would prohibit the development, production, possession, transfer and use of chemical weapons, they agree that it must contain more effective methods of verification than those which underpin the BW Convention.

Finally, chemical weapons have acquired a fresh significance with the resurgence of interest in the balance of conventional forces in central Europe. For nearly a generation, American superiority in nuclear weaponry had more than offset the massive conventional armies retained by the Soviet Union. Only in 1971 did the Soviets attain the same number of missiles (but not warheads) as the United States. A continuing surge of qualitative improvements has enabled them to claim (and have ratified in the SALT accords) an approximate parity in strategic systems. As Henry Kissinger perceived, once 'strategic parity approached, the historical Soviet advantage in ground forces in Europe would grow more ominous'.[21] Chemical weaponry is one facet of that advantage; it warrants close analysis.

In evaluating this weaponry, its tactical utility will be of prime concern. The experience of the First World War warrants examination to establish the various modes in which poison gas was employed, as well as its impact and effectiveness on the field of battle. Equally important are the inter-war attempts to proscribe the use of chemical weapons, especially the difficulties which bedevilled the quest for measures of disarmament. Despite the signing of the Geneva Protocol (1925) several states preserved a limited chemical warfare capability, and many expected its widespread employment during the Second World War. That this did not occur was significant; it indicated not merely a persistence of limited stocks and logistical problems but also a policy of deterrence based upon the fear of retaliation in kind. Although lessons should not be glibly drawn from previous wars, since most conflicts are anomalous and the lessons cited are often based upon the preconceptions of the writer, this experience is important. When coupled with the use of chemical weapons in local wars both before and after the Second World War, it provides a context for the current debate. It might not suggest how or if these weapons would be employed in the future, but it could indicate some of the minimum requirements for their effective employment, control, or deterrence.

Soviet chemical warfare capabilities will be examined, including their possible value as a form of tactical pre-emption instead of nuclear release. In face of this threat, NATO's range of responses will be considered: the adequacy of her anti-chemical defences, the credibility of America's limited offensive capacity in chemical warfare, and the expectations which may be held realistically of arms control, given the intrinsic difficulties of reaching a satisfactory agreement and the abject state of Soviet–American relations. Ultimately NATO's concept of deterrence will be reconsidered to assess whether it is currently adequate and, if not, can it be improved?

2 Chemical Warfare 1914–18

During the First World War 124 200 tons of poison gas were used in battle. Compared with the expenditure of 2 million tons of high explosive and the 50 000 million rounds of small arms ammunition, this was a fairly small total. But gas was a new weapon. Once introduced on a significant scale (3870 tons) in 1915, it was employed in increasing quantities thereafter (16 535 tons in 1916, 38 635 tons in 1917 and 65 160 tons in 1918).[1] New and more potent gases were introduced; although irritants (both lachrymators which produced tears and sternutators which caused sneezing) were used to harass adversaries throughout the war, the lethal agents – including chlorine, phosgene and later mustard – became the primary instruments of chemical warfare. The methods of disseminating gas were also refined as were the techniques of gas protection. Chemical warfare organisations appeared in the various armies, supported by extensive research and development in their respective countries. 'As a result,' wrote Major Victor Lefebure (a wartime CW expert who later held an executive post in Imperial Chemical Industries Ltd), 'the history of chemical warfare becomes one of continual attempts, on both sides, to achieve surprise and to counter it by some accurate forecast in protective methods. It is a struggle for the initiative'.[2]

Chemical weapons, particularly irritant or poisonous smoke, had been used on many occasions before 1914. During the siege of Platea and Velium (431–401 BC), the Spartans had tried to reduce the cities with sulphur fumes. Although various toxic smoke clouds were employed in medieval warfare,[3] it required the emergence of a sizeable chemical industry before such weapons became significant as military propositions. New chemical weapons including organoarsenical and phosphorus shells were proposed during the Crimean War, and clouds of hydrogen chloride and glass grenades containing arsenicals in the American Civil War.[4] Although none of these ideas was acted upon, poisonous and asphyxiating weapons became prominent issues in the

13

peace conferences of 1868, 1874 and 1899. At the Hague Peace Conference of 1899, various rules and limitations on the conduct of war were agreed. All principal countries, with the exception of Britain and the United States, affirmed that they would 'abstain from the use of projectiles the sole object of which is the diffusion of asphyxiating or deleterious gas'. Britain later adhered to a similar declaration at the Peace Conference of 1907.[5]

Despite these pronouncements, research continued into the possibilities of chemical weaponry. In Britain, the concept of a shell, containing a small portion of a lachrymatory substance, was investigated but set aside. It was thought to infringe the spirit, if not the letter, of the Hague Declaration.[6] Nevertheless, the War Office still authorised tests on the irritants – chloroacetone and benzyl chloride – in the spring of 1914.[7] Military experiments with chemical agents were also conducted in pre-war Germany, though apparently without any positive results.[8] The French developed the first practical chemical weapon – a hand grenade containing ethyl bromoacetate, a mildly suffocating and non-toxic lachrymator, which was used by the French police from 1912. By August 1914 the French army had procured some 30 000 26 mm cartridges filled with the liquid agent, weighing about ½lb and fired by special rifles (*fusils lance-cartouches éclairantes*). These were used on the Western Front in 1914. Hand grenades, containing the same substance, were soon developed and were used in the Argonne sector in March 1915.[9]

Military appreciation of chemical weapons varied considerably. In September 1914, Lieutenant-General the Earl of Dundonald apprised Lord Kitchener of the various plans left by his grandfather, Admiral Sir Thomas Cochrane, for the use of sulphur dioxide clouds to drive an enemy from a fortified position. Kitchener at once discounted them as did Admiral Sir Arthur Wilson. Only Winston Churchill's imaginative interest kept the scheme alive, and eventually a modified version of Cochrane's proposal was put into practice, not as lethal gas clouds but as naval smoke screens.[10] Even when line officers returned from France and inquired about the possibility of using 'stink bombs' to clear enemy dug-outs, the response was unfavourable. Some lachrymatory substances were examined at the Imperial College of Science, and, unofficially, 'stink bombs' were offered to Sir John French in case the enemy resorted to similar methods. The Commander-in-Chief brusquely rejected the offer.[11]

German interest in chemical munitions quickened after their set-back at the Marne in September 1914. Dwindling stocks of powder and shell, coupled with complaints about the ineffectiveness of high-explosive shells, persuaded the high command to authorise the production and experimental usage of chemical agents. Initially, non-toxic irritants were fired but they proved ineffective. Neither the shelling of the French at Neuve-Chapelle with 3000 rounds of Ni-Schrapnell (27 October 1914) nor the pounding of Russian positions at Bolimow with 18 000 T-Stoff shells (31 January 1915) had any decisive impact. Accordingly, as bottle-necks still existed in the German shell production, the military authorities were prepared to test the proposal of Professor Fritz Haber for the firing of chlorine gas in clouds from cylinders emplaced in front-line trenches.[12] The decision was not universally popular. Many German infantrymen disliked the additional work involved and the danger of leakages from damaged cylinders. Some senior commanders deprecated the use of such an 'unchivalrous' weapon, while Crown Prince Rupprecht of Bavaria perceptively observed that if the Allies retaliated with gas on the Western Front, they would benefit from the prevailing winds.[13]

General Erich von Falkenhayn, the Chief of the General Staff, held fairly modest expectations of poison gas. Although willing to approve a practical trial, he was not prepared to support the venture with substantial resources. His caution was understandable, if hardly inspired. Previous tests with gas had proved unpropitious. Any successful offensive, based upon cylinder gas, would depend entirely upon suitable weather and could as a consequence be prone to recurrent delays (as it was in this instance). Also the laborious installation of cylinders would consume valuable time (nearly two months were required to emplace 6000 cylinders along a front of 6 kilometres) and could hardly be concealed from the enemy. In any case, by April 1915, Falkenhayn was principally concerned with developments on the Eastern Front. He regarded the gas attack on the Ypres salient as merely a diversionary move; it would help 'to cloak the transportation of the [German] troops to Galicia', and so facilitate a massive assault by German and Austrian forces against the Russians in the Gorlice–Tarnow area.[14]

In the late afternoon of the 22 April, around 5 p.m., the Germans launched the first gas cloud attack against the French and Second Army positions at Langemarck. On this warm and sunny day, the two greenish-yellow clouds spread laterally, merged, and moved quickly before a light wind. The bulk of the cloud drifted over the French defences, manned by the recently deployed 45th (Algerian) Division and the 87th Territorial Division. Both units broke and retreated to the West bank of the Yser Canal. They had opened a gap of four and a half miles and had left Ypres unprotected. The German infantry cautiously advanced behind the drifting gas clouds. Encountering some resistance on their flanks, they made uneven progress but still captured sixty guns and a substantial tract of territory. They also lacked the reserves with which to press on to Ypres, only 2500 yards from their positions at nightfall. By choosing to dig in, they allowed the Allies time to recuperate, to cover the gap with ten battalions, and to begin a counterattack on the following day and so commence the second battle of Ypres.[15]

Generals Falkenhayn and Balck accepted, in retrospect, that the German High Command had seriously underestimated the impact of gas. As Falkenhayn recalls: 'Its surprise effect was very great. Unfortunately we were not in a position to exploit it to the full. The necessary reserves were not ready. The success achieved, however, was considerable.'[16] The Germans achieved this surprise despite ample warnings of their gas preparations. The Allies had learnt of the deployment of cylinders from deserters and prisoners and from their reconnaissance airmen. They had captured impregnated gauze/cotton waste respirators and had ruptured cylinders by their shell fire.[17] Yet the attack of the 22nd, and a second gas attack upon Canadian-held positions near St Julien on 24 April, came as a complete surprise. An official British report confirmed:

We were aware of the fact that the Germans were making preparations for this discharge of gas for several days previously . . . Nobody appears to have realized the great danger that was threatening, it being considered that the enemy's attempt would certainly fail and that whatever gas reached our line could be easily fanned away. No-one felt in the slightest degree uneasy, and the terrible effect of the gas came to us as a great surprise . . .[18]

Moreover, the impact of the gas was maximised because its initial victims were inexperienced troops bereft of any means of personal protection. By the 24th the Canadians, though still lacking any respirators, had at least improvised some protection, using handkerchiefs, towels, and cotton bandoliers impregnated with water. Although many men succumbed, the majority held their line and the Germans made only minor gains of ground.[19]

Four more gas attacks occurred in May (on the 1st, 6th, 10th and 24th), accompanied by massive artillery and infantry assaults. Tactically, the results were minimal. Germany inflicted losses nearly double those which she suffered herself, and managed to disrupt the Allies' plans for a 'Spring Offensive', but the Ypres salient remained in Allied hands, so confirming that Falkenhayn and his advisers had wasted the cloud gas initiative.[20] The Allies had also been 'blooded' in the techniques of gas warfare. They had significantly reduced their casualty rates by the issue of respirators and later cloth helmets – the so-called 'hypo helmets' – which were chemically impregnated against chlorine. They had observed, too, that respirators and helmets were insufficient protection unless the men were properly trained in their use (specifically in the redipping of respirators into water while under attack).[21] Above all, they had glimpsed the horrendous potential of chemical warfare.

Shock was the initial reaction. Squadron Leader E. D. Kingsley, then serving with the 2nd Battalion Seaforth Highlanders, recalls his first experience of gas on 6 May 1915: 'I stood up on the back of the trench and saw a cloud rolling towards us, so thick that one was unable to see through it. We were all so stupefied by the sight that we just watched to see what would happen . . .'[22] The impact was frightfully severe: those who lacked protection reeled and began to choke and cough, with their eyes watering and sore. Severe casualties were removed to a dressing station, where Sergeant Cotton recollects the appearance of a dozen such men: 'all gassed – their colour was black, green and blue, tongues hanging out and eyes staring – one or two were dead and others beyond human aid, some were coughing up green froth from their lungs'.[23]

Mingled with the horror was a profound sense of outrage. Sir John French castigated the Germans for playing 'a very dirty "low down" game' in 'shooting out that damnable "gas"'.[24] Kitchener was equally appalled; in a telegram revealing more anger than accuracy, he deprecated 'the use of asphyxiating gases' as 'contrary to the rules and usages of war'.[25] The cloud gas attacks, though unprovoked and contrary to the customs of war, had not broken the letter of international law. The Hague Declaration of 1899 had merely forbidden the 'use of projectiles' the sole object of which is the diffusion of asphyxiating gases, not the emission of cloud gas. Germany might have disregarded the spirit of the declaration but had not contravened its wording.

Such legal niceties, however, did not prevent the Allies from mounting a massive propaganda campaign over the use of gas. For nearly a week following 22 April, the Fleet Street editors refrained from denouncing gas (possibly for fear of panicking their readers), but, as soon as the official report of Dr J. S. Haldane was published on 29 April, confirming that the gas was lethal, the press promptly exploited the atrocity aspect. Germany, wrote *The Times*, had devised 'an atrocious method of warfare' which would 'fill all races with a new horror of the German name'.[26] Wellington House, the propaganda bureau of the Foreign Office, publicised the 'inhuman' methods employed by the enemy, clearly hoping to influence neutral opinion in the United States.[27] 'Eye-Witness', the British government's official war correspondent, described how a German officer had laughed at the sufferings of gassed British troops, an account supplemented with gruesome accounts of the 'incredible tortures' involved in gassing. Such reports when bracketed with other atrocity stories – the crucifixion of the Canadian soldier, the publication of the Bryce report and the sinking of the *Lusitania* – ensured that gas became a central issue in Allied propaganda. Despite the readiness of the Allies to retaliate in kind, and to introduce new engines of war – the flame thrower and the projection of cans of boiling oil and containers of gas – Germany would be arraigned for introducing gas as one of the thirty-two war crimes by the Commission of Responsibilities at the Peace Conference.[28]

Moral outrage did not prevent the Allies from seeking to retaliate with chemical weapons. After the first gas attack, Sir John French telegraphed the War Office to request not only a supply of suitable respirators but also a capacity to retaliate with 'similar means of the most effective kind'.[29] The High Command never regarded the provision of defensive equipment, though vitally important, as remotely adequate in itself. They wished to exploit the offensive potential of poison gas. Lieutenant-General Sir Henry Wilson, displaying his usual *sang froid*, believed that the enemy had stolen a march on the Allies: 'the Germans,' he wrote, 'did this by those noxious gases and without reinforcements, for they have none, and so it was a very fine performance'.[30] British commanders were also deeply concerned about morale. Should the Germans be allowed to continue their chemical attacks without any Allied response, they feared for the morale and confidence of the front-line forces. Such fears were raised in the press, and were pressed upon senior members of Asquith's cabinet.[31] As the latter were already concerned about the shortage of munitions, retaliation was quickly approved. *The Times* saw little alternative. Once prohibited weapons were in use, it declared, 'the question is no longer a question of right, but merely a question of expediency'.[32]

Retaliation was a formidable undertaking, rendered even more daunting by the feeble state of the British chemical industry. Only one firm in the country, the Castner–Kellner Alkali Company, could expand its output of liquid chlorine to produce bulk supplies. Presenting even more problems than the production of gas was its projection or discharge into the open air. Commercial containers could not be used as they were too bulky to be installed in trenches. Consequently a group of Royal Engineers, advised by prominent scientists, was established to devise and test a cylinder method of discharge. While the factory output was greatly increased, and portable containers designed and manufactured, special Companies of Royal Engineers (largely recruited from chemistry students and graduates) were formed in France. Commanded by Major C. H. Foulkes, this élite force – all of whom held the rank of corporal at least – specialised in the handling of the cylinders which were to be the basis of Britain's first chemical attack.[33]

While the British laboured upon their secret preparations, the Germans employed gas to support their advance on Warsaw. Ludendorff recalled that he 'anticipated great tactical results from its use, as the Russians were not yet fully protected against gas'.[34] At the end of May 1915, some 12 000 cylinders containing 264 tons of chlorine were discharged over the Bolimov sector, spreading the gas over a 12 kilometre front. Although the winds were generally favourable, and the gas was emitted as planned, the artillery and infantry failed to co-ordinate their subsequent assault. Surprised by the resilience of the Russian gunners, who continued firing in places, the Ninth Army assumed that the gas attack had failed. Gas had already proved unpredictable in Russian conditions, especially when the cold weather blunted its effects, but, in this attack, it still inflicted some 8934 casualties, of whom 1101 died.[35]

British senior commanders shared Ludendorff's optimism about the tactical utility of gas. On 16 June 1915, Sir John French formally requested the provision of sufficient gas to mount a surprise attack from cylinders over a front of 5000 yards which could be sustained for thirty minutes. He also hoped that the production of gas bombs and gas shells could begin quickly.[36] Sir Douglas Haig, having seen a trial discharge of gas at Helfaut on 22 August, favoured a heavy gas attack upon the German positions near Loos. As gas could have a 'great moral effect', he urged his commanders to feed the attacks con-

tinuously from the rear and 'to gain as much ground as possible in the
first advance'. He also pressed Sir William Robertson, who was Sir
John French's Chief of Staff, to insist upon the gas factory working
night and day to make special arrangements for expediting the delivery
of gas. He maintained that:

> On the one hand, with gas, decisive results were to be expected – on
> the other hand, without gas, the fronts of the attacks must be
> restricted, with the result of concentrated hostile fire on the
> attacking troops, considerable loss, and small progress! In my
> opinion the attack ought not to be launched except with the aid of
> gas![37]

By 19 September nearly 5500 cylinders, containing some 150 tons of
chlorine, had been distributed along the British front. After four days
and nights of a preliminary artillery bombardment, and an anxious
watch of the weather, the first British gas attack was launched on 25
September 1915, so commencing the battle of Loos.

Sir Henry Rawlinson, commander of the IV Corps, watched as 'a
huge cloud of white and yellow gas rose from our trenches to a height
between two hundred and three hundred feet, and floated quietly away
towards the German trenches'.[38] After about half an hour, his assault
troops left their trenches, dashed against the enemy's lines and overran
their forward positions. Eighteen guns were seized and over 3000
prisoners taken. The secret deployment of cylinders, the use of smoke
as a cover, and the sudden discharge of gas had caught the Germans by
surprise. Captured prisoners confirmed that some men had failed to
don their respirators, and that others had panicked and run. But the
effectiveness of gas had varied considerably along the front. The wind,
though generally favourable, had varied in strength and direction. It
undoubtedly facilitated the rapid advance of the 15th and 47th
Divisions on the extreme right and the capture of the Hohenzollern
redoubt in the centre. In other places the wind slowed, veered, and
even drifted back towards the British trenches. On the front of the 2nd
Division, the discharge had to be aborted at once and gas never
reached the enemy's trenches. Over the next three weeks some 2500
British troops were reported as casualties of their own gas, ten fatally
and fifty-five severely.[39]

Both sides learnt from the battle of Loos. To counter the surprise
effect of gas, improvements in anti-gas training and discipline were
realised as necessary as well as the introduction of more efficient

respirators. The Germans had already tested a new respirator, which relied upon layers of charcoal as the absorbent. First issued to the troops in October–November 1915, its distribution was completed early in the following year. The British, anticipating recourse to more lethal agents such as phosgene or prussic acid, developed the new P helmet which was impregnated with phenate solution. Known as the 'Tube' helmet, when fitted with a mouthpiece for exhaled air, it was issued to all officers and men by 18 November. The later addition of hexamine, a Russian idea, improved its efficiency against phosgene and led to the issue of the PH helmet from January 1916. To provide additional protection against prussic acid, the British eventually introduced the small box respirator (SBR), in which the mask was connected by a flexible rubber tube to a filter containing charcoal and sodium permanganate-lime granules. More effective than the German respirator, the SBR was also more complicated to manufacture and was not fully issued until January 1917.[40]

Having captured German plans in November 1915, the British were forewarned of the next gas attack. It was to be launched in Flanders in early December and would use various gases including phosgene. Suitably alerted, the British accelerated and completed the introduction of the P helmet. When the gas was discharged at 5.15 a.m., on 19 December 1915, along a front which extended $3\frac{1}{2}$ miles in length, some 25 000 men of the 49th, 6th and 17th Divisions were exposed to the gas. They did not panic, as implied in one recent commentary;[41] indeed, Major S. J. M. Auld recalled that 'there was absolutely no confusion and the men put on their helmets at once and lined the parapets within a minute'.[42] Difficulties were more apparent in the support and reserve trenches, where the gas cloud, moving at very high speed, was smelled before any receipt of warning. The gongs and klaxon horns which were used to warn the front-line trenches could not be heard in the rear because the noise of rifle and gun fire. The gas was felt as far back as Vlamertinghe, some 8500 yards behind the line. Although the men suffered heavily from having to wear their helmets for two hours, and were soon exhausted if they had to march even 400 yards with their helmets on, the helmets proved remarkably effective. Only 1069 men were gassed, of whom 116 died. As Lieutenant-General Sir Nevil Macready, the Adjutant-General, concluded, 'the number of persons seriously affected was very low in proportion to those exposed to the gas, and . . . the Anti-gas Helmets proved of great efficacy in withstanding the gas'.[43]

In this attack, the Germans employed phosgene mixed with chlorine (to produce the necessary volatility) and projected it as a cloud gas. About six times more toxic than chlorine, phosgene was also much more useful. It was practically odourless, emitting only a faint smell of new mown hay. It could be inhaled in fatal doses without undue discomfort or coughing (which often limited the intake of chlorine). It also had a 'delayed action' effect, whereby the victim, having experienced only mild irritation of eyes and throat upon exposure, suddenly collapsed and died three to twenty-four hours after an attack. Tactically, this delayed action effect and the visibility of the gas were drawbacks. The gas also presented logistical dangers, particularly the loading of so volatile a substance into projectiles. Yet phosgene was highly regarded as an 'offensive' gas; it became the main battle gas used by the Allies, comprising over half of the tonnage of chemical agents used by the French.[44] It evoked considerable fear and respect. As recalled by a warrant officer of the 8th Bavarian Infantry,

the English gas is almost odourless and can only be seen by the practised eye on escaping from the shell. The gas steals slowly over the ground in a blueish haze and kills anyone who does not draw his mask over his face as quick as lightning before taking a breath.[45]

Innovation was not confined to the choice of agent and the means of protection. Neither the Germans nor the French nor even the British latterly were enamoured of gas clouds as a mode of attack. Such attacks were inherently unpredictable because they always depended upon the speed and direction of the wind. The Germans were additionally handicapped since the prevailing winds in Flanders came from a westerly direction. To mount the attacks required immense organisation and consumed valuable labour, not least in the furtive night-time installations. Commanders on both sides reported the intense dislike of the labour involved and the danger to their own troops from the proximity of the cylinders. The task of penetrating the increasingly proficient anti-gas defences, over a wide front, became increasingly complex. It involved the discharge of higher and higher concentrations of cylinder gas, often at night, with the aim of causing casualties by exploiting the element of surprise.[46] As the effects of these attacks could not be quickly assessed, infantry commanders became reluctant to proffer immediate and substantial support. Devoid of any other purpose, attrition became the main objective of the cloud gas attacks, not simply the losses inflicted but also the demoralisation and fatigue associated with the protracted wearing of gas masks.

To obviate dependence upon cloud gas, whose effects varied with the direction and strength of the wind, the French and Germans sought alternative means of delivery. The Germans had experimented with tear gas shells in the autumn and winter of 1914, and the French followed suit with a 75 mm tear gas shell in March 1915. By August 1915, German batteries were firing sufficient quantities of tear gas shells to warrant the authorisation of employment directives by the General Staff. Henceforth non-persistent shells (K-Stoff) would be fired against an enemy position immediately prior to assault, while persistent shells (T-Stoff) would be used to harass positions which were not to be attacked directly.[47] But these early shells were inherently limited. Based upon traditional artillery shells, each relied upon a large explosive charge which reduced the volume of gas per shell and increased its dispersal on impact. The French surmounted this problem in their phosgene shell, which was introduced successfully in the defence of Verdun (February 1916). By employing only sufficient high explosive (25 grams) to open the shell and liberate its contents, the French shell could carry a larger payload of gas, reduce the area over which the chemical was dispersed and ensure a greater concentration of gas. French artillery fire, using their formidable 75 mm guns to deliver phosgene shells and later Vincennite, a hydrocyanic gas mixture, was much more effective at this time than fire from German gas artillery.[48]

Most belligerents were impressed by the French initiative. By May 1916, the Germans deployed their first lethal gas shell – the Green Cross shell, containing diphosgene instead of phosgene. With the advent of these shells, large-scale gas bombardments were begun, the first being the German bombardment of French positions at Fleury (22 June 1916) when 110 000 rounds were fired in six hours. Further refinements of the Green Cross shell included a special casing for chemical fillings (longer than the HE shell and with thinner walls) and their adaptation for the entire range of German field artillery by August 1917. Sir Douglas Haig, the new British Commander-in-Chief, was also attracted by the potential of gas shells. On 16 May 1916, in preparation for the Somme offensive, he requested the production of 40 000 rounds within the next month and 10 000 rounds per week thereafter. This was quite impractical. The British war effort was still bedevilled by munition supply problems, and chemical production had to compete with demands for the production of HE shell. Haig, as a

consequence, had to rely upon French batteries for his gas bombardments. On 31 July 1916, he increased his requirements to 30 000
rounds per week in the proportions of 6:4:1 for the 4.5 inch howitzer,
60-pounder, and 4.7 inch gun respectively. Production, however, still
had to wait upon research and development. By the end of 1916,
Britain possessed only 160 000 shells filled with lethal or partially
lethal agents and discharged less than one-third of her toxic gases by
artillery (whereas Germany, France, Austria, Hungary, Italy and
Russia used artillery to deliver some 75 per cent of their chemical
agents).[49]

Nevertheless, Britain kept in the forefront of gas warfare. To
support the war effort, an experimental installation was established in
January 1916 on some 3000 acres of downland on the southern rim of
Salisbury Plain. As the problems of chemical warfare multiplied,
Porton Down, as it came to be called, more than doubled in size and
employed over 1000 scientists and soldiers. New ideas could thereby be
tested, developed, and converted into operational weapons. Among
the British innovations were the 4 inch Stokes mortar and the Livens
Projector. The mortar was the first weapon specifically intended to
deliver a chemical projectile. Used initially at the battle of Loos, it
could fire twenty rounds per minute for short bursts or a sustained rate
of five rounds per minute. It was mobile, comparatively silent to
operate, and could establish very heavy concentrations of gas over a
target in the minimum of time. Its main limitation was a maximum
range of 1075 yards. The Livens Projector, invented by Captain F. H.
Livens, was a remarkably simple but effective device. The projector
was a steel tube: it came in two sizes, a shorter version, 2 ft 9 in in
length, weighing 100 lb, and having a maximum range of 1375 yards;
and a longer version, 4 feet in length, weighing 150 lb, and having a
range of 1700 yards. Once embedded in the ground at an angle of 45°,
it was fired remotely by means of an electrical charge, usually in
batteries of twenty-five. The charge propelled a drum from each tube
containing 30 lb of chemical (normally pure phosgene). Although
neither mobile nor particularly accurate, and extremely laborious to
install, the Livens Projector could deliver a massive quantity of agent
over a target with the maximum of surprise.[50] Its virtues were readily
conceded by the Germans when the projector was first used in a
full-scale attack during the battle of Arras (9 April 1917). From a
captured document, belonging to the 111th German Division, it was
admitted that:

The enemy has combined in this new process the advantages of gas clouds and gas shells. The density is equal to that of gas clouds, and the surprise effect of shell fire is also obtained . . . Our losses have been serious up to now, as he has succeeded, in the majority of cases, in surprising us, and masks have often been put on too late.[51]

From April 1917 onwards, the chemical struggle intensified considerably. The Germans, having failed to invent anything to equal the Livens Projector, relied primarily upon artillery bombardment. Both sides experimented with new gases (chloropicrin, for example, was widely used as a casualty-producing gas and a strong lachrymator). They also employed huge quantities of gas shell, but found that the efficiency of the respirators and improving gas discipline had rendered gas less effective. The Germans broke this deadlock by shelling the Allies with the Yellow Cross vesicant, mustard gas. During the night of 12/13 July 1917, they bombarded Ypres with 77 mm and 105 mm gas shells. The British 15th and 55th Divisions did not immediately recognise that they had been gassed. Although some men noticed the slight smell, describing it as 'unpleasant', 'oily', 'like garlic' or 'like mustard', they experienced few immediate symptoms. The majority had gone to sleep after the attack only to wake a few hours later with acute conjunctivitis and, in some cases, temporary blindness. Sneezing and nausea followed, often accompanied by marked and persistent vomiting. Some found that the gas had even penetrated their clothes, burning their skin and leaving patches of painful blisters.[52]

Mustard gas proved extremely effective, even in low concentrations. Its slight odour, coupled with its persistence and many-sided action, defied defensive precautions. Although its most fatal effects could be obviated by wearing a respirator, it still produced a massive number of casualties. In the first three weeks of Yellow Cross shelling, the British incurred more casualties (14 276) and almost as many deaths (nearly 500) as they had suffered from all previous gas shelling. From 21 July 1917 to 23 November 1918, British clearing stations admitted 160 970 gas casualties, of whom 1859 died. Seventy-seven per cent of these were victims of mustard gas.[53] Tactically, the persistence of mustard gas was its principal asset. This enabled the Germans, when fighting on the defensive, to render vast areas impassable, such as Bourlon Wood in November 1917 or Armentières in April 1918. General Ludendorff acknowledged that gas had made a vital contribution to his artillery bombardments. In driving the British back over a front of fifty miles between Arras and La Fère, he claimed that short and powerful artillery bombardments, relying upon gas for effect, had served 'to paralyse the enemy's artillery and to keep the infantry in their dug-outs'.[54] The allies could only advance if willing to accept severe casualties from German gas shelling. The American attack upon the St Mihiel Salient in September 1918 exemplified the problem; indeed gas accounted for 70 752 American soldiers or 27.4 percent of America's total casualties of 258 338.[55]

During the final year of the war, gas was used in unprecedented quantities. The Germans relied upon three types of gas shell: Yellow Cross, Green Cross, and Blue Cross which contained at different times diphenylchloroarsine, diphenylcyanoarsine and other arsenic compounds. The non-persistent gas was supposed to penetrate Allied respirators, prompt their precipitate removal by intensely irritating the nose and throat, and enhance the scope for the more lethal Green Cross shell. In their massive offensives of March 1918, the Germans sealed the flanks of a projected attack with mustard gas, while bombarding the enemy positions for several hours before the assault with Blue and Green Cross shells. So substantial were these assaults that the normal establishment of a German ammunition dump contained some 50 per cent of gas shell by July 1918. Consumption exceeded supply when the Germans were forced onto the defensive and tried to stem the Allied attack by drenching large areas of ground with mustard gas. Although the penetrating gases, particularly the Blue Cross shells, proved comparatively ineffective, the Yellow Cross shell was an excellent defensive weapon.

Gas also assumed an increasing importance in the Allied armouries, if only to counter the German initiatives. By June 1918, the French had produced substantial quantities of mustard gas with which they inflicted heavy casualties upon the Seventh German Army and the 11th Bavarian Division.[56] The British and later the Americans increased their production requirements, with the British launching their first mustard gas attack in September. By the Armistice, chemical shells comprised an estimated 35 per cent of the French, 25 per cent of the British and 15 per cent of the American ammunition expenditures. Had the war continued, both the British and Americans planned to expand their gas shell programmes considerably.[57]

Despite the increasing use of gas, the development of more lethal agents, and recourse to more effective methods of delivery, gas was never a decisive weapon in the First World War. None of the belligerents, not even Germany, invested heavily in chemical warfare. Throughout the conflict, gas shells comprised a mere 4.5 per cent of the artillery ammunitions expended, and specialised chemical troops constituted 2 per cent of the total engineer strength.[58] Armies, in short, placed a much higher priority on the provision and employment of high explosive ammunition.

Reflected in this preference was the persistence of several problems which bedevilled chemical warfare. The most basic was the shortage of any chemical capacity in all countries, with the exception of Germany. She alone possessed a remotely adequate chemical industry, namely the eight chemical combines of the *Interessen Gemeinschaft*. By exploiting this productive capacity, she could procure the complex chemical compounds required by her army quickly and in quantity. The German army employed some 57 600 tons of toxic gases during the war, nearly one half of the total tonnage expended by all belligerents.[59] Nevertheless, even the German industry failed to meet the full requirements of the military, especially when these mounted rapidly in 1918. France produced about one half of the German tonnage and Britain barely a fifth. The British predicament was all too clearly demonstrated in February 1916, when Russia requested the supply of 2700 tons of chlorine and 1600 tons of phosgene from Britain. At that time British industry could not even meet the requirements of General Haig: throughout 1916, British forces only discharged some 1700 tons of gas.[60]

To manufacture mustard gas, the French and British had to build specialist chemical plants, and, in these plants, production proved extremely slow and hazardous. At Roussillon, the main French plant, which supplied three-quarters of the Allied-fired mustard gas, conditions were unpleasant and hazardous. Some 90 per cent of the workforce were voiceless and about 50 per cent coughed continuously. Conjunctivitis was almost universal, and most employees suffered from red, peeling skin which was intensely itchy and rendered sleep 'nearly impossible'.[61] At the main British plant in Avonmouth, the Medical Officer reported over 1400 illnesses directly attributable to the work among a work force of 1100. In a period of six months, there were 160 accidents and over 1000 burns.[62] Despite these risks, it still took nearly a year before the French received any battlefield supplies of mustard gas, while the British had to wait for another three months before her stocks arrived.

Compounding these problems of supply was the military's reluctance to assimilate gas as a weapon of war. Dislike of gas as an additional burden and danger persisted throughout the war. Cylinders were especially loathed. They were cumbersome to carry, had to be installed at night, and then had to remain in the parapet until a favourable wind appeared. Accidents and losses recurred from leaks, from bursting cylinders, and from the shrapnel and high explosive shells which invariably greeted any gas attack. As a captured German pioneer recalled, 'the infantry are all very glad to be away from the front-line trench when the cloud is sent over'.[63] Foulkes would claim that these fears, which were also apparent in British trenches, were '(largely) imaginary'. In the six months after 1916, the British kept 20 000 cylinders in their front line with only twenty-five burst by shells, killing thirty-one men. In 110 cloud attacks, drift-back occurred only once, killing nineteen men as a consequence. Yet the fears, however unreasonable, remained: they were 'almost as destructive in chemical warfare as the chemical itself'.[64]

Gas instruction was perfunctory, extremely dull and boring for instructors and men alike. Soldiers spent about one week in gas schools, with about one hour immersed in a cloud gas and thirty seconds exposed to tear gas. A. E. Hodgkin, recalled that his job as a temporary Chemical Advisor assigned to the Fifth Army headquarters was 'rather dull', with 'no chance of progression'. It involved 'a certain amount of instruction which hardly ever varies' and the tedium of lecturing before disinterested audiences. 'Most of the audience,' Hodgkin recalled, 'go to sleep: those who do not are only kept awake by the intense cold'.[65] Gas instructors complained bitterly about the lack of interest shown by their audience. 'Never, never', wrote Hodgkin, 'will the mysteries of gas warfare penetrate the brain of the regular soldier.' Commanding officers and their staffs were often as culpable; indeed, Hodgkin found that the staff of the 62nd Division, despite two years of training, knew 'about as much about gas as a new-born babe!'[66]

Gas equipment was regularly misused. Troops used their box respirator satchel to carry 'rations, knives and forks, ammunition, private knickknacks of all kinds', irrespective of the damage which such items might do to the respirator or the problems they could pose for using it quickly.[67] Proper anti-gas precautions were sometimes ignored or neglected, and basic instruction was occasionally missed by new recruits. Whenever training was neglected gas casualties mounted, particularly among those who were exposed to the persistent effects of mustard gas.[68] The chemical officers felt aggrieved and frustrated. 'The paid expert (myself),' wrote Hodgkin, 'should either be sacked, or else his views should be acted on: one can't both have one's cake and eat it.'[69] But the British gas officer had one enduring source of comfort; his frustrations and disappointments were not unique. German chemical officers were equally dismayed by the repeated failures of gas discipline in the German army. A gas officer of the Sixth German Army complained that the gas casualties in the winter of 1916 'were mainly due to the men being surprised in dug-outs, to the neglect of gas discipline, masks not being at hand, to faulty masks, and to the use of old pattern drums which could not afford protection against the type of gas employed by the enemy'.[76] Even improved equipment could not counter the threat posed by the Livens Projector. Because the gas was fired in lethal concentrations without warning, all German working parties had to wear gas masks when within 1000 yards of the front line on any night when an Allied gas attack could be launched. Morale undoubtedly suffered as the troops laboured under this imposition.

Logistics, finally, proved a persistent problem in gas warfare, especially for the British in mounting their cylinder attacks. The infantry deeply resented the additional work involved in night-time installations which had to be quietly and carefully completed in order to preserve the secrecy of the operation. The British never fully solved this problem. A cable-based ropeway was devised and tested, but the lengthy period of experimentation precluded its use before the Armistice. Although a trench tramway was introduced, its labour-saving properties were limited. As Hodgkin recalled:

All our material is brought up to the line by light railway which is never repaired much and which is consequently jerky, to say the very least of it. Each truck goes up separately being pushed by 5 or 6 men: every 100 yds or so it hops off the line and has to [be] unloaded, replaced on the line, and loaded up again. My vocabulary has been improved wonderfully by the exercise, but that of the men is becoming rather threadbare.[71]

These problems might have seemed of less importance had commanders been able to assess immediately the effectiveness of gas attacks. This was never possible. Nor were the early wartime agents likely to produce a decisive breakthrough. Shortages of chemicals, the deficiencies of the munitions, and the limitations of the early modes of attack were palpable shortcomings. They were compounded by improvements in protective devices and in anti-gas training. Gas was largely reduced to the rôle of attrition, inflicting casualties upon the enemy and hampering his movements. By using the gas shell in this rôle during the period from July 1916 to July 1917, the Germans largely wasted its potential. Instead of concentrating upon the surprise bombardments of important targets, they distributed their fire over wide areas with the aim of 'neutralising' the enemy's effectiveness. This tactic derived from earlier attacks with tear gas which had proved an adequate means of harassment, but scattered area shelling wasted the lethality of lung irritants which required higher concentrations of agent to ensure a casualty dosage. Only in December 1917 did the German General Staff formally alter these tactics. While retaining area shelling as a means of harassment, it revised neutralisation to include sudden concentrated fire upon comparatively small targets and envisaged mustard gas as a weapon of area denial.[72]

Even with improved tactics, however, gas was never a decisive battlefield weapon. Only in the initial attack upon Ypres, when the Germans gained ground which they held for another two and a half years, was a specific gain directly attributable to gas. As the war progressed, gas became merely one of several new weapons and was employed, like the tank and combat aircraft, on an increasingly large scale. It undoubtedly contributed to the outcome of particular operations, notably the capture of Riga in September 1917; the German offensive of March–April 1918, including the seizure of Armentières without any loss of life; and the German defensive actions of September–November 1918. Whether it was as influential in these operations as J. F. C. Fuller argues, is debatable,[73] but gas was clearly perceived as an increasingly valuable weapon, capable of causing heavy casualties or at least of undermining morale, by forcing troops to work for long periods encumbered by anti-gas equipment.

Much more passion would be expended over the morality of using chemical weapons than over their tactical effectiveness. In the post-war years, those who sought to proscribe these weapons described them as peculiarly 'inhumane'. The Allied governments had partially contributed to this perception by their vehement denunciations of the German gas attack of April 1915, and by shrouding subsequent gas operations in considerable secrecy, both the German successes and Allied activities. To counter criticisms of gas, chemical officers, scientific advisers and later military historians began to argue that gas was actually more humane than other weapons, even 'the most humane method of warfare ever applied on the battle field'.[74]

Although war is hardly a humane exercise, it can be prosecuted by methods which do not cause excessive or needless suffering. Humaneness, in this context, may be measured by the degree of suffering at the time of injury, the degree of permanent after-effects, and the proportion of deaths caused by comparison with other weapons. Generally, gas caused less suffering than wounds from other weapons. Although chlorine caused strangulation, considerable pain and a high mortality among unprotected troops, it was rendered comparatively innocuous by gas mask protection. The more effective lethal gases caused much less initial suffering. While phosgene, when it took effect, caused instant collapse with relatively little pain, mustard gas inflicted pain in proportion to the levels of concentration, length of exposure, and parts affected. The delay of several hours ensured that the many casualties could be treated by the time the symptoms appeared. By the end of the war British medical officers reckoned that some 80 per cent of the mustard gas casualties who were evacuated from the front could be made fit for duty after eight weeks of treatment, and a 'considerable proportion could be cured within 4 weeks'.[75] Although some casualties would suffer for the rest of their lives from war gassing, many more would make a relatively quick recovery and at least emerge from the experience with their body and limbs intact. In the American army, gas caused 26.8 per cent of all casualties but only 11.3 per cent of the total discharges for disability. The period of hospitalisation of gas casualties was about one half, on average, of the period which non-gas casualties spent in hospital.[76] Finally, the mortality rate of gas appears to have been much less than that of other weapons. Prentiss, in his authoritative comparison of the official statistics, records that Britain suffered only 4.3 per cent of deaths from gas while 24 per cent of her non-gas casualties died; France had 4.2 per cent deaths from gas compared with 32 per cent deaths from non-gas weapons; the United States had 2 per cent deaths from gas as against 25.8 per cent deaths from conventional arms; and Germany 4.5 per cent deaths from gas compared with 36.5 per cent deaths from other arms. Such data provided the basis for the case that gas was considerably less cruel in its effects than high-explosive shells and other conventional armaments.[77]

These arguments are still disputed. Some of those who advocate the proscription of chemical weapons stress that their horrific potential was concealed by the official statistics. Noting the absence of data on the first German gas attack, they quote the post-war German claim that the Allies suffered 5000 dead and 10 000 wounded. They also maintain that the official statistics grossly underestimate the numbers of men who were killed and wounded by gas. British statistics, write Harris and Paxman, omit those who were gassed in 1915 for whom no records exist; any gas victims captured by the enemy; any soldiers killed outright by gas on the field of battle; any gassed soldiers among the quarter of a million who were listed as missing in action; any men retained in Field Ambulances with relatively minor injuries; any gas casualties who died after evacuation to Britain; and any gas casualties who died of illnesses precipitated by exposure to gas. Finally, they insist that the long-term effects of gas poisoning were much worse than the official data imply. 'Exceptionally harsh' criteria were established, so limiting the number who were eligible to receive a disability pension. Many thousands of men continued to suffer from the effects of wartime gassing for the rest of their lives.[78]

Had this analysis possessed more consistency, and a sense of perspective, it might have carried more conviction. Medical records were incomplete, with inadequate British data for 1915, German statistics which terminate on 31 July 1918 and unreliable information for the Eastern Front. Although a lack of reliability is generally true, it is particularly true of the early German cloud gas attacks. The post-war claim that the Germans killed 5000 men and injured many thousands more lacks any substantiation. Indeed, what fragments of information exist suggest that these figures are much too high.[79] Undoubtedly, the official statistics underestimate the number of men who were killed and injured by gas, but lack of precision was not peculiar to the recording of gas-related injuries; it applied across the whole spectrum of medical evidence, which had perforce to exclude the captured, missing, and killed in action. Similarly, the pension settlements are inaccurate, a shortcoming which applies to all classifications and not simply to victims of poison gas. Many injured ex-servicemen received less than they should have or even nothing: some signed themselves A1 in health simply to escape the army. Conservative though the numbers may be, the proportions are significant at least for the purpose of comparing gas with other weapons. By March 1926, only 683 men were receiving pensions for gassing while, as late as 1929, 65 000 others were still languishing from 'shell shock' in mental hospitals.[80] What these proportions reflect is not the 'humanity' of using gas but the limited, and largely auxiliary, rôle of gas on the field of battle.

Gas, as a consequence, was hardly a war-winning weapon in the First World War. Even on the Eastern Front, where it inflicted heavy casualties upon the poorly protected Russians (475 000 injured and 56 000 fatalities), its tactical impact was all too often blunted by the extreme cold.[81] On the Western Front, its effectiveness was also localised and limited. 'Gas,' wrote Brigadier-General Edmonds, 'achieved but local success; it made war uncomfortable, to no purpose.'[82] This view, though endorsed by another historian who served in the trenches at Ypres,[83] is probably too dismissive. Gas was effective locally and suggested a potential utility for future conflicts. Should the principles of surprise and concentration be realised, and appropriate targets chosen, gas still offered, in the view of Brigadier Hartley, 'brilliant possibilities'. He recognised, nonetheless, that the potential of gas, especially its effect on morale, could be greatly exaggerated: 'theoretical victories,' he added, 'might well be won with other weapons on the same assumptions'.[84]

3   The Failure of Disarmament

German acceptance of the Armistice on 11 November 1918 occasioned immense relief from war-weary peoples and widespread hope that peace could now be secured on a lasting basis. President Woodrow Wilson, having led the United States into a 'war to end war', cherished the expectation of realising a permanent peace. Once the war had ended he envisaged the creation of a new international order, rooted in a League of Nations, which would be able to guarantee the rights and peace of all nations, whether large or small. At the peace conference in Versailles (1919), he gained the endorsement of the concept, with some modifications, by the other victorious powers and the approval of a Covenant which committed the League to see 'the reduction of national armaments to the lowest point consistent with national safety' (Article 8). This initiative, coupled with the drastic reduction of the German war machine, including its chemical capability (Versailles Treaty, Article 171), seemed to portend a new era in international relations. At the very least, it required each of the major nations to reassess its policy on chemical warfare.

As early as 25 March 1919, senior officers within the British General Staff had expressed alarm lest the peace conference should prohibit gas warfare. To preserve this tactical option, they had sought the aid of the French and had prepared a paper for circulation at Versailles. Drafted by Major-General Sir Arthur Lynden-Bell, the Director of Staff Duties, and Major-General Percy P. de B. Radcliffe, the Director of Military Organisation, this memorandum questioned the value of international proscription in view of the failure of the Hague Declaration and the impossibility of verifying another ban completely. Britain, they added, had benefited from the recourse to gas in the recent operations and, by utilising the prevailing westerly winds, she had increasingly used chemical weapons. Had the war continued, 'one shell in every four that left our lines . . . would have been a gas shell, and tanks would further have been using it freely'.

Henceforth Britain could employ gas in her minor colonial campaigns, both non-lethal tear gases and mustard gas, to impede the movement and fighting power of unprotected tribesmen. As Lynden-Bell and Radcliffe concluded,

> Whatever adversary is contemplated, whether highly or semi-civilized, it would be unthinkable to commit our troops to the field without the best possible gas protection, no matter what undertakings had been given by the enemy. We must therefore continue the study and science of gas in all its forms, primarily with a view to protection, secondly with a view to retaliation.[1]

Winston Churchill, then Secretary of State for War and Air, quickly endorsed these sentiments, and agreed that Britain should act in concert with the French.[2] Marshal Ferdinand Foch needed little persuading. Convinced of the potential importance of gas warfare, he shared Britain's concern about Germany's chemical manufacturing capacity. 'Chemical warfare,' he later wrote, should 'enter into our calculations and our preparations for the future, if we wish to avoid a formidable surprise.'[3] On 15 April 1919, Britain formally proposed that Germany should transfer all chemical processes which had been used for producing munitions to the Allies. Robert Lansing, the American Secretary of State, adamantly opposed this suggestion, implying that the British motives were essentially economic and not military.[4] Unable to allay this suspicion, the British delegation accepted the compromise formulation: 'The use of asphyxiating, poisonous, or other gases and all analogous liquids, materials or devices being prohibited, their manufacture and importation are strictly forbidden in Germany' (Article 171).

Like so many aspects of the treaty, this article proved unsatisfactory and merely compounded the German sense of grievance. It lacked any substance as a measure of disarmament. As Major Lefebure repeatedly argued, the chemical combine, IG, had fuelled the German war effort and had an unparalleled productive capacity. Unless it was controlled, the Allies could not assume that Germany was effectively disarmed and could not proceed towards mutual disarmament.[5] Nor did the article provide any reassurance that gas warfare could not recur, a suspicion reflected in the findings of a War Office committee, chaired by Lieutenant-General Sir Arthur Holland. Reporting in July 1919, less than a month after the treaty was signed, the committee maintained that 'a Nation which is unprepared for Gas Warfare lays itself open to sudden and inveterate disaster'. It recommended that Porton should be retained, and that scientists of 'the right type' should be attracted by substantial salaries, security of tenure, pensions, liberal allowances of leave as well as the rights to publish the results of work which was 'not of military importance' and to attend meetings of learned societies.[6] The British War Cabinet, though still hopeful of progress towards disarmament once the League was established, accepted the main thrust of these arguments. On 16 October 1919, it resolved to retain the gas organisation because 'no other military Power' had taken the initiative in chemical disarmament. Five months later, on 4 March 1920, it determined to raise the issue at the Council of the League of Nations, hoping to put 'an end to such warfare'.[7]

The Chemical Warfare Service also survived in the United States. This was an extremely new body as provision for chemical warfare had not been anticipated before the United States entered the war (6 April 1917). It was not until August 1917, when some 12 000 American troops were deployed about thirty miles from the German lines, without gas masks or anti-gas training, that a Chemical Warfare Service, headed by Lieutenant-Colonel Amos A. Fries, was established. Even so, an American-based organisation able to support the Gas Service in France was not formed until May 1918. Under the direction of Major-General William L. Sibert, this body co-ordinated all aspects of the American gas effort, both offensive and defensive. It was the Interior Department (Bureau of Mines) and not the War Department which initiated the research and production of toxic agents. A massive research and production plant, known as the Edgewood Arsenal, was established in 3400 acres 20 miles east of Baltimore, Maryland. By 1 October 1918, 233 officers, 6948 enlisted men and 3066 civilians were working at Edgewood. Located within the grounds were 550 buildings, some 15 miles of roadway, 36 miles of railway and production plants for phosgene, chlorine, chloropicrin, mustard gas and sulphur chloride. In addition a new chemical compound, called lewisite after its discoverer, Captain W. Lee Lewis, had been discovered. This was an arsenic compound which had many of the vesicant properties of mustard gas but was quicker acting. It not only blistered the skin and caused excruciating eye pain, but could, if the dosage were large enough, penetrate the skin and poison the body. The first 150 tons of lewisite was at sea, *en route* to Europe, when the Armistice was signed.[8] Although the navy never used chemical weapons in the First World War, a defensive policy was established requiring individual protection and the provision of gas-proofing and decontamination devices aboard ship. A special navy board reported in June 1918, advocating the development of an armour-piercing shell with a non-lethal gas filler – a plan which was never implemented.[9]

As soon as the war ended, the War Department mounted a campaign to disband the Chemical Warfare Service. General Peyton C. March, the Chief of Staff, abhorred the effects of gas warfare, particularly the sufferings of women and children whom he had seen among the gas casualties in Paris. Feeling that such warfare 'reduces civilization to savagery', he pressed for the abolition of the Chemical Warfare Service.[10] Newton D. Baker, the Secretary for War, heeded his advice and proposed relegating the study of gases and of protective devices to a section of the Engineer Corps. Only the intensive lobbying of Fries on Capitol Hill, supported by a massive publicity campaign, preserved the Chemical Warfare Service as a separate body in the 1920 National Defense Act.[11]

Despite their retention by the major powers, the gas warfare services soon encountered a multitude of problems. Many political leaders wished to contain their remit and, if possible, to abolish gas warfare altogether. When the British General Staff, strongly supported by Churchill, wished to use poison gas against the Afghan tribesmen,[12] they met with vehement opposition from the authorities at home and in India. Edwin Montagu, the Secretary of State for India, feared for the 'very serious political and moral' consequences of using gas,[13] while neither Lord Chelmsford, the Viceroy, nor Sir Charles Monro, the Commander-in-Chief in India, saw any need for gas as the army had just triumphed in the Third Afghan War (April–May 1919), using conventional weapons. Although Brigadier-General Foulkes eventually converted Chelmsford and Monro – after an extensive tour of the frontier and a campaign promoting the tactical utility of mustard gas – the Indian Office remained firmly opposed. Indeed Montagu gained the support of several Cabinet colleagues, including Lord Fisher, the President of the Board of Trade. In a lengthy memorandum Fisher maintained that the initial response to gas warfare was right: 'the British public thought that poison gas was a low game and they think so still'. He argued that since another war was not imminent the army should desist from employing or developing its stocks of gas until the prospects for abolition have been 'thoroughly explored'.[14] Austen Chamberlain, the Foreign Secretary, endorsed this reasoning. 'It was', he suggested, 'undesirable that we should proceed with our studies of the use of gas without first making an effort to induce the world generally to abandon its use.'[15]

This opposition was only deflected by a ruling of the League of Nations Permanent Advisory Commission on Military and Naval Technical Questions. On 20 October 1920, the Commission decided that it would be 'useless' to seek to restrict the use of gases in war by prohibiting their research or manufacture in peace. The Cabinet promptly increased its funding on chemical warfare research from £52 000 in 1920–1 to £135 130 for 1921–2.[16] Such expenditure, though much less than the sum proposed by the Holland Committee (£500 000 in capital outlay and £330 000 in annual recurring costs), at least sustained Porton and the Chemical Warfare Committee. In view of the draconian economies which were being imposed on the armed services, this was a significant achievement. The Cabinet was implicitly accepting the Holland Committee's view that, whatever the eventual ruling of the League of Nations on the legitimacy of gas warfare, nations would be compelled 'in the interests of safety' to continue their research into the offensive and defensive methods of this warfare, if only to avoid a 'recurrence of the events of April 1915'.[17]

Political hostility was even more apparent in the United States. Throughout the inter-war period, successive Presidents sought the abolition of gas warfare. Leading international opinion towards this objective became a consistent aim in American foreign policy, following the precept of Warren G. Harding that the United States should 'help humanity throughout the world to reach a little higher plane'.[18] Such lofty sentiments coincided with a desire to meet the expectations of various peace groups in the United States and to curb expenditure on the military in general and on the Chemical Warfare Service in particular. Although successive administrations accepted the necessity of retaining a defensive chemical capability, pending the realisation of total disarmament, they favoured neither an expansion of its remit nor a significant increase in its funding. As late as 1937, Franklin D. Roosevelt vetoed a bill to alter the title of the Chemical Warfare Service to Chemical Corps, lest the change 'dignify' a Service whose extinction was his ultimate objective.[19]

What further hampered research into chemical warfare were the ambivalent attitudes which it aroused within the scientific community and the military establishments. The scientific divisions were the less important. On the one hand, Sir Edward Thorpe undoubtedly spoke for many colleagues in describing the recourse to poison gas during the First World War as a 'degradation of science'. In his presidential address to the British Association for the Advancement of Science on 7 September 1921, he affirmed that 'Civilization protests against a step so retrograde. Surely comity among nations should be adequate to arrest it.'[20] On the other hand, Sir William Pope argued that the use of 'gas was more merciful than high explosives', and that chemical weapons could become 'the sole deciding factor in future wars'. Similar ideas would be amplified in the trenchantly argued and widely read *Callinicus: A Defence of Chemical Warfare*, written by John B. S. Haldane.[21] Such divisions of opinion did not prevent either Porton or Edgewood from recruiting teams of engineers, technologists, and specialists in most branches of physical science. Many chemical manufacturers assisted the various research programmes and several universities undertook government-sponsored research. The British Chemical Warfare and Research Department regularly filled its membership quota of nine eminent scientists. Above all, in the United States the Chemical Society strongly supported Fries in his periodic lobbying of Congress to ensure the continuation of the Chemical Warfare Service.

Military reluctance to assimilate gas into its training, tactical, and operational requirements was much more significant. Gas contradicted several basic premises in the military code of conduct, particularly the belief that war should be restricted to combatants only. When Foulkes toured the North-West Frontier, assessing its potential for gas warfare, he heard critics maintain that gas would conflict with the traditional chivalry of frontier fighting, that it would encumber the logistics of military operations, and that it was basically unnecessary since conventional weapons had always proved their worth. Military opinion was split, with some frontier commanders proving more sympathetic towards the use of gas than the High Command in Simla. The latter was worried not merely about the tactical implications of using gas but also about any political repercussions in view of Britain's condemnation of Germany for having introduced gas in 1915.[22] Within the home army, Captain Auld perceived a widespread and 'dangerous apathy' about the potential rôle of gas. He ascribed it to a 'marking time' approach by the General Staff, pending an international ruling on the legitimacy of gas warfare; to a widespread ignorance of gas among senior and junior officers (partly because gas personnel had been largely drawn from the ranks of non-regulars during the war); and to a 'lack of sympathy with the subject *in toto*, resulting from a natural feeling that it is a rotten way of fighting anyhow'. Given the secrecy which had shrouded the Allies' gas operations, Auld felt that the military had tended to 'decry the effects of gas on the one hand or to magnify its brutality on the other'.[23]

Faced with a malaise so profound and pervasive, gas zealots like Fries, Foulkes and Auld and army reformers like Fuller and Liddell Hart campaigned vigorously to 'educate' opinion. Throughout the 1920s they produced a profusion of lectures, articles and books, advocating more study of gas as a weapon of war. Their arguments were essentially fourfold. In the first place, gas could have proved decisive in the last War had it been used more efficiently or had larger stocks been available at appropriate moments. Testifying to this importance, they argued, was the development of ever more potent gases and the increasing prominence of gas within the arsenals of the Allies. Secondly, gas had achieved its effects without causing as many fatalities or permanent disabilities as high explosive. Official medical statistics were quoted repeatedly to prove the relative 'humanity' of gas as compared with conventional munitions and to indicate that even non-lethal gases and smokes could prove tactically useful. Thirdly, gas was described as a weapon of the future, irrespective of international attempts to proscribe it. A weapon, so easily produced and versatile in its properties, could be used in land, sea and, above all, air operations. Indeed the future combination of the gas bomb and the aeroplane, directed against cities and rear area targets, seemed potentially the most effective and menacing use of gas. Finally, gas could still be used both offensively and defensively in the mobile operations, based upon the tank and mechanical means of transport, which it was hoped would replace the linear battlefield of the Great War.[24] Admittedly expectations varied considerably over the impact of gas at this level; whereas Fuller anticipated that gas-tight tanks would dominate future battles, the gas zealots demurred, claiming that gas might prove 'the Achilles' heel of the tank'. None doubted, though, that gas would prove immensely important: 'there is a strong probability', argued Foulkes, 'that gas will displace H(igh) E(xplosive) as a shell filling almost as completely as HE has displaced black powder'.[25]

The reformers' criticism of their military establishments was not entirely fair. Both Generals John J. Pershing and Sir Henry Wilson, the Chiefs of Staff in the United States and Britain, sought to maintain their respective chemical warfare capabilities, despite in Pershing's case a strong personal antipathy to gas warfare.[26] Neither could ignore – and Pershing positively supported – the diplomatic initiatives which were aimed at curtailing the need for such a capability. The United States launched the first of these initiatives when it invited Britain, France, Italy and Japan to a conference in Washington on the Limitation of Armaments, which lasted from November 1921 until

February 1922. The Harding administration had several objectives in sponsoring the conference, principally naval disarmament, a disengagement of Britain from her pre-war alliance with Japan, and the resolution of outstanding Sino-Japanese disputes. Gas warfare was a comparatively minor issue, but the Harding administration still sought another international prohibition of poison gas to reaffirm international law, improve upon the Hague Declaration, and produce a statement which the American Senate could ratify (since it had failed to ratify the Treaty of Versailles).

Several subcommittees were appointed to make recommendations to the main committee. A technical subcommittee, composed of members from the five principal powers, examined the 'Utilization of Poisonous Gases' and 'Rules for the Conduct of War'. It concluded that neither research on, nor the manufacture of, poison gas could be prohibited, restricted or supervised, and hence that no nation dare risk entering into an agreement which an unscrupulous enemy might break if he found his opponents unprepared to use gases both offensively and defensively. It only accepted that the use of gases should be prohibited against cities and other large bodies of non-combatants in the same manner as high explosives. But another committee which advised the American delegation took a contrary view. Composed of various public officials and private citizens, it took evidence from pacifist associations and other bodies, testifying to the outrage felt by segments of American opinion. It also organised a poll of public opinion, recording that 366 795 respondents favoured the abolition of chemical weapons, while only nineteen approved their 'retention and restriction in use'.[27] Although the committee, chaired by Pershing, accepted that there were arguments in favour of the use of gas, it deplored the prospect of aerial gas bombardments. Claiming to represent the 'conscience of the American people', it advocated the total abolition of chemical warfare and its classification with unfair methods of warfare such as poisoning wells and spreading germs of disease. A third report was submitted by the General Board of the United States Navy. It asserted that the employment of gas in the First World War had infringed two principles of warfare, namely, that unnecessary suffering should be avoided and that innocent non-combatants should not be destroyed.[28]

Deviating from its practice in respect of submarines, aircraft and the disposition of naval vessels, the American delegation set aside the findings of the technical subcommittee. Having aroused expectations about banning chemical weapons, it would not douse them with a careful and guarded recommendation. On 6 January 1922, Elihu Root formally proposed that the conference should recognise the condemnation of gas warfare by 'the general opinion of the civilized world', and that its prohibition should be 'universally accepted as a part of international law'. Arthur Balfour, heading the British delegation, had hoped that this issue would not be raised, and suspected that it had been 'rather hastily adopted'. On the one hand, he believed that the research and production of poison gas could not be curtailed by international ruling, that no nation could allow its safety to depend upon other states adhering to such a ruling, and that Britain would have to take the same precautionary measures whether or not the conference condemned gas warfare. On the other hand, he accepted that the American statement was merely a reaffirmation of the Treaty of Versailles, and that the other powers were likely to endorse it. Britain, therefore, could only agree lest the rejection of the proposal 'be laid wholly at our door'. Britain, he feared, would be 'charged with appealing to sentiments of humanity when it suits them – as it does in the case of submarines – and being indifferent or hostile when their interests are specially concerned'.[29]

At the 17th Meeting of the Washington Conference, on 7 January 1922, Balfour heartily endorsed the American proposal. Nonetheless, he echoed the reservations of Albert Sarraut of France that merely affirming a law without any sanctions would not relieve nations from taking precautions against those who might break the law. He added, too, that it was impossible to prevent a nation, bent upon using gas in war, from making its preparations to do so. 'No nation,' he concluded, 'could forget that it was open to attack by unscrupulous enemies; no nation therefore could forego that duty of examining how such attacks could be properly dealt with and effectively met'.[30] With these remarks minuted, the delegates duly approved the American resolution which later became Article V of the Treaty:

The use in war of asphyxiating, poisonous or other gases, and all analogous liquids, materials or devices, having been justly condemned by the general opinion of the civilized world and a prohibition of such use having been declared in the Treaties to which a majority of the civilized Powers are parties,

The Signatory Powers, to the end that this prohibition shall be universally accepted as a part of international law binding alike the conscience and practice of nations, declare their assent to such prohibition, agree to be bound thereby as between themselves and invite all other civilized nations to adhere thereto.[31]

Initially the disarmament clauses of the Washington Treaty were hailed as an immense success. Unlike those clauses in the peace treaties with Germany, Austria, Bulgaria, Hungary and Turkey, they were not imposed on defeated countries. As measures freely agreed, and of universal application, they were approved by the American Senate on 29 March 1922, so representing the first American endorsement of an international ruling on gas warfare. But the treaty proved a lamentable failure. It never came into force because France failed to ratify it on account of the submarine clauses. Moreover, Article V represented the worst form of disarmament agreement since its wording never strayed beyond pious platitudes. By ignoring the issues raised in the technical subcommittee, it failed to consider the tasks of monitoring, verifying, and enforcing an agreement. Even worse, by referring to the 'general opinion of the civilized world' in the heady post-war atmosphere of the early 1920s, it raised expectations that gas would not be used in a future war. Setting aside the careful caveats of Sarraut and Balfour, the US War Department used the treaty to justify its deletion of the training of fighting troops in offensive chemical warfare. And in Britain Sir Robert Horne, the Chancellor of the Exchequer, proposed curtailing the expenditure on Porton because of the treaty, and argued that it should be closed altogether if other powers agreed to follow suit. More prudent counsel prevailed once the Committee of Imperial Defence had received the protests of the War Office and Admiralty, as well as the intelligence estimates of a potential German chemical warfare capability, unchecked by the Treaty of Versailles.[32]

In default of any binding agreement, and pending further action by the League of Nations, the major powers retained their chemical warfare capabilities. France, though willing to abide by the gas clauses of the Washington Treaty, kept its stocks of gas shell and approved the study of offensive gas tactics at its Staff College and Centre of Higher Military Studies. The American Chemical Warfare Service, despite a greatly reduced budget, preserved its research facility at Edgewood Arsenal, assisted in the training of troops in anti-gas techniques, and retained the 1st Gas Regiment which undertook limited training in the offensive use of gas. Within Britain, research continued on all aspects of gas warfare at Porton, various universities and several hospitals. In deference to the Washington Treaty, the army accepted that gas should only be a weapon of retaliation, and that training should be primarily defensive. The training was also extremely limited as the army had dispensed with any specialist gas troops and had utterly inadequate stocks of equipment (although it had some half million face pieces in store, most of which were made in 1918 and were all unserviceable by 1924). Only in 1923 were courses begun at Porton, enabling twenty staff and senior officers as well as eighty regimental instructors to receive training in gas defence each year. What provided a vital spur to these efforts were the reports emanating from Germany of continued research into gas warfare, the refusal to surrender gas masks to the Inter-Allied Control Commission, and the prominence of gas tactics in her military manuals.[33]

Hopes of progress towards disarmament centred upon the League of Nations. With the aim of arousing public concern about gas warfare, the Third Committee of the League recommended that a report should be prepared on the probable consequences of chemical discoveries upon future warfare. Agreed by the Fourth Assembly on 29 September 1923, a sub-committee was established, comprising chemists, physiologists and bacteriologists from eight different countries. They had access to the findings of the technical committee which had reported to the Washington Conference. After examining a wide range of gases and their effects, the committee concluded that poison gases, if not bacteriological weapons, were extremely formidable, that they conferred an immense advantage on any power with hostile intentions, and that their manufacture could be easily camouflaged. These findings were incorporated in the Temporary Mixed Commission's report on chemical and bacteriological weapons. Issued on 30 July 1924, the report warned 'that all nations should realise to the full the terrible nature of the danger which threatens them'.[34]

On 27 September 1924, the Fifth Assembly of the League of Nations acted upon this report. It requested that the Council should circulate the draft convention, prepared by the Temporary Mixed Commission, relating to the control of the international trade in arms, munitions and weapons of war to the governments of members and non-members of the League. Following this exchange of correspondence, a conference was convened in Geneva on 4 May 1925 to consider the 'Supervision of the International Trade in Arms and Ammunition and in Implements of War'. This conference was also required to examine proposals for the prohibition of the use of chemical and bacteriological warfare.

At the first meeting, held on 7 May, Theodore E. Burton, the

American representative, seized the initiative. He stressed that President Calvin Coolidge wished to secure an international agreement upon the prohibition of the export of poison gas. He submitted a draft convention before the general committee of the conference which virtually reproduced the wording of the Washington Treaty, only adding that the conference should agree to prohibit the export of asphyxiating, poisonous or other gases and analogous liquids which were designed or intended for military usage.[35] While most countries applauded the principle and sentiments of the American proposal, several fears were immediately raised. Non-producing countries noted that failure to constrain the producing states, who could still manufacture and employ gases, would preserve the existing inequalities. Other smaller countries claimed that the means of defence against chemical warfare should be excluded from the prohibition. Poland insisted that the prohibition should cover bacteriological as well as chemical warfare. Once the issue was referred to a Military, Naval and Air Technical Committee, even more difficulties arose. The British delegation, supported by the Polish and Italian delegations, carried the committee in arguing that merely banning trade in chemical and bacteriological weapons would not prevent their use in future wars, and would constitute a menace to the security of non-producing states. In his report to the general committee, Colonel Lohner insisted that a larger political issue was at stake, namely the effective means of prohibiting chemical and bacteriological warfare, and that a conference on the arms trade was not the proper body to proclaim new principles of international law in regard to war.[36]

Once again technical advice had confounded the hopes raised by an American initiative. Nevertheless, several nations dreaded the consequences of the conference adjourning without some pronouncement on chemical and bacteriological warfare. Burton quickly harnessed this feeling; he proposed another general declaration based upon Article V of the Washington Treaty or, failing that, the convocation of another special conference in Washington to draft a convention on chemical warfare. While the Earl of Onslow endorsed the second approach, Paul-Bancour, in a speech which 'made women weep and men tremble with emotion', sketched vividly 'the horrors and sufferings of the great war and the awfulness of gas warfare'. As so many Frenchmen had suffered from 'the marvels of science in the sphere of destruction', he supported any initiative which could prohibit chemical warfare.[37] The majority of the general committee agreed, and, by 17 June 1925, the conference approved a protocol. It stated that

the use in war of asphyxiating, poisonous or other gases, and of all
analogous liquids, materials or devices, has been justly condemned
by the general opinion of the civilized world; and . . . the prohibition
of such use . . . shall be universally accepted as part of International
Law, binding alike the conscience and the practice of nations.

This protocol also encompassed bacteriological methods of warfare.[38]

Forty-one powers, including the United States, France, Germany,
Poland, Italy, Japan and the British Empire, signed the Geneva
Protocol. They had merely signed a declaration which reproduced the
injunctions of the Washington Treaty, extended to cover bacteriologi-
cal as well as chemical warfare. The Protocol neither contained any
sanction for non-compliance nor applied to a war with non-signatories.
It also had to be ratified, with a clear lead expected from the United
States. Frank Kellogg, the Secretary of State, assumed that ratification
would follow in view of the Senate's endorsement of the Washington
Treaty and General Pershing's declared antipathy to poison gas.
Indeed, Senator William E. Borah, in trying to sway his colleagues,
quoted the general's statement that 'Chemical warfare should be
abolished among nations as abhorrent to civilization. It is a cruel,
unfair, and improper use of science. It is fraught with gravest danger to
noncombatants and demoralizing to the better instincts of humanity.'[39]
But Fries had marshalled his opposition much more effectively than in
1922. He had supplied senatorial opponents, led by James W.
Wadsworth, with masses of information demonstrating, as the latter
claimed, that 'compared with other weapons used in warfare, gas is the
least cruel, not only in its effect at the time of its use but in its after
effects'.[40] Fries had also ensured that senators were deluged with
telegrams, denouncing the Protocol, from the American Legion,
Veterans of Foreign Wars, the Association of Medical Surgeons and
the American Chemical Society. So formidable was the lobby that
Borah, Chairman of the Senate Foreign Relations Committee, withdrew the treaty from Senate consideration. (It remained with the
Committee until 1947 when President Truman withdrew the executive's request for Senate action on it. Resubmitted by President Nixon
on 19 August 1970, it was eventually ratified in 1975.)

American equivocation hardly enhanced the credibility of the
Protocol. Japan followed America's example and refused to ratify
while the European countries carefully considered their respective
positions. Of the major powers, France took the initiative and ratified
in 1926. Two years later Italy and the Soviet Union followed suit, but it

was not until Germany ratified in 1929 that Britain felt able to do so. Only on 9 April 1930 did Britain ratify the Protocol and, following the example of France and Russia, she added two reservations: first, that this commitment only applied *vis-à-vis* other states which had ratified the Protocol, and second, that this commitment would cease should any enemy fail to respect the Protocol.[41] In short, Britain regarded the Protocol as merely a ban on the first use of poison gas or germ warfare and retained the right to retaliate should she be attacked.

Sceptical writers assert that these declarations had little practical significance. They claim correctly that research on offensive and defensive aspects of chemical warfare was continued in the major countries, and that the 'public' was cynically deceived. Harris and Paxman quote selectively from the official history of Porton to buttress this thesis. They reproduce the following passage:

> On the offensive side of chemical warfare, the Government's pronouncement following ratification of the Geneva Protocol meant that any actual development of weapons had to be done 'under the rose'. As a gesture, the Offensive Munitions Department at Porton changed its name back to 'Technical Chemical Department' and in 1930 the term 'Chemical Warfare' was expunged from official language and titles and 'Chemical Defence' was substituted. Thereafter all offensive work was done under the heading 'Study of chemical weapons against which defence is required'.

However, that passage continues by describing the critical constraints which were placed upon British research – constraints omitted by Harris and Paxman.

> The practical effects of this were that funds for weapon research were limited, weapon trials could not be done openly and hence were restricted in scope, and finalization of designs was delayed by absence of the impetus which is imparted by manufacturing contracts and target dates. Moreover, as the Services were not in a position to say what chemical weapons they might need in a future war, the limited offensive effort had to be spread thinly over a very wide range of investigation and development.[42]

Signing and later ratifying the Protocol constrained British gas policy in several respects. In the first place, the Foreign Office regarded the British condemnations of poison gas at Washington and

Geneva as binding declarations of policy. When this was challenged in the Committee of Imperial Defence in 1926 by the War Office and the India Office, then headed by Lord Birkenhead, Sir Austen Chamberlain was adamant. To counter arguments that gas was a legitimate form of warfare, and should be used on the North-West Frontier, he insisted that the government could not execute 'a complete somersault', admitting 'that all the moral strictures which had been passed on the Germans for making use of this barbarous method of war were quite unjustifiable'. He deprecated 'the launching of any campaign in favour of gas till a longer time had elapsed and our charges against Germany were less present in the minds of the public'.[43] Even the more modest request from the Governor of Southern Rhodesia to use tear gas against a native rebellion was rejected. Although France and the United States had used tear gases in riot control, Stanley Baldwin, the Prime Minister, was unwilling to countenance the use of gas 'until it had been used by some other Power first'.[44] Subsequent allegations that Britain used gas against the Afghans in the 1920s, first aired by Italian propaganda during the Abyssinian war and still believed by some commentators, lack any documentary verification and run counter to the Cabinet decisions and policy statements of the British government.[45]

Secondly, successive governments used the Protocol to underpin their policy of financial stringency. Expenditure upon chemical research was hardly lavish; from a peak of £200 320 in 1929, it dropped to £155 390 in 1933 before rising gradually through the remainder of the 1930s.[46] Although this funded improvements in many First World War weapons, and facilitated development studies on new concepts, such as mustard gas spray from aircraft, gas bombs, airburst mustard gas shell and gas grenades, research was considerably hampered by lack of funds. Two particular requirements emphasised by the Committee of Imperial Defence in January 1925 were the capability to produce gas in bulk and the retention of stocks of gas in reserve. By 23 June 1936, when Italian action in Abyssinia (Ethiopia) had revived interest in chemical warfare, the Chiefs of Staff Subcommittee ruefully remarked that, 'Owing to financial stringency, however, no action could be taken on the second of these decisions, and no stocks or bulk manufacturing establishments now in fact exists.'[47]

Thirdly, the Protocol provided a perfect cloak for deferring any action on civil defence against gas attack. The Chemical Warfare Committee repeatedly urged that this issue should be considered, and that a political initiative should be taken. Neither Conservative nor

Labour governments were willing to do so. Given the good relations between Germany, Britain and France in the late 1920s, symbolised in the 'spirit of Locarno', the Marquess of Salisbury, Lord Privy Seal in Baldwin's government, insisted that Germany must be recognised as a 'friendly government now . . . a government of good faith and good will'. As a consequence, he saw real danger in 'over-alarming the public mind and even of panic' in respect of gas defence.[48] Ramsay MacDonald, when Prime Minister, was even more specific. On 9 July 1929, he stated, 'In view of the recent ratification of the Geneva Gas Protocol of 1925 by most of the important European States, including this country, I do not think this is a moment to press the local authorities to develop plans for the protection of the civil population against gas attack.'[49]

Notwithstanding these financial and other constraints, the continuation of research and development in Britain and elsewhere only fuelled anxieties among those who favoured disarmament. Neither the Washington Treaty nor the Geneva Protocol met their expectations; indeed the likelihood of states ignoring these undertakings in time of war, just as they had ignored the Hague Declaration, only prompted demands for a new framework of international relations based upon disarmament, the compulsory arbitration of disputes, and collective security under the League. Such feelings reflected a deep horror of war, kindled by memories of recent sufferings. Gas still evoked a peculiar fear and revulsion, so vividly captured in the poetry of Wilfred Owen (*Dulce et Decorum est*). Lurid descriptions of gas-related injuries, disdaining any reference to official medical statistics, comprised a basic element in the disarmer's rhetoric.[50] These descriptions were then linked to two related assumptions – that gas would inevitably be used in future conflicts and that its effects would be utterly devastating. Underpinning these assumptions were fears of scientific discovery, especially of more potent gases and their properties (lewisite, in particular, aroused some fantastic calculations of the fatalities it could cause)[51] and of the impact of gas bombing upon civilian communities. Various military authorities were quoted to testify that the bomber would 'get through', and that gas bombs would complement high explosive and incendiary bombing. But the alarming speculations of Lord Halsbury, former chief of the wartime Explosives Department, were possibly the most widely quoted. His favourite assertion that a single gas bomb dropped on Piccadilly Circus 'would kill everybody in an area from Regent's Park to the Thames', though highly questionable, was repeatedly quoted.[52]

Disarmers feared not only what might happen should these weapons be retained, but also what would happen since they believed that competition in armaments inevitably led to war.[53] Convinced that this had caused the outbreak of the First World War, they regarded the reduction and limitation of armaments in general, and the total prohibition of more offensive weapons like poison gas, as absolutely essential. Few doubted the intrinsic difficulty of the task, often turning to Major Lefebure's proposals for internationalising the control of the chemical industry,[54] but they generally insisted that disarmament could not be effective without a curb upon the potential of chemical warfare.

Although support for disarmament during the 1920s and early 1930s cannot be quantified precisely, it was probably substantial and, more importantly, was believed to be substantial by governments, by disarmers, and by their opponents. Yet the prohibition of gas warfare was simply one of many objectives in disarmament; it was neither a prominent issue in party politics nor a topic which aroused much public protest. Such passion as it aroused, particularly in Britain, was exacerbated by concern over animal experiments at Porton. Nevertheless, a petition which coupled anti-vivisection as its first priority with the abolition of gas warfare, attracted a mere 160 000 signatures before its submission to Parliament.[55] Only ministerial backing, particularly from the incoming Labour government in 1929, enabled disarmament to be considered again at an international level. Arthur Henderson, the new Foreign Secretary, was eager to implement the pledges of Article 8 of the League of Nations Covenant and of Part V of the Treaty of Versailles. He secured the assistance of Lord Cecil whose support of the League had earned him international renown, and pressed the Council of the League to convene a World Disarmament Conference. To allow the League Secretariat and the various governments to prepare for the negotiations, the 6 February 1932 was chosen as the first date of the conference.

The timing was hardly auspicious. By 1932 the Labour government had fallen and Henderson, who had been appointed president of the conference, was neither Foreign Secretary nor even a Member of Parliament. His authority would be significantly diminished as a consequence. Relations between the two crucial states, France and Germany, had deteriorated rapidly with the rise of nationalist parties and the collapse of the economy in Germany. Even worse, Japan had embarked upon her expansionist policy in Manchuria, so exposing the inadequacy of the League's provisions for collective security. For disarmers like Philip Noel-Baker, however, who had waited for the conference for thirteen years, the darkening international scene merely ensured that the conference had to succeed. They were heartened by the opening address of Cecil, who attended not as a British delegate but as President of the World Federation of League of Nations Societies. In a concise and lucid speech he argued that the conference should seek to reduce all armaments to the minimum needed for national defence and to abolish all weapons, including poison gas, which could assist the offensive. Should the conference bolster each nation's defences, it would reduce the risk of a surprise attack which would break the Covenant and so give the League more time to settle international disputes. As these principles were largely embodied in the opening speech of Sir John Simon, the British Foreign Secretary (and later in the plan submitted by President Herbert Hoover), a seemingly clear approach had been adopted.[56]

As soon as the plenary sessions convened, however, the prospects for prohibiting poison gas began to recede. The principle of prohibition was not disputed, especially as the powers agreed that chemical weapons posed a serious threat to civilians. It was accepted, too, that any ban should cover the wartime use of all gases, including tear gas, as well as biological and incendiary weapons. But it proved impossible to agree how this ban should be realised, monitored and enforced. Representatives argued over whether the ban should be absolute or relative, that is, whether a state should retain the right to retaliate in kind if attacked. They differed over whether the ban should cover peacetime preparations for chemical, biological and incendiary warfare, and should proscribe the manufacture and storage of toxic substances as well as military training in their usage. At issue was a willingness to open national chemical industries to international inspection and to desist from research and training in offensive and defensive chemical warfare.[57] To make these concessions required complete confidence in the process by which an agreement was to be monitored and policed.

Differences over these questions reflected not merely the technical difficulty of devising appropriate safeguards but also conflicting political priorities. While Germany insisted upon equality of treatment on this issue, as on others, France would not countenance an agreement without provision for her own security, that is, enforcing an agreement by 'extended supervision' and sanctions.[58] Neither Britain nor the United States could approve the latter's request. As no process of verification could be absolutely reliable, a system of effective sanctions had to be established in advance. Only collective reprisals could meet this requirement, an undertaking which neither Britain nor the United States could approve. Such an omission was clearly apparent when MacDonald presented Britain's draft disarmament convention at Geneva on 16 March 1933. The proposed ban upon either the preparation or the use of chemical, incendiary or biological weapons was coupled with the creation of a Permanent Disarmament Commission, charged with powers of investigating any complaints that this ban had been violated. Yet conspicuous by its absence was any additional military commitment by Britain to Europe or the suggestion of any dilution of national sovereignty in a collective security arrangement.[59] Henry L. Stimson, the American Secretary of State, also precluded any commitment by his government. He warned H. R. Wilson, the American delegate at Geneva: 'although public opinion in this country would align itself against the violator of the chemical warfare treaty, I do not think it would be possible for this Government to pledge itelf to affirmative action'. Hence he believed 'that the simpler the treaty, the easier will be its acceptance; similarly, the more it depends on the good faith of its signatories, the better will be the chances of its observance'.[60] Fortunately, these sentiments were never put to the test; when Germany, in October 1933, withdrew from the conference and notified her withdrawal from the League, the prospects of an agreement, however inadequate, collapsed.

Nevertheless, the disarmament illusion was not readily set aside. Even after Hitler's departure from Geneva, other governments were reluctant to follow suit. Although unwilling to formulate coherent disarmament policies, involving a necessary sacrifice of national sovereignty, they had raised public expectations about the possibility of securing peace, at an economical cost, through disarmament. Consequently the moribund conference lingered on into 1934, diminished in stature and bereft of purpose. While the draft convention remained official British policy, the government responded tentatively to the adverse trend of events in the Far East and on the Continent. In November 1933, it abrogated the 'ten year rule', by which defence planning had been based on the premise that no major war was likely to occur for ten years, and appointed the Defence Requirements Subcommittee which was to lay the foundation for all subsequent measures of rearmament. With Neville Chamberlain, the Chancellor of the Exchequer, playing an increasingly prominent rôle in the formulation of defence policy, the key priority was upon deterring the outbreak of war *per se* as distinct from fighting a particular kind of war. In these circumstances there would not be any massive increase of funding for research into aspects of gas warfare. Only in 1935 were the War Office and Air Ministry able to reconsider their requirements for offensive gas operations, while civil defence received its initial funding – £92 000 for Air Raid Precautions (ARP).[61]

Chemical warfare did not resurface as a political issue until the reports of Italian gas attacks in the Italo-Ethiopian war (1935–6). After Emperor Haile Selassie had protested to the League of Nations about these attacks on 30 December 1935, a torrent of accusations followed from the Ethiopian government, Red Cross officials and war correspondents. The Committee of Thirteen, a body established by the Council of the League to examine the Abyssinian conflict, received accounts of further attacks, medical testimony, photographs of mustard gas wounds, and details of Italian shipments of gas and bombs through the Suez Canal. As this evidence coincided with graphic reporting of aerial gas attacks, it could not be ignored.[62] Italy, after initially refusing to confirm or deny the charges, implicitly admitted them by asserting the right of reprisal against Abyssinian atrocities and by alleging that Britain and Spain had already used gas in colonial conflicts.[63]

The governments of Britain and France were embarrassed by the Ethiopian protests. Both had tried to appease Mussolini during the conflict: Britain felt unable to intervene without the full military support of France in the Mediterranean, which was never forthcoming since the war had deeply divided opinion in France. Both governments simply supported the Committee of Thirteen's report, which reminded the belligerents of the 'importance' of their commitments under the Geneva Protocol. Like the half-hearted imposition of economic sanctions against Italy, this response represented another nail in the coffin of collective security. Yet the military significance of Italy's action had been perceived. In an extensively reported speech Stanley Baldwin asked the crucial question: 'if a great European nation, in spite of having given its signature to the Geneva protocol against the use of such gases, employs them in Africa, what guarantee have we that they may not be used in Europe?'[64] Paul-Bancour, speaking two days later before the Council of the League, seemed even more fatalistic; once a war had erupted, he argued, it would be impossible to humanise it or to predict the limits within which it would be waged.[65]

Lending credibility to this renewed concern were the intelligence reports, chronicling developments in research and training for chemical warfare by potential adversaries. Germany was known to have taken the potential threat of chemical warfare extremely seriously. By 1929, British intelligence had monitored the formation of a gas inspectorate attached to the Reichswehr ministry, the construction of an experimental gas station, extensive practice and training in gas defence, collaboration with the Russians in testing mustard gas, and the retention of a substantial productive capacity, syndicated under the name of I. G. Farben. More alarming, by 1936, were reports of experiments with various methods of gas projection and the establishment of two or three offensive gas battalions. Subsequent reports amplified the substantial research investment (at the Technische Hochschule, Berlin, at the Kaiser Wilhelm Institute and at several state and commercial laboratories); a massive air defence network which was assessed as 'too well developed for aerial gas attack to be effective'; the formation of 'gas attack' troops and mechanised smoke columns; the extensive testing of ground contamination apparatus; and the investigation of biological warfare, albeit primarily from a 'defensive aspect' to counter a perceived threat of germ warfare from the Soviet Union. But lacking in these reports was any sense of German anxieties about chemical warfare, following the restrictions imposed upon her capabilities in the early twenties, and the lack of funds and interest to develop them properly until Hitler's accession to power. British intelligence never grasped the German feeling of being fifteen development-years behind her potential rivals in respect of productive capacity or in the training of the Wehrmacht and the civil community. Nor did the British perceive that Dr Gerhard Schrader, in the course of research into new insecticides, had discovered the nerve gases – tabun in 1936 and sarin in 1938. Instead they confidently quoted a Polish assessment that 'no highly effective new gases have been discovered'.[66]

Italian capabilities were considered as formidable, too, especially after the Abyssinian war. They were based upon an industry able to produce stocks of mustard, lewisite, phosgene, chloropicrin and adamsite, and a research network located in various universities and experimental stations, directed by the Office of Chemical Warfare in Rome. The Military Chemical Service had its own regiment; chemical companies were attached to each Army Corps and anti-gas sections to each regiment. Methods of projection included ground spray from chemical lorries, 81 mm mortars, rifle and hand gas grenades; gas shell from six types of gun, ranging from 75 mm to 305 mm; and, above all, aerial spray which is 'considered the most effective form of gas attack using vesicants, persistent or semi-persistent gases'. British intelligence concluded 'that in a future war she (Italy) would employ the gas weapon unless special circumstances render such a course inadvisable'.[67]

Much less was known about Japanese preparations for chemical warfare. They were thought to possess a large range of poison gases, including chlorine, phosgene, mustard, lewisite, adamsite, bromoacetone, and cyanic acid. They were reported to have developed various methods of projection – aerial bombing and spraying, gas shell, and ground contamination apparatus (mines, mortars, cylinders, projectors, toxic smoke boxes, tank carts and portable contaminating devices). 'In time of war,' it was believed, 'chemical shell will constitute 20–25% (other versions say 30%) of the total quantity of shell in the ammunition ration.' Japanese troops were known to be specially trained for gas operations, with the principal centre of training in offensive and defensive gas warfare being the Army School of Chemical Warfare at Narashino. The reports of Japanese gas attacks upon the Chinese in 1937 and 1938, though not confirmed to the satisfaction of British intelligence, merely fuelled concern about Japanese capabilities.[68]

Soviet interest in chemical warfare had been much more apparent. Having suffered more gas casualties than any other power in the Great War, the Soviet armed services had resolved to cope with the demands of fighting in a chemical environment. The Chief Chemical Committee of the 'Revvoensoviet' advised on all technical questions, drafted mobilisation plans, directed training, and inspected factories. A subcommittee, the Central Institute of Gas Defence in Moscow, supervised all aspects of gas defence, both civil and military. Anti-gas platoons were attached to rifle and cavalry units, while an independent chemical corps, consisting of mechanised chemical battalions, was capable of undertaking offensive operations. Instruction and field training were exceedingly thorough. Several schools and courses were available not merely to gas specialists but also to regular officers in the army, navy and air force. The range of gas weapons seemed particularly impressive: shell for all calibres, mortars, projectors, mines, lorries, portable cylinders and toxic smoke generators for the army; a heavy investment in smoke generation by the navy; a wide array of bombs and a limited, mainly low level, aerial spraying capability for the air force. The range of gases appeared to be considerable including mustard, phosgene, diphosgene, chlorine, chloropicrin, several arsenicals and harassing agents, and lewisite, with a mixture of lewisite and mustard seeming an attractive proposition in the Russian winter.

Yet British intelligence remained sceptical about the productive capacity of Soviet industry, and reckoned that only 'moderate stocks' of gases were held.[69]

Anti-gas measures, particularly the protection of the civilian community, became a prime concern in Britain and France. Originally Baldwin's National Government had hopes that the local authorities would voluntarily shoulder the burden of civil defence. In its first ARP circular, issued in July 1935, it had promised technical and administrative advice, some stocks of anti-gas equipment and the training of instructors, but maintained that the protection of the civil population 'must be organised locally'. Some local authorities responded vigorously but others procrastinated, reflecting the broad division of opinion over the whole rearmament problem. The government, as a consequence, gradually assumed an ever widening range of responsibilities. It established Anti-Gas Schools (at Falfield on 15 April 1936 and Easingwold on 27 December 1937) to train instructors who could then train volunteers in the ARP services; formed the Air Raid Wardens Service in March 1937, which recruited some 200 000 citizens by the middle of the following year; authorised the mass production of civilian respirators; and secured the ratification of the Air Raids Precautions Act 1937, which compelled local authorities to prepare measures of local defence. So rapid was the progress that the government could distribute 38 million gas masks to local authorities during the Munich crisis (September 1938). By the outbreak of war, 50 million gas masks were available for the whole population as well as 1 400 000 anti-gas helmets for babies, and more elaborate personal protection for the 2 million members of the ARP services, police and fire brigades.[70]

The French ARP measures were also quickly developed, but the approach differed from that pursued in Britain with more emphasis upon collective protection and the defence of the capital. By the end of 1938 the warden organisation was complete. Public shelters were constructed at various points in the Paris Metro. Some 60 000 cellars were passed as reasonable shelters, and an evacuation scheme was prepared for Paris. The manufacture and sale of respirators to the public was under strict governmental control and the standard of efficiency of filtration units was subjected to stringent regulations. Yet the standard of civilian instruction and training seemed less than satisfactory to British observers; it certainly paled by comparison with the German Air Defence League which had 13 million members, aided by 5000 schools and 28 000 instructors, and which regularly conducted practical exercises.[71]

Refurbishing an offensive capability proved a more ponderous process. To facilitate the possible use of gas as a retaliatory weapon required, in the first instance, political backing. In Britain this came from the Committee of Imperial Defence when it met on 10 July 1936 to approve the request of the Chiefs of Staff for the manufacture and storage of reserves of poison gas. Five months later Duff Cooper, the Secretary of State for War, reaffirmed this commitment. He assured Sir Cyril Deverell, the Chief of the Imperial General Staff, that

I am strongly in favour of the most rapid progress possible being made in every form of defensive and offensive gas warfare – and shall always be prepared to defend it in the House of Commons.[72]

Thereafter choices had to be made about weapons, gases, tactical units, and tonnage requirements. Already, at a meeting held at Porton on 11 September 1935, eight specialist chemical weapons had been tentatively listed as worthy of future development. These included an improved Livens Projector with a range of 2500 yards, chemical lorries, bombs, grenades and several other devices. By November 1936, the General Staff had halved this list to avoid overloading Porton's limited facilities and 'to utilise existing weapons as far as possible'. As Deverell proposed to limit the proportion of gas shell retained in the ammunition reserve to 10 per cent of the stocks for the 25 pounder field gun, and 30 per cent of the stocks for the 6 in. howitzer, his priorities seemed clear. In preparing for mobile war, in which the significance of chemical weapons could not be predicted, he appeared 'reluctant to divert any large portion of the scanty financial and industrial resources available to the War Office away from areas of more certain need'.[73] Deverell also favoured simplifying the gas production requirements by developing only mustard and arsenical gases. But a series of trials held in the first quarter of 1937 proved that a persistent tear gas, known as BBC, could act more effectively as a harassing agent than arsenical smoke. By changing his gas requirements accordingly, Deverell was able to delete the hand bomb which would have contained arsenical gas from his weapon requirements. He deleted the 6 in. mortar, too, preferring to improve the existing stocks of Livens Projectors by adding a stand, base block and drum to each projector. Even so he warned that the production of the remaining apparatus, scheduled to begin in 1938, could only be undertaken if it did not interfere 'with other more important items of equipment'. Eventually further cuts in the tonnage requirements eliminated the chemical lorry, so leaving the army dependent upon the Livens Projector as the main weapon for the two Chemical companies of the Royal Engineers attached to the Field Force.[74]

The War Office and Air Ministry agreed that the principal war gas had to be mustard.[75] They wished to develop two types of mustard – HS which had proved itself in the Great War and the new improved agent, HT, which had the advantage of being less liable to freezing (and so more useful in aerial spraying). At an inter-departmental committee, established to assess these requirements, the War Office and Air Ministry submitted proposals to Treasury officials. At a meeting on 16 December 1937, the War Office requested a production capacity of 40 tons HS per week and 2 tons HT per week, while the Air Ministry required 290 tons HS per week and 180 tons HT per week. To produce this gas, the War Office proposed using its pilot plant at Sutton Oak, near St Helens, and constructing two larger plants (one at Kemet on Merseyside and the other at an unspecified site). It estimated that the construction of Kemet would cost £1 436 247 and the second factory about £1 600 000. The Treasury immediately challenged the hypotheses on which these proposals were based, claiming that they broke 'fresh ground' since they provided, 'not only for the manufacture of the stock of gas which would enable this country to retaliate without delay, but also for the production of gas in wartime at a rate – 512 tons a week – which assumed that gas would be continuously used in bombing operations'.[76] The Chancellor of the Exchequer endorsed these reservations. He insisted that these recommendations would require Cabinet approval since, if implemented, they could not be kept secret and would require political justification. He questioned, too, whether gas bombing would prove as effective against civilian populations as bombing with incendiary and high explosive.[77]

In a memorandum submitted to the Committee of Imperial Defence, the War Office and Air Ministry explained their gas policy. Germany, they stressed, was preparing thoroughly for gas warfare and, in this respect, was 'very much ahead of this country': she would 'possess the ability (though not necessarily the intention) to employ gas against the civil population'. As a weapon of retaliation, gas would complement high explosive and incendiary bombing. While incendiary bombs would extend the effect of high explosive bombing, gas could hamper the work of rescue, repair and fire-fighting services and could add seriously to the strain upon civilian morale. Gas spraying would also be useful in reducing the mobility of an army in the field and in dislocating its assembly at ports, entraining or embussing centres. In essence, though, the possession of an offensive gas capability represented 'a strong deterrent'. The military chiefs argued that it complemented the anti-gas measures and so reassured the domestic populace while deterring gas attacks from potential enemies abroad. 'Positive knowledge that we do *not* possess gas,' they added, 'is likely to be dangerous and to encourage its use against us.' This argument, however, could be used to reduce the priority accorded to gas. 'It would be illogical,' they conceded, 'to reduce our offensive or defensive capacity in more important directions in order to include an ideal scale of provision for a weapon which it is hoped will never be used. Gas provision is therefore a direction in which some risk might legitimately be taken.'[78]

Endorsed by the Committee of Imperial Defence on 6 October 1938, the provision of additional capacity for gas production gained the approval of the Cabinet on 2 November 1938. Yet the Cabinet, doubtless heeding the objections of the Treasury, only authorised a manufacturing capacity of 300 tons of gas per week in peacetime and a total reserve of 2000 tons of gas. The provision of gas was to be split between the War Office and the Air Ministry in the ratio of 50 to 250 tons. Implementing this decision would prove slow and cumbersome. Although the Treasury had approved a 220 ton capacity and a reserve of 500 tons in October 1938, it failed to sanction the full amount of manufacturing and reserve storage capacity until 6 February 1939. All this production was to be concentrated at Sutton Oak and Kemet, which required the construction of additional plant, charging units, roads, rail and sewage facilities (at an estimated cost of £1 906 000). Even after the installation of these facilities, delays continued to bedevil the production process leaving the armed services with a minimal capability of about 500 tons when war broke out. The stock of mustard gas only reached 2000 tons in January 1941.[79]

French capabilities augmented this deterrent. When the first Anglo-French staff talks were held in May 1939, significant differences were apparent in their thinking about chemical warfare. Unlike the RAF, the French did not anticipate high level aerial spraying and were confident that their anti-aircraft defences could cope with low level attacks. They regarded artillery as the primary land-based weapon, although they had developed a projector with a range of 3000 metres. Above all, they still believed in phosgene, using it to fill their shells, projectors and large aircraft bombs. They proposed to use mustard only as air-launched grenades, to be dropped in clutches of fifty at a time. They had 4½ million grenades ready to be filled and ample mustard with which to fill them.[80]

Although the prospective allies entered the war with a good defensive capability and a minimum deterrent, they could not expect any assistance from the United States. American foreign policy had consistently eschewed specific commitments to European powers and her army languished after years of neglect. The United States retained an immense potential for chemical warfare, and her Air Corps had perfected the techniques of low level aerial spraying, but British intelligence feared that 'it would appear that the C.W.S. is fighting an uphill battle in their efforts to arouse active interest in gas tactics and defence among the other branches of the Land Forces'. The British criticised aspects of American equipment, the absence of anti-spray appliances 'on the lines of our capes and eyeshields', and the lack of gas awareness shown by unit commanders and troops during the autumn manoeuvres of 1938.[81]

By the eve of war, deterrence in chemical warfare had clearly replaced any notion of disarmament as a policy for the major powers. Disarmament had failed for numerous reasons. Abolishing gas warfare had never been a primary concern of all the major powers: all too often it had been launched as an initiative by the President of the United States, and the credibility of such initiatives was severely damaged by the Senate's refusal to ratify the Geneva Protocol. Despite the anguish periodically expressed over the use of gas in the First World War, and the often exaggerated claims for gas bombing in a future war, chemical warfare was not a major issue of political debate and popular protest. When the Disarmament Conference was convened in the midst of the Depression, Stimson ruefully admitted that 'the people are so much more interested in other troubles at present . . .'[82] Similarly, when the British government began spending large sums of money on anti-gas measures, and gave the topic the widest publicity in pamphlets and newsreels, it encountered little response. As the service chiefs noted in July 1938, the 'public reaction to these grim realities, far from being alarmist or panicky, has until recently been somewhat apathetic'.[83] Also, there was little likelihood that the restraints upon poison gas, as proposed at various international gatherings, would prove effective. The grandiose declarations of the Washington Treaty and Geneva Protocol may have stigmatised recourse to chemical weapons but they had little further substance. Admittedly, the Protocol defined a range of prohibited conduct and gave the prohibition a legal status. It compounded any existing constraints within the military bureaucracies by adding attitudes and inhibitions associated with the law, and so ensured that political considerations would be imposed upon military ones in chemical warfare planning. Even to ignore the prohibition would involve a choice, and this alone would introduce a new factor into the decision.[84] Whether this was a 'major obstacle' to the assimilation of chemical weapons is arguable; more important is the point that it was a self-imposed obstacle, with the degree of imposition varying from country to country.

Moreover, the Protocol was not perceived as an adequate obstacle in the late 1920s. Some powers reserved the right to retaliate if attacked by an enemy using gas, others sought further measures of disarmament. But when they assembled at Geneva to draft a gas convention which could be monitored, verified and enforced, these powers found the task beyond them. A treaty might have been agreed which relied upon the 'good faith' of the signatories, but any agreement which was more realistic, incorporating the threat of sanctions or of collective reprisals, was utterly unacceptable. The great powers were neither prepared to make commitments nor willing to constrain their foreign policies for the sake of a gas convention. Lacking a disarmament agreement, the Protocol was left dependent upon its power to inhibit the assimilation of gas as a weapon and upon the nebulous concept of collective security. Both were revealed as woefully inadequate by Italy's recourse to gas in Abyssinia and by the flaccid international response.

Not only had the quest for disarmament proved illusive, but various powers, in pursuing disarmament as a declaratory goal, had constricted or let wither their chemical warfare capabilities. Such neglect flourished amid the general curbs upon military expenditure in the 1920s and early 1930s. It also reflected the failure of chemical warfare specialists to become fully assimilated within their respective military establishments. Having struggled merely to retain an infrastructure of research and testing, with small chemical formations in certain armies, the chemical services faced an equally daunting task in seeking an appropriate allocation of resources once rearmament began. Nevertheless, some measures of offensive and defensive gas rearmament had become inevitable once Japan, Italy and Germany exposed the hollowness of collective security. As international relations worsened, first in the Far East and later in Europe, the major powers turned from disarmament to deterrence, still hopeful of preserving their countries from the horrors of poison gas.

4 Avoiding Chemical Warfare 1939–45

When the Second World War erupted there was a widespread, and quite reasonable, expectation that poison gas would be used. Various gases had been employed in an increasingly extensive fashion during the later years of the Great War, and, despite the signing of the Geneva Protocol, poison gas still seemed a potent weapon, especially in view of its use in Ethiopia and its reported use by the Japanese in China. The great powers prepared for the worst; they feared that their opponents possessed either large stocks of chemical weapons or the potential to produce such stocks. They strove to improve their own defences, both civilian and military, and to acquire the means of deterrence through a retaliatory capability. As the threat of gas was ever present, it proved a lasting concern for political leaders and their military advisers. What warrants analysis is not simply why these weapons were not used – in respect of the balance of incentives and disincentives (an analysis already expertly done)[1] – but also how the policy of deterrence evolved and developed during the conflict.

At the outbreak of war Britain and France issued a joint communiqué through the Swiss government, intimating that they would abide by the terms of the Geneva Protocol. Hitler, in a typically bombastic speech before the Reichstag, replied: 'whoever fights with poison gas will be fought with poison gas. Whoever departs from the rules of humane warfare can only expect that we shall do the same'.[2] To this extent the Laws of the War had served a purpose. All the principal belligerents, apart from Japan and the United States who entered the war in 1941, had signed and ratified the Protocol. By claiming to be honour-bound to abjure such weapons, the adversaries preserved a degree of operational constraint. But legalistic and humanitarian considerations were not decisive in and of themselves; they simply provided a rhetoric which concealed more pragmatic anxieties.

None of the powers possessed sufficient stocks of chemical munitions with which to launch a decisive attack. In Britain, only the defensive preparations for gas warfare were fairly complete. A War Office memorandum, compiled shortly before the war began, regarded British gas protection, detection and decontamination equipment as 'among the best in the world'. On the other hand, it regarded Britain's offensive capability as woefully inadequate; the Field Force had still not received the bulk of its authorised chemical munitions, while the Royal Air Force had just begun to charge bombs and spray tanks with mustard gas. Gas production capacity still languished at 120 tons a week, leaving Britain with an arsenal 'insufficient for gas warfare on a large scale'. Compounding these fears was the belief, based upon the latest intelligence reports, that German 'defence preparations, military and civilian, are well advanced and they are capable of introducing offensive gas warfare on a large scale if and when they consider it desirable'. As Japan was also thought to have made 'considerable progress' in the defensive and offensive aspects of chemical warfare, the report concluded: 'There seems, therefore, to be little doubt of the ability of our probable enemies to conduct gas warfare and of their will to do so if they think it will be to their advantage.'[3]

These worst case assumptions, though understandably cautious in interpreting fragmentary evidence and enemy intentions, were wildly inaccurate. Admittedly, the Wehrmacht had endeavoured since about 1934 to prepare thoroughly for chemical warfare. By the outbreak of hostilities the army was probably as well equipped and organised for this form of conflict as any of its enemies, but the Luftwaffe, the main offensive arm, was ill-prepared in several respects. Trials of apparatus and munitions at the Heeresversuchsstelle, Raubkammer, had revealed failures of fuse-setting (with the air-bursted KC 250 II Gb bomb, loaded with thickened mustard) and the inflaming of bombs filled with more than 0.5 kg of prussic acid. Even low level spraying, a success in the trials, was vetoed by the General der Schlachtflieger because of the danger to aircraft and crew from ground attack.[4] There were important gaps, too, in civil defence, particularly shortages of civilian gas masks which would grow more ominous as the war progressed.[5] The large stock of chemical warfare agents – some 10 000 tons of blister, choking and harassing gases – testified to the immense German potential for gas warfare, but much of this output was still stored in bulk and not in filled munitions.[6] The new nerve gases were not available either; the tabun plant at Dyhernfurth, started in September 1939, would not begin production until April 1942, and the construction of a 100 tons per month sarin plant was not authorised until 1942–3, with the production scheduled to commence in March 1945.[7] Finally, Germany's intelligence seemed to be no better informed than Britain's. The legacy of those fifteen years before the mid-1930s, in which it was assumed that the other powers had greatly improved their capabilities to wage gas warfare, left the German authorities haunted by the spectre of retaliation. As General Lieutenant Herman Ochsner, a former general of the smoke troops, recalled, 'The general impression held in Germany was that in all matters pertaining to gas warfare we lagged seriously behind foreign powers.'[8]

Germany had taken the Soviet threat seriously, particularly in view of the high priority which the Red Army had accorded to its CW programme throughout the inter-war period. The Soviet Military-Chemical Army Administration, founded in 1924, authorised research in military laboratories as well as in the laboratories of the Academy of Sciences, universities and large chemical factories. Utilising the nation's burgeoning chemical industry, especially the Bandyuzhsky chlorine works, Chapayevsk near Kuibyshev, and the centres at Berezniki, Khibinogorsk and Karanganda, numerous agents were manufactured. These included the choking gases – phosgene, diphosgene and chloropicrin; poisonous gases – hydrogen cyanide and cyanogen chloride; blister gases – mustard and nitrogen mustard (HN-3); and harassing gases – chloroacetophenone, adamsite and diphenylchloroarsine. The armed services had trained extensively in the tactics of gas warfare and had developed various means of disseminating chemical agents (aircraft spray and bombs, artillery shell and mortars, chemical tanks and smoke candles). They possessed, too, an impressive range of anti-gas equipment, so entering the war reasonably equipped for chemical hostilities.[9] From a German point of view, the Nazi–Soviet pact (24 August 1939) obviated the possibility of such hostilities occurring immediately.

France was certainly not able to assume the offensive in chemical warfare. In 1922 she had centralised her research and development studies at the *Atelier de Pyrotechnie du Bouchet* near Paris and could test agents at the proving grounds of Satory, Entressen, Chalai-Meudon and, by 1939, at Beni Ounif in the Sahara desert. Defensively, she had built anti-gas installations into the Maginot Line and collective shelters in Paris. There were production facilities for adamsite, mustard and lewisite at Le Bouchet,[10] but the Soussens plant, designed for the large-scale production of adamsite and lewisite, remained uncompleted by July 1940. Although the army and air force possessed the systems which could deliver chemical munitions, the CW policy was circumscribed by the broader assumptions of French military strategy, in particular by the belief that a lengthy defensive phase of operations would precede any assumption of the offensive.

Nor was Japan able to consider initiating chemical warfare when she began attacking British possessions and American bases in the Far East in 1941. Never having experienced poison gas in the First World War, the Japanese Army had only begun to study its battlefield potential in 1919 (with the navy and air force following suit in 1923 and 1931 respectively). But it was not until the early 1930s that the army and navy commenced their manufacturing programmes – the former at the Tadanoumi Arsenal and the latter at the Sagami Naval Yard.[11] The navy and air force lagged behind the army in the quality of their research personnel, equipment and training for chemical warfare. The air force in particular suffered from a high command which was indifferent to the subject and reluctant to allocate money or materials to it. The air force possessed neither an official chemical warfare training school nor a training course until 1939. The first gas protection course for the air force, held at the Mito Military Air Force School, was not begun until April 1940. From 1940–2 it organised sixteen courses, training 200 officers and 150 non-commissioned officers. The courses were then reduced from four to three months and transferred to the Hamamatsu Military Air Force School, where 200 officers were trained from August 1942 to March 1944. Eventually, four-month courses were restored and held at the Mikatogahara Air Force Chemical School.[12]

The Japanese Army was much better trained and organised for gas operations. The Commandant of the Narashino School held to his conviction that students should undertake long courses and receive a thorough training in gas operations (only under extreme pressure in the 1940s would he reduce the length of his courses slightly). Various gas units also gained operational experience in China and Manchuria. A field gas section of 119 officers and men was activated in China in 1937; it used portable gas sprayers and toxic smoke candles to disseminate blister gas and smoke. In the same year the Morita Detachment (a battalion of 1031 officers and men) was attached to the Central China Expeditionary Force; it saw action, using toxic smoke candles in campaigns around Süchow, Hankow, and south of Shanghai until August 1940. Four chemical mortar battalions also saw service in China (two operated near Hankow and one was at Wowak): a large chemical section (1555 officers and men) accompanied the Kwantung Army from March 1941 till the end of the war; and a smaller section

(79 officers and men) joined the China Expeditionary Force in February 1945.[13] But gas was still not assimilated fully as a battlefield weapon. Field commanders resented the 'loss' of officers and non-commissioned officers to the Narashino courses and, in some instances, thwarted gas officers who tried to institute gas training within their units. Chemical warfare was never organised as a separate service within the army, and intelligence was lamentable with virtually nothing known of British, German, Russian or American research and development. The armed services were not lavishly equipped with gas munitions, as they had not utilised civilian university or industrial personnel and facilities to any appreciable degree. They had failed to develop new gases or chemical weapons; their protective clothing was incapable of sustained wear and could not protect against blister gases; and their gas masks could not protect against the newer and highly toxic gases (initially the charcoal bed and filter were placed in the wrong order within the canister – a potentially fatal defect which was later corrected during the war). Japan's production facilities also failed to sustain efficient high volume production.[14] As a consequence, Japan was only able to undertake chemical operations against the Chinese, who were woefully deficient in anti-gas protective equipment and lacked a retaliatory capability. After the attack on the United States, Japan reduced the number of her gas attacks in China, apparently on the Emperor's order, in case they provoked American retaliation.[15]

In their early operations neither Germany nor Japan had any need to employ gas, having obtained sweeping successes with conventional arms. Indeed gas attacks seemed to contradict the tactics of *blitzkrieg*, in which Germany relied upon surprise, speed and the shock power of aeroplanes and panzers to overrun her enemies. Her logistics would have been encumbered by bringing gas supplies, defence equipment and decontamination units to the front. Her advance might have been slowed had the enemy retaliated by means of gas barriers and of gas attacks on her spearhead formations. Although gas might have facilitated an initial breakthrough, unless used on a massive scale and directed against rear area as well as frontal units (reserve formations, centres of command and communications, etc), it would have given time and incentive to retaliate in kind, so frustrating tactics which were based essentially on speed.[16]

For countries forced onto the defensive, gas was a more plausible option. Although the British General Staff would consider whether a combination of various gases would be more effective than mustard and phosgene,[17] British planning assumed that the latter would be the principal gases. Writing a fortnight before the German attack on the Low Countries (10 May 1940), the British Chiefs of Staff accepted that the army could not 'undertake any large scale gas operations before the Spring of 1941'. They recognised, too, that their main gas weapon – high level aerial spraying – was 'indiscriminate', and that 'its use in the event of a German advance through the Low Countries would inevitably entail the gassing of Belgian or Dutch civilians'. Should either this tactic or more localised retaliation, using gas bombs and low level spraying over strictly military targets in a limited area, be authorised, the military required prompt authorisation from the British and French governments.[18] Such authorisation was never forthcoming, partly because the Germans did not attack with gas and partly because the French political authorities, shaken after the bypassing of the Maginot Line, seem to have had no desire to compound the chaos by launching a large-scale gas attack.

Once France had fallen, and Britain faced the threat of imminent invasion, gas became seriously considered as a defensive option. Writing on 15 June 1940 in the wake of the Dunkirk evacuation, Sir John Dill, the Chief of the Imperial General Staff, questioned the whole basis of British gas policy. Instead of waiting until Germany seized the initiative, he proposed a pre-emptive gas attack upon the enemy forces wherever they landed and crowded onto the beaches. Low level aerial spraying, he argued, along with the 'contamination of beaches, obstacles and defiles by liquid mustard would have a great delaying effect'. He recognised that a gas initiative could alienate American sympathy and provoke German gas retaliation, but reckoned that these risks were acceptable especially if the initiative was presented as a response to invasion, and the well-disciplined populace took cover during air attacks. Frankly, he saw little alternative: 'At a time when our National existence is at stake when we are threatened by an implacable enemy who himself recognises no rules save those of expediency, we should not hesitate to adopt whatever means appear to offer the best chance of success.'[19]

Major-General Kenneth M. Loch, the Director of Home Defence, matched these emotional overtones in a brief retort. He deplored the prospect of 'throwing away the incalculable moral advantage of keeping our pledged word for a minor tactical surprise', and feared the ultimate effects of enemy retaliation upon 'this overcrowded little island'.[20] A more substantial and carefully reasoned reply came from Brigadier Kenneth N. Crawford, the Inspector of Chemical Warfare. He analysed the various tactical options, preferring low level spraying and gas bombing to any other method of using gas. Germany's population, he argued, would be more vulnerable to attack than Britain's but her stock of gases was larger, and Britain would be vulnerable not only at home but also to attack by Italy upon her possessions in the Mediterranean and the Middle East. He accepted 'that important and possibly decisive immediate tactical advantages could be obtained by the surprise use of gas', but feared that these tactics would alienate American public opinion, leave Britain's limited means of chemical production vulnerable to attack, and deflate public morale by initiating a form of warfare which could not be continued effectively while exposing Britain to enemy retaliation.[21]

Churchill, who was becoming increasingly concerned about the Enigma messages revealing German preparations for a possible invasion, suddenly intervened. On 30 June he requested a report from Major-General Hastings Ismay on 'the amount of mustard and other variant' in store. Churchill inquired whether it could be used in air bombs as well as fired from guns, sought details of the output per month, and stressed that it should certainly be 'speeded up'. He then added:

Supposing lodgments were effected on our coast, there could be no better points for the application of mustard than these beaches and lodgments. In my view there would be no need to wait for the enemy to adopt such methods. He will certainly adopt them if he thinks it will pay. Home Defence should be consulted as to whether the prompt drenching of lodgments would not be a great help. Everything should be brought to the highest pitch of readiness, but the question of actual employment must be settled by the Cabinet.[22]

Dill replied that Britain retained at home 410 tons of gas, 1000 spray tanks and 39 000 bombs – a fraction of the German arsenal. He accepted this disparity as 'part of the price we have to pay for having been unprepared for war', but insisted that it should not inhibit a pre-emptive attack. By leaving Germany with the initiative, 'we lose any advantage we might have gained from the surprise use of this weapon'. Dill asserted that Britain could launch a gas attack from 5 July, using Lysander, Battle, Blenheim or Wellington bombers, loaded with spray tanks or gas bombs. 'Low spray,' he surmised, 'would be the most effective method for dealing with troops on beaches . . . Bombs would be useful for contaminating specific points, such as piers, and so interfering with the landing of guns and equipment'. An aerial gas attack, added Dill, using existing stocks, could spray a strip 60 yards wide and some 4000 miles long, but an attack on this scale could only be sustained for 'a limited period'.[23]

Backed by the Chiefs of Staff, Churchill swept all reservations aside. Desperately concerned about the possibility of a German gas attack, he immediately authorised an accretion of British stocks. On 14 July 1940, he advised Ismay 'that everybody should be made to look to their gas masks now,' adding 'I expect a great many of them require overhauling, and it may well be Hitler has some gas designs upon us'.[24] Yet Churchill refused initially to seek chemical supplies from the United States lest this request embarrass the Roosevelt administration. When Herbert Morrison, the Minister of Supply, raised this issue, the premier agreed that 'it would be better to leave the United States out of this particular line'.[25] He still expressed 'great anxiety' about the rate of producing gas and projectiles, particularly the failure to implement the pre-war targets (a productive capacity of 300 tons of mustard gas per week and a reserve of 2000 tons). He ordered an inquiry into the reasons for the Randle factory failing to work at full capacity and demanded weekly reports on gas production.[26]

For the next two years Churchill provided the drive and determination which had been missing from the British CW programme. Even when the immediate threat of invasion had receded, he still read the weekly reports of gas production, frequently exhorting or chivvying officials with phrases like 'Press on. We must have a great store. They will certainly use it against us when they feel the pinch'.[27] The Royal Air Force refined its plans for employing gas. No longer concerned simply about checking an invasion with mustard gas, the RAF Committee on Chemical Warfare considered retaliation against civilian targets where 'there was a definite case for using phosgene'. It requested that 5000 250 lb LC bombs should be earmarked for phosgene filling (a request quadrupled by the end of 1940).[28] Once backed by the War Cabinet for its counter-city policy,[29] the Air Ministry urged Bomber Command to ensure 'that all preparations for the use of gas in retaliation against the enemy civil population should be in as advanced a state of readiness as possible'. It now approved the provisioning of equal quantities of 250 lb LC bombs filled with phosgene and mustard, and accepted Bomber Command's view that bombs would prove more effective than spraying because they produced a higher degree of contamination. The Air Ministry also agreed that mustard should still be the primary agent for countering an invasion, and, in Plan Y (completed by 14 October 1941), Major-

General Crawford proposed charging the new 65 lb LC bomb with mustard for use against beach targets.[30]

Such planning presumed the provision of gases and munitions in sufficient quantities, a requirement heavily dependent upon the premier's leadership. His harrying and injunctions eventually bore fruit. Not only did the rate of British production improve but the lifting of the initial embargo on American supplies of phosgene (manufactured in private American plants and shipped to Europe in foreign-registered vessels)[31] ensured a gradual accumulation of stocks. By 26 December 1941, Britain had 15 262 tons of mustard, phosgene and other gases (so approaching the target of 18 546 tons). Both the Army and Royal Air Force had a plentiful supply of gas-filled weapons.[32]

Army	*Target*	*Stock* (31.12.41)
25 pdr. shell	1 050 000	477 170
5.5 in. shell	45 000	8 619
6 in. shell	45 000	45 004
chemical drums	100 000	96 851
RAF		
30 lb bomb	181 104	177 906
65 lb bomb	100 000	56 132
250 lb bomb	81 946	60 367
500 lb container	6 467	6 467
1000 lb container	2 915	2 915
Special drums	65 399	42 321
Bulk storage		
mustard		4 351
phosgene and other gases	5 500	137

The Royal Air Force could now mount a retaliatory strike with mustard gas bombs at five hours' notice and with phosgene bombs or spray containers at twelve hours' notice. Four Blenheim and three Wellington squadrons had been trained to use these weapons: 15 per cent of the British bomber effort could be employed in gas warfare.[33]

Complementing the accumulation of offensive stocks was the

maintenance of Britain's gas defences. Churchill frequently urged his military advisors and the Ministry for Home Security to check that anti-gas equipment had not fallen into disrepair, and that civilians had not become too complacent about the threat from poison gas. Equipment was not the main problem. By February 1941, the Ministry of Supply confirmed that the early warning systems and the ground decontamination apparatus, which had recently been overhauled, were satisfactory. Some 70 million respirators, along with their 'contex' attachments (to give improved protection against toxic smoke) had been distributed. Unfortunately, some public apathy had set in: many people no longer carried their respirators nor had them at hand. Although the Cabinet approved more publicity by the Ministry of Home Security, it limited the new campaign 'for fear of causing panic and of giving the enemy an excuse to initiate the use of gas'.[34]

Meanwhile, Porton Down sustained its programme of research and development, despite the loss of access to the French experimental ground in North Africa. Accepting an offer of help from Canada, it established the new Suffield Experimental Station in Alberta. Porton also experimented with new gas and smoke weapons, particularly those which might be used for attacking tanks, bunkers and pillboxes. It designed gliding bombs, the 'Flying Cow', capable of raining gobbets of mustard gas, and the 'Flying Lavatory'; an elongated mortar bomb for smoke ('Frankfurter'); grenades, portable projectors, and generators; and, most ingeniously, an anti-tank projectile which could pierce a hole through armourplate by high explosive and then squirt sufficient liquid hydrogen cyanide through the hole to kill the crew. None of these projects was ever fully developed and, in fact, most of the accelerated offensive effort was concentrated upon completing the pre-war programmes – airburst shell, aircraft spray tanks and various bombs, all for spraying mustard gas. Several universities, notably Cambridge, assisted in the search for new toxic substances – an immensely complex and time-consuming task. Some new compounds reached the stage of experimental production and preliminary field assessment but none completed all the stages of field trials, manufacturing development, bulk manufacture, weapon design, charging into weapons and operational assessment.[35] Even so, Britain had developed, by the spring of 1942, a remarkable readiness for chemical warfare – an extensive civil defence organisation, a greatly improved production process, a flourishing programme of research, a trained bombing capability ready to retaliate, and a stock of 18 283 tons of poison gas.[36] The rate of progress testified to the prodigious impact of Churchill as a war leader.

While Britain amassed her stocks of gas and munitions, her declaratory policy remained circumspect. It rested upon the original statement made in September 1939 and reflected an understandable concern about the adequacy of her offensive capability and hence her deterrent. When the Chiefs of Staff were informed that Italy might use poison gas to quell an Abyssinian revolt in December 1940, their dilemma was all too evident. The Joint Planning Staff, fearful lest British retaliation should lead to 'widespread gas warfare', recommended that Britain should 'neither take nor threaten retaliation against the Italians, nor give publicity to their use of gas. The Ministry of Information has been provisionally asked to stop any reference in the Press to gas warfare in Abyssinia'.[37] Appalled by this policy, Lieutenant-General Sir Archibald Wavell, Commander-in-Chief in the Middle East, protested that only the threat of British retaliation would deter the Italians and reassure the Abyssinian chiefs. Neither the Chiefs nor Churchill would agree; the former advised Wavell to 'temporise with the chiefs, leaving Whitehall to arrange a "calculated leakage" to deter the Italians, possibly giving the impression . . . that we possessed a new and potent form of gas which would be available for use against them'.[38]

By 1942 such ruses seemed neither adequate nor appropriate. The possibility of gas being used arose on several fronts, involving a wide range of adversaries. Of most concern were the rumours that Germany might employ gas in her spring offensive against Russia, especially as she seemed to anticipate that Russia would defend herself with gas munitions. When Stalin informed Churchill that he expected a German gas attack, the latter sought to reassure him. With the approval of the Defence Committee, he promised that Britain would retaliate 'without limit' should Germany use gas against the Soviet Union. 'This,' he apprised Roosevelt, 'we are in a good position to do.'[39]

Such confidence was quickly dampened. As the Japanese Fifteenth Army moved north through Burma towards Mandalay, threatening to cut the Burma Road to China, the prospect of gas warfare being introduced in the Far East and used elsewhere thereafter aroused acute British anxiety. The Chiefs of Staff advised the Defence Committee that any recourse to gas warfare would be a 'grave disadvantage' to Britain. Japan, who had never ratified the Geneva Protocol, could now 'use gas on advantageous terms against India, where no serious preparations were possible'.[40] Britain's chemical defence research in India had been located at Rawalpindi, so facilitating the study of the problems of using chemical weapons in a hot (but mainly dry) climate. Any fighting with Japan would be conducted in a tropical jungle, where the atmosphere was warm and humid and the terrain covered with vegetation. To assess the impact of these factors required the relocation of chemical research (eventually centred upon Cannanore, India; Innispail and later Prosperine, northern Australia; and two American tropical stations – Bushnell, Florida and the island of San Jose off the Panama Canal).[41] Meanwhile, the avoidance of a precipitate gas conflict seemed imperative.

Unfortunately, the chances of gas being used seemed increasingly likely. British intelligence, though bereft of any positive information about German intentions, was convinced that Germany would use gas if it could advance her military prospects.[42] Whitehall was now concerned not merely about the German threat but also about the possibility of Russia alleging a German gas attack in order to bring forth British retaliation. In the hope of deterring both combatants, Churchill delivered a carefully worded broadcast on 10 May:

> I wish now to make it plain that we shall treat the unprovoked use of poison gas against our Russian ally exactly as if it were used against ourselves, and, if we are satisfied that this new outrage has been committed by Hitler, we will use our great and growing air superiority in the west to carry gas warfare on the largest possible scale far and wide upon the towns and cities of Germany.[43]

On 5 June 1942, President Roosevelt, responding to Chinese complaints of Japanese gas attacks, issued a similar warning:

> I desire to make it unmistakably clear that, if Japan persists in this inhuman form of warfare against China or against any other of the United Nations, such action will be regarded by this Government as though taken against the United States and retaliation in kind and in full measure will be meted out.[44]

Conspicuously absent from this threat was any mention of timing. After years of neglect America's chemical warfare capabilities had seriously deteriorated; indeed, on 18 May 1942, Major-General William N. Porter, Chief of the Chemical Warfare Service (CWS), had submitted a report describing the inadequacies of America's offensive and defensive preparations. Immediate retaliation, he argued, could only at best be on a limited scale, and he recommended a massive increase in America's productive capacity for toxic agents along with improvements in training, the provision of defensive kit, the ratio of chemical battalions per division, and increases in the numbers of personnel trained in the CWS Officer Candidate School and the Chemical Warfare Replacement Training Centre. Within a week the Operations Division had approved these proposals, merely cavilling about the proportion of chemical battalions. It proposed the activation of fourteen by the end of 1942 and twenty-eight by 1944. The General Staff quickly approved, so instituting a rapid overhaul of America's capacity for chemical warfare, with the Far East receiving first priority in the distribution of matériel.[45]

The United States and Great Britain, by the declaratory statements of Roosevelt and Churchill, had enunciated similar deterrent policies. Thereafter they moved quickly to ensure some co-ordination between these parallel policies. The Combined Chiefs of Staff proved the natural centre of liaison, advised by an *ad hoc* chemical warfare subcommittee headed by the Chief of the American CWS. The subcommittee duly proposed that gas warfare could be undertaken by the US and British Commonwealth forces on the order of the Combined Chiefs of Staff, if approved by the British and American governments, or independently by either force in the case of retaliation. It recommended, too, that the Combined Chiefs should be informed whenever the enemy had used poison gas or if independent retaliation had been authorised. On 14 November 1942, the Combined Chiefs of Staff approved the report.[46]

To implement this policy required agreement upon a wide range of criteria (including potential production capacities, adequate levels of stocks, minimum standards of individual and collective anti-gas protection, the logistics of moving anti-gas kit, weapons and munitions and some standardisation or interchangeability between British and American chemical warfare equipment). Initially, General Porter had anticipated that these standards would be settled jointly through a committee composed of British and American chemical officers. But Lieutenant-Colonel Humphrey Paget of the Royal Engineers objected to the creation of any supranational committee. He proposed liaison at staff level between the British Inter-Service Committee on Chemical Warfare and a similar body in the United States. By 6 May 1943, this concept of parallel joint committees was accepted and the United States Chemical Warfare Committee established. The organisational arrangement reflected real differences of opinion about the likely use and effectiveness of gas warfare. Whereas the American representatives, especially those from the CWS, regarded gas as a potentially strategic weapon able to achieve decisive results if dispersed in sufficient quantities at the right places and at the right time, the British military tended to view gas as a supplementary tactical weapon to be used in conjunction with high explosives and incendiary weapons.[47]

Over the next two years the two committees co-operated extensively, with a continual exchange of information and periodic visits by official personnel. Of most benefit, as a consequence, were the co-ordination of supply and procurement programmes. Until large-scale American production was feasible, the British agreed to furnish US forces with smoke pots (later the US would supply United Nations forces with floating smoke pots); she also supplied the US Eighth Air Force in Britain with 10 000 phosgene-filled 500 lb bombs and facilitated the procurement of 15 000 tons of tropical bleach, so saving American shipping space. More extensive co-operation was hampered by the lack of surplus British material and by the lack of standardisation between British and American equipment. Although it was too late by 1943–4 to arrange the distribution of standardised kit, interchangeability could be promoted by training British and American troops to use each other's protective equipment. Some items, especially aircraft munitions (the 500 lb bomb and 1000 lb non-persistent gas bomb but not the British 65 lb mustard bomb) were made interchangeable. The colours of smokes for signalling were standardised between the respective armies, navies and marines, but the quest for a common gas mask proved abortive. Co-ordination of research and development was more successful, particularly the study of gas warfare in the tropics.[48]

Underpinning this transatlantic co-operation was a vast expansion of America's capacity to produce, test, and manufacture chemical weapons. Thirteen new plants were constructed between 1942 and 1945, including the Pine Bluff Arsenal, Arkansas, which employed some 10 000 people in the production of filled munitions and agents and the Rocky Mountain Arsenal, Colorado, which produced 87 000 tons of toxic chemicals by the end of the war. In 1942, the Americans also opened a new test site, known as the Dugway Proving Ground, Utah, which occupied a quarter of a million acres. It facilitated testing on a huge scale and enabled the US Air Force to experiment with high altitude spraying techniques.[49] Once buttressed by a massive production base and testing facilities, the Joint Chiefs of Staff could consider

plans by which the United States could implement Roosevelt's threat
of retaliatory chemical warfare. In approving the report of the Joint
Logistics Committee (JCS 825/4) on 16 October 1944, the Joint
Chiefs accepted that gas would have to consume 25 per cent of the
bombing tonnage in strategic attacks upon Japan, the Ryukyus and
Bonin islands, and that gas could only be employed tactically in other
Asiatic and Pacific areas.[50] Although the details of America's
expanded CW capability were concealed from her enemies, and
massive logistical problems would have to be overcome before the gas
could be deployed in the Far East, the potential capability leant
credibility to America's deterrent posture.

Fears of gas warfare still persisted, repeatedly fuelled by intelligence
reports. In February 1943, following the fall of Stalingrad, these
forebodings were compounded by an Enigma decrypt indicating that
all the respirator containers of the German army (save for the units in
Germany, Poland and Czechoslovakia) would be changed by 1 April
1943. So radical a departure in practice alarmed both Churchill and
General Sir Alan Brooke, his new CIGS. Their concerns were
heightened by further signals from Russia, based upon captured
documents and interrogated German prisoners of war, all of which
suggested that Germany might use gas in the near future. The
evidence, though fragmentary, was worrying: thirty to forty trains of
gas containers had been sent to the Russian front; the German army
had begun fitting its gas masks with new filters; German troops were
carrying these masks at all times; German prisoners, in private
conversations which their captors had overheard, supposed that gas
would soon be used; certain equipment had been captured; and the
chemical plant at Ludwigshafen appeared to be operating at full
capacity.[51] The Joint Intelligence Committee (JIC) noted that none of
these reports revealed anything about German gas intentions. It
concluded that the danger of gas warfare remained slight so long as the
decision rested with the German military, but it could not discount a
desperate act by Hitler himself. On 20 March, the Chemical Warfare
Committee endorsed this view, adding that Japan would probably be
deterred by her shortage of air power, and that Italy might be deterred
even more than Germany by the threat of retaliation.[52] Once the
subject had been considered by the Joint Planners and the Anglo-
American Combined Intelligence Committee, the Chiefs of Staff
formally advised Churchill that 'the chances' of Germany starting
chemical warfare 'though less remote than hitherto, are still small'.

They warned that it was possible: 'Hitler, faced with imminent military disaster might order it to be introduced.'[53]

Churchill reassured Stalin and repeated his public warning of British gas retaliation in the event of a German gas attack on Russia. As reported on 22 April 1943, the warning added ominously that 'British resources and scale of delivery have greatly increased since last year'.[54] On 8 June 1943, Roosevelt repeated his warning of American gas retaliation but pledged 'categorically that we will in no circumstances resort to the use of such weapons unless the first use of them is by our enemies'.[55] These threats were broadened to include the Italian theatre when Italy surrendered in September 1943. General Dwight D. Eisenhower was authorised by the Chiefs of Staff to warn that any German use of gas against the Italians would 'call forth immediate retaliation upon Germany with gas, using to the full the Allied air superiority'.[56]

Germany responded to these threats with similar rhetoric. Officials from the Wilhelmstrasse characterised Churchill as 'mad with desperation' in May 1942 and suspected him of trying to conceal a British first use of gas against Germany. Should this occur, they warned, 'the British people would suffer a fearful revenge because German industry is infinitely better equipped than the British for gas warfare. The German army has made the most minute preparations, and all civilian gasmasks have been overhauled only a few weeks ago'.[57] In April 1943, German spokesmen reiterated their previous declarations. Unnamed 'military circles', however, were reported as arguing that Germany would not engage in gas warfare because unless it proved 'immediately effective and decisive' Germany would not escape retaliation in kind.[58]

If not Germany's sole concern, fear of retaliation had always been a principal anxiety and it became increasingly dominant as the Allies gained air superiority during 1943. Based upon intelligence estimates which exaggerated Allied capabilities, and even assumed that they possessed nerve gases,[59] it ensured an extremely careful policy in respect of chemical weapons. The High Command prohibited either the deployment or the storage of gas munitions outside Germany to prevent their unauthorised usage by local field commanders and their capture in case of retreat. The German army took similar precautions before it evacuated the Italian town of Foggia in September 1943. Dr Ehmann was flown into the town to arrange the destruction of the mustard and diphosgene plant at the Sabonia chemical works.[60] The

Germans, in short, wished to avoid any incident which might give the Allies a pretext for chemical warfare.

Admittedly, there were other significant inhibitions not the least of which was Hitler's dislike of poison gas. Possibly derived from his experience of being gassed at Ypres in October 1918,[61] Hitler's aversion was profoundly felt and widely known. Several Germans confirmed this impression in post-war interrogation, with Professor Karl Brandt, Hitler's former surgeon, providing the most convincing testimony. He stressed that Hitler, who never visited the CW testing range at Raubkammer, always opposed the use of gas except in retaliation against the Allies.[62]

Tactical priorities and logistical difficulties also blunted the offensive utility of gas. Just as gas had seemed an inappropriate adjunct to the *blitzkrieg* strikes upon Poland and France, so it would have complicated an invasion of Britain and possibly retarded the assault on Russia. Using gas in an amphibious operation would have complicated its planning. The operation could not have been launched until the wind and weather was favourable, while additional shipping space would have been required to carry gas munitions and decontamination kit. In the attack on Russia speed was imperative as the German assault armies sought to envelop and annihilate entire army groups before pressing on towards Moscow and the industrial heartland. Using chemical weapons would only have impaired this mobility and strained a supply service which was already struggling over inadequate roads and railways at a great distance from Germany. When the German advance was halted and reversed, gas seemed more attractive especially as a means of countering the partisan groups who attacked the German rear. As the latter operated from caves, catacombs and innumerable bunkers, the widespread dispersal of mustard gas could have rendered these bases inaccessible. By 1943–4, however, such action would have enabled the Allies to use their growing air superiority to retaliate on all fronts and against Germany itself.[63]

Similar concerns almost certainly inhibited the defensive use of gas to impede the Normandy landings. Superficially this might have seemed a tactically useful and technically feasible proposition. Large sectors of the coastline could have been drenched with mustard gas, so requiring the enemy to encumber his invasion force with decontamination equipment, specialist chemical units and vast quantities of decontamination agents. Landing forces could then have been harassed with gas from mines, shells, bombs and spray cylinders. The troops would have had to wear gas masks and protective clothing, and their morale might have been seriously impaired had the attacks been concentrated upon a narrow front for a number of days, leaving no space for retirement. But the Allies, by the summer of 1944, had secured complete mastery of the skies. Had Germany employed chemical weapons, the Allies planned to launch two 400 plane retaliatory attacks within the next forty-eight hours, each carrying 100 per cent toxic agent payloads.[64]

German gas defences seemed less and less adequate as the Allied air threat grew more formidable. By June 1944, the production of respirators had met only 7 per cent of the children's requirements and 35 per cent of the adult requirements. When all protective items were considered (respirators, capes, decontamination equipment etc) only about 19 per cent of the necessary issues had been made in the period from 1939 to 1944. Dr Brandt, who was specially appointed to rectify these deficiencies, planned the production of 45 million new Peoples' gas masks. Although gas mask production eventually exceeded 2 300 000 per month, a large proportion of Germany's urban population remained unprotected.[65] Compounding this problem were the huge losses of military respirators on the Russian front (some 6 to 7 million had been lost from a total production of 15 million). During the last year of the war, 7 500 000 replacements were sought but supply difficulties reduced this target to 3 500 000 and later to 1 500 000.[66] Gas production, finally, was hampered by the increasing shortages of raw materials, notably chlorine and ethylene, and of suitably trained labour.

Germany had amassed a substantial stock of gas, possibly 70 000 tons by 1945,[67] but she had become so exposed to aerial attack that any initiation of gas warfare would have been suicidal. As a last desperate option, the use of gas still had its advocates, notably Josef Goebbels, Martin Bormann and Robert Ley. Hitler, apparently, even considered it briefly as a counter to the Soviet advance but the idea evoked little enthusiasm. Brandt was alarmed about the state of civilian defences, especially the shortage of medical supplies. The German General Staff was opposed to the use of gas, and Albert Speer, then Reich Minister for Armaments and War Production, had ignored the Fuehrer's order and curtailed production of war gases. Speer believed that Germany with her cities unprotected, and facing the threat of massive retaliation, could not employ gas. To do so, he stated, would have been 'utterly insane'.[68]

The Germans had always anticipated that the Allies could use gas, especially the Russians in defence of their homeland. Lack of source

material precludes any informed speculation on the Russian reluctance to employ gas, yet fear of German capabilities, buttressed by
memories of the First World War, were almost certainly factors.
During the first months of the war, the Soviet army command even
forbade the use of smoke-screens lest they be used as a pretext by
Germany to launch gas attacks. Commanders of chemical units were
required to destroy all training toxic substances including smoke
candles in their retreat from the Western Front. Some equipment was
still seized including the Russian VAP 500 spray apparatus, and the
chemical discipline of troops and commanders began to deteriorate
under pressure of combat. In these circumstances, finding the transport and organisation to mount an effective gas attack would have
been extremely complicated. Any retaliatory action by the enemy
would have merely compounded the disorder within the army and the
rear areas.[69] Stalin, too, seems to have doubted that Soviet chemical
stocks were adequate. When he requested Allied assistance in the
spring of 1942, Churchill could proffer a mere '1000 tons of mustard
and 1000 tons of bleaching by the first available ship'.[70] When Russia
eventually assumed the offensive, whatever tactical advantages may
have accrued from the use of gas (and these had to be balanced by a
likely slowing of the advance owing to the contamination of road and
rail junctions and by the moving of large gas stocks over the
lengthening lines of communications), they were more than out-
weighed by the diplomatic and strategic disadvantages. Stalin knew
that the Allies had renounced the first use of gas. Had he broken ranks
and thereby legitimised gas warfare, perhaps spreading it to other
theatres, he would have complicated the planning for the Normandy
landing and possibly delayed its implementation. As the opening of a
Second Front had been his prime concern, and insistent request,
initiating gas warfare could have been immensely counter-productive.

Although any change of gas policy was complicated by broader
strategic issues and Alliance considerations, a British gas attack was
considered in view of the V-1 attacks upon London, which caused
extensive damage, injury, and loss of morale within the capital. The
Chiefs of Staff requested a report from the Joint Planning Staff (JPS)
on the utility of gas attacks upon the V-1 installations or as a means of
retaliation against Germany. On 5 July 1944 the JPS replied,
deprecating gas retaliation as unlikely to curb the launching of V-1
weapons, as impossible to limit once used so precipitating the
widespread use of gas, as militarily detrimental inasmuch as the
Germans could respond with gas attacks upon the Allied forces in

Normandy, and as dependent upon the agreement of the United States, Dominion and Soviet governments. The Chiefs of Staff endorsed these conclusions, advising Churchill that 'the use of gas at present would be militarily to our disadvantage'.[71]

Churchill was not easily dissuaded. He had already raised the question of gas retaliation with Herbert Morrison, the Home Secretary, when he envisaged only two possible objections: that the attacks on V-1 bases might injure some French – 'my answer would be that they ought not to be there' – and that the Germans might retaliate by filling their flying bombs with poison gas. He accepted that experts would have to weigh the advantages and disadvantages, and that any use of gas would want 'careful handling'.[72] Unimpressed by the JPS report, he demanded another inquiry based upon purely military considerations and bereft of moralistic or diplomatic concerns. 'I shall of course have to square Uncle Joe and the President', he confidently affirmed, belying Britain's diminished influence in Allied counsels by 1944. Instead, he pressed the Chiefs of Staff to consider why the Germans had refrained from using poison gas even against the tempting target of the Allied landings. The explanation, he suggested, was not 'moral scruples or affection for us . . . (but) because it does not pay them'. Fear of retaliation, added Churchill, can only explain their abstention: 'what is to their detriment is to our advantage'. He made his own inclination abundantly clear:

> I may certainly have to ask you to support me in using poison gas. We could drench the cities of the Ruhr and many other cities in Germany in such a way that most of the population would be requiring constant medical attention. We could stop all work at the flying bomb starting points. I do not see why we should always have all the disadvantages of being the gentleman while they have all the advantages of being the cad. There are times when this may be so but not now.
>
> I quite agree it may be several weeks or even months before I shall ask you to drench Germany with poison gas, and if we do it, let us do it one hundred per cent. In the meanwhile, I want the matter studied in cold blood by sensible people and not by that particular set of psalm-singing uniformed defeatists which one runs across now here now there.[73]

When the Chiefs of Staff discussed the minute, Sir Charles Portal, Chief of the Air Staff, doubted that a gas attack would stop the flying bomb attacks. Viewing gas as merely a tactical weapon to be used in combination with high explosive, he doubted that 'a heavy concentration of gas over a large area' could be achieved. The Chiefs required the Vice Chiefs of Staff and the JPS to consider all aspects of the Premier's minute, including the possibility of biological warfare.[74] (Originally, Britain's highly secret BW programme, which operated under the auspices of Sir Maurice (later Lord) Hankey's Microbiological Warfare Committee, had studied the defensive aspects of bacteriological warfare. Once the war began, it responded to fears of German and Soviet interest in offensive BW by developing an anthrax bomb in 1941 and testing it on Gruniard Island in 1942. Britain had begun the manufacture of anthrax-filled cattle cakes,[75] should it prove necessary to retaliate against a German BW attack and, in March 1944, the government had ordered half a million 4 lb bombs from the United States as the first instalment for filling.)[76]

By 27 July, the JPS completed its extensive review. It doubted that either Germany or Japan would initiate chemical warfare, especially Japan on account of her 'technical inferiority', but insisted that Germany would retaliate if attacked. It accepted, too, that the available stocks of British and American gas in the United Kingdom were sufficient to produce 'a formidable scale of gas attack on Germany'. In a concentrated assault, leaving only 25 per cent of the payload as high explosive, Bomber Command could drop phosgene on the scale of '16 tons per square mile' against either 1000 tactical targets or 20 German cities. It could drop mustard gas upon either 1500 tactical targets, 1500 localised centres of communications or 60 cities.[77] Should a stalemate occur in Normandy, the JPS accepted that gas, if used as a weapon of surprise, could ensure 'decisive local results' even facilitating the penetration of German defences. In other operations, though, gas would impair the fluidity of offensive movement whether in northern or southern France or in Italy. It would, too, have unpredictable consequences upon morale; unprotected civilians might prove less adaptable than soldiers, and the use of gas could undermine the support of resistance groups in France, Italy and the Balkans. In other theatres, gas warfare seemed even less practical as Britain lacked sufficient stocks of gas weapons in the Far East and could not wage offensive operations in both the European and Far Eastern theatres. The new defensive equipment which would protect against gas in tropical conditions would not be issued for another six to twelve months. In the Far East, finally, future actions would require a series of amphibious assaults without decisive air superiority; in these circumstances, 'the use of gas by the enemy would materially reduce the prospects of success'.[78]

Strategic usage, that is the gas bombing of large German cities, was even more unpredictable, particularly the effects upon civilian morale and the consequences of German retaliation (either reprisals against prisoners of war or the gas bombing of London and southern England). Such action could impair British morale which was already 'less resilient' after 'nearly five years of war and five weeks' experience of the flying bomb'. The JPS feared that 'the public' might resent 'being subjected to gas attack if it felt that this could have been avoided'. Although Britain would reap an advantage over Germany by virtue of her heavier scale of attack on industrial centres, gas bombing was beset by uncertainties: 'we should be substituting an untried form of attack for the present incendiary and H. E. bombing which is well tried and is known to be achieving a very grave effect upon German war production, particularly on oil, aircraft and ball bearings'.[79]

Finally, the JPS dismissed the impact of gas attacks upon the flying bomb and rocket sites, estimating that the effects would be 'negligible'. Only biological warfare, it argued, could alter materially the war situation. Civilian populations were especially vulnerable as a prophylactic treatment against anthrax had not been found. Twenty 500 lb aircraft cluster bombs, each containing 106 4-lb bombs charged with anthrax, could contaminate a flying bomb site of one square mile; 2000 bombs could devastate a 'large town' within an area of twenty-five square miles. The American production programme, however, had encountered difficulties and it was now unlikely that half the initial order of 500 000 4-lb bombs would be available by the end of 1944. Although an accelerated programme was promised for the new year, the JPS doubted that 'a sustained attack' would be 'possible much before the middle of 1945'.[80]

Having studied this report, the Chiefs of Staff added their own criticism. Significantly, they chose to stress not the tactical and logistical problems of using gas but the repercussions of German retaliation. The fragility of public support remained their overriding concern:

There is no reason to believe that the German authorities would have any greater difficulty in holding down the cowed German population, if they were subjected to gas attack, than they have had during the past months of intensive high explosive and incendiary bombings.

The same cannot be said for our own people, who are in no such inarticulate condition.[81]

Faced with advice so pessimistic in tone, Churchill gave way. 'I am not at all convinced,' he wrote, 'by this negative report. But clearly I cannot make head against the parsons and warriors at the same time. The matter should be kept under review, and brought up again when things get worse.'[82]

Gas remained a persistent concern. The Allies could never discount the possibility of Hitler authorising recourse to chemical warfare. Admiral William Leahy, Roosevelt's chief of staff, described such action as 'illogical' from a 'purely military point of view', but he accepted that Hitler could still order the use of gas despite the retaliation which the Allies threatened.[83] Indeed, as the Allied armies pressed upon Germany, the Joint Intelligence Subcommittee monitored reports of German gas preparations. Even after the crossings of the Oder and the lower Rhine, it continued to warn that the employment of gas was possible, although very unlikely in view of Berlin's vulnerability to air attack. As late as 23 April 1945, the Committee advised that Germany was still capable of launching chemical attacks on a 'limited scale' in a 'last reckless throw'.[84] This prudence seemed warranted when the Chiefs of Staff reported upon the state of German gas preparations in the wake of the Third Reich's surrender (7 May 1945). Not only had the Germans developed tabun and begun experiments on sarin and soman, but their general state of preparedness 'was well advanced and their stock of equipment and weapons, all of high quality, was larger than had been anticipated'.[85]

In the Far Eastern theatre, the first use of gas warfare was never seriously considered by the dominant Allied power – the United States. Until 1945 American gas policy has been aptly described as one of minimum deterrence, aimed at inhibiting initiation by the Axis nations. This limited objective reflected Roosevelt's fierce opposition to gas warfare and his declaration that America would never employ it initially. It also derived from a reluctance by the military to divert scarce resources to improve their gas readiness in the Far East. By January 1945, the United States possessed sufficient munitions to launch a gas attack but the bulk of them remained in the United States. Neither of the Pacific Theatre Commanders had allocated the requisite shipping space to transport the gas munitions overseas. In the Pacific Ocean Area, Admiral Chester Nimitz retained only about 5 per cent of the authorised stocks while in the Southwest Pacific Area General

Douglas MacArthur held about 50 per cent, but the available munitions were widely deployed and some were deteriorating in the tropical conditions.[86]

Such incapacity had not prevented general discussion of the possibility of using toxic agents. A British study, known as the Lethbridge report, examined the feasibility of gas warfare in tropical conditions to find that the temperature, humidity, and low air movement decisively favoured the offensive. It proposed that the Japanese could be overwhelmed by a completely ruthless attack 'upon a vast scale, employing a mixture of chemical agents'.[87] Although this report was set aside, the issue kept recurring. While *en route* to the Honolulu conferences of July 1944, Admiral W. D. Leahy recalls a spirited discussion of bacteriological warfare in the President's cabin. He advised the President that using gas or germ warfare 'would violate every Christian ethic I have ever heard of and all of the known laws of war. The reaction can be foretold: if we use it, the enemy will use it.'[88] Only with Roosevelt's death (12 April 1945), which removed his passionate opposition to gas warfare, was it possible to reconsider the use of gas. Furthermore, the defeat of Germany in May 1945 removed the problem of dividing resources. It also lifted the fear of escalation and German retaliation against Great Britain, while leaving the United States as the dominant decision-maker in the Alliance. Finally the prospect of overcoming fanatical Japanese resistance, already demonstrated at Iwo Jima and Okinawa, revived interest in any tactical alternative to costly amphibious assaults. As extensive tests had shown that non-persistent agents would be effective in reducing cave defences, the employment of toxic agents was reconsidered.[89]

Reconsideration, however, merely involved another assessment of the readiness for retaliatory gas warfare. Initiation was not proposed as a serious option before the end of the war. On 5 March 1945, the Joint Chiefs of Staff recognised that the Pacific, Southwest Pacific and China Theatres did not possess their authorised stocks of gas munitions because of a 'lack of shipping and higher priority needs'.[90] During April and May the Joint Staff Planners reviewed the problems of moving existing munitions to the Pacific, of providing adequate storage facilities, and of resuming the production of bomb cases without disrupting the high explosive and incendiary bomb programmes. Setting 1 November 1945 as a target date, the Planners proposed that sufficient stocks should be moved forward to permit strategic and tactical retaliatory gas warfare over a period of seventy-five days in the Pacific Theatre and of ninety days for the India–Burma and China Theatres. But no directive was thought necessary about the shipment of these additional stocks (some 113 500 short tons or sixteen shiploads); Theatre Commanders still had to give priority to their 'directed' operation, namely the conventional requirements of operation OLYMPIC.[91]

Compounding the problems of transportation were the increasing number of targets as the Japanese heartland came within range of American air forces. Although doubts would be expressed about the adequacy of planned expenditure rates and the production of gas munitions,[92] gas deterrence seemed to have worked. By mid-1945 the Joint Staff Planners admitted that they were planning 'for a contingency which now appears unlikely to occur, except in isolated incidents'.[93] Policy remained wedded to retaliation because of confidence that other strategies would succeed (the low level incendiary bombing raids began in March 1945, the possibilities of the atomic bomb which was tested successfully on 16 July, and the implementation, if necessary, of operation OLYMPIC).

Japanese gas policy was distinctive but cautious. Her senior army commanders regarded gas as a useful battlefield weapon; they had authorised its usage in China and so had disregarded the fear that such action would lead to gas warfare elsewhere. Numerous Chinese reports, endorsed on occasions by independent medical and military opinion, alleged the use of lethal agents, but General Tojo, Field Marshal Shunroku Hatu and other Japanese officers maintained that Japanese forces had only employed tear and sneezing gases. They insisted that non-lethal gases were permissible under international law.[94] Nevertheless, Tojo conceded that he had taken Roosevelt's declaration of 1943 seriously, fearing an adverse outcome should chemical munitions be used against American forces. Apparently the Army High Command often disputed this view, urging the use of gas, notably in the fighting for the Mariannas, but Tojo forbad it completely. He was supported in this view by Field Marshal Sugiyama who succeeded him as War Minister in July 1944. Japan refrained from gas warfare, claimed Tojo, because of her commitments under international law, an industrial production which could never equal the output of the United States, and her vulnerability as a densely populated island empire.[95]

Whether these explanations given in post-war interrogation are an accurate reflection of earlier priorities is possibly moot. Her wartime leadership had hardly evinced much respect for the finer points of international law, whereas the country's vulnerability to retaliation was all too evident by 1944. Major-General K. Akiyama added that the Japanese not only feared recourse to gas but believed that it would be used on a large scale by the United States to hasten the end of the war. The Japanese, he explained, were particularly concerned lest the Americans spray their rice fields with mustard or lewisite or, worst of all, arsenic trichloride. Those tactics, he asserted, would have been as effective as dropping the atomic bomb.[96] Substantiating these reflections was the decision of the Japanese army in the summer of 1944 to recall all stocks of gas munitions from the field to prevent the possibility of a local attack. Once the invasion of the home island had become imminent, Japanese gas stocks were too small to permit extensive operations and her aeroplanes were too limited in number to use gas effectively. Japanese cities were utterly exposed, as demonstrated by the effects of incendiary bombing from B-29 and carrier-based aircraft. Japan could not withstand gas attacks, possessing only four public gas shelters, no suitable protective clothing for prolonged wear, and 9 656 200 civilian gas masks – all of a fairly inadequate quality. Having lost the military initiative by the middle of 1944, she had to avoid gas warfare if at all possible. The combined threat from American industrial capacity and air power, coupled with her own abject vulnerability, served as a powerful deterrent.[97]

No single all-embracing factor can explain the non-use of gas in the Second World War. The attitudes of political leaders were important. Both Hitler and Roosevelt instinctively disliked gas; they neither encouraged their respective gas services nor required their military commanders to plan seriously for the employment of chemical weapons. A collapse of effective centralised authority, as in France during the summer of 1940 was equally inhibiting; any paralysis of political initiative generally prevented a reassessment of gas as an effective weapon. On the other hand, neither international law nor public opinion posed a significant constraint. Churchill, for example, was quite prepared to consider the initiation of gas either in defence of Britain or in retaliation for the V bomb attacks. His dynamic leadership undoubtedly transformed British gas capabilities during the war, but it was not sufficient in itself to occasion the first use of gas.

The non-assimilation of gas by military commanders had proved a more powerful constraint. Some senior officers deplored the prospect of gas warfare; others doubted its strategic potential or its capacity to achieve decisive tactical results; others simply accepted that gas was designated as a weapon of retaliation against a hypothetical threat, and so accorded priority to the accretion and deployment of conventional munitions to meet an immediate threat. Whenever initiation was considered, some complained about the logistic burden of moving gas munitions and defensive equipment as well as the problems of storing such items and of coping with retaliation in kind. In the early years of the war the Axis powers achieved rapid and notable successes without recourse to chemical weapons. When the Allies recovered, and gradually gained air superiority, they too succeeded with high explosive and incendiary bombing, although their bomber commands almost certainly exaggerated the achievements of conventional strategic bombing, at least over Germany. Yet it was significant that commands which held such views and those like the Japanese, which regarded chemical weapons as legitimate battlefield weapons, at least against the Chinese if not the Americans, exploited more profound fears to inhibit the initiation of chemical bombing.

For all belligerents, save the United States, the threat of counter-city retaliation was the most powerful deterrent to gas warfare. It reflected a peculiar combination of fears and assumptions – misperceptions about enemy gas potential, inferences about possible enemy intentions derived from capabilities, and a conviction that any enemy, if attacked with gas, would retaliate in kind and on a massive scale. Compounding these forebodings was the dread of escalation – an assumption that gas, once used, would become accepted as a legitimate weapon and so employed in all theatres of war. The Allies, therefore, could not consider the option of gas in isolation; they had to take account of the anxieties voiced by their co-belligerents and the possible effects of their action upon Allied strategy. Of particular concern were the possible repercussions of gas retaliation upon civilian morale, even within well-protected countries like Great Britain. The threat loomed more ominously still for countries lacking adequate protection or vulnerable to air attack. In these circumstances, countries could only avoid the possibility of incurring gas attacks, or of their allies incurring such attacks, by refraining from chemical attacks themselves.

5 Gas and Third World Conflicts

The battlefield utility of poison gas was not seriously undermined by the mutual restraint displayed by the Allies and Axis powers during the Second World War. From the inter-war period there had been reports, which varied considerably in their degrees of accuracy, about the employment of gas in small colonial conflicts.[1] Gas was used in Abyssinia and China and would be used again in post-war encounters, notably in Vietnam and allegedly in the Yemen, South-East Asia and Afghanistan and most recently in the Gulf War. All these incidents occurred in Third World conflicts, where the belligerents neither encountered any credible deterrent nor felt constrained by the Geneva Protocol. In these circumstances gas seemed a useful weapon, and more light may be shed on this utility by the study of three examples: the Italo-Abyssinian War, the Sino-Japanese War and the recent allegations of chemical warfare in Laos, Kampuchea and Afghanistan.

Each of these examples was, and in the last case still is, highly controversial. Unlike the American use of riot control agents and herbicides in Vietnam, which was openly admitted and has been extensively examined,[2] these allegations of gas warfare were persistently disputed. They became embroiled in the claims and counter-claims of various governments. The search for evidence from the battle zones proved almost as difficult as assessing the purpose, extent and effectiveness of the military operations. Still more hazardous was the deriving of lessons from campaigns between foes of grossly unequal strengths, often conducted over desert, mountainous or jungle terrain and sometimes in tropical climates. Yet these campaigns should not be ignored; they raised questions about the battlefield utility of poison gas, the efficacy of disarmament measures, and the intentions and capabilities of the powers involved.

As early as 1925, Benito Mussolini had authorised contingency planning for a full-scale military invasion of Ethiopia whenever events in Europe afforded him the opportunity to do so. Although he ratified the Geneva Protocol in 1928, he was not remotely inhibited about the use of poison gas; indeed, he had authorised the gas bombing of Libyan rebels in the late 1920s, albeit under conditions of the strictest secrecy.[3] The Italian army sustained its interest in chemical warfare, allotting organic mobile chemical units to each division. The Office of Chemical Warfare of the Ministry of War and the National Association for the Commerce of Asphyxiating Gases directed the production of poison gases. Italy, in short, was well equipped for gas warfare when Mussolini resolved upon the 'total conquest of Ethiopia' in December 1934.[4] Poison gas bombs were stockpiled in Eritrea and in Italian Somaliland. Between 25 June and 25 December 1935, 265 tons of asphyxiating gas, 45 tons of mustard gas and 7483 gas bombs were sent through the Suez Canal. On 4 January 1936, the SS *Sicilia* passed through the Canal, carrying 4700 asphyxiating and tear gas bombs.[5]

When Mussolini launched the invasion on 2 October 1935 the army knew that poison gas could be used,[6] and that victory was expected before the onset of the next rainy season in the north (that is, by about June 1936 as it would be extremely difficult thereafter to undertake decisive fighting and to maintain a large army in the field). Having taken a keen interest in gas warfare, the Italian military could experiment with tactics which it had only practised in manoeuvres. It could use various types of agent and methods of delivery, particularly aerial delivery. Of the agents used, the irritants were found to be none too successful. Chloroacetophenone (CN), diphenylchloroarsine (DA) and phenyldichloroarsine were delivered by bombs, and possibly by shells, but the difficulty of creating high concentrations ensured that they had to be used intermittently and on a small scale.[7] The local meteorological conditions also militated against the use of non-persistent agents, like chlorine, phosgene or chloropicrin. Cloud travel was unpredictable in conditions where sudden and gusty winds alternated with dead calm, or in desert areas where the hot equatorial air would rise in the daytime to diffuse vapour clouds, or where sudden torrential showers could 'wash' the gas from the air. Mustard, therefore, although it volatised rapidly in the hot sun, became the principal agent,[8] and aircraft, exploiting Italy's total air superiority, became the principal mode of attack. Initially, metal drums (frangible bombs) were dropped whose thin walls ruptured on contact with the ground to release a puddle of 70 to 200 lb of agent. Although this mode of attack inflicted casualties, the puddles could be avoided by experienced warriors. The ground-bursting of 100, 200, and 500 kg bombs with explosive bursters was found to be more effective; it was capable of spattering agent over a larger area (up to 200 yards in radius). Finally, aerial spraying was introduced to spread the agent more accurately and evenly over a wider area.[9]

The Italo-Abyssinian War was essentially a two front conflict. The major Italian invasion was launched from Eritrea in the north, under the commands of General Emilio De Bono and later Marshal Pietro Badoglio, with the objective of capturing Addis Ababa, the Ethiopian capital. A smaller force, led by General Rodolfo Graziani, invaded from Italian Somaliland in the south; its main aim was to engage as many Ethiopian forces as possible to prevent their employment in the north. The first report of a gas attack came in October 1935 from Ras Nasibu, an Abyssinian commander in the Ogaden desert on the southern front.[10] Although there were further reports of episodic attacks in the south, gas remained a minor factor on this front.[10] The main gas attacks were to be delivered in the north after Badoglio had replaced De Bono in late November. Alarmed by De Bono's dilatory tactics, Mussolini had installed Badoglio as commander with instructions to press forward, using whatever methods were necessary, not only the bombing of villages but also the use of gas and flamethrowers 'on a vast scale'.[11] Badoglio, having employed gas initially at the Takkaze river (22 December 1935),[12] where it relieved the pressure on the II corps, used it increasingly thereafter.

Gas was required for three distinct purposes. In the first place, it was used defensively to protect the flanks of the Italian forces as they moved through the mountains. It compensated for the inability of Badoglio's men to apply the normal light infantry methods of mountain warfare. Instead of picketing the heights, the areas bordering the flanks were gassed so ensuring that the bare-footed Abyssinians would be burned whenever they entered these protected zones. Secondly, gas was used to interdict enemy supply columns, which probably caused few troop casualties but destroyed many cattle and pack animals as well as terrorising the camp followers who accompanied the columns. Thirdly, gas was used with other weapons to promote battlefield offensives. While his machine-gunners held off the enemy advance, Badoglio gassed the area in the enemy's rear as well as their obvious lines of retreat. He then drove the Abyssinians back by high explosive bombing and artillery fire, and turned retreats into routs as the bare-footed warriors, bereft of any anti-gas protection, passed through the contaminated defiles.[13]

Mussolini mounted an extraordinary campaign to conceal the extent and nature of Italy's gas attacks. Having portrayed Italy as a civilised country intent upon subduing a barbarous opponent, he tried to hide the facts from the public at home and abroad. Nor did he wish observers to think – as some of them did –[14] that Italy had won the war only by recourse to illegal methods. He dreaded both the tarnishing of fascist prestige and the loss of secrecy about a weapon he was willing to use again. Rumours of Italian gas attacks were denied in Italy, the press censored, and stories fabricated about the Ethiopians using gas against the Italians.[15] In the League of Nations, when questioned about the Ethiopian accusations, Italy did not explicitly deny the use of gas. Her representatives argued that the Protocol had not modified the existing legal situation concerning the right of reprisal. They then listed the Ethiopian crimes, including the torture and decapitation of Italian prisoners, the emasculation of the dead and wounded, the abuse of the Red Cross emblem, and the use of dum dum bullets.[16] These counter-accusations were not simply instruments of propaganda, they had some semblance of truth: Abyssinian atrocities had enraged Mussolini and his military commanders who promptly retaliated with further gas attacks.[17] Yet these charges were not legally sound (the Protocol was absolute and contained no provision about the use of gas as a reprisal), and they hardly detracted from the point that Mussolini wished to win the war quickly and was willing to use any means to do so.

The effectiveness of gas in contributing towards the fulfilment of the objective has been extensively debated. As the fascist authorities sought to conceal all evidence of the gas attacks, and Badoglio destroyed his operation plans,[18] there is little evidence with which to make an assessment. The Ethiopians kept few, if any, combat records, and the reports from the Emperor Haile Selassie and his ministers to the League of Nations have to be examined cautiously since publicising Italian gas attacks was one means by which they hoped to arouse sympathy and receive aid from other countries. Gas bombing was only one of several atrocities which the Ethiopians claimed had been perpetrated against them (the others included the bombing of Red Cross ambulances and the bombing of open towns and villages), but it was one which they emphasised in the early months of 1936 and almost certainly exaggerated (for example, the claims that Makale had been gas bombed on 31 December 1935 and 21 January 1936, whereas the Italians had occupied it since 8 November 1935).[19] Doctors, journalists and foreign military attachés could confirm that gas attacks had occurred or that gas victims had been treated, but they could not assess the military effectiveness of these attacks.

War correspondents might have provided an independent assessment but they encountered severe restrictions throughout the conflict. Although 120 journalists assembled in Addis Ababa in October 1935, they found little to report. As the Emperor could not guarantee their safety beyond the limits of his capital, they were all confined to Addis. As only one of their number spoke Amharic, they had to rely upon paid informers and lacked any regular sources of information other than official handouts. As the Abyssinian authorities not only censored the news but manipulated it too, 'leaking' decidedly optimistic reports to favoured journalists like George Steer of *The Times*, few journalists were willing to remain. By January only twelve of the original 120 were still in Addis. The correspondents who accompanied the Italian forces experienced similar difficulties. Their reports were stringently censored and their movements were closely controlled. Of the 150 who had originally joined the Italians, a mere twenty-four were left at Christmas, only four of whom were not Italians. One of the latter, Herbert Matthews of *The New York Times*, found an additional frustration, namely that people would not believe his dispatches especially when he predicted an Italian victory. Because most newspaper editors wanted the Abyssinians to win, they gave undue weight to the reports from Addis Ababa. As the consequence, the collapse of the Abyssinian forces, followed by the Emperor's flight and the capture of his capital on 5 May 1936, came as a surprise, leading to glib explanations that gas had been a decisive weapon.[20]

Such assessments cannot be accepted without data on the number of gas casualties and the proportion of gas to other casualties – information which is simply not available. Undoubtedly there were severe casualties whenever the Abyssinians, always barefoot and clad only in togas and cotton trousers, passed through a contaminated area or were struck by mustard spray. Under the tropical heat, the mustard burns appeared more rapidly than in the First World War,[21] and the troops lacked either masks or protective clothing. Not until 6 April 1936 were the first 1800 gas masks made available by the Ethiopian Women's Work Association. Only late in the war did the Ethiopian government import medicines to treat the gas burns.[22] Casualty records were not kept, apart from the men, women and children who received treatment from the Red Cross units. As the latter were few in number and were scattered across both fronts of the war, they could treat only a small proportion of the wounded, without gaining any impression of the total number involved. Members of the British Red Cross Unit, however, were quoted as saying that they alone had

treated 'at least 2500 cases of gassing' after a month in the field.[23]
After sifting various medical and news reports, Matthews concluded:

> when you add them all together what do you get? At best several
> thousands of peasants and soldiers burned more or less badly by
> mustard gas.
> . . . I cannot conceive how any thoughtful person, using the available
> facts, could reach the conclusion that the Italians broke the
> Ethiopian resistance with gas.[24]

Yet Matthews, who neither saw any gas attacks nor met the victims
of those attacks, could not assess the effects of gassing upon
Abyssinian morale. He maintained that the Ethiopians could not have
been demoralised because the Emperor's army had fought so bravely
at the final battles of Mia Chio and Lake Ashangi.[25] Such reasoning is
not wholly convincing. Colonel Konovaloff, Haile Selassie's military
adviser, preferred an entirely contrary view. Having watched the
Emperor's forces near Quoram endure a month of regular mustard
attacks from the Regia Aeronautica, he argued that the Emperor had
to seek battle because his army was in danger of melting away. The
army, he observed, 'was exhausted by the continual spraying with
yperite, which burnt their shoulders and feet, blinded them, and burnt
the mouths of their pack animals when they chewed infected grass. The
Shoans were saying that they wanted to go home . . .'[26] Mass desertions
had already occurred from the armies routed at Amba Aradam,
Tembien, and the Shire. By the end of March Everett Colson, the
Emperor's American adviser, told George Steer that the survivors
from the armies of Ras Imru and Ras Ayelu had already gone home
'because they said they could not fight against gas'.[27] Although
fragments of these forces joined Haile Selassie's army in its final assault
at Mia Chio (31 March), the results were only too predictable. Once
the Italians had held and decimated the attack by shell and machine-
gun fire, they counter-attacked with seventy aircraft using mustard gas
and high explosive. Three days later, the Ethiopians were completely
scattered at the massacre of Lake Ashangi.

Having employed gas in these battles, and in the bombing of several
towns, the Italians clearly regarded it an ideal weapon for terrorising
the enemy. In the wake of their victory at Lake Ashangi, they
subjected Quoram to four days of gas bombardment (4 to 7 April), in

which the town was 'said to have been literally drenched with gas'.[28] Several doctors who had treated the victims of these attacks agreed that gas had had a disproportionate effect on the tribesmen's morale. J. W. S. Macfie described how the people, though used to high explosive bombing, 'seemed stunned by the effects of "gas". It was something outside experience, a mysterious devilish thing'. John Melly was even more appalled: 'This isn't a war – it isn't even a slaughter – it's the torture of tens of thousands of defenceless men, women and children, with bombs and poison gas.'[29] Sir Sidney Barton, the British Minister in Addis Ababa, feared that gas would have decisive tactical implications. On 10 April 1936, he sent a telegram to the Foreign Office, warning that the Italians 'for more than a month past have been relying upon intensive use of gas to drive Ethiopian forces from their prepared positions in the hope of securing decisive results before the League of Nations intervenes. The use of gas represents their best chance of attaining this end'.[30]

Although such comments were impressionistic and must be treated with as much reserve as the Emperor's impassioned speech before the League of Nations Assembly (where he described mustard gas as 'death-dealing rain' which had inflicted 'tens of thousands' of casualties),[31] gas seems to have impaired Abyssinian morale. It was not a 'war-winning' weapon, in the sense that Badoglio would not have won without it. Indeed he had a well-trained, well-equipped army with an abundance of armaments and a devastating superiority in airpower. He would have won anyway but he had to win quickly (both to avoid the rains and to minimise the consequences of the economic sanctions imposed by the League of Nations). Poison gas was an asset in fulfilling this aim. Its effects, though rarely fatal, were appalling to experience and to observe; almost certainly they assisted in hastening an inevitable end and in contributing to the speed of the Italian victory. Mussolini required little convincing that poison gas had been useful; once Addis Ababa had fallen, he authorised his generals to continue using gas to pacify the rest of the country.[32]

This utility reflected both the inability of the Abyssinians to protect themselves and the absence of any credible deterrent. The Italians were neither threatened with serious retaliation by the Abyssinians nor with intervention by other powers. Only Britain and France could have posed any threat but neither was prepared to act against Italy, a Locarno power, to uphold the principle of collective security. Although the League of Nations had responded to Italy's invasion by imposing economic sanctions (18 November 1935), it could never secure agreement over closing the Suez Canal to military traffic or over the banning of oil supplies. While Britain felt unable to take naval action without the support of France, French opinion was split: Pierre Laval's Right-wing government wished to uphold the Italian alliance but the Radicals, on whom it depended for support in the Chamber of Deputies, favoured the League and collective security. Anglo-French relations, already strained by the recent Anglo-German Naval Agreement (18 June 1935) were damaged still further by the British repudiation of the Hoare–Laval Plan, which would have given Mussolini much of what he wanted in Abyssinia.[33] Finally, Hitler's reoccupation of the Rhineland (7 March 1936) ensured that European issues would take precedence, and that France, even under a new government, would not provoke Italy. In these circumstances the gas allegations, first referred to the League on 30 December 1935, could hardly have come at a less opportune moment.

They caused great public indignation, particularly in Britain where newspapers were deluged with letters condemning the Italian tactics. Even the *Daily Mail*, which sympathised with Mussolini's colonial ambitions, denounced the use of gas.[34] But governments felt unable to act. Although the British Cabinet possessed 'overwhelming' evidence in support of the Abyssinian charges, (including liquid from an Italian bomb which fell near Daghabur on 30 December 1935 which was found to be 'the vesicant ingredient of ordinary mustard gas' by the Chemical Defence Research Department),[35] ministers dared not reveal it for fear of admitting 'that nothing could be done to secure compliance with the terms of the Convention'.[36] The Cabinet preferred to raise the issue with the Committee of Thirteen (a body appointed by the Council of the League to examine the situation in Abyssinia as a whole) and to seek an independent inquiry into the allegations. Anthony Eden, however, found little support for his proposal save from the representatives of Portugal, Denmark and Australia. 'Hardly anyone,' he informed the Cabinet, seemed to be thinking about 'Abyssinia and Africa at all.'[37] Paul-Bancour blocked any meaningful inquiry by insisting that all the wartime atrocities, including the Abyssinian use of dum dum bullets, should be investigated. The Committee duly adjourned, issuing a brief report which reminded the belligerents of 'the importance' of their commitments under the Geneva Protocol.[38] So pusillanimous a response still served a purpose. When Eden was pressed in the House of Commons about Britain's failure to act over the gas allegations, he replied that British policy had been 'based upon collective action through the League, and (the government) cannot therefore take any unilateral action in this matter'.[39]

If the Italo-Ethiopian War revived fears of poison gas being used in future conflicts, it merely confirmed the expectations of the Chinese High Command. These forebodings reflected Japan's non-ratification of the Geneva Protocol and the disdain for international law displayed by the commanders of the Kwantung Army during the Manchurian and Shanghai incidents of 1931–2. In the planned reorganisation of the Chinese defences, accepted by the government in 1933 and due to be completed within five years, there was provision for the establishment of five regiments of chemical troops, large-scale production of gas masks, the formation of air defence corps with anti-gas capabilities, and the training of cadets and officers in anti-gas defence at the Central Military Academy. Financial, industrial and political constraints ensured that these plans were never fully implemented. By the spring of 1937 only thirteen cities had completed their air defence organisations. Gas defences had hardly been a foremost priority in view of the shortages of conventional weaponry, ships, and planes, the lack of fortifications in key strategic areas, the deficiencies of transportation and communication, and the tardy introduction of conscription (only begun in 1936). When the war erupted (7 July 1937) the Japanese armed forces were vastly superior in equipment, training, organisation and even manpower (at the beginning of the war, a far greater proportion of the Japanese population had been mobilised in the war effort).[40]

From the outbreak of hostilities the Japanese Army moved chemical units into China. In October 1937, the Japanese Army established a field chemical warfare laboratory in Shanghai to collect intelligence on the state of Chinese preparedness for chemical warfare. In the same year it deployed a field gas section of 119 officers and men, armed with portable sprayers and toxic smoke candles; four chemical mortar battalions, each equipped with twelve 90 mm light mortars; and the Morita Detachment, a battalion of 1031 officers and men, which was attached to the Central China Expeditionary Force and later to more than twelve different divisions.[41] The Chinese Gas Defence Department of the Ministry of War recorded nine gas attacks in the first six months of the war. It claimed that tear and sneezing gases had been used in the battles of Shanghai and Sinkow (1937); that tear gas hand grenades had been captured by the victorious Chinese soldiers after the battle of Taierhchwang (March–April 1938); and that recourse to gas had increased considerably after the success of various gas attacks

along the Tientsin–Pukow railway. Not only were more gas groups
added to Japanese front-line units but they were also armed with
asphyxiating as well as irritant agents.[42]

In May 1938, the Chinese government warned the League of
Nations that the Japanese were 'on the point of using poison gas on a
large scale in disregard of international law and convention'. It
reported that two mechanised units had just left Japan for the
Shantung front, and that both contained chemical warfare troops.[43]
Although the Council duly responded by recalling 'that the use of toxic
gases is a method of war condemned by international law' which
should 'meet with the reprobation of the civilized world',[44] such
protestations from an impotent organisation had negligible impact. By
the autumn the Chinese returned with allegations of extensive gas
attacks, supported by the testimony of Dr H. Talbot, a British surgeon
in the Nanchang General Hospital, a signed report from five Red Cross
doctors, and captured Japanese documents.[45] On 30 September 1938
the Council proposed the formation of a 'Commission of Neutral
Observers in China' to investigate the poison gas allegations, and
invited those Council members who had official representatives in
China to consider the practicality of implementing this recommendation. R. A. Butler, Britain's reprsentative at the Council, accepted the
resolution but stressed that the evidence on this subject was 'very
diverse and conflicting' and so his government maintained 'an attitude
of some reserve in regard to certain of the Chinese representative's
observations'.[46]

Verifying the Chinese charges, however legally necessary, was more
pedantic than practical. Even if an independent commission had been
allowed to gather information in the war zone, verification would not
have ensured subsequent action either by the League nations collec-
tively or by any great power. As Butler informed the House of
Commons, the British government endorsed the Council's reprobation of gas warfare as a 'sufficient' reflection of its views.[47] Apart from
the intrinsic difficulty of taking action in view of the state of Britain's
defences and the ominous developments in Europe, the military
significance of the gas operations was not entirely clear. The gas
attacks were being used, quite understandably, as an issue in China's
diplomatic and propaganda offensive. They were only one of many
atrocity charges, and they were causing far fewer casualties than the
aerial bombing of civilians or the appalling slaughter which followed
the fall of Nanking (an estimated 150 000 inhabitants killed in six
weeks).[48] The reports, too, were often imprecise, lacking accurate

details about the agents used and their medical effects. As partial, confused, and sometimes contradictory reports emanated from China throughout the campaign, and as their particulars could not be confirmed fully by British and American military sources, they complicated the task of intelligence assessment.[49]

Despite the confusion and inaccuracies, there was little doubt that gas in various forms had been used. Even General the Honourable Sir Harold Alexander, when General Officer Commanding in Burma, accepted that the Japanese had used 'arsenious toxic smoke and tear gas in China', although he suspected that the Chinese sometimes alleged gas attacks to explain their retreats.[50] In post-war testimony Japanese officers confirmed that their forces had used gases but only irritant agents on the assumption that non-lethal gases were permitted under international law.[51] But the multitude of Chinese reports, coupled with photographic evidence and testimony from journalists, Red Cross doctors and a CW observer from the 14th United States Air Force,[52] strongly suggests that lethal agents were employed.

Chinese reports allege that the Japanese employed gas in China from 18 July 1937 to 8 May 1945. They also allege that the Japanese used diphenylchloroarsine (DA), diphenylcyanoarsine (DC), chloroacetophenone (CN), chloropicrin, hydrogen cyanide, phosgene, mustard and lewisite.[53] By the end of 1941, Chinese sources claim that over 1000 gas attacks had been delivered. Although the statistics are not necessarily reliable (since there are discrepancies between the various reports), the data from the Chinese Gas Defence Department reveals an interesting pattern of usage:

Year	No. of attacks	Proportion of Agents Used					Casualties	
		Tear	Sneezing	Asphyxiating	Vesicatory	Unknown	Killed	Wounded
		%	%	%	%	%		
1937	9	40	40			20	20	50
1938	105	35	48	10		7	293	2 708
1939	455	41	37	8	4	10	634	12 556
1940	259	39	37	8	9	7	71	6 288
1941	231	34	46	10	10		930	5 000
	1 059						1 948	26 602[54]

While this report underlines the Japanese recourse to a wide variety of agents, it does not confirm the wilder assertions from Chungking of a rapid increase in the use of vesicatory gases.[55] On the contrary, it indicates that the Japanese continued to rely upon irritant agents in the early years of the war, for which the army was adequately equipped. Prior to 1942, it had manufactured 1067 metric tons of diphenyl-cyanoarsine (DC), its principal irritant, to be used as a fine-particle aerosol (smoke).[56]

Whether generated by candles and pots or by artillery and mortar projectiles, 'special smoke' figured prominently in several important battles, notably those of Wuhan and Hankow in 1938. Mustard gas was allegedly used for the first time in bombing raids upon villages in southern Shansi in the autumn of 1939. A particularly intensive gas attack occurred at Ichang from 8 to 10 October 1941. It was launched in response to a powerful Chinese assault upon Japanese positions near the city. As the Japanese retreated towards Ichang, guns on the flank of the Chinese advance pounded their units. On 8 October thirty gas shells were fired, on the following day another ten as the 26th Regiment seized Yentimpao, and on 10 October, as the main force of the 9th Division attacked the city, Japanese guns fired gas shells over a period of four hours, supported by Japanese planes dropping over 300 gas bombs. A mixture of gases may have been used, including tear, sneezing and lewisite (consistent with a 'smell like flowers', rapid onset of symptoms, blisters, and later paralysis and vomiting). Chinese reports claimed that the gases accounted for 1600 casualties of whom 600 died. Although there were inconsistencies in these reports, gas victims were treated by a Red Cross doctor and they were interviewed and photographed by journalists. As a Porton analysis stated, 'there seems a solid basis for the conclusion that the Japs did use either lewisite or a lewisite mixture on a fairly large scale'.[57]

Captured Japanese documents, like *Lessons from the China Incident no. 7* (April 1939) and *Collection of Combat Examples of the use of smoke and others* (TN war gases) (June 1943), present assessments of CW operations. Where failures occurred, there were two principal explanations. Sometimes there was a lack of confidence in the effectiveness of gas or undue misapprehension about the toxic qualities which resulted in a failure to make a timely attack through the smoke-screen. On other occasions attacks had foundered because of a lack of co-ordination between the smoke units and other forces. Nevertheless, 'special smokes' had been used effectively in many operations, especially when the enemy was inadequately protected and lacked training and experience in chemical warfare. In the early mountain battles of the Hankow campaign, smoke had often had a decisive psychological effect: 'Often the enemy took to their heels at the mere sight of smoke before we launched upon any actual offensive action.'[58]

By 1943 the Narashino school compiled a list of examples from the Chinese experience, exemplifying how gas (i.e. red candles or red shells) could be used effectively and how failures could be minimised. When the enemy held a strong position and could not be dislodged by ordinary gunfire, red shells could be used often in conjunction with smoke or artillery to facilitate an infantry assault. In encounter battles when a small punitive force engaged a numerically superior enemy, the firing of a small number of red candles could 'surprise the enemy and gain battle advantage'. Night attacks were more hazardous; heavy losses had occurred because the firing positions had been improperly selected and had drawn enemy fire upon ignition. Yet red candles could be used to mount a surprise attack after the force had closed in on the enemy under the cover of darkness or had concealed its movements by the discharge of smoke. Gas could also be employed in defending positions or narrow fronts. The co-ordinated use of red candles, gunfire and close combat could 'trap and destroy' the attacking units by drawing them into the fire net. When fighting over special types of terrain, gas could be used effectively if care was taken over special meteorological and topographical conditions. Before attacking defences on mountainous summits, allowance had to be made for valley winds and temperature inversion (i.e. the formation of a layer of cool air beneath a mass of hot air which occurs in valleys when the flow of air is interrupted by the surrounding peaks). In river combat, once the enemy had been checked at the front and his envelopment completed, the projection of red candles could be decisive. As a surprise weapon, it could 'throw him into confusion' and bring about his destruction in 'one blow'. Red candles could also be used to dislodge adversaries from villages or caves, so enabling the main force 'to destroy the fleeing enemy'. Finally, they could be employed in defensive combat to surprise an enemy and launch a counter-attack.[59]

The effectiveness of the Japanese gas operations cannot be determined accurately. The offensive gas units were using China and Manchuria as 'testing areas' and an element of experimentation seems to have persisted throughout the campaign. British military intelligence, in reviewing a report of seventeen gas attacks in North China during 1942 (when 772 shells killed 245 people and wounded another 927), commented that 'the practice of firing a few rounds into villages seems to have no real use and can only be experimental'.[60] Nor was the army able to employ gas on a large scale over a long period of time. Prior to 1942 it had produced only 138 metric tons of hydrocyanic acid, 1067 tons of DC, 40 tons of CN, and 3062 tons of mustard and lewisite (it had to procure any phosgene or chloropicrin from commercial sources).[61]

Relying primarily upon irritant gases, usually in small-scale attacks, the infliction of casualties was not the primary aim. Indeed, the gas-related casualty tally, as claimed by the Chinese, was derisory as a proportion of her overall casualties (officially estimated at 362 000 dead and 1 087 000 wounded by February 1940 – and possibly as many as 2 million casualties by the middle of 1940).[62] More important was the effect of gas upon morale or as a temporary incapacitant, especially in the early battles. General Li Han-Yuan feared that the Chinese lines would not hold should the Japanese start using gas on a large scale. 'Even when it is only tear or mustard gas,' argued General Tang En-po, 'it lays our men out for long enough to enable the enemy to come and bayonet them as they lie gasping for breath.'[63] Yet gas could never be used in a decisive mode. The stocks of gas were insufficient, and the Chinese armies prudently avoided the 'conclusive battle' so eagerly sought by the Japanese invaders. By trading space for time, the Chinese forced their adversary to spread his resources including his gas capabilities. Gas could only be used tactically and against specific targets. British military intelligence concluded that the Japanese carefully husbanded their gas resources, and that they only used gas 'when they are up against it either in attack or retirement'.[64]

Both Britain and the United States monitored the gas reports from China and tried to deter Japan. Using the diplomatic services of Argentina, Britain reminded the Japanese government that her predecessors had accepted Article 171 of the Treaty of Versailles and Article V of the Treaty of Washington (1922). Britain intimated that she would 'observe the Protocol strictly so long as it continues to be observed by Japan' and reserve 'full liberty of action' should Japan infringe the Protocol.[65] On 5 June 1942, President Roosevelt issued a public warning of 'retaliation in kind and in full measure' in the event of Japan persisting with gas warfare 'against China or against any other of the United Nations'. One year later he reiterated the threat in more general terms, adding that the United States would 'in no circumstances resort to the use of such weapons unless the first use of them is by our enemies'.[66]

These warnings which were conspicuously vague about the mode and timing of retaliation contained an element of bluff: neither Britain nor the United States could have mounted effective gas operations in the Far East in 1942 or 1943. Nor did it appear that the threats had succeeded. The Chinese continued to report gas attacks until as late as May 1945, including an account of a particularly extensive and prolonged attack in the battle of Changteh (November–December 1943).[67] Only the prospect of direct conflict with American land and air forces, coupled with the loss of air superiority in 1944, induced some caution in the Japanese High Command. Aware of America's potential capability in gas warfare, General Tojo and Field Marshal Sugiyama argued successfully against any use of gas in combat with American forces.[68]

Nevertheless, the possibility, however remote, of the Allied governments wishing to act upon their threats required that reports from Chungking had to be scrutinised with care. Allied intelligence agencies repeatedly bemoaned the lack of precision in the Chinese accounts and the absence of independent corroboration by trained CW officers. British military scepticism even persisted when there was a report from a CW officer of the 14th US Air Force, indicating that the Japanese had used mustard and lewisite in their Hengyang advance.[69] Not until the United States had established field teams in China in 1945, which were competent to assess the gas reports, was British intelligence convinced that reliable independent evidence would be forthcoming. Hitherto, argued the Director of Military Intelligence, the reports had been 'largely propaganda to excuse the poor showing of the Chinese forces against the Japanese'.[70]

By 1945 it was much too late to investigate the gas reports thoroughly. Japan's gas production had diminished sharply in the previous year, and her main concern was to avoid giving the United States any pretext for embarking upon chemical warfare.[71] Conclusive evidence would have been difficult to gather anyway since the Japanese Army had endeavoured to conceal the extent of its gas operations. A captured Japanese order, 'Command No. 38', issued by Lieutenant-General Matsuura Junrokuro at Huhanchen on 25 August 1938, authorised the use of 'special smoke' but only under strict conditions. It was not to be used where nationals of a third power were in evidence and all empty shells were to be destroyed. All enemy soldiers affected by 'special smoke' were to be killed and not allowed to escape; the red shell markings should be erased from shell cases; and printed matter on 'special smoke' should be carefully kept.[72]

Such attention to detail had assisted in obfuscating the truth about the Japanese gas operations. The Chinese were left to cope with the attacks as best they could, protesting somewhat forlornly to the rest of the world. Although some of their units had gas masks,[73] their level of anti-gas protection was woefully inadequate, compounded by the absence of any credible deterrent or means of retaliation. Admittedly Japanese gas attacks never represented a strategic threat, although they were probably effective tactically in some encounters. The limitations were largely self-imposed, reflecting a shortage of gas supplies, non-assimilation by some officers, and an inadequate aerial capability. Ultimately the gas effort only began to contract when Japan's military resources became increasingly stretched and the conflict with the United States became more ominous.

In the post-war period gas warfare has recurred. The United States employed riot control agents and herbicides in Vietnam. Egypt was strongly suspected of attacking Royalist forces with chemical weapons in the Yemen (1963–7).[74] More recently, there have been reports of chemical attacks by the Lao People's Liberation Army and Vietnamese forces upon the H'Mong tribesmen in Laos, by the Vietnamese and later the People's Republic of Kampuchea forces against the Khmer Rouge in Kampuchea, and by Soviet and Afghan forces against the *mujahidin* in Afghanistan. The allegations began emanating from Laos in the summer of 1975. H'Mong refugees, having fled into Thailand from Laos, described aerial attacks upon their villages. These tribesmen claimed that air-bursted rockets or aerial spraying had released clouds of vapour over their villages, which were coloured yellow or white but sometimes red or green. The yellow clouds were dubbed 'Yellow Rain' by Western journalists because small particles in the clouds sounded like raindrops as they settled on the roofs of huts and in surrounding fields. Following these attacks, the villagers experienced a bizarre range of medical symptoms. Some died, while others who were on the periphery of the attack or who ate contaminated food and water experienced dizziness, severe itching of the skin, the formation of small hard blisters, nausea, bloody diarrhoea, and the vomiting of copious amounts of blood. Such reports were fragmentary in 1975 and 1976 but they increased alarmingly in the next two years, especially from refugees fleeing from the H'Mong strongholds in the mountainous Phou Bia area. In 1978, similar reports began to emerge from Kampuchea (where the Vietnamese were alleged to be delivering chemical attacks by 60 mm mortars, 120 mm shells, 107 mm rockets, M-79 grenade launchers, mines, T-28 aircraft and the poisoning of water) and in 1979 from Afghanistan (where apparently helicopters were extensively employed along with fixed wing aircraft, artillery, mines and the pumping of yellow gas into waterways).[75]

The United States, under successive administrations, sought to confirm and publicise the allegations of chemical warfare, intending thereby to stop the attacks and to secure a verifiable treaty which would ban the production and stockpiling of chemical weapons. In the summer of 1979 the State Department compiled the first systematic record of interviews with refugees from Laos, and in the following autumn a US Army medical team visited Thailand to conduct further interviews. By the winter of 1979 the United States, who had expressed its concern about H'Mong human rights to the Laotian government as early as October 1978, felt able to raise the reports of chemical warfare with the governments of Laos, Vietnam and the Soviet Union. All three governments denied the validity of these reports. Dissatisfied with these replies, and in possession of further accounts of gas attacks from Kampuchea and Afghanistan, the Carter administration began to raise the issue in Congress and the United Nations. In August 1980, it published a 125 page compendium of reports and declassified intelligence information on the alleged attacks.[76] In December 1980, the United Nations General Assembly responded to pressure from the American, Canadian and other delegations to vote in favour of establishing a UN investigation (Resolution A/35/144C approved by 78 votes to 17 with 36 abstentions).

Investigating and analysing the evidence had proved difficult for the State Department. Its cautious movements prompted critics to charge that the Carter administration had only belatedly supported the inquiry, lest its findings jeopardise the negotiation of an arms control agreement with the Soviet Union.[77] But bureaucratic problems persisted under the Reagan administration. As Richard Burt, then director of the Bureau of Politico-Military Affairs, admitted, 'It took us a while, obviously, to lash up the governmental system, people in the Pentagon, people in the Intelligence community, people in the State Department' to create a functioning team which could examine the issue effectively.[78] The scientific analysis proved especially daunting. Carolyn Stettner of the Arms Control and Disarmament Agency recalls that there was 'no formal mechanism' at the beginning with which to assemble a 'team of experts'.[79] Nor was it clear which chemical agents had been used. Tests on the original samples collected from alleged attack sites (and often carried by foot over a period of several weeks to the nearest international border) failed to reveal any traces of known chemical agents. Although medical symptoms indicated that irritants, incapacitants (including a highly potent, rapid-acting 'knock-out' chemical) and nerve agents, possibly in non-persistent forms, may have been used, the combination of symptoms was unusual in many cases (particularly the lethal haemorrhaging) and indicated that other agents perhaps in addition to traditional ones were possibly being employed. Only in mid-1981 did medical and toxicological experts start testing samples for the presence of mycotoxins, poisons produced by several species of fungi. Samples of vegetation (a leaf, leaf parts and a twig from an alleged Yellow Rain site in Kampuchea) were found to contain three of these mycotoxins from the trichothecene group (109 parts per million (ppm) of nivalenol, 59.1 ppm of deoxynivalenol and 3.15 ppm of T-2 toxin) by Dr Chester J. Mirocha of the Department of Plant Pathology, University of Minnesota. He analysed these samples, unaware of their provenance, using his computerised gas chromatography/mass spectroscopy method in the selected ion-monitoring mode. He detected no trichothecenes in the negative control sample and concluded that 'the concentrations found and their combination are not normally found in nature and it would appear that these mycotoxins found their way into the environment by the intervention of man'.[80]

These findings were only part of a much larger body of evidence. The testimony of eyewitnesses – those who claim to have seen, experienced or suffered from chemical weapon attacks – was checked (in respect of date, place and type of attack) against information from defectors, journalists, doctors, international organisations, and 'national technical means' to pinpoint the time and place of the reported attacks. Testimony was gathered from military defectors, including a Laotian pilot who flew chemical warfare missions before defecting in 1979, Vietnamese Army defectors, numerous Afghan Army defectors and a captured Soviet military chemical specialist, Yuriy Povarnitsyn. It was buttressed by intelligence gathered from radio intercepts and other technical means, correlated with knowledge about the Soviet chemical and biological warfare data base and with information from the corresponding data base of the United States. There was film evidence, too. Bernd de Bruin, a Dutch journalist, filmed an Mi–24 helicopter dropping canisters over a village in the Jalalabad area on 15 and 21 June 1980 which produced a dirty yellow cloud. De Bruin entered the village after both attacks, incurring personal injuries on each occasion, to photograph the effects including a victim with blackened skin, discoloured by extensive subcutaneous bleeding five hours after the attack. Further physical samples were also gathered from attack sites in Kampuchea. Trichothecenes were found in the blood, urine and other tissue samples from alleged victims, in samples of water, and in yellow powder scraped from rocks. T-2 toxin was also found on the outer surface of a Soviet gas mask found near Kabul (but not on the filters) and several trichothecene toxins on the hose connections from another gas mask removed from a dead Soviet soldier. From this massive body of evidence the United States listed a minimum of 261 separate chemical attacks in Laos, causing a minimum of 6504 deaths from the summer of 1975 to autumn 1981; 124 attacks in Kampuchea, causing 981 deaths, from 1978 to autumn 1981; and 47 attacks in Afghanistan, causing over 3000 deaths, from the summer of 1979 to the summer of 1981.[81] The State Department reported that similar attacks had occurred in 1982, that trichothecene toxins had been found in twenty biomedical samples by August 1983, that the attacks had continued in South East Asia through 1983 (but had diminished in number in Laos and in lethality in Laos and Kampuchea), and that gas attacks in Afghanistan, though reported in 1983, had not been confirmed, although a senior Afghan chemical officer has since claimed that they continued until as late as January 1984.[82]

In its diplomatic *démarches* the United States emphasised the involvement of the Soviet Union. It claimed that Soviet advisers and technicians had participated in the preparation and loading of chemical weapons, the unloading of Soviet shipments of 'deadly toxic chemicals' in the port of Ho Chi Minh City and the flying of aircraft by 'caucasian pilots' (one dead Soviet pilot was found in a crashed plane). Two Vietnamese corporals from the 337th and 347th Vietnamese Army Divisions described how Soviet advisers trained personnel in the use of Soviet-supplied weapons and equipment, including chemical artillery shells and gas masks.[83] Defecting Afghan officers, particularly those who had been trained in the use of chemical weapons by Soviet advisers, provided 'very precise information about types of agents employed, where they were employed, where they are stored, the methods used'.[84] They indicated that the Soviets had provided supplies of lethal and incapacitating agents, and that Soviet planes, helicopters and land-mines had been used to disseminate chemical agents. Soviet chemical defence battalions remained with the three motorised rifle divisions at Qonduz, Shindand and Kabul, despite the removal of 5000 troops and 'nonessential' combat equipment. In a sweep operation through the Konar Valley and near Shindand in 1980, personnel decontamination stations and chemical decontamination units were both observed. Soviet personnel were also seen wearing chemical protective equipment. The testimony of captured Soviet soldiers amplified these accounts. Yuriy Povarnitsyn, a military chemical specialist from Sverdlovsk, explained that he had a mission to examine villages after chemical attacks to determine whether they were safe to enter or required decontamination.[85] Anatoly Sakharov, a young conscript, claimed that he had seen three different kinds of chemical weapons stored – 'picrine', possibly picric acid; various asphyxiating gases; and an agent known as 'smirch' which blackened human flesh and atrophied limbs (effects which tallied with previous doctors' descriptions).[86]

The discovery of toxins buttressed suspicion of Soviet involvement. Soviet agriculture has had long experience of fungal poisonings often derived from mouldy grain. Since the 1930s trichothecenes have been the subject of intensive Soviet scientific investigation. In the winter of 1943–4, an epidemic of the disease then called Alimentary Toxic Aleukia swept the Orenburg district, killing some 300 000 people. Numerous industrial microbiology plants have been identified in the Soviet Union. Many are engaged in the perfectly legitimate production of single-cell protein for fodder additives, some produce antibiotics and other microbial products, but some produce 'products that are quite unknown'.[87] The physical and chemical properties of toxins, especially their stability in solid form, make them practical weapons which could be mass-produced. The State Department noted that a significant proportion of Soviet literature on toxins is concerned with defining the optimum conditons for biosynthesis of the compounds (from a sample of fifty Soviet articles on trichothecenes twenty-two focus on biosynthesis). Mycotoxins can be produced in good yield from fungi, employing the same techniques which produce some antibiotics. Fusaria, finally, are produced in the Berdsk Chemical Works, which the State Department describes as 'long reported in the open literature as being a suspected biological warfare agent production and storage facility'.[88]

The plausibility of such circumstantial evidence depends on the possible utility of toxins as military weapons. The State Department reckoned that they were probably cheaper and easier to store, handle, and transport than nerve agents which require elaborate and costly safety precautions.[89] On the other hand, trichothecenes are much less lethal than nerve agents and would have to be delivered in substantial quantities to have lethal effects. The scientific estimates of the lethality of trichothecenes in humans vary considerably[90] (partly because much of the data concerning their toxicological effects is derived from animal experiments, using pure compounds administered by oral, subcutaneous or intravenous routes). Dr Sharon Watson, a toxicologist from the Office of the US Army Surgeon General, claims that the lethal dose of T-2 toxin could be as low as 35 milligrams for a 70 kilogram man, which is considerably lower than other estimates. She argues that the toxicity of trichothecenes appears to increase when crude extracts and combinations of toxins are used and when a solvent, specifically DMSO, is applied. An even smaller dose could be fatal if inhaled, which could account for the pulmonary and gastric haemorrhaging. Nevertheless, nerve agents would have the same lethal effects at one-thirtieth of this concentration,[91] and some believe that trichothecenes would be even less effective as an anti-personnel weapon. They could only inflict casualties if dispersed in sufficient quantities against an unprotected enemy, but they have some attractions in the difficulty of detection, resistance to prophylaxis and therapy, and difficulty of attribution. As Stuart Schwartzstein observed,

> There are great advantages in using weapons that are either very subtle and perhaps not even noticed as weapons – indistinguishable from natural phenomena or simply inexplicable, even if suspected – or where verification and identification is so difficult that arguments continue to rage over whether or not allegations of use are true.[92]

Finally, the State Department considered why the Soviet Union might use weapons which are illegal as it would risk, if exposed in such warfare, a further deterioration in its relations with the Third World. The Soviet leadership was not oblivious of these points; it firmly denied the early American protests, then tried to explain the presence of trichothecenes by reference to the American seeding of elephant grass in Indo-China (a theory which commands little scientific credibility),[93] and later refused to permit an investigatory team from the UN to enter Afghanistan. The State Department suspected that the Soviets and their allies might have thought that they would not be exposed; that the agents would be difficult to detect and identify; that incontrovertible evidence could not be easily compiled from inaccessible areas in South-East Asia and Afghanistan; and that they could refute successfully any charges which were less than utterly conclusive. Moreover, chemical weapons are a cost-effective mode of combating guerillas, entrenched in jungles or in mountainous terrain. Compared with conventional artillery or with high-explosive bombing or with sweep operations, chemical weapons are more economical, minimise the assailant's losses, and are probably more effective: 'chemical clouds can penetrate the heavy forests and jungle canopy and seep into the mountain caves'.[94] They can also be employed as a terror weapon, especially if the adversary has complete control of the skies (as over Laos) and if the agents leave bizarre and horrific symptoms. As a means of driving the H'Mong from their highland sanctuaries, chemical weapons would seem to be particularly useful. Against opposing resistance forces, whether in Kampuchea or Afghanistan, chemical weapons could be used tactically to protect the flanks of moving columns, and to attack otherwise inaccessible forces which lack anti-chemical protection. Even experimentation could have been a partial motive, using these campaigns to test and evaluate older as well as more recently developed agents under operational conditions. After some attacks, Soviet personnel were observed collecting samples of soil and tissue as well as holding any survivors for further examination.[95] Notwithstanding the value of such tests, the tactical utility of chemical weapons was probably more important: it would enable attacks to be mounted in remote areas with minimal losses.[96]

Initially the presentation of this evidence was none too impressive. On 13 September 1981, Secretary of State Alexander Haig revealed that the United States had gathered physical evidence to substantiate its allegations of chemical warfare, specifically samples which contained 'abnormally high levels of three potent mycotoxins – poisonous substances not indigenous to the region which are highly toxic to man and animals'.[97] He inserted these remarks into a speech before the Berlin press association to pre-empt a leak about the mycotoxin evidence due to be published in *Time* magazine and the imminent publication of *Yellow Rain* by Sterling Seagrave. There had been little preparation for charges of such magnitude. At a briefing on the following day, Walter J. Stoessel, Under Secretary of State for Political Affairs, explained that 'a leaf and stem sample' from Kampuchea had revealed abnormally high levels of mycotoxins of the trichothecene group. He added that 'it is highly unlikely that such levels could have occurred in a natural intoxication. In point of fact, these mycotoxins do not occur naturally in Southeast Asia'.[98]

Various reporters and scientists were highly sceptical. The insertion of the charges into a speech designed to bolster support for NATO and to offset European criticism of the Reagan administration seemed somewhat contrived. The physical evidence – 'a leaf and stem' – seemed meagre, prompting some scientists to query the apparent absence of control samples and the lack of data about how the evidence was gathered and sent to the United States (as it could have been contaminated *en route*). Also the firm assertion that mycotoxins could not have occurred naturally surprised some *Fusarium* experts, who noted that *Fusarium* could be found almost anywhere, including the tropics (although whether they produce toxins in the tropics was unknown).[99] On 10 November 1981 Richard Burt, the director of the Bureau of Politico–Military Affairs, assisted by Drs Watson and Mirocha, tried to meet some of these criticisms in testimony before the Senate Foreign Relations Subcommittee on Arms Control. Burt presented the physical evidence in a broader historical context, revealed further findings of toxin in samples taken from Laos and the negative results from control samples taken 'from near the same area in Kampuchea' as the leaf and stem. He also modified some of the State Department's previous scientific observations; he argued that the trichothecenes which had been found 'do not occur naturally in the combination identified in Southeast Asia'. Stressing the link between these poisons and the symptoms reported, he insisted that 'the fit . . . was perfect'. 'We now have,' he concluded, 'the smoking gun'.[100]

Professor Matthew Meselson, a Harvard biochemist, testified before the same committee. He conceded that 'the preliminary evidence' indicated that trichothecene mycotoxins may have been used in South-East Asia, but cautioned against premature over-confident statements. He questioned whether the samples could have been 'spiked'; whether mycotoxins, if disseminated in coarse particules or droplets as described by Burt, would cause massive haemorrhaging and death; and whether it was wise to preclude a natural explanation since nothing was known about mycotoxins in South-East Asia. Indeed, he noted that a recent study of a Brazilian shrub had revealed another type of trichothecene in concentrations much higher than those found by Mirocha.[101] Unimpressed by the scientific premises of the State Department's case, critics persisted with their scepticism. Some accepted that the volume of testimony was too large to be ignored, and that chemical warfare of some kind, though not necessarily involving trichothecenes, was being practised.[102] Others agreed with J. P. Perry Robinson that nothing could yet be concluded from the evidence publicly presented.[103] Gene Lyons was even more doubtful, refusing to accept 'the shaky evidence on faith' in view of previous 'intelligence hoaxes'.[104]

Had the United Nations been able to investigate the allegations effectively, some of these charges might have been answered. However, the Group of Experts, led by Major-General Dr A. E. Ezz, head of the Scientific Research Branch, Egyptian Armed Forces, was fatally hindered in its activities. It was organised slowly, lacked adequate resources, and found itself hampered by the due processes of UN bureaucracy as well as an extremely tight schedule (it had to report to the thirty-sixth session of the General Assembly). It met only three times in 1981 (for four days in April, fifteen in July and nearly a month over October–November including a brief visit of ten days to Thailand). Above all, it was denied access to the countries of Afghanistan, Laos and Kampuchea. In Thailand, the Group found it difficult to conduct 'meaningful interviews through interpreters' (and was much criticised for its attitude towards the H'Mong).[105] Although the Group gathered physical samples from the refugees, it was reluctant to derive final conclusions from the analysis of samples whose source it could not ascertain. Unable to reach a final conclusion,[106] the Group found its remit extended for another year by the General Assembly (with 86 votes in favour, 20 against and 32 abstentions – resolution 36/96C of 9 December 1981).

The second investigation was more thorough and comprehensive in scope. The Group evaluated the written submissions of various governments, cross-checking the information as best it could (although the reinterviewing of witnesses was difficult because of the time lapse between the interviews – six months in one instance). It reviewed the trichothecene hypothesis, particularly the possibility of a natural occurrence of high concentrations in Laos and Kampuchea. From the scientific literature studied by the Group, 'it had not come across any report of a natural occurrence of trichothecenes of the vomitoxin type or of the T-2 and diacetoxyscirpenol type in a concentration exceeding 50 ppm (parts per million) in any of the areas surveyed for this purpose'.[107] On the other hand, it failed to detect any positive evidence of trichothecenes from samples of vegetation, blood, and military materials gathered from Pakistan and Thailand. This was none too surprising since the samples which were handed to the Group had been collected several weeks or months beforehand. Moreover, two of the six laboratories even failed to detect trichothecenes in the spiked control samples.[108] Once again the Group could not conduct any on-site investigations and had to content itself with interviews in

Pakistan and Thailand. From the mass of evidence gathered, none of which was entirely conclusive, the Group concluded that 'it could not disregard the circumstantial evidence suggestive of the possible use of some sort of toxic chemical substance in some instances'.[109]

While the UN team conducted its investigations, a mounting volume of evidence was published. ABC News organised its own expedition to South-East Asia and found a sample, containing three trichothecenes as well as a derivative of polyethylene glycol, a material which does not occur in nature.[110] It presented this evidence in a programme entitled 'Rain of Terror' on 21 December 1981. During the following year the State Department unfolded an even more extensive case. It revealed an analysis of blood samples from two 'Yellow Rain' victims in Kampuchea, revealing HT-2, a metabolite of T-2 trichothecene toxin. It published a thirty-two page report in March, which represented the most comprehensive account hitherto of American intelligence findings, and an updated report in November 1982, cataloguing the data of trichothecene mycotoxins found in sixteen biomedical and five vegetation samples, as well as on the Soviet gas mask. In testimony before a subcommittee of the House Committee on Foreign Affairs (30 March, 1982), Dr Sharon Watson and Dr Chester Mirocha provided scientific support for the State Department's charges. And in June 1982 Canada submitted an unofficial report to the United Nations, reflecting the findings of Dr H. Bruno Schiefer, one of Canada's foremost authorities on mycotoxins, who had visited Thailand in the previous February. From his visits to refugee camps and study of control samples, he concluded that 'it is highly improbable that the events reported by the refugees could be due to natural circumstances' (although he thought that there were more similarities between Stachybotryotoxicosis and 'Yellow Rain' than between ATA and 'Yellow Rain').[111]

By the end of 1982 the steady accumulation of evidence, corroborated by some respected American and Canadian scientists, had converted many in the US Congress and media. It was the totality of the evidence which seemed so convincing, a theme underlined by US Ambassador Kenneth Adelman when he addressed the UN Assembly's Political and Security Committee on 8 December 1982. It might be 'easy', he declared, 'to discount individual bits of evidence . . . But when the body of evidence accumulates, as it has in Afghanistan and South-East Asia with the various components independently confirming chemical warfare, it is no longer possible to do so'.[112]

Scepticism persisted, nonetheless. It thrived upon several different issues and apparent anomalies. The first was the chain of evidence,

inasmuch as the State Department refused to disclose full details of
when and where the samples were collected and of how and by whom
the control samples were chosen. Also, without a description of how
the samples were maintained in transit from the collector to the
analyst, critics argued that contamination could have occurred in
transit or in the laboratory since the findings of Mirocha and Dr. J.
Rosen (for ABC News) lack confirmation by other scientists and
another sixty samples tested by the Army's Chemical Systems
Laboratory have proved negative.[113] Secondly, the finding of T-2 toxin
in human tissues weeks after an alleged exposure conflicted with most
animal studies, which indicate that T-2 toxin is excreted from the body
within forty-eight hours when the toxin is administered orally or by
intravenous injection. In the only reported autopsy (upon Chan Mann,
a Kampuchean soldier) high levels of aflatoxin B1 (a mycotoxin
endemic in South-East Asia) and of trichothecenes were found in the
gastrointestinal tract. As the stomach and intestines are the first organs
of entry for ingestion, this discovery prompted some to argue that
Chan Mann died from eating mouldy food within the previous day or
two.[114] Thirdly, the presence of pollen in some Yellow Rain samples
analysed by Thai, Canadian and Australian scientists warranted an
explanation. Meselson noted that in shape, size, colour, texture and
high pollen content, the spots of Yellow Rain closely resembled the
natural excreta of bees of the genus *Apis*. These bees generally
defecate in flight and are known to swarm in India from mid-February
to mid-April, the period when twenty-three of the twenty-six samples
containing trichothecenes were collected. Should bees also swarm at
this time in South-East Asia, this would coincide with a time when the
hill tribesmen of Laos and Kampuchea turn from eating rice to other
food, like corn, which is a good substrate for *Fusarium*. Meselson and
some colleagues argue that there could have been a natural coinci-
dence: at a time when people are eating mouldy food and becoming ill,
bees swarm and defecate and so the two actions were erroneously
linked and buttressed by rumours of chemical warfare.[115]

Originally proposed at the national meeting of the American
Association for the Advancement of Science in Detroit (31 May
1983), the bee theory aroused considerable controversy. Meselson
initially did not argue that the State Department was wrong, only that
its evidence, as publicly presented, lacked adequate controls and left
'serious room for doubt'; that the bee theory was possible; and that
further research was necessary.[116] The theory has been bolstered
indirectly by subsequent findings. A paper written by four Chinese

geologists in 1977 describes the descent of bee excrement for periods of up to twenty minutes over areas as large as twenty acres in Northern Jiangsu in 1976. Also two pathologists, writing in a pre-war volume of the *Philippine Journal of Science*, explained that disease-producing fungi could be carried on pollen grain from infected banana plants to healthy ones.[117] Moreover, Meselson's suspicions of chemical warfare rumours spread by 'mass psychic suggestion'[118] has been endorsed by an Australian sociologist, Grant Evans, who reinterviewed some of the H'Mong refugees. He criticised previous investigators for asking leading questions, noted inconsistencies in the accounts of various refugees and defectors, and dismissed all stories from the Pol Pot military structure 'which has a clear-cut motive for lying'. He suggested too that rumours or a 'great fear' of 'Yellow Rain' could have served to explain the deaths, illness and crop failures, bind the H'Mong together in their common predicament as displaced refugees, and buttress the H'Mong ex-CIA leadership.[119]

The State Department and its scientific advisers have responded to these charges. Understandably, they have refused to name their sample collectors (especially refugees who could still have families in Laos) or to describe the modes of sample retrieval (since this could jeopardise similar operations in the future). Dr Watson insisted that appropriate controls had been applied. Samples had been gathered from areas adjacent to the attack sites, species of plants matched, and additional samples of soil, rice, corn, water and vegetation collected. She admitted, though, that the collection process could never emulate the requirements of a 'laboratory situation', and that control samples had to be gathered when it was safe to do so.[120] To explain the protracted presence of T-2 toxins in human tissues, Mirocha proffered several theories: the T-2 and other poisons could damage the body's normal processes of elimination; the victims may have been exposed continuously to T-2, possibly from small deposits in their hair or lungs; or T-2 may bind in some unknown way to proteins in the body only to be released over several days (this is unproven, but another fungal poison (ochratoxin) has been reported as binding to proteins and so achieving a half-life of three days in the body).[121] These are only theories but little is known about the effects of trichothecenes when inhaled by humans. Extrapolation from animal data poses problems, and the compounds involved seem to vary considerably in their composition.

To account for the pollen, several theories were adduced. In the first place, some American and Thai officials suspected that the pollen could be part of a disinformation campaign, intended to discredit the charges of chemical warfare.[122] Later it was suggested that pollen could have been used as 'a carrier' for the toxins because pollen grains are the correct size for maximum retention in the body. Toxin-coated grains could be used because they are caught in the nose and throat (not the lungs) and filtered into the digestive system. Although Emery W. Sarver, chief of the methodology research team investigating Yellow Rain samples for the army's chemical research and development centre at Edgewood, Maryland, did not preclude Meselson's hypothesis, he thought it unlikely.[123] Others were much less charitable. The State Department retorted that one sample of Yellow Rain weighed 300 milligrams which was too large for a bee to drop, that some samples – taken from water and from the Soviet gas mask – contained mycotoxin but no pollen, and that the Yellow Rain had been limited to the war zones and had not been observed throughout the region.[124] The bee theory did not explain the presence of trichothecene mycotoxin in samples of blood, urine and tissues of alleged victims and on the gas mask. It did not explain the reports of illness and death, nor the reports of Yellow Rain following overflights or aircraft attacks or attacks by artillery and rockets. Nor could it account for the presence of polyethylene glycol in one sample[125] (save for the unproven supposition of contamination in transit or in the laboratory). The bee theory only focuses upon one part of the State Department's evidence, albeit a part which was emphasised by departmental spokesmen without the support of a thorough epidemiological survey of the areas in question. The second report which the Canadian government submitted to the United Nations substantially redressed this oversight; its authors concluded that 'epidemiological data indicates the use of an incapacitant against the Khmer Rouge in Cambodia and a different group of agents, possibly mycotoxins, in Laos, Cambodia and Thailand'.[126] Had a natural contamination occurred, it would presumably have been a widespread phenomenon and not merely confined to the war zones in question and to the victims of alleged attacks.

Eyewitness testimony was also important, and the State Department tried to confirm its veracity wherever possible. Evans's book only refers to the testimony of the H'Mong but the Haig report stresses that 'in all three countries instances were identified in which eyewitness accounts could be corrolated with information from other sources'. Aware of the propaganda activities of Pol Pot's Democratic Kampuchean resistance, 'special efforts' were made to confirm any Kampuchean allegations.[127] Several anthropologists who have worked with the H'Mong in Thailand and Laos dispute Evans's description of them as prone to rumour and panic. 'That's not the nature of the people', claims Jeanne Guillemin, 'they are very pragmatic.'[128] Nevertheless, some of the refugee reports could have been exaggerated and some of the charges may have been fabricated. Despite this probability Professor Schiefer argues, quite reasonably, 'one has to give serious attention to the apparently never-ending flow of reported incidents. It appears highly unlikely that the essentials of all the reports are products of imagination, fabrication or propaganda'.[129]

Had it been possible to produce incontrovertible evidence – intact munitions, remnants of used munitions or samples of chemical compounds used exclusively as chemical warfare agents – this largely speculative debate could have been avoided. Finding such evidence would have required timely and unhindered access to the sites of the reported military action by neutral observers. This has not been possible. Moreover, the alleged attacks have often occurred in fairly remote areas (with the exception of Kampuchea), so ensuring a considerable lapse of time (sometimes twenty days or more from Laos) before victims can seek medical treatment or refugees can bring samples for analysis. Nor have the methods of attack facilitated subsequent investigation. Although there have been reports of shelling by artillery and rockets in Kampuchea, most of the attacks in Laos have been air-delivered often involving spraying from planes like the AN-2s and captured American L-19s. Such operations leave neither munitions nor canisters for post-attack retrieval. The Vietnamese, apparently, seem to exercise tight security over their chemical munitions, so inhibiting access by untrained and unprotected personnel.[130] In short, the task of collecting, analysing and presenting convincing evidence has proved extremely difficult, whether undertaken by a national government or an international team.

On account of this difficulty, the international response to the American charges has been tepid. Several governments have conducted their own investigations, but only Canada has published a substantive account of its findings. A committee of Asian lawyers has reported 'that evidence of employment of chemical warfare . . . is of such a nature that reasonable men must agree that such weapons have been used against people in Kampuchea and Laos'.[131] Although some Western governments and NATO foreign ministers have endorsed aspects of the American case,[132] the lack of utterly conclusive evidence has been inhibiting. There was an impression, too, that the initial presentations by the Reagan administration were maladroit and premature, so eroding their credibility and compounding suspicions about the administration's policy on arms control.[133] Once the United States had taken up the issue, and accused the Soviet Union, the topic became highly politicised. Neither allies nor the non-aligned wished to become involved in a propaganda struggle between the superpowers. As Marious Grinius, a Canadian diplomat, remarked, the issue had become 'a political hot potato'.[134] Finally, some governments were worried about how the presentation of this issue would effect their defence policies and the chemical arms control talks in Geneva.

Since 1968 numerous countries have committed themselves to seeking an absolute ban on the development, production and stockpiling of chemical weapons. The 'Yellow Rain' allegations merely confirmed the inadequacy of the Geneva Protocol and the Biological and Toxin Weapons Convention (1972). Neither includes satisfactory measures of verification; indeed the latter simply provides for the investigation of a complaint by the UN Security Council (an investigation which could be vetoed by any one of the five permanent members of the Council, including the Soviet Union). Having charged the Soviet Union with breaking both agreements, the Reagan administration did not abort the quest for further measures of arms control. Instead, it sought to buttress any chemical weapons convention with more stringent measures of verification to produce 'real, equitable and fully verifiable arms control'.[135]

Although these three case studies cannot be compared in any meaningful historical sense, they still highlight important issues. In the first place, they confirm the perceived utility of chemical weapons in conflicts where one adversary lacks either adequate means of defence or a credible deterrent. Revelations from the Gulf War, including the use of tabun and mustard gas,[136] merely underlines this point. Whether chemical and biological weapons constitute a 'poor man's atomic bomb' is arguable, but their potential utility as terrorist weapons and in certain Third World conflicts[137] seems widely recognised. Secondly, their usage or suspected usage raises acute questions for great powers interested in the particular conflict or in the possible ramifications of smaller powers employing such weapons. A response on their part will be fraught with difficulties – other policies may suffer by an initiative, the task of investigating reports which may be partial, confused or exaggerated will not be easy, and the presentation of evidence could be decisive in influencing opinion. Thirdly, should the great powers respond by seeking a more effective arms control regime, with more stringent methods of verification, this would still leave one question

unanswered: 'after detection what?'. Asked over twenty years ago by
Fred C. Iklé, this question has been revived in the wake of the 'Yellow
Rain' controversy.[138] If international law cannot be upheld and
properly enforced, chemical weapons could proliferate and chemical
warfare recur despite any further measures of arms control. The
prospects for proliferation will depend, at least partially, upon the
perceived utility of chemical warfare, an assessment which could be
influenced by the policies of the superpowers and their retention or
otherwise of offensive chemical weapons.

6 The Soviet Chemical Warfare Posture

In his annual report to Congress for Fiscal Year 1983, Caspar W. Weinberger, the Secretary of Defense, described the Soviet Union as 'much better prepared than the United States or our allies to wage chemical warfare and fight in a chemically contaminated environment'.[1] American military authorities have repeatedly sounded the tocsin on this issue. They have warned that Soviet forces are 'the best equipped and prepared forces in the world to employ chemical weapons'; that the Soviet advantage in 'offensive chemical weapons . . . may be the Achilles heel of NATO's defence'; and that the Soviet chemical warfare capability is 'truly scary'.[2] Their concern reflects the priority which the Soviet forces attach to their chemical warfare capabilities. Soviet ground, air and naval forces, along with those of other Warsaw Pact countries, have developed the doctrine, organisation, training and protective equipment to employ chemical weapons in conjunction with either conventional or nuclear weapons.[3]

The Soviet interest in chemical warfare is not a new development. It derives from Russia's horrendous experience in the First World War (when she incurred an estimated 475 340 gas casualties, of whom some 56 000 died),[4] the extensive efforts of the Red Army to develop a chemical capability in the inter-war period (including clandestine collaboration with the German Reichswehr); and the impressive preparations for gas warfare during the Great Patriotic War (1941–5). German intelligence estimated that the wartime gas production of the Soviet Union was at least 8000 tons per month, that intensive troop-training in chemical warfare was sustained throughout the war, and that the Red Army could employ chemical weapons in any conditions even those of extreme cold. The Germans, understandably, 'feared Soviet CW capabilities more than those of any other Allied nation'.[5] These capabilities were augmented at the end of the war by the seizure of large stocks of chemical agents from Germany, as well as the technology and equipment to make tabun and sarin. Captured

120

German nerve gas plant was dismantled and removed (with personnel) to the Soviet Union where it was reassembled (one such plant was relocated in the Volgograd chemical combine).[6] As the United States enjoyed nuclear superiority from the end of the War until the 1970s, the Soviets may have regarded chemical weapons as a means, however limited in scope, of offsetting this nuclear domination.

Soviet investment in chemical warfare expanded considerably in the post-war period. The Military Chemical Forces (VKhV) are a separate arm of the military establishment. Commanded by a three-star general (Colonel-General V. K. Pikalov), these 'specialist troops' consist of units and subunits with responsibilities for chemical defence, radiation and chemical reconnaissance, the operation of flame throwers and smoke generators, the identification of enemy chemical weapon sites and other targets for Soviet chemical strikes, and for the decontamination and deactivation of personnel, weapons, equipment, structures and terrain exposed to radioactive and chemical agents. Apart from the employment of smoke and flame equipment, these chemical troops are trained and equipped for defensive purposes: they are not responsible for the delivery of chemical munitions.[7]

The VKh V is the world's largest corps of NBC specialists. Estimates of its size vary considerably; frequently quoted as 80 000 to 100 000 men, some recent estimates from the US Department of Defense suggest a 'line strength' of about 60 000 peacetime chemical troops which would be increased to about 138 000 in wartime.[8] Officers of the chemical troops are usually graduates of one of three primary higher officer schools or military chemical academies: Saratov Higher Military Engineer School of Chemical Defence, Tambov Higher Military Command Red Banner School of Chemical Defence and Kostroma Higher Military Command School of Chemical Defence. Saratov offers courses of up to five years for engineer officers, preparing them for duty with the chemical troops. Tambov and Kostroma prepare officers 'of a command profile' for chemical duty after four years of study. Graduates from Saratov are commissioned as 'Lieutenant-Engineers' and are qualified as 'Engineer-Chemists'. Graduates from the other two are also commissioned as lieutenants. The training at these schools aims to inculcate a detailed knowledge of NBC procedures and involves an extensive amount of field work. More advanced study can be undertaken at the Military Academy for Chemical Defence in Moscow, named after Marshal Timoshenko. This Academy offers a wide range of courses, including a five year degree programme leading to a Master's or PhD, a Senior Officers of

Chemical Troops course (twenty-eight months) and an advance course for chemical service officers (thirty months). Chemical non-commissioned officers are trained in six month courses at chemical training battalions.[9]

Chemical defence units are drawn from the Chemical Troops and comprise an organic element in every Soviet military command. In the ground forces the basic unit is the chemical defence company attached to tank and motorised-rifle regiments. With an authorised strength of about thirty-five to fifty men, the company has responsibility for reconnaissance, dosimetric control and decontamination of personnel and weapons. Each tank and motorised-rifle division has a chemical defence battalion of approximately 200 men. It comprises a headquarters element, two decontamination companies, and probably chemical reconnaissance and service platoons. At tank and combined arms army level, there are larger chemical defence battalions organised into a headquarters and services unit, three chemical defence companies and a chemical reconnaissance company. Finally, the largest unit is the chemical defence brigade, incorporating at least three chemical defence battalions and a chemical reconnaissance battalion. These compositions, particularly at army and front levels, will vary according to the formation's strength and mission. Lavishly equipped with reconnaissance vehicles and truck-mounted decontamination systems, the Chemical Troops aim to minimise the delays imposed by operating in a chemical environment.[10]

All Soviet Air Force units from headquarters down to company level have chemical warfare officers. A Chemical Biological and Radiological (CBR) section is attached to air bases. It is responsible for detecting CBR agents at airfields, for the decontamination of aircraft, runways, personnel and equipment and for training. The airfield technical services, under the administrative command of the Rear Services, provide personnel and material support for the CBR defence section. The office of the regimental Chief of Chemical Services, subordinate to the Chief of Chemical Troops, provides technical and training support for the CBR defence section.[11]

Each of the four Soviet fleets has its own chemical service which advises the fleet commander on CBR matters, trains chemical officers and sailors, maintains CBR material and depôts, and supervises naval CBR units. Each warship, submarine and naval squadron has a chemical officer assigned to it, and most if not all surface ships, from small patrol boats to the largest surface ships, contain some degree of CBR protection. Naval collective protection systems include citadels which can be hermetically sealed with filtered air overpressures, water washdown systems and supplementary equipment (including periscopes for conning from sealed bridges). The Soviets are also providing ships with items of individual protection, including masks, clothing, personal decontamination kits and medical protective devices. Naval personnel carry out CBR defence training on a regular basis.[12]

Reconnaissance and decontamination are the primary duties of the Chemical Troops (apart from the operation of smoke and flame equipment). Personnel from other arms support these endeavours; engineers are responsible for water purification and the preparation of sites required for decontamination facilities; medical services treat the casualties of chemical agents; and rear services are responsible for supply.[13] Yet this massive defensive effort is neither an end in itself nor simply concerned with protecting individuals and their equipment. Its real significance is operational, namely maintaining or restoring the combat effectiveness of front-line units in a chemical environment and thereby sustaining the speed and momentum of the advance. In other words, the essential purpose of CBR reconnaissance is to support the principal tactical requirement of Soviet doctrine – the rapid advance of combat forces.

Warsaw Pact Ground Forces, Soviet and non-Soviet, are amply endowed with equipment for reconnaissance, protection and decontamination. In each instance the equipment is intended to meet specific Soviet priorities. Reconnaissance must be prompt and accurate; it must be undertaken across the whole front and the entire depth of deployment. Combat troops require timely warning of the approach of a vapour hazard or of an area of contamination in their line of advance. Chemical troops must mark the boundaries of such areas and determine whether a decontaminated path can be driven through them or the degree of contamination likely to be incurred by units who have to cross them (and hence whether these units have to be decontaminated on emerging from these zones). From a sample of eighty-nine articles on the Soviet Chemical Troops in the *Military Herald* (January 1974 to April 1978), Major S. Z. Kovac has concluded that the emphasis is overwhelmingly on 'speed both of reconnaissance and of reporting results'.[14] Chemical reconnaissance platoons operate with the most advanced patrols and far to the rear in case of enemy interdiction strikes. Each platoon is equipped with four BRDM rkh vehicles, carrying GSP-11 automatic chemical agent detector alarms and PPKhR chemical agent detectors as well as flag pickets (to mark safe lanes or contaminated areas) and firing devices.[15]

Chemical Troops are not solely responsible for chemical reconnaissance. They undertake their duties alongside conventional reconnaissance squads under the direction of the unit chief-of-staff. All combat subunits, whether in the first echelon or the reserve, are also required to conduct chemical reconnaissance. While a platoon would be expected to post a soldier upwind as a chemical agent sentry, armed with detector papers, each company has a specialist detachment, equipped with a VPKhR kit to detect and identify chemical agents. A recent model of this kit weighs 2.3 kg and uses only three indicator tubes to detect mustard, phosgene, diphosgene, hydrogen cyanide, cyanogen chloride and the G- and V-type nerve agents. Should a subunit detect a hazard and identify its nature, it would send its warnings by radio and/or signal flares.[16]

All regular soldiers possess personal masks and protective clothing. The standard mask (ShM) consists of a strapless headpiece which covers the entire head and is connected by a hose to an external canister. The ShM allows the wearer to exchange canisters rapidly, and the hose attachment contains a double outlet valve to reduce back leakage. But the mask is heavy and uncomfortable in hot weather; it lacks voice transmitters, corrective lenses, and openings for eating and drinking. Signal troops have their own version equipped with a voice-emitter and uncovered ear area. Another version, the ShMS, has optically corrective lenses, facilitating the use of binoculars and rangefinders. For wounded soldiers, the ShR can be worn which has a double inlet valve designed to prevent suffocation if one valve becomes blocked with blood or vomit. The ShM and ShMS protect the head, eyes, and respiratory tract against blood and choking agents, but they are visually poor, and a new more comfortable respirator with canister attached is expected to be in service soon.[17]

To protect against blister and nerve agents, for which the mask alone is not sufficient, the Soviet forces have a wide range of protective clothing. The L-1 suit comprises a jacket with hood, trousers with integral overboots and gloves made from butyl rubberised fabric. Designed to be donned quickly, it is issued to reconnaissance troops and provides full protection (with the ShM mask) against vapour, aerosol and liquid agents. The OP-1 is a one-piece garment with hood, which can be worn as a cape or a coat, or, with boots and gloves, for full protection against liquid agents. Unlike the L-1, the OP-1 is not airtight and so it has to be worn with impregnated undergarments to protect against vapour hazards. Although heavy and cumbersome, weighing about 3 kg apiece (more than twice as much as the air-permeable British Mk3 suits), these outfits provide better protection against penetration than do the fabric suits worn by NATO armies. Decontamination troops wear an even heavier one piece suit made of rubberised fabric with gloves and rubber boots weighing about 6.5 kg.[18] Only the reconnaissance and decontamination units would have to wear their suits constantly, combat forces, unlike their NATO counterparts, would neither expect to spend lengthy periods in their suits nor to respond instantly to general alerts. As a surprise chemical strike from NATO is extremely unlikely (in view of NATO's doctrine and America's very limited offensive capability in West Germany), and as CBR reconnaissance is expected to provide timely and accurate warning of any downwind hazard, Soviet troops 'can be ordered to put on the minimum of protective equipment consonant with safety'.[19]

Soviet Ground Forces have even more significant compensations. All their modern tanks and armoured personnel carriers have protective seal-out liners and positive-pressure filtered air systems. These features enable their crews to operate in 'a shirt sleeve environment' at periods when NATO forces would require full individual protection.[20] Soviet armour is fully capable of riding over and across contaminated ground and, after rapid decontamination, is able to resume the advance. Other fighting vehicles, including support vehicles, missile transporters, and command vehicles possess either air filtration systems (in the more modern models) or individual protective equipment for their crews. Collective protection facilities, like the PP-2, are also a prominent part of the Soviet inventory. Once erected in the field, these centres enable work to be undertaken without protective clothing or allow soldiers to eat, rest, and complete other bodily functions. They may serve various purposes, for example, as centres for command and communication and as medical aid posts.[21]

Medical treatment kits (MSP-18) are issued to each soldier. These contain five red syrettes for treating nerve agent contamination, six tablets for lung irritants from toxic smoke, a pain killer, a syrette and ampoules to counter hydrogen cyanide poisoning, and atropine syrettes for high-speed personal injection against nerve agents. The nerve agent antidotes give protection against soman, which is a Soviet nerve agent, as well as sarin and VX, the main American nerve agents. By providing protection against hydrogen cyanide, toxic smoke and soman, which are Soviet and not NATO weapons, this suggests a readiness to move through or to fight in environments contaminated by Soviet chemical agents.

Finally, Soviet and non-Soviet Warsaw Pact forces are amply supplied with decontamination equipment. Soldiers are issued with individual decontamination kits (the 1PP kits) which are used to treat small areas of skin contaminated by nerve agents or vesicants. They are also issued with an 1DP decontamination kit for clothing and personal weapons. Subunits each possess an 1DP-S decontamination pack and an 1DPS-69 decontamination and degassing kit (often vehicle mounted), which are capable of decontaminating five to ten infantry weapons (small arms) and ten sets of uniforms.[22] Front-line personnel will also be able to clean themselves in the AGW-3M decontamination stations. Specialist equipment also exists for larger weapons; the PM-DK kit for cleaning machine-guns and mortars, the ADK for artillery pieces, and the DKV, consisting of seventy-eight cylindrical tanks, each with a capacity of 30 litres, carried on a track and trailer for decontaminating vehicles. Should more thorough decontamination be required, the chemical troops would be summoned with their truck-mounted systems. Of these vehicles the most versatile is the ARS-14 (now replacing the older ARS-12U) which is mounted on a Z1L-131 truck chassis and carries a 2700 litre storage tank. Capable of decontaminating thirteen tanks, it can also decontaminate roads and terrain and supply water for smaller devices, like the DDA-53, which steam cleans contaminated clothing and serves as a field shower for personnel. The TMS-65 is another vehicle decontamination system. It consists of a modified turbojet aircraft engine mounted on a swivel base on a truck chassis, with two 1500 litre tanks carried on the vehicle and another 4000 litres being towed behind in a trailer. Operating in pairs, the TMS-65s inject water or decontaminent fluid into the hot exhaust from the gas turbines and direct the steam at vehicles driving slowly past (alternatively, the TMS-65s can drive along a stationary column of vehicles and decontaminate them with their jet exhausts). The treatment of each vehicle will take from one to three minutes depending on the type and degree of contamination.[23]

An approach to chemical protection which is so comprehensive in scope and extensive in provision has several attributes. In the first place, it should enhance the ability of Warsaw Pact forces to conduct sustained operations. First echelon units on emerging from a contaminated area would be expected to decontaminate partially and to continue the advance. If this was not practical, they could move aside while second echelon units rode through decontaminated zones to maintain the momentum. The original assault units could then be decontaminated rapidly (in about four hours for a battalion)[24] before following on in the attack. Secondly, the reconnaissance provisions, collective anti-chemical protection systems, and the vast array of decontamination equipment should minimise the amount of time that any soldier has to spend in his protective suit. It should reduce the degree of performance degradation involved in wearing such suits (additional heat load in high temperatures, difficulties of communication, and a loss of visual acuity, manual dexterity and manoeuvrability). Thirdly, the Soviet investment of resources, equipment and drills suggests a very different approach to chemical warfare from that adopted by the NATO armed forces. The Soviet posture would seem ideally suited to a force which knows when, where, and what agents have been used and which is fully equipped to exploit this knowledge.[25]

Underpinning this investment of resources and specialist provision is an extensive programme of training for chemical warfare. Such training pre-dates military service, beginning at school and continuing through the courses and field exercises of the civil defence system and the DOSAAF (Voluntary Society for Assistance to the Army, Air Force and Navy).[26] Most conscripts enter the armed services with a rudimentary knowledge of Nuclear Biological and Chemical defence. Their training involves instruction on how to don individual equipment, use personal decontamination and medical kits and operate portable decontamination devices. It then graduates to undertaking military duties while wearing partial or full protective clothing and to field exercises by day and night in realistic chemical environments. There are training ranges at all levels, albeit of varying complexity and facilities, to permit training in chemical conditions. Realism has been a feature of the specialist training exercises, inculcated by the use of simulated chemical agents, smoke, and even live, if usually diluted, toxic agents. Thinned nitrogen mustard has been used to produce minor blisters on troops wearing their protective clothing improperly.[27] Fatalities sometimes occur,[28] but the extensive exercises continue with the aims of increasing the soldier's psychological preparedness, improving his combat efficiency while in protective clothing (including operations at night), and developing confidence in the effectiveness of protective clothing and equipment.[29]

The effectiveness of this training has been vigorously debated in the Soviet military press and Western journals. Apparently complaints about laxity, oversimplification and lack of effort recur in Soviet accounts of the field exercises, and doubts about the overall level of training attained by the non-specialist conscript have been expressed by Western authorities.[30] Such criticism, however, has to be placed in perspective. Training will vary considerably from the field exercises of particular units to the teaching and training at specialist areas, which exceed 200 in number,[31] where the Chemical Troops teach and train forces to operate in highly realistic chemical environments. The training programme benefits, too, from the presence of specialist chemical troops with each unit, the provision of large quantities of excellent equipment (save for the mask and suit), and the relevance of its drills and operating procedures. Finally, complaints about chemical defence training, like army training generally in the Soviet Union, indicate little sense of complacency. Attempts are doubtless under way to correct the perceived deficiencies.[32]

The United States Army did not realise the extent of Soviet preparedness for chemical, biological and radiological warfare until it studied the Soviet equipment captured after the Middle East War of 1973. The army's analysts, explained General Creighton W. Abrams, were surprised by the 'sophistication, completeness and extensiveness' of the defences found; they concluded that 'chemical, biological and radiological defences were now standard on all Soviet weapons and thus had to be included on the equipment sent to Egypt and Syria'.[33] So massive an investment of resources, coupled with the extent of Soviet CBR training, aroused concern that the motivation was not purely defensive but was prompted by a desire to exploit the results of their own offensive chemical operations.[34] In 1980 a Defense Science Board of twenty-five members, chaired by Professor John M. Deutch of the Massachusetts Institute of Technology, completed a six month review of chemical warfare. Having had access to sensitive information and intelligence data, it concluded

that the Soviets have attempted not only to provide complete protection for their forces but also to minimize the degradation in force effectiveness they would experience in a chemical environment. The latter, of course, is an important objective for any offensive, as well as defensive capability.[35]

In subsequent Congressional testimony Professor Deutch was even more emphatic; 'the evidence is quite overwhelming,' he argued, about 'their capability and their intent to use CW in a NATO war'.[36]

Professor Matthew Meselson, in reviewing the Defense Science Board's report, questioned this fundamental assumption. Although he agreed that 'We know a considerable amount about Soviet anti-chemical protective posture. It is pervasive and well exercised. This,

however, provides no measure of Soviet offensive chemical preparations.'[37] A strong defence, he added, was only to be expected in view of
Russia's experience in the First World War, the large increase of
America's chemical weaponry in the 1950s and 1960s and the
reluctance of the United States to sign the Geneva Protocol until 1975.
He also feared that 'worst case interpretations' (of the Soviet offensive
threat), based on 'highly questionable' assumptions, could have an
adverse effect upon US policy-making. 'Prudence,' he concluded, 'not
definite knowledge, dictates that we assume the existence of a
substantial chemical threat.'[38]

Such scepticism, which is shared to some degree by several scientific
commentators,[39] reflects the persistence of gaps in Western knowledge
about Soviet intentions and capability. The lack of firm evidence about
several important issues permits a wide spread of opinion and
interpretation. Soviet intentions are not clear; serving Soviet officials
have neither spoken nor written openly about their chemical weapons
since 1938.[40] Nor is there precise data about every aspect of their
offensive capability; indeed US Department of Defense officials have
repeatedly admitted that their intelligence has 'gaps', albeit gaps of the
'same order' as on 'other Soviet activities'.[41]

Open data on the Soviet research and development (R&D)
programmes is extremely sparse. Formerly these were described as
'extensive' and 'continuing in all areas of chemical warfare activities'.[42]
But Dr T. S. Gold, Deputy Assistant to the Secretary of Defense
(Chemical Matters), has since stated that the Department does not
know very well 'the size and shape of their CW/BW R&D effort',
although it does know that the programme is 'active . . . and probably
includes development of new agents'.[43] In 1975, it was revealed that
the Soviets had been constructing larger additional test grids and test
sites to conduct field tests of thickened soman. This seemed significant
because defensive testing could have been completed in a chamber,
whereas test grids were required to test the patterns of dispersing
chemicals.[44] Several new chemical agent/weapon test grids have been
constructed at the Shikhany Chemical Proving Ground since the late
1970s. Shikhany, first established in the late 1920s as part of the
collaborative Reichswehr/Red Army programme, was a testing centre
in the pre-war period and has since grown in 'size and sophistication'.
The new grids have a distinctive circular or rectangular pattern
(depending on the type of munition or agent being tested). When the
munitions are exploded (leaving visible impact craters), the agent can
be measured in its concentration and pattern of dispersal by sampling
devices positioned downwind.[45]

Neither production nor storage facilities are thought to be 'limiting factors' in the Soviet chemical capability. The large chemical industry has had a history of producing war gases since the late 1920s, and the large civil chemical complexes which contain closed central areas are thought to be centres of toxic agent production. Although one German authority has suggested that this chemical industry could supply about 30 000 tons of chemical munitions annually, this may be a fairly conservative estimate (since it would presume annual production of some 3000 to 5000 tons of agent, and during the Second World War Soviet output was estimated to be 8000 tons of agent per month).[46] More recently, officials from the Department of Defense have claimed that the Soviets have fourteen chemical warfare production centres and 'at least seven biological warfare centres'.[47]

Chemical agents are apparently stored in a network of military depôts across the Soviet Union and in Eastern Europe. There appear to be at least nine depôts in the Soviet Union, which contain not merely agents in bulk containers and in filled munitions but also gas masks, protective suits, decontamination solutions and decontamination vehicles. Highly secure military installations, they are ringed by security fences and guard towers, and many have railway lines to permit the rapid mobilisation of chemical warfare materials. From satellite reconnaissance it would appear that 'the amount of agents, weapons, and material in storage at these depôts has increased significantly' since the late 1960s.[48]

The Soviet Union has accumulated a wide range of chemical agents. These are said to include stocks of blood, blister and choking agents of First/Second World War vintage, that is hydrogen cyanide; mustard, lewisite and a mixture of the two; phosgene, diphosgene and chloropicrin. Having captured German stocks of tabun, the Soviets have apparently developed more toxic nerve agents – sarin, soman and VR-55, a thickened form of soman.[49] There are claims, too, that the Soviets may have expanded their range of additional agents beyond temporary irritants like adamsite to include 'among others the hallucinogenic compounds such as BZ and LSD and mycotoxins'. Such speculation has been fostered by the reports of a rapid-acting knock-out gas being employed in Afghanistan and of trichothecene mycotoxins being used in Afghanistan and South-East Asia.[50]

The actual size and specific composition of the Soviet chemical stockpile is unknown, just as the exact composition of their conventional stockpile is unknown. Although American defence spokesmen have repeatedly made this admission over the past decade, they have still insisted that the Soviets have a substantial stock, representing a formidable capability.[51] Published estimates range from 20 000 tons of nerve agent to 350 000 tons of all agents to over 700 000 tons.[52] There is a French estimate of 120 000–150 000 agent tons, corresponding to 600 000–750 000 tons of munitions; an official British estimate of a stock of agent in excess of 300 000 tons; and a German estimate of 200 000 to 700 000 tons of chemical munitions.[53] These wide differences may reflect not only the differing assessments of national intelligence agencies but also the all-embracing Soviet concept of chemical weaponry, including as it does poison gas, irritants, incendiaries, defoliants and smoke.[54] There are vast disparities, too, between the estimated proportions of weapons (shells, rocket warheads, bombs etc) carrying chemical warheads. They range from 10–15 per cent of Warsaw Pact shells to 'as much as 50 per cent of all filled munitions for missiles and bombs stockpiled by Warsaw Pact forces in East–Central Europe'.[55] The percentages are not precise in and of themselves (not least because the total numbers of munitions is not exactly known), but they are still significant: they reflect a widespread belief that a considerable proportion of Soviet munitions are loaded with chemicals. As Dr Gold avers, 'even the low estimate of useable agent tons provides a substantial military capability'.[56]

The Soviet Union has the capability to deliver chemical munitions in ground, air, and naval combat. Just as in the Second World War, Soviet armed forces maintain a wide variety of potential delivery systems, including aerial bombs, spray tanks, tactical missiles, mines, rockets, artillery and mortar projectiles.[57] The Department of Defense claims not only that the Soviets have such systems but that they have also 'developed the firing data' on the utility of chemical weapons 'in battle situations', that is

the types and numbers of weapons required to attack various targets under a variety of weather and combat conditions. They continue today to explore and test systems with improved dissemination, larger payload, increased range, and better accuracy. This gives them greater target flexibility and deeper strike capability.[58]

Of the weapons listed in Table 6.1, the anti-personnel mine, designated KhF, is described in an American military manual as a 'bounding chemical mine', capable of spreading 'liquid agents over the ground'.[59] Any mortar or artillery piece with a calibre in excess of 100 mm is capable of delivering chemical munitions. Mortar bombs

TABLE 6.1 Possible Soviet chemical delivery systems

Weapon	Designation	Calibre	Maximum range (km)	Maximum Rate of fire (rounds per min. unless specified otherwise)	High explosive projectile weight (kg)	Weapon payload (kg)
Land-mine	KhH					
Mortar	M-43	120 mm	5.7	15	15.4	
Howitzer	D-30	122 mm	15.3	7–8	22	
Howitzer	D-20	152 mm	17	4	43.5	
Gun/howitzer	S-23	180 mm	30	less than 1	84	
Field gun	M-46	130 mm	27.5	5–6	33.4	
Multiple rocket launchers	BM-21 (40 rounds)	122 mm	20.5	40 rds/20 secs	19.4	
	BM-27 (16 rounds)	220 mm				

Free flight rocket	FROG-7	60–70	450
Surface to surface missile	SS-1C SCUD B	280	860
	SS-12 SCALEBOARD		megaton range
Attack helicopter	MIL Mi-8/HIP E	800 465	1500 (CW munitions)
Strike aircraft	SU-17 Fitter D/H	700	3000 (bombs)
	MiG-27 Flogger D/J	1200	3000 (bombs)
	SU-24 Fencer A	1800	2500 (bombs)

SOURCES FM30-40 *Handbook on Soviet Ground Forces* (1975); C. Foss (ed), *Jane's Armour and Artillery 1983–84* (Jane's, London, 1983); R. T. Petty (ed.), *Jane's Weapon Systems 1983–84* (Jane's, London, 1983); R. Bonds (ed.), *The Soviet War Machine* (Purnell, London, 1977); US DOD, *Continuing Development of Chemical Weapon Capabilities in the USSR* (Washington, 1983); *Soviet Military Power 1984*.

carry a larger proportion of chemical fill (about 10 per cent) than artillery shells (about 5 per cent) and, on account of their lower velocity, lose less agent as they do not bury on impact. Mortars, though limited in range, possess a higher rate of fire and could be used to engage the forward positions of an enemy. To attack targets within 20 kilometres, the 122 mm BM-21 multibarrelled rocket launcher (MRL) would be particularly effective. The 18 MRLs of a Soviet motor-rifle division could fire 720 rounds (about 15 per cent of each would be chemical fill) in some thirty seconds. By delivering agent in such large quantities and in so short a period of time, the MRL could blanket an area with effective concentrations of fast-acting and quickly evaporating lethal agents, like sarin or hydrogen cyanide.[60] Tube artillery could support and extend the range of the MRL attack, notably the 130 mm gun with its range of 27 kilometres and the 152 mm howitzer with a shorter range of 17.3 kilometres but heavier shell. These guns, dispersing more persistent nerve and blister agents, could be used for purposes of area denial. A battalion salvo, comprising one minute's intense fire from eighteen 152 mm howitzers, could deliver over 270 kilograms of chemical agent.[61]

For longer range tasks, Soviet armed forces are equipped with a variety of missiles and rockets. Each division has four Frog 7 free-flight rockets, capable of delivering a chemical warhead over a range of 65 kilometres. At army level the Scud B, a surface-to-surface missile (SSM), can deliver a chemical warhead of about 1100 lb (500 kilograms) over a range of 280 kilometres. And at front level, there is possibly a chemical warhead for the larger Scaleboard missile, with a range of 800 kilometres. There are apparently two types of weapon for these tactical missiles – bulk agent and small bomblets which can be released in flight, 'creating a lethal rain over several square kilometres'.[62] Hitherto these tactical rockets and missiles compensated for their lack of accuracy by their large warheads. But their replacements (the SS-21 for the Frog, SS-22 for the Scaleboard, and the SS-23 for the Scud) are thought to combine even longer ranges with larger payloads and much greater accuracy. These missiles are also credited with a chemical capability,[63] so extending the chemical threat throughout the entire theatre including rear area ports, airfields, railway centres, logistical depôts, material storage sites, and command and control facilities. There is even a report that the SS-20, with its 5000 kilometre range, has a chemical capability,[64] although this lacks confirmation from other published sources.

Finally, the Soviets could complete their target coverage by employing helicopters and modern ground attack aircraft. The Mi-8/HIPE attack helicopter could carry up to 1650 lb (about 750 kilograms) of chemical munitions on each wing,[65] and even more versatile in range and payload are aircraft like the SU-17 Fitter C, MiG-27 Flogger D and SU-24 Fencer A. Carrying payloads in excess of 2500 kilograms, and flying in a hi-lo-hi mission profile, they could launch chemical strikes on targets in the west of mainland Europe. The Su-24 could even attack the major operational air bases in the United Kingdom. In such chemical strikes, these aircraft could maximise the element of surprise. If the weather was favourable they need not overfly their target but could release their agent upwind from spray tanks, letting it drift down upon the intended victim. Some 4000 kilograms of sarin, if sprayed across wind over a range of 6 kilometres, could decimate a force located about 5 kilometres downwind. If the troops donned their respirators when they felt the first symptoms, and used efficient countermeasures, they could still anticipate 20–30 per cent severe or fatal casualties and 70–80 per cent light casualties. Without effective precautions, these casualty rates could soar to 80 and 20 per cent respectively.[66]

The Soviet Navy could also assume the offensive and impose a chemical warfare environment in naval engagements. Almost all their tactical weapons, whether air-to-surface or surface-to-surface missiles could carry chemical munitions. Indeed, chemical attacks could prove particularly effective in the context of amphibious operations, not merely against the amphibious forces but also against the supporting naval forces. Soviet weapon systems have the range to implement such attacks, and the stocking of 'chemicals near the piers and storage places' lends credibility to the belief that they have a capability to mount chemical attacks at sea.[67]

Neither the existence of a Soviet delivery capability nor its qualitative and quantitative expansion in the 1970s is seriously contested. But critics still dispute whether the Soviets have expanded their arsenal of chemical weapons – as distinct from their delivery capability – in the 1970s and 1980s (that is, during the period in which the United States imposed a moratorium on its own production of chemical munitions). On 16 September 1980, Senator Gary Hart declared that 'there is not one concrete bit of evidence' to support the 'statements about the massive Soviet build up of chemical warfare agents'.[68] Although Department of Defense officials have generally referred to an expansion of the Soviet chemical warfare capability in the 1970s,[69] some statements have been more explicit. Under ques-

tioning from Senator Sam Nunn, Harold Brown, the former Secretary
of Defense admitted that America's moratorium has 'not . . . had a
restraining effect on the Soviets'.[70] The recent Department of Defense
report is even more forthcoming; it asserts that 'chemical agents
produced over the past five decades are stored in a network of military
depots located across the Soviet Union'. Since the late 1960s, it adds,
'the amount of agents, weapons, and material in storage at these
depots has increased significantly, and this build up continues'.[71]

Even more fundamental is the debate over the purpose of the Soviet
chemical warfare posture. Some sceptics question whether the offensive and defensive capabilities are intended to support a first use of
chemical weapons in a war with NATO. Initiation, they argue, would
involve immense risks and require calculations about the influence of
ground and weather upon chemical strikes (despite the accuracy of
modern micrometeorology); the efficiency of the enemy's chemical
defence equipment and his training to fight while encumbered by NBC
protection; and the possibility of either retaliation in kind (forcing
Soviet soldiers to don their rubberised suits) or escalation to a nuclear
exchange. Apart from the meteorological factors, these imponderables hardly applied in Afghanistan, and so any usage against the
mujahidin, if true, is hardly a precedent for a war in Europe.[72] Soviet
intentions, so the sceptics imply, could be much more modest, namely
the maintenance of a strong defence and specific operational
capabilities (partly to deter attack by threatening retaliation in kind,
partly to preserve tactical options which could be used in favourable
circumstances, say in a war with China or in a selective attack upon key
targets in NATO's rear area).[73]

As Soviet intentions on the use of chemical weapons are not clearly
and openly stated, these interpretations cannot be disproved. But their
plausibility may be questioned, especially in view of America's limited
offensive chemical capability which, whatever its merits or lack of
them as a deterrent, cannot be considered as a first strike threat. Nor
are America's allies in Western Europe, of whom only France
possesses any offensive chemical warfare capability, able to pose a
significant threat to Soviet forces. Nor are the risks of nuclear
escalation in the wake of a chemical strike particularly credible, at least
in an era of nuclear parity when NATO has every incentive to keep the
nuclear threshold as high as possible.[74] On the contrary, the possibility
or even 'strong probability' that the Soviets would initiate chemical
warfare in a conventional war[75] must be taken seriously: it reflects an
apparent change in Soviet attitudes towards chemical weapons, a

recognition of their tactical utility, the relevance of their usage to Soviet military doctrine, and the massive advantage which the Soviets retain over the United States in this area of warfare.

Formerly the Western perception of chemical weapons followed the Soviet description of them 'as weapons of mass destruction', whose employment would only be possible in an all-out war. An American military manual, issued in 1975, described Soviet CBR defence as 'tailored to fit the nuclear battlefield concept'.[76] Soviet military strategy, however, no longer appears to assume that the 'decisive' clash between the socialist and capitalist systems must begin with nuclear pre-emption, and accepts that the conflict could begin with a phase of conventional operations. Since the late 1970s, a shift appears to have occurred in Soviet military writings, with a diminution of the emphasis upon the other 'weapons of mass destruction' (nuclear and biological) but with a continuing interest in chemical conflict. Some major exercises have also been conducted with the use of chemical weapons unaccompanied by nuclear weapons.[77] If it is too extreme to assert that chemical weapons have moved from a separate category to that of a conventional one, it would seem reasonable to claim that the Soviets have not precluded the use of chemical with conventional weapons. In 1978, the Department of Defense reckoned that it was 'likely that the Soviets could consider using a combination of chemical and conventional weapons, as well as a combination of chemical, nuclear and conventional weapons'. By 1984, the Department affirmed that 'the Soviets have developed the doctrine, plans, personnel and equipment to support their use of chemical weapons. They believe that the user of chemical weapons would gain a significant military advantage in a conventional conflict'.[78]

The tactical attractions of chemical weapons derive at least partially from the deficiencies of NATO's protective and retaliatory capabilities. Inherently flexible, chemical weapons could contribute towards the realisation of a quick battlefield success, by which the Soviets hope to pre-empt NATO from deploying her transatlantic reinforcements or from authorising nuclear release. So important is this objective that it would seem to dwarf any political costs associated with initiating usage (such as contravening the Geneva Protocol or offending non-involved opinion). Once approval had been sanctioned, responsibility for using chemical weapons would devolve primarily upon divisional commanders.[79] They would be able to select the type of agent and mode of delivery system. They would know where and when the strike was launched, and, if their troops had to cross contaminated areas, they would benefit from the advice, reconnaissance, and decontamination provided by the specialist chemical troops.

Several major tactical missions could be facilitated by employing chemical munitions in support of conventional or nuclear weapons. To breach NATO's forward defences, especially her anti-tank defences, chemical weapons could be used with smoke and high explosive artillery bombardment to maximise the element of surprise with the aim of opening up attack corridors for Soviet armoured columns. In this role hydrogen cyanide, if delivered in sufficient concentrations from multibarrelled rocket launchers, could be highly effective. The agent is difficult to detect, acts very quickly (in sufficient quantities it can prove effective within thirty seconds), is highly lethal and dissipates within ten minutes after the attack. Advancing motor-rifle troops would not even need to don their respirators, let alone protective clothing, if they allowed ten minutes to elapse before moving through the target zone. Persistent agents, such as mustard gas could be employed in the rôle of area denial, so protecting the flanks of a Soviet advance. Unlike conventional weapons, a persistent agent provides a continuous contact and (locally) a vapour hazard. Depending upon the type of agent used, the concentrations of the attack and the weather conditions, this area denial could range from several days to several weeks. If successful, these tactics could reduce the mobility of the enemy, hinder his ability to resupply and reinforce forward positions, and possibly channel his movements through areas intended by the Soviets as killing zones. Similar tactics could enable the Pact armies to bypass some fortified areas and defensive strongholds. Neutralising those centres with chemical weapons would involve less time and less expenditure of men and material than required by direct assault.[80]

Suppressing NATO's nuclear capabilities which are widely dispersed over Western Europe in air bases and supply depôts is another major Soviet priority. Should nuclear weapons be withheld, persistent chemical agents, such as thickened soman, delivered by SCUD missiles, could be extremely effective. After a few repeated strikes, these bases could be rendered inoperative for an extended period of time or reduced in readiness as time was consumed in elaborate decontamination. Chemical weapons could also be employed in fulfilling another basic principle of Soviet operations, namely attacks upon the enemy throughout 'the entire depth of this deployment'.[81] The targets would include air bases, command, control and communication facilities, harbours, airports and other transportation centres.

By interdiction strikes the Soviets might hope to hamper the mobilisation and movement of European reserves, while delaying the reinforcement process from Britain and the United States. As chemical weapons only attack living organisms, the negligible degree of collateral damage (to equipment and installations) would be an added bonus. While the agents could deny certain facilities (like roads, runways and bridges) to NATO, they might permit Soviet forces to seize and utilise them subsequently, if necessary after large-scale decontamination.[82]

Another attraction of chemical weapons is their ability to reduce the efficiency of enemy forces. Even troops who are fortunate enough to don their protective equipment in time (so disregarding any problems which might arise from defective equipment and inadequate training) face numerous physical and psychological problems. If compelled to fight in their 'current chemical protective gear', American troops face 'at least a 30–50 per cent decrement in operational effectiveness due to the restrictions imposed by protective equipment and procedures'.[83] Even the most modern individual equipment will restrict the serviceman's vision, muffle his voice, reduce his tactile dexterity, and impair his freedom of movement. Should the temperature soar above 70° Fahrenheit, a soldier in full ensemble would almost certainly experience heat stress and physical fatigue (although the degree would vary from individual to individual and with the nature of his particular duties).[84] Arguably the most severe problems could be psychological, including the damaging effects upon morale and unit cohesiveness. Unless troops were well trained and prepared for the experience, leadership could be especially daunting. Squad leaders could find difficulty in communicating with their men, identifying them (because they all look the same in protective clothing), motivating them, and even keeping their attention. A chemical strike would be a decisive test of peacetime training: in such circumstances, argues Lieutenant-Colonel Eifried, 'poorly trained soldiers let their minds defeat their bodies'.[85] To fulfil these tactical missions and degrade the enemy's effectiveness, would not depend upon lethal doses of chemicals delivered over the entire target. A volatile nerve agent would create both a liquid and a vapour hazard in the immediate target area, as well as a downwind vapour which would gradually thin out. Those downwind of the strike could be incapacitated by sublethal doses of nerve agent, including optical pain and miosis (the contraction of the pupil of the eye, producing dimmed vision, which could seriously impair tasks like aiming, sighting, instrument reading and flying). The effects upon air crews could be extremely severe, contributing thereby to a reduction of NATO's sortie rate.[86]

The nature of the war itself lends credibility to the prospect of chemical warfare. It would be the 'decisive' clash between the socialist and capitalist systems and it seems highly unlikely that the Soviets would demonstrate much restraint. Marshal V. D. Sokolovskiy, one of the Soviet Union's foremost strategic writers, supports this contention. 'A war,' he writes, 'must be conducted decisively and with the best methods using the necessary forces and means to achieve the set political and military goals . . . The need for success,' he asserts, 'is incompatible with the requirement for limiting the scale of combat operations.'[87] Sokolovskiy expects 'the employment of chemical and bacteriological weapons' in a future war, adding that their development is being given 'great attention in the Western countries especially the United States'.[88] Yet using chemical weapons in a first strike on a massive scale to maximise surprise would seem perfectly compatible with Soviet military doctrine. V. Ye Savkin emphasises that surprise is 'a most important principle of military art' – it 'brings success in a battle or operation'. Historically, 'military toxic chemical substances' have been weapons of surprise, and

> the degree of influence of new means of warfare on methods of conduct of combat operations is directly related to the number and quality of these means. New forms of weapons and military technology employed in small numbers cannot have a substantial influence on the character of combat operations.[89]

Finally the Soviets would hardly overlook the relative advantage which their forces enjoy in this form of warfare. The potential effectiveness of some of the aforesaid tactical missions reflects, at least partially, upon the limitations in NATO's preparedness or in her ability to retaliate in kind, that is, her ability to inflict similar degradation upon Soviet forces throughout the depth of their offensive deployment. In 1983, the Department of Defense estimated the Soviet advantage over the United States as 5:1 in ground capable delivery systems; 25:1 in large mobile reconnaissance and decontamination vehicles (assuming that the Soviets now possessed 20 000 to 30 000 vehicles); 11:1 in chemical personnel and in training facilities; and 14:0 in production facilities.[90] Although the United States, like her allies in NATO, has begun to pay increasing attention to chemical-related training and to improve the individual and collective protection of her armed services, she has not produced any new chemical munitions since 1969. The Soviet offensive advantage remains awesome and could be exploited in a non-nuclear attack. As two Pentagon aides have testified, 'The Soviets are so immersed in chemical weaponry, tactics, doctrine, equipment and personnel, and so much of their training centers around the use of lethal agents, that it would be odd, from a military standpoint, if they did not employ them.'[91]

7 NATO's Preparations for Chemical Warfare

NATO has renounced the option of initiating the use of chemical weapons, a policy reflected in the adherence of all allies to the Geneva Protocol and reaffirmed by General Bernard Rogers, NATO's Supreme Allied Commander Europe.[1] NATO seeks to deter recourse to such weapons by its strategy of flexible response (a flexible and balanced range of responses to all levels of aggression or threats of aggression). Within this overall deterrent the NATO allies make provision for anti-chemical protection, enabling personnel not merely to survive an attack but to operate as effectively as possible in a contaminated environment. The Alliance does not possess a chemical retaliatory capability, but the United States and France retain limited offensive chemical forces which could retaliate if NATO incurred a chemical attack. The adequacy of these provisions was brought into question by the revelations from the Yom Kippur War (1973), particularly the supply of comprehensive and highly sophisticated NBC protective equipment by the Soviet Union to Egypt and Syria. As the Soviet Union had apparently standardised these features on all its weapons, and so had had to include them on the equipment sent to Egypt and Syria, General Creighton W. Abrams concluded that the United States Army was 'well behind' its Soviet counterpart in its chemical warfare protection.[2] How the United States and her allies in NATO have responded to these findings warrants review.

By the mid-1970s America's chemical warfare preparedness had suffered from nearly a decade of neglect. During the late 1960s chemical weapons had aroused considerable controversy, with protests over the morality, legality, and military utility of using riot control agents and herbicides in the Vietnam War, complemented by criticism of the hazards posed by the storage, transport, disposal, and testing of chemical munitions. A series of incidents involving chemical weapons occurred, including the accidental release of chemical agent from a storage site on Okinawa, the disposal at sea of obsolete or leaking

142

chemical munitions, and the death of several thousand sheep near the Dugway Proving Ground, Utah, in 1968.[3] Congress responded to these accidents by passing Public Laws 91-441 and 91-121, which prohibited the open-air testing of chemical munitions and restricted their movement, disposal and deployment.

On entering office, President Richard M. Nixon ordered the National Security Council to review America's chemical and biological warfare programmes – the first such review in fifteen years. In light of the review, he announced on 25 November 1969 that the United States would renounce the use, and destroy all stockpiles, of biological weapons and confirm its pledge not to initiate the use of lethal chemical weapons, extending this renunciation to include incapacitating (but not riot control) agents. He intimated, too, that the Geneva Protocol would be submitted to the Senate for ratification.[4] The US Army also responded to the public protests by ceasing further production of unitary chemical munitions, in the expectation that the safer binary munitions would be produced in the early to mid-1970s. Procurement levels for defensive equipment, with the exception of respirators, declined sharply, and the Chemical Corps barely survived the post-war economies. The Chemical Corps School at Fort McClellan, Alabama, was closed and the chemical training functions were transferred to the US Army Ordnance School, Aberdeen Proving Ground, Maryland. Chemical units were disestablished and their missions were dispersed throughout the Army Training and Doctrine Command, so diluting the quality and quantity of expertise devoted to chemical warfare.[5]

But the neglect of the chemical warfare programme cannot be solely attributed to the Vietnam War and the concern aroused by the accidents of the late sixties. The programme was a victim of its own image, a lack of assimilation by the military, and competing diplomatic priorities. When bracketed with the other 'weapons of mass destruction', chemical weapons seemed somewhat old fashioned and of much less significance than nuclear missiles. Chemical warfare preparedness seemed a fairly minor component of the deterrent strategy, so eroding still further the realism and incentive of unit training.[6] The traditional military dislike of chemical weapons persisted, not merely the feeling that such weapons were unchivalrous and repugnant but also scepticism about their comparative effectiveness (notably the problem of predicting target coverage).[7] American intelligence, moreover, appears to have seriously underestimated Soviet capabilities in chemical warfare; indeed, the Nixon administration may have been the victim of a Soviet disinformation campaign. In 1969, it was apparently misinformed about Soviet CBW capabilities by the Soviet double agents, known as Fedora and Top Hat.[8] The Nixon administration also gave priority to avoiding any semblance of an arms race in chemical weapons and to promoting the prospects of arms control (in authorising the unilateral disarmament of biological weapons, it seems to have rated these weapons as more useful in arms control than as warfighting instruments).[9] Arms control has remained a corner stone of American policy: the Ford administration secured the Senate's ratification of the Geneva Protocol in 1975, and began bilateral discussions with the Soviet Union about chemical arms control which the Carter administration continued until 1980. The Reagan administration, though unwilling to resume the bilateral talks, has taken initiatives in the multilateral forum at Geneva, including the submission of the draft CW treaty in 1984.

Within this context the US Army, supported by the other two services, has sought to arouse support for its renewed concern over chemical warfare. American deficiencies covered almost every aspect of chemical warfare defence. The army required a new nerve agent antidote, more sophisticated decontamination equipment, additional stocks of protective gear and an improved mask and decontamination kit for the individual soldier. It lacked a remote area warning alarm and collective protection for vehicles, command and control facilities and forward medical treatment. The active strength of its chemical personnel numbered a mere 1600 soldiers in 1975.[10] American air bases in Europe were found to be extremely vulnerable to attacks with chemical weapons. The safety of air and ground crews was potentially at risk, so limiting the ability to sustain high sortie rates during combat operations. The US Air Force, as Lieutenant-General John W. Pauly observed, now had 'to play catch-up ball'.[11] It required more sophisticated protective clothing, decontamination apparatus, detection alarms, and, above all, collective protection centres for rest and relief, for medical facilities, and for work areas where equipment could be repaired and maintained.[12] The Marine Corps identified similar shortcomings in its protective, decontamination and medical equipment. When coupled with a shortage of qualified chemical specialists and perfunctory unit training, these deficiencies left the Marines without 'the capability to survive, fight, and win in a sophisticated chemical warfare environment'.[13] The US Navy was ill-prepared, too. Its warships needed area protection alarms and its sailors more modern protective equipment. Its water washdown systems, which could decontaminate ships reasonably quickly, were not optimised for chemical conditions. Finally, American warships unlike those of every other major navy in NATO or the Warsaw Pact, did not possess any collective protection citadels.[14]

Some improvements in America's defensive capabilities would be authorised, at fairly modest cost, from 1974 onwards. A new nerve agent antidote and decontamination kit for the individual soldier were quickly procured. Some 200 000 British Mark III suits and boots were bought, pending the production of American counterparts. Research was begun on new detector/alarms, a new protective mask, and collective protection facilities.[15] In its funding proposals for Fiscal Year 1978, the Carter administration requested $111 million to improve chemical defences, a significant increase on previous funding levels. It augmented this request annually until it reached $259 million in FY 1981. New NBC Defence Companies were constituted in FY 1978, with the aim of conserving combat strength by providing nuclear, biological and chemical reconnaissance and decontamination for combat brigades. By March 1982, the army had approximately 7400 chemical personnel – a force projected to increase to 11 200 by the end of FY 1987 with a target strength of over 21 000. With the issue of protective equipment, chemical training improved. It was integrated into the annual programmes of companies, batteries and battalions; it was also a feature of the major exercises such as MOBEX and REFORGER 78.[16] Under the Reagan administration, funding levels for all chemical warfare programmes were substantially increased from $532 million in FY 1982 to nearly $1 billion for FY 1984 with plans to spend between $6 billion and $7 billion during the period FY 1984 to 1988 (some two-thirds of which would be spent on chemical protection). Qualitative and quantitative deficiencies, argued Dr Theodore Gold, Deputy Assistant to the Secretary of Defense (Chemical Matters), still had to be overcome. These included protective clothing which was not debilitating in its own right, collective protection systems, adequate detection and warning devices, a monitoring capability able to assess the extent and location of a contaminated area, decontamination equipment, and the ability to treat large numbers of chemical and conventional casualties in a toxic environment.[17]

The American programme was not promoted in isolation. The United States co-operates extensively with her allies in NATO on all aspects of chemical defence. They have agreed standards for protective equipment, training, organisation, and procedures which are formalised in a series of Standardisation Agreements (STANAGS). The implementation of these STANAGS is embodied in the Long-Term Defence Programme (LTDP). Several NATO organisations review matters pertaining to chemical defence, particularly the Panel V11-NBC Defence, the Military Agency for Standardisation and Panel X1, Tactical and Logistical Concepts. Within these groups, the allies exchange information on equipment, technology training, exercises, and procedures. The allied armed forces train together in exercises, tactical evaluations and at the NATO NBC School. These arrangments are complemented by bilateral exchanges within the Alliance, ranging from discussions between governmental officials to those between scientists and military officers.[18]

Despite these arrangements, the defensive chemical provisions of the NATO allies vary considerably. Some West European countries, notably Britain, France and West Germany, are better equipped than others, but all countries have had to procure their equipment within tight budgetary constraints and with reference to competing military priorities. Amoretta Hoeber, though willing to praise British CW efforts, describes NATO's general preparedness to counter NBC warfare as 'dismal', while Dr Gold regards NATO's 'overall ability to conduct chemical or biological defensive operations' as 'unsatisfactory'. Gold accepts that improvements have been made in recent years, particularly in the ability to survive an initial chemical attack on the Central Front, and that progress has been made in improved training and inspection standards and in updating concepts and doctrine. But he recognises that significant shortcomings persist, especially on the flanks where 'it is unlikely that any country will have its full complement of individual and unit protective equipment until late in the 1980s, for some countries it may even be later'.[19] These deficiencies reflect not merely financial constraints but also a lack of consensus about the threat posed by Soviet CW capabilities and of how best to respond to it. Danish governmental officials concede that their country lacks certain chemical defensive provisions but stress that it possesses a well-developed civilian defence which includes defence against chemical attack. Norwegian military officials reject the view sometimes propounded by American military spokesmen that northern Norway is distinctly vulnerable to a chemical attack; they contend that the climatic conditions would make the use of chemical weapons unpredictable and even dangerous to attacking Soviet troops.[20]

NATO, nonetheless, has agreed certain basic principles of NBC defence, namely:

(a) To mitigate the effects of enemy nuclear, biological and chemical attacks and their associated post-attack hazards.

(b) To enable NATO forces to operate in an NBC environment.[21]

The prompt and accurate detection of a chemical attack is a pre-requisite to fulfilling these requirements. It should enable military personnel to don their full protective gear only when necessary, to identify the agent and so select either the correct antidote or decontamination agent, and to decide when it is safe to unmask. As harmful concentrations of the largely odourless and colourless nerve agents are virtually undetectable by the human senses, NATO armed forces have deployed a variety of automatic detection alarms. The M8 and M8A1 alarms, used by the US Army and Air Force, are to be replaced by the Advanced Chemical Agent Detector Alarm, the XM22, which is still under development. In France, the Detelac automatic chemical agent detector is produced in two forms, one 'portable' (though it weighs 18 kilograms) and the other intended for use at static locations. In the United Kingdom, NAIAD (Nerve Agent Immobilised-enzyme Alarm and Detector) is in widespread service with the Army and Royal Air Force and is due to replace the Ship Installed Chemical System on Royal Navy ships. NAIAD comprises a point-sampling detector unit and a remote alarm unit which can reproduce the detector's audible and visual alarm signals at distances of up to 500 metres. The detector monitors continuously the voltage across an electrochemical cell in which covalently immobilised cholinesterase is irrigated with the ester butyrylthiocholine: nerve gas in the sampled air inhibits the enzyme, as it would in the human body, resulting in a change in the rate and magnitude of the electrode potential, which triggers the alarm. By using an efficient chemical filtration system and advanced electronics, NAIAD has a lower false alarm rate and greater sensitivity (measuring nerve agent concentrations as low as $0.005–0.05$ mg/m^3) than the M8 system.[22]

These alarms, though classified as portable, are essentially large items (Detelac weighs 18 kilograms and NAIAD 12.5 kilograms) which are normally held at section level or above. More simple and portable pieces of kit – basic go/no go devices – are distributed to individual soldiers. Detector papers, like the American M8 and M9 and the British No 2 Mk2, are issued in booklets to each soldier. They act as alarms by means of a colour change whenever in contact with minute droplets of liquid chemical agent. Coated with adhesive on one side, they can be attached to an individual's NBC clothing or to equipment such as vehicles. Detector kits, like the British No. 1 Mk 1, American M256 and French TDCC, are also issued to service units. Manually operated, and designed for usage by an operator in full protective clothing, these kits monitor the residual vapour in the atmosphere from chemical agents. But these tests take time to complete, about ten minutes in the case of the M256.[23] The Chemical Agent Monitor (CAM), now undergoing trials with the British armed forces, represents a considerable advance in the realm of agent-monitoring. A completely dry instrument which relies upon the ionisation process to detect mustard and nerve gases, it provides a 'real time' post-attack measurement (i.e. a measurement which is received in sufficient time to ensure that the information can be used with maximum effect). Weighing only 1 kilogram, it can be passed over or around an object to reveal whether it is clean or contaminated and so facilitates a multitude of repair, maintenance and decontamination tasks.[24]

All these detectors are essentially 'point-sampling' devices, that is, they detect the presence of an agent at the point of sampling. They cannot give adequate preliminary warning unless arranged in a network upwind with a secure chain of communications. To provide genuine remote detection, the American armed forces have several systems under research and development. The Automatic Liquid Agent Detector System includes two components: the XM85 central alarm unit and several XM86 detector units. When the detector units identify liquid nerve agent, mustard gas or lewisite, their signals are passed to the central alarm. Thereupon estimates can be made of the size, speed, and drift direction of, say, an aerosol cloud, so enabling commanders to determine the areas which are likely to be affected. Another new device is the XM21 remote-sensing chemical agent alarm. Mounted on a tripod, it scans an arc of 60° out to ranges of three to five kilometres and detects the presence of nerve gas by monitoring variations in the infra-red spectrum. This equipment is due to be introduced by the US armed forces at company level from 1988.[25]

Personal protection will enable individuals to survive a chemical attack and to continue fighting thereafter. Several NATO nations, including Canada, Belgium, Britain, France, Italy, West Germany and the United States, have commercial companies experienced in the production of protective clothing and respirators. Protection is normally provided by an overgarment for ground and naval personnel and an undergarment or 'innerall' for aircrews. When worn with neoprene or butyl rubber gloves, overboots and the respirator, the suits provide excellent protection against biological and chemical agents and some defence against the thermal effects and residual radiation of a nuclear attack. Britain has pioneered the development of protective clothing. The current No. 1 Mk 3 suit, introduced in 1975, has a shelf-life of at least four years and is normally issued on a scale of three per man. Durable and air permeable, it can be worn for at least four weeks by a soldier carrying out his normal duties and protects him against vesicant or nerve agents for at least twenty-four hours. The suit is composed of two layers: an outer layer of non-woven nylon/viscose material which is flame-retardant and water-repellant and an inner layer uniformly coated with finely powdered activated charcoal. Should droplets of liquid agents fall on the suit, they will spread out over the outer surface (the so called 'wicking' effect) to increase the rate of evaporation while the charcoal beneath absorbs any vapour from the agent. The American OG suit has similar properties but is slightly thicker because it has a layer of polyurethane-foam material, coated with activated charcoal, lying between a nylon/cotton outer fabric and a nylon inner fabric. As these materials are combustible, the suit is to be replaced by a fire-resistant version. The French company, Paul Bayé, has already produced an air-permeable but fire-resistant NBC suit which is being issued to the French Army. The British are also seeking improvements in the durability and shelf-life of their Mk 4 suit, currently under development, and possibly the addition of a disruptive camouflage pattern.[26]

The crucial item in individual protection is the gas mask with filtered canister, designed to prevent the wearer from inhaling toxic and irritant vapours. Properly fitted gas masks can reduce the concentration of chemical agents in inhaled air by a factor of at least 100 000. The filters contain activated charcoal for vapour absorption and paper or other material to retain particulates. Small molecule agents, like hydrogen cyanide, can be neutralised by a variety of additives such as copper compounds and other reactants. The special requirements of aircrew, especially the supply of oxygen for breathing at altitude, can be met by the attachment of ventilators – both in the cockpit and in transit to the aircraft – as well as an intercom unit. The various gas masks used by NATO forces can be quickly donned, within nine to twelve seconds, and worn thereafter for long periods, even in sleep.[27]

Deficiencies persist, nonetheless, in respirator design. Research in several countries has sought to improve vision through the mask, so enabling optical sights and equipment to be used more effectively, to ease breathing within the face piece, and to improve speech transmission. The French model ANP 51 M53 is now in production, with one version fitted with a built-in microphone which can be plugged into communications equipment. The British S10, which is due to be produced by the end of the 1980s, will have a new filter unit with lower breathing resistance, a separate speech transmitter and a drinking facility. It should be much cheaper than the S6 and more quickly manufactured.[28] But replacing the current American masks (the standard M17A1, M24 (for aircrews), M25A1 (for tank crews) and the M9A1 special purpose mask) has proved extremely difficult. The XM30, developed by the Chemical Systems Laboratory, between 1974 and 1982 at a cost of $50 million, was intended to replace these masks. It had a voice transmitter, a drinking facility, an externally mounted canister which could be placed on either side and a resuscitation capability. It had a large flexible polyurethane lens, weighed 40 per cent less than the M17A1, and had thinner cheeks so purportedly improving the ability to fire many modern weapons. Yet the US Army decided against procurement because the mask failed to produce the expected performance improvements in testing and because the lens material was susceptible to damage from petroleum, oil and lubricant products, discolouration, deformation in storage, and scratching. The US Air Force, on the other hand, found that the XM30 had significant advantages over the standard mask in protection, comfort, fit, communications, and field of view. While it approved an initial order of 10 000 masks per year for fiscal years 1983 and 1984, the army approved the development of a new prototype, the XM40, which is supposed to incorporate the best features of several designs (i.e. the better fit, protection and standard NATO filter canister of the XM30, with the proven rigid lens system of the M17A1). The new mask should be ready for production in March 1985.[29]

Servicemen, however well trained, can only undertake strenuous duties wearing their full protective clothing for a limited period of time. They will experience physiological and thermal stress, especially in temperatures above 70° Fahrenheit. They will require rest and relief. They will have to complete various bodily functions and to shave, eat and drink. There are emergency drills to permit some of these activities, especially drinking, in a toxic environment but they are hardly ideal. Certain military specialists, moreover, like doctors, simply cannot perform their tasks in a contaminated, toxic environment. To meet these requirements, collective protection centres have to be established within buildings, vehicles and shelters, whether permanent or transportable. The internal areas are sealed by providing a filtered supply of clear air, by maintaining an overpressure within the area, and by using airlocks to control the points of exit and entry.

Toxic-free areas can be secured on modern warships by incorporating internal citadels in their design. Several NATO navies, including the British and Dutch, have required that their ships contain pressurised citadels, so enabling them to operate in a contaminated environment.[30] Collective protection centres have also been constructed within many of the static air bases in the Central Front. In these bases, entry into the semi-hardened combat operations centres is through a Contamination Control Area (CCA), wherein personnel can remove their contaminated clothing, decontaminate themselves and each other, before proceeding into the toxic free areas. The French AMF-80 concept of modular bunkers is installed in numerous military airfields in France and a small number have been procured by the US Air Force for trial use in Europe.[31] Aircraft, such as the Harriers and helicopters which operate from forward deployment sites, will have to rely upon mobile off-base support from transportable shelters, lined in anti-gas fabric, with air filtration systems. Similarly army units, which have to be mobile, can only expect a limited degree of collective protection. They may use shelters, such as the British Field Shelter Mk2, as command posts, observation posts, casualty-clearing and first aid centres and as storage posts. Some of their vehicles will be protected, too. Modern British armoured vehicles have been equipped with NBC collective protection systems. The German *Leopard 2* main battle tank also has an overpressure system with filters which can be changed by the crew from inside the fighting compartment. But NBC filter systems have not been fitted into all NATO vehicles, especially the armoured personnel carriers. Installation is expensive, adding some 30–40 per cent to the cost of some models, and might not be appropriate for armies who expect their infantry to dismount frequently and to fight on foot.[32]

Within all branches of the American armed forces, the lack of collective protection shelters has been described as 'a major and significant shortcoming'. By June 1982, the US Army still required another 2000 protective shelters for forward medical treatment, as well as a capability to operate inside combat and command and control vehicles without protective masks and clothing.[33] Remedying these deficiencies has proved, and will continue to prove, among the more expensive aspects of the American programme. Retro-fitting positive pressure systems into ships is much more expensive than incorporating them into the original design, hence the first two zone prototype citadel is being installed in the amphibious assault ship (LHA), with a view to installing a similar system in all new ships. Expenditure on shelter development will also consume the bulk of projected air force spending on chemical defence.[34] The US Army has purchased, and plans to continue purchasing, M-51 protective shelters (ten man shelters for use by forward medical teams); proposes to improve its Modular Collective Protection Equipment (MCPE) in vehicles, vans and shelters; and will equip the new M1 Abrams tank with a hybrid system of collective protection, combining an overpressure unit with ventilated face masks for the crew. The M3 Bradley (an armoured reconnaissance vehicle) is being fitted with an overpressure system but not the M2 infantry fighting vehicle.[35] In the late 1970s, the US Army completed a review of its collective protection facilities and confirmed its preference to fight 'hatch open' from combat vehicles. It assumed that the NATO forces would be the recipients of the first chemical attack and so had to be flexible in response (whereas the Soviets, by being able to select the time and place to use chemical agents, could traverse the area rapidly 'in a buttoned-up mode . . . then unbutton and fight'). Dispensing with collective protection seemed tactically appropriate and financially prudent: the army found that it would cost 'one-sixth as much to do it our way'.[36]

Decontamination procedures and equipment constitute a third component of anti-chemical protection. They clean individuals, their personal equipment, and crucial combat and support equipment, so facilitating movement from contaminated to clean areas. Such measures, if administered promptly, may also guard against agent penetration since permeable NBC suits, though highly effective against vesicants and nerve agents, can only sustain this protection over a fairly limited period.[37] Personal decontamination can range from the removal of spots of agent on skin, clothing and small arms by the soldier's personal decontamination kit (PDK) with its absorbent powder such as Fuller's earth, to mass decontamination by showers. Research undertaken by the German firm Alfred Karcher, has found that the traditional showering/lathering/showering process merely tends to spread the droplets of chemical agent over the skin. Karcher has duly pioneered new procedures for mass decontamination, involving an initial showering of the whole body with a chemical decontaminant followed by washing the skin clean with a lateral shower spray, using pulsating jets of water. Yet even this technique will not succeed unless the decontamination is carried out within ten minutes of the chemical attack.[38]

Vehicle decontamination is an even less certain process. Trials at the Chemical Defence Establishment, Porton Down, have revealed that persistent agents can penetrate the joints, cracks and paintwork of a vehicle unless it is decontaminated within a few minutes of an attack. Crew members could be lulled into a false sense of security if they thought, erroneously, that subsequent decontamination had been fully effective. Should they remove their respirators, they could succumb to residual vapours as the decontaminants were desorbed from the cracks by warming from the sun or the vehicle's engines. The British, accordingly, have eschewed large-scale decontamination (for which in any case, they lack the equipment and surplus manpower), doubting that it could be applied effectively on the battlefield. They believe that time and weathering are the only wholly reliable methods of decontamination, and, unlike their allies, have concentrated on protecting the individual while accepting that his equipment may become contaminated. Described as 'fighting dirty', this is a slight misnomer since British forces are expected to decontaminate themselves and those pieces of kit which they use repeatedly (doors, hatches, seats, ammunition etc.) when it is essential, and to do so quickly and efficiently. They could clean parts of armoured and the larger 'B' vehicles with a nine litre fire extinguisher, filled with water and soluble decontaminant, using an extension hose and car wash brush. 'Fighting dirty', however, is only part of a broader concept of contamination control, whereby the British hope to limit their period of exposure to chemical hazards, employing the techniques of avoidance or of limited removal from contaminated zones wherever possible. The utilisation of CAM should assist in implementing these aims, not least in finding areas where personnel can seek rest and relief from the burden of wearing their full protective kit.[39]

France and West Germany have pursued a more traditional approach. Both have established units of NBC defence specialists and attached them to their front-line forces. Both have invested in a wide array of decontamination apparatus. The French have a trailer-mounted system in service, which carries 600 litres of a decontaminant solution and uses a high pressure pump to decontaminate personnel, equipment and enclosed spaces. They also have apparatus for decontaminating terrain, the temporary decontamination of equipment and clothing, and field showers for the temporary decontamination of personnel. Equally extensive is the range of equipment possessed by the *Bundeswehr*. All vehicle crews are equipped to provide limited immediate decontamination of the points of contact on their vehicles.

All units at battalion level and above are supported by heavy decontamination equipment, including the TEP (Truppen-Enlstrahlungs-, Entseuchungs- und Entgiftungs-Platz) vehicles, which are 5 ton trucks capable of decontaminating personnel, clothing and terrain. In addition the NBC defence battalions are able to provide large-scale decontamination services at truck-mounted decontamination centres, known as HEPs (Haupt-Entstrahlungs-, Entseuchungs- und Entgiftungs-Platz). These systems are being modernised, notably by the replacement of low pressure jets on the TEP and HEP by high pressure ones, which produce smaller quantities of potentially dangerous waste water.[40]

More sophisticated decontamination techniques have also been developed. New German methods involve pre-washing with hot, high pressure water containing non-corrosive additives (to dissolve oil and grease and emulsify chemical agents), followed by the application of a decontaminating foam containing calcium hypochlorite (to chlorinate the chemical agent and render it harmless), with a solvent (to bring chemical agents back to surface by diffusion) and a surfactant (to reduce the surface tension at interfaces between liquids), and completed by a steam spray (to remove the corrosive calcium hypochlorite and solvent from the surface of the equipment). These techniques are incorporated into the *Decojet*, the fastest of the Western decontamination systems. Mounted on a Daimler-Benz four-wheel drive vehicle, it can travel over rough terrain, draw water from rivers, streams and lakes up to five metres below the level of the pump, and decontaminate thirty to forty persons and six trucks in one hour. It can also be used as a fire-fighting vehicle and in the maintenance and servicing of armoured vehicles, aircraft and helicopters. Another German innovation, which is still being developed, is the *Decocontain* system. It incorporates all the necessary equipment for decontaminating equipment, personnel, clothing, vehicles and terrain within a standard 20 foot container. As the container is movable by truck or by Chinook helicopter, it can be used to provide decontamination services close to the front.[41]

The US armed services, though equipped with stocks of portable power-driven decontamination apparatus, lacked adequate equipment and supplies for sustained operations, and their vehicle decontamination capabilities were labour intensive and time-consuming.[42] Prototypes have now been produced of the XM16 Jet Exhaust Decontamination System (JEDS), using J-60 engines mounted on 5 ton trucks. A smaller portable system, the XM17, is being evaluated to assess whether it meets the requirements for a lightweight decontamination system. Another portable device, the M13, which is scheduled to reach field units in 1985 will be carried on most vehicles. It comprises a pre-filled disposable container holding 14 litres of non-caustic DS-2 decontaminating agent, a manual pump, wands and brushes. An Interior Surface Decontamination System, the XM15, is also being developed to remove contaminants from sensitive surfaces, like electronic devices, by using heated air.[43]

Despite NATO's array of detection, protective and decontaminant equipment, casualties will occur from chemical attacks. These victims will include those who are poisoned by the agents directly, as well as conventional casualties from contaminated areas, whose NBC protection has been penetrated in the course of being wounded. As exposure to a single drop of sarin is lethal within ten minutes, first aid treatment is essential. It takes several forms, including the taking of prophylactic pills at regular intervals whenever a chemical attack becomes imminent. Formerly the British forces took oxime (P_2S) tablets but these were only one-tenth as effective against soman as they were against sarin. The new pyridostigmine pills, which have to be taken every eight hours, are much more effective against soman.[44] Should symptoms of nerve gas poisoning appear, soldiers are equipped with autoinjectors, with which they can inject themselves or wounded colleagues. The injection may include either atropine or a mixture of atropine and oxime (in the L2A1 Cambopen injector) which provides additional protection against sarin. Should breathing cease, artificial resuscitation would be required, using equipment like the Leyland Mk2 portable resuscitator. It consists of a face mask, inhalation and exhalation valves, a filter, and a bellows hand-pump with a capacity of 2.5 litres. These treatments, if promptly and properly applied, may save lives but only of the victims of nerve gas poisoning. The effects of hydrogen cyanide and the various toxins cannot as yet be countered medically, while the best defence against mustard gas remains physical protection and decontaminants. Ultimately, medical treatments may boost morale and reduce the proportion of fatalities, but they are unlikely to reduce significantly the number of casualties, that is, soldiers who are put out of action.[45]

Although deficiencies in their anti-chemical defences still exist, NATO countries, particularly those with forces on the Central Front, have endeavoured to correct them. These efforts reflect two basic elements of NATO doctrine: a no first use policy on chemical weapons, which requires that NATO forces must be able to withstand an enemy attack with chemical weapons, and a commitment to forward defence whereby NATO forces cannot yield territory even if it has been contaminated (although they might try to avoid fighting in contaminated areas, if it was tactically possible to do so). Anti-chemical defences, though vital in both respects, would impose grave limitations upon NATO's fighting ability. They would degrade the performance of servicemen, encapsulated in NBC kit, divert personnel to purely defensive duties, encumber NATO's chain of logistics, and expose Western Europe's acute vulnerability in civil defence.

Military performance will be degraded whenever the armed services don their full protective equipment and try to conduct operations in a chemically contaminated environment. The causes are twofold: the burdens of individual protective gear and unit defensive procedures. When troops are clad in their full ensemble, dubbed by the Americans 'mission oriented protective posture 4', they are subjected to physiological, thermal, and psychological stresses. The degree will vary according to the individual, the nature of his task and the ambient temperature, but some loss of performance will occur. It will be compounded by the loss of manoeuvrability due to wearing the overboots, a loss of visual acuity and impaired communications caused by wearing the mask, and a loss of tactile dexterity caused by wearing the gloves. Delicate operations like sighting a rifle or using optical guidance systems on some anti-tank missiles or punching keys in radio communications systems will be impaired.[46] As the suits do not allow bodies to dissipate heat effectively, heat stress will occur especially in hot and humid temperatures, such as those which may prevail in armoured personnel carriers and tanks, bereft of collective protection facilities.[47] Finally, the problems of battlefield command will be exacerbated as everyone looks alike, communications will be hampered, and motivation could prove difficult as levels of endurance begin to ebb.

Compounding the personal degradation will be a loss of effectiveness at unit level. Should chemical attacks be launched, NATO units would have to undertake additional tasks including contamination avoidance and, apart from the British army, large scale decontamination of personnel and equipment. They would have to transfer substantial numbers of men from their primary duties to the purely defensive requirements of chemical reconnaissance, decontamination and casualty-handling. They would also require, on a daily basis, vast quantities of additional defensive equipment and supplies.[48] Above all, military units would find that time – a critical commodity in most wars – was all too readily consumed in even the most perfunctory of duties.

Moving headquarters, rearming helicopters, replacing tank transmissions, building bridges, sighting missiles, even digging foxholes would take considerably longer, sometimes double the normal time or much longer.[49]

Estimating the degree of degradation is difficult because so many imponderables have to be considered. US Army estimates range from 30–50 per cent,[50] with the more extreme results occurring in temperatures over 70° Fahrenheit (although such temperatures only occur, on average, for three months of the year in the NATO Central region, the services must be able to fight in all conditions). US Air Force estimates are even higher than those of the army because their units operate from static bases and cannot adopt the contamination avoidance procedures of the army. Of the air force estimates the more modest suggest that sortie rates could be cut by 'a factor of two or three', and that larger quantities of better protective equipment, especially collective protection facilities, would still leave airfield operations (that is, maintaining, arming, launching and flying an aeroplane) degraded by 50 per cent.[51] These are aggregate estimates: some tasks will be impossible to perform while others will be barely affected. The estimates, moreover, only apply to men in full protective posture. At a lower state of readiness, when the overgarment alone is required, the soldier can remain in his suit for several days (save for the completion of bodily functions) in temperatures of less than 70° Fahrenheit. In colder weather he may even welcome the suit as an extra layer of clothing.[52] As soon as he adds the gloves, boots and mask, the degradation will increase considerably, reaching a level which can be mitigated marginally by training and appropriate operational procedures but never removed entirely. The implications, as summarised by Dr Richard L. Wagner, are serious:

> If we are forced to operate encumbered by protective systems while the enemy is allowed to operate unencumbered in a clean environment, chemical weapons can offer him the same results as a high casualty rate, even if he kills no one. This is a decisive advantage and is an invitation to use chemical weapons against us.[53]

In these circumstances chemical warfare training is of critical importance. The major NATO countries have NBC training schools: Grenoble in France, Sonthofen in West Germany, Winterbourne Gunner in Great Britain, CFB Borden in Canada, Breda in The Netherlands and Fort McClellan which was reopened in the United

States in 1979. At these centres junior officers and non-commissioned officers (NCOs) can be trained to lead and to instruct their men in NBC defence, senior officers can be briefed and updated on the problems of command and control in a chemical environment, training methods and operational procedures can be developed, and new equipment evaluated (usually in conjunction with research centres like Porton Down or the Aberdeen Proving Ground, Maryland). As a consequence, most NATO units contain a small group of officers and NCOs who have trained in NBC defence in addition to their normal duties. The major NATO armed forces, except the British, also maintain specialist NBC units, required to assist in peacetime training and in the tasks of detection, reconnaissance and decontamination in war. The West German NBC corps, for example, provides a company of 145 men of all ranks for each division of the *Bundeswehr*. Each company provides three platoons, one for reconnaissance and two for the decontamination of personnel and equipment. The staff of the Sonthofen school would provide a NBC defence battalion for each corps, and another six independent companies and seven battalions would be activated within the territorial command in time of war.[54]

Organisation and equipment would be of little avail without regular and realistic training. Like so many aspects of America's chemical warfare defence, training waned in the early 1970s. Live agent training ceased in deference to public laws and environmental safety regulations.[55] The realism of training was diluted still further by the inadequate quantities of protective equipment, so compelling soldiers to train in leather gloves and galoshes and not in the debilitating kit they would use in war. CW training had become, as the late Senator Henry Jackson remarked, 'largely rudimentary, infrequent and unrealistic'.[56] Such weaknesses were highlighted by several studies of the NBC posture of the US armed forces in the mid-1970s, prompting a renewed emphasis upon the importance of integrating chemical warfare training into all facets of mission-oriented training. New army training and evaluation programmes (ARTEPs) stressed mission accomplishment in a chemical situation. Major exercises, such as REFORGER 78 and MOBEX, included chemical warfare events.[57] Army units, particularly those which were based in Europe and had priority in the issue of protective clothing, began training for chemical warfare more regularly and intensively. By 15 March 1982, Major-General N. J. Fulwyler could claim 'that every soldier in every unit now is getting some kind of chemical training at least once a week'.[58]

Training should enable soldiers to become familiar with their NBC kit, to learn basic survival skills (like donning a respirator properly within nine seconds) and to grasp what can and cannot be done in full protective clothing. Once they have realised how to make the necessary adjustments, training should boost the soldier's confidence and his ability to complete the prescribed mission under additional stress.[59] To fulfil these aims, the training has to be as realistic as possible. Several simulators or dispensers are used to project gas attacks with CS (to prevent 'cheating' by participants in NBC kit) or liquid agent attacks with CATM (chemical agent training mixture). In 1979, a carefully constructed Battle Run was opened at Porton Down, upon which various units, including light armoured forces, can train in company strength under combat conditions. Over a period of forty-eight hours, soldiers move through wooded terrain with which they are not familiar, encountering simulated mortar, artillery and aircraft (when available) attacks by day and night, involving persistent and non-persistent agents as well as nuclear blast. The Battle Run has its limitations. The exercise lacks the element of surprise (save in the precise timing of the simulated attacks) since units will anticipate NBC training whenever they move to Porton. Only twenty to twenty-four 'runs' are possible per annum as the ground is required for other purposes. The waiting list testifies to the general army interest, but requests to use the Battle Run depend upon the priorities of individual battalion commanders. More battle runs are planned for the United Kingdom, and, ideally, some should be created in West Germany but the paint-damaging properties of CATM and the strength of the German environmental lobby have hindered development hitherto.

Air force and naval units also train extensively for chemical warfare, in the latter instance often within the scope of damage control drills. Naval training is still hampered by the lack of a fully effective simulant (that is, one which triggers alarms and imposes a penalty but does not damage paintwork and equipment). All American Air Force personnel stationed in West Germany from four star generals down to civilian employees are required to undergo familiarisation training in a chamber filled with CS within thirty days of their arrival and to repeat this training once a year. American Air Force bases conduct unit training exercises in chemical gear and must be able to complete chemical defence exercises in their Operational Readiness Inspections.[60] In addition, their stations or squadrons, like those of all NATO air forces, can be subjected to Tactical Evaluation (TACEVAL), that is, a test by SACEUR without notice of a full wartime alert. The Evaluation Team will simulate almost every incident, including chemical attack, which could disrupt the task of air defence. It tests thereby the readiness of aircrew, the strength of the logistic and other supporting facilities, and the ability of all units to survive and operate in hostile air and ground conditions. Bases can prepare extensively for TACEVALs and even meet the criteria of the exercises despite flaws in drill (since the Evaluation is a random sample of procedures). Nevertheless, the reports on operational effectiveness are taken seriously and any deficiencies in a station's drill are sent to the national commanders-in-chief and to SACEUR.

Despite the improvements of recent years, chemical warfare training is still intrinsically limited. Technical problems persist, particularly the lack of realism and the continued search for better simulants, prompting the US Army to express an interest in renewed toxic agent training, at least for chemical specialists.[61] The time allocated to training varies considerably between different units, not least between American units in Europe and those based in the United States, excluding the airborne forces (in 1982, it ranged from 16 to 100 hours per annum, compared with 100 to 400 hours per annum in the Soviet forces).[62] Some NATO conscript armies (with the notable exception of the *Bundeswehr* where NBC training is extensive) could undoubtedly profit from additional training. But time is restricted as conscription lasts for only twelve to fifteen months in Norway and nine months in Denmark and the reservists of both armies are recalled for so little time that they are preoccupied with conventional kit and drills.[63] In the southern flank, there may also be problems of NBC comprehension among conscripts drawn from agrarian communities. Even in the volunteer armies of NATO, the belief still lingers in some quarters that NBC defence is a separate skill which should be tested as an additional contingency in planning and exercises. Only if chemical weapons are fully integrated into military planning – as a routine aspect of every exercise – will commanders appreciate fully the constraints and choices involved in a chemical war: the effects of contamination upon his ability to move, on his resupply requirements, and on his options for countering and responding to a chemical attack.[64] Inculcating a greater sense of gas awareness remains the aim; although improvements have been made, much remains to be done.

NATO's chemical defences and training, though bolstered in recent years, can neither conceal nor offset Western Europe's glaring vulnerability in civil defence. Contemporary chemical weapons are probably not intended for the purpose of large-scale strategic bombing, if only because the bombing of cities with chemical weapons could trigger nuclear retaliation. Tactical chemical strikes, nonetheless, are likely to produce heavy civilian casualties. Numerous targets exist in NATO's rear area, including command and communications centres, mobilisation depôts, weapon storage sites, railway junctions, ports, harbours and airfields, many of which depend – in varying degrees – upon skilled and unskilled civilian labour. Chemical attacks on these facilities could inflict casualties, and disrupt operations severely, unless the civilian employees are protected and trained to work in a contaminated environment. Chemical attacks on front-line military units would also produce a downwind vapour hazard and, depending upon the agents used, could leave the terrain contaminated long after the fighting had ceased. Should such attacks occur, heavy civilian casualties would be expected.[65]

Civil defence is a purely national responsibility, although NATO proffers guidance to the member states through its Civil Defence Committee. Only Norway, Denmark and The Netherlands have made any significant provisions to protect their citizenry against chemical attack. Most West European countries maintain extremely modest civil defence programmes without even a policy on chemical warfare protection.[66] Several options are possible. Governments could follow the British example in the 1930s and distribute respirators nationwide, or even complete anti-chemical kits. Although fairly expensive (each British S6 respirator costs £60 and a complete NBC kit about £150), the equipment could be considerably cheaper than the military kit since there would be less need to preserve mobility.[67] Issuing the equipment, however, would not in itself constitute an adequate defence: people would have to be trained in its use, be willing to maintain it, and to keep it at hand. As a consequence, the option is usually considered impractical; indeed Norway, the only NATO country to retain a respirator policy in the 1970s, has abandoned it in favour of a collective shelter programme, based upon shelters with chemical filters in large urban areas. Of the NATO countries, only Norway, Denmark and The Netherlands have pursued this approach on a remotely adequate scale. By 1980, the proportions of their populations for which shelters were available ranged from 80 per cent in Norway to 60 per cent in Denmark to 54 per cent in The Netherlands, compared with less than 10 per cent in most other countries.[68] Building shelters is expensive and may only be practical in small countries with comparatively affluent populations. A more feasible, if minimal, policy would aim to provide protection and training for those civilians upon whom NATO's logistic chain depends.

However politically contentious, this would seem a prudent response by responsible governments to a chronic weakness in NATO's defences.

These defensive shortcomings have ensured that NATO's deterrent is based upon a mix of offensive and defensive capabilities, including a limited stock of chemical munitions. As possessed by France and the United States, these offensive chemical weapons are not assigned to NATO and only about 10 per cent of the American arsenal is deployed in West Germany.[69] All members of the Alliance have signed the Geneva Protocol, thereby renouncing the first use of chemical weapons. Several countries have reserved the option to retaliate in kind if subjected to a chemical attack, but Denmark, Greece and Italy have apparently renounced the option of retaliation and Iceland, Luxembourg, Norway and Turkey will only consider it as a legal reprisal. West Germany and Italy are precluded by treaty commitments from producing or possessing such weapons, and the Dutch government, in 1982, foreswore the use of chemical weapons by its own forces and the storage of such weapons in The Netherlands.[70]

The differing national policies and legal commitments have undoubtedly hampered the process of policy formulation within the Alliance. So long as governments are bound by radically different commitments, NATO cannot evolve formal procedures about how chemical weapons could be employed in war – a shortcoming which has vexed General Bernard Rogers, NATO's supreme commander.[71] The lack of clear political directives has at least not foreclosed any tactical option – a flexibility reflected in the policy of West Germany. Having renounced the production of NBC weapons in the Brussels Treaty (1954), the Federal Government has reiterated this commitment on numerous occasions but the obligation only relates to her partners in the Western European Union, and it does not affect the deployment of foreign chemical weapons on German soil. Indeed the Federal Government has strongly supported the retention of chemical agents by NATO forces. In the *White Paper 1983*, it stated that

> as long as the threat posed by chemical weapons continues, the Federal Government, like those of our allies, considers it indispensable for NATO not only to improve its defence capabilities against such weapons, but also to maintain a capacity for reprisals, albeit limited in size, in order to deter any aggressor from using chemical weapons in violation of international law.[72]

NATO's offensive deterrent rests upon the American stockpile of chemical weapons, whose capability has aroused acute controversy. Department of Defense spokesmen have echoed the anxieties of their military advisers, describing the elderly arsenal as 'inadequate' for the purposes of deterrence.[73] By adhering to the moratorium on production, the United States has not produced any chemical munitions since 1969. The current stocks were designed to have a shelf-life of twenty years,[74] but many of the items have either reached or exceeded that figure. The last stocks of mustard gas were manufactured between 1952 and 1959; production of sarin was completed in 1957; and VX was manufactured from 1961 to 1967. The newest munitions in the inventory – Mk 116 Weteye bombs containing sarin – were produced between 1961 and 1968.[75] The exact size of the American arsenal remains classified, but various estimates range from 28 000 to 42 000 tons of poison gas (the data coming from 'informed sources' or from particulars released by the Defense Department in Congressional testimony). The stock contains mustard gas and the nerve gases, sarin and VX. Over 60 per cent of the agent tonnage is stored in 1-ton bulk containers, with the balance loaded reportedly in about 3 million munitions including shells, rockets, mines and bombs.[76]

The sheer size of the stockpile belies its utility as a deterrent. The bulk agent cannot be readily converted into filled munitions. There are no filling facilities for the mustard gas, and the filling facilities for sarin and VX have not been operated since 1969. Set aside on a 'laid away' and not a maintained basis, these facilities would require extensive renovation before the charging of munitions could recommence. Some 11 per cent of the total agent is formally declared unserviceable or obsolete. Within this category are some defective and leaking ammunition as well as the M-55 rockets for which the compatible multiple rocket launchers have been phased out of service. Most of the remaining systems were designed and produced in the 1950s and early 1960s in accordance with contemporary military capabilities and tactical doctrine. As a consequence, the vast majority of current chemical munitions suffer from the obsolescence of their delivery means. Some are being phased out; others simply fail to meet the requirements of the Air Land Battle doctrine of the 1980s, with its emphasis upon highly mobile, combined arms operations throughout the entire depth of the battlefield area.[77]

Limitations in range and agent composition characterise the current stockpile (Table 7.1). Some 22 per cent of the agent stocks vary in range from mines, which must be hand-emplaced, to 8 inch artillery

TABLE 7.1 Capability of the US chemical stockpile

Unserviceable	Bulk	Short range <25 km		Deep strike nonpersistent	Deep strike persistent
		TOTAL	(Useful)	TOTAL	TOTAL (Useful)
11%	61%	22%	(6%)	4%	2% (0%)
Mostly rockets Also leakers, gun shells and a bad lot of 155 mm howitzer projectiles	6% VX 14% GB 41% Mustard no filling facilities exist	Mines; 105 mm and 155 mm mustard and nerve agent projectiles; 8-inch nerve agent shells; 4.2 inch mustard mortar rounds	155 mm and 8 inch nerve agent projectiles	Nerve agent bombs	VX spray tanks

SOURCE Hearings before a subcommittee of the Committee on Appropriations US House of Representatives, *Department of Defense Appropriations for 1984*, 98th Congress, first session (12 April 1983) p. 448.

projectiles which can be fired to about 23 kilometres. Of these systems, the majority are being phased out, including the 4.2 inch mortar (M30) with its 4 kilometre range and the 105 mm howitzer (M102), although a few 105 mms will remain with the marines and army airborne units. Of the usable projectiles, 58 per cent are filled with persistent agents including a substantial quantity of mustard artillery (M110). This is of limited utility because of its persistency (a desirable characteristic for deep strike attacks but not for firing into areas over which friendly forces might wish to manoeuvre) and because it freezes at 58° Fahrenheit (although solid mustard still emits an effective vapour, the frozen agent causes an unbalanced shell and unpredictable flight). Only 6 per cent of the artillery systems – the 155 mm and 8 inch nerve agent artillery shells (M121/M121A1 and M426) – are considered as potentially useful (and even many of these are filled with less useful persistent agent or cannot be fired to maximum range from the new howitzers).[78] There were fears that these shells, which have not been field-tested since 1969, might have begun to deteriorate.[79] A blue ribbon panel has since examined the stockpile, finding that neither leaking shells nor metal deterioration were serious problems, and that the military utility 'has not been perilously degraded to date'. On the other hand, it found that some GB agent had begun to deteriorate (not least because the stabilisers inserted to inhibit this process are almost consumed) and that the 'remaining lifetime is uncertain'.[80]

Several Congressmen and scientists have taken comfort from the current utility of the artillery stockpile. They contend that the United States could respond to a Soviet chemical strike by a chemical barrage, comprising 5 per cent of all rounds, and sustain that retaliation over a period of thirty days. They note that this response would consume about 200 000 chemical artillery rounds, and that the existing stockpile is substantially greater than this requirement.[81] But the US Army has not accepted the 5 per cent assumption; it would prefer to retaliate by firing at least one chemical round out of every six rounds fired by a battery and occasionally by firing some all-chemical rounds. Though unwilling to specify an exact requirement, it would prefer to fire 'several times the 5 per cent', as constituting an effective mix of conventional and chemical weapons.[82] Moreover, the critical deficiency in the current stockpile is the inability to deliver persistent agent beyond artillery range. Only 6 per cent of the agent is deliverable by air and two-thirds of that proportion is composed of bombs filled with non-persistent nerve agent. At 60° Fahrenheit, the contamination pattern for a bomb containing sarin would last from about two minutes at the fringes to about forty minutes in the heaviest area. As a consequence, it would require neither extensive decontamination nor prolonged protective measures.[83] A mere 2 per cent of the agent stockpile is persistent agent, VX, loaded into Air Force TMU-28/B and Navy Aero 14/B spray tanks. Formerly aerial spraying was an excellent method of disseminating agent in a uniform pattern, by flying straight and level over the target. With the advent of modern air defences, this approach is now too high, too slow, and too long and would be extremely hazardous. In addition the spray tanks are inordinately cumbersome (each weighs 2000 lb and has to be carried in a shipping container weighing 4000 lb to ensure safety standards). They can be moved safely, but only as a massive logistical burden.[84]

The Department of Defense has instituted several programmes to mitigate these shortcomings. It has begun a demilitarisation programme to destroy the obsolete and unserviceable munitions which now exceed 700 000 items. By constructing a pilot project, the Chemical Agent Munition Destruction System (CAMDS) at Tooele depot, Utah (which will destroy 130 000 munitions in a twelve phase programme by the end of 1987), it hopes to develop the technological procedures for large-scale demilitarisation.[85] It has also undertaken a maintenance programme by which it plans to repair large calibre nerve agent munitions and upgrade them to a 'ready-for-use' status. The maintenance consists of inspection, derusting and painting, and the replacement of missing or faulty components. It will ensure, too, that aerial spray tanks are compatible with modern aircraft. These endeavours, though useful, are limited in scope. They will not alter the decline in usable munitions due to the phasing out of delivery systems, nor allow the use of bulk agent nor produce an effective strike capability against rear echelon targets. Similarly, maintenance cannot affect the intrinsic limitations of munitions designed in the 1950s and 1960s, halt or reverse their deterioration, and guarantee a viable stockpile into the 1990s.[86] Accordingly the Department, strongly supported by the Reagan administration, has sought to modernise the stockpile by producing binary weapons and by revising its offensive tactical doctrine. The objective, as emphasised by Dr T. S. Gold,

is to maintain the safest, smallest stockpile that denies a significant military advantage to any initiator of chemical warfare. We need not match the Soviets in agent/munition quantities and types. Rather, our stockpile requirements are driven by the need to force the initiator of chemical warfare to operate encumbered by protective clothing and burdened by the logistics and redirection of combat power necessary to sustain operations in a CW environment.[87]

Binary munitions contain two relatively non-toxic chemical components which are mixed during the flight to their targets to produce standard nerve agents. Although the US Army plans to develop an Intermediate Volatility Agent (IVA), which would have a volatility between those of sarin and VX and would be sufficiently volatile to be inhaled while still sufficiently persistent to be absorbed through the skin, the first binaries which could be produced would emit sarin or VX. The most advanced projects in their stage of development are the 155 mm GB-2 artillery projectile (M687) and the Bigeye VX-2 bomb (BLU/80/B). In the M687 the two components are contained in separate canisters separated by rupture discs. When the shell is fired, the g-force drives the upper canister, containing methylphosphonyl difluoride (DF), onto the lower canister, containing a solution of isopropyl alcohol and isopropyl amine. The liquids rapidly mix with the rotation of the shell to produce sarin plus about 25 per cent of a by-product, hydrogen fluoride. In the 500 lb Bigeye bomb, a core of sulphur is separated by a steel diaphragm from a surrounding liquid, ethyl 2-diisopropylaminoethyl methylphosphonite (QL). When a gas generator in the bomb is started, it ruptures the diaphragm allowing the sulphur to mix with the liquid to produce VX and some isomers. In flight a time-delay fuse will ignite to cut the ports in the bomb casing, whereupon air, which enters through 'scoops', will force the liquid agent to spray out of the ports as the bomb falls.[88]

Pentagon spokesmen, in urging the production of binary weapons, have emphasised that these two systems would constitute the first phase in a modernisation programme. The present stockpile, containing twelve systems capable of delivering chemical munitions, would be replaced by 'four or five systems', of which the M687 projectile and the gravity Bigeye bomb would be the first that could be produced. The smaller stockpile would be more effective militarily; it would include a more appropriate matching of agent and mission (hence the priority accorded to Bigeye as a bomb capable of delivering a persistent agent against second echelon targets); provide a more credible naval retaliatory capability (the navy is responsible for developing the Bigeye bomb for use by air force, marine corps and navy fixed-wing aircraft); extend the range of the US chemical threat (hence the interest in developing the Multiple Launch Rocket System (MLRS) and the Corps Support Weapon System (CSWS) – the latter being potentially able to deliver a stand-off attack capability against rear area targets),[89] and deliver a larger tonnage of agent in retaliation (Senator Carl Levin stated that the JCS had considered building a stockpile of 25 000 to 30 000 tons overall, with 19 000 tons earmarked for Europe, but Secretary of Defense Brown refused to confirm these estimates, implying that they were excessive).[90]

The safety features of binaries have been emphasised to explain why the stockpile should be modernised by their production and not by the filling of more unitary munitions. The army and navy plan to produce, store, and transport the two components of each agent separately. They would only place them in juxtaposition at a shell-filling or bomb-filling facility in a forward area prior to firing. This process would minimise the chances of a disastrous accident occurring in the manufacture, storage, maintenance, transport, and handling under combat conditions. It would reduce the cost and security requirements involved in producing, storing and moving chemical weapons. It would facilitate the forward movement of binaries in times of crisis and would reduce the hazard if American munition areas were damaged in an attack (an especially severe hazard on naval vessels carrying chemical weapons). Finally binary weapons, which do not produce any toxic agent until used, would be more easily and more safely destroyed in their eventual demilitarisation.[91]

Stressing the safety aspects of binaries was clearly intended to pre-empt protests from those who might oppose production by raising pollution and other environmental issues. The furore over such issues in the late 1960s persuaded Congress to impose severe restrictions upon the movement, testing, deployment, and disposal of chemical weapons. Similar protests were likely to greet the production of a new generation of chemical weapons, not merely in the United States but also in Western Europe.[92] The safety issue had to be addressed, and binary munitions are inherently less likely than unitary munitions to cause an unintended release of nerve agent. Yet this argument was unlikely to prove conclusive in and of itself. In the first place, the existing unitary munitions have a long and excellent safety record; they have been stored and transported (with fuses packed separately) without a serious accident in over a generation.[93] Secondly, any new chemical weapon, whether unitary or binary, was bound to arouse political controversy. By seeking a technical solution to the safety issue, the armed services were responding to the symptom and not the source of public disquiet.

The chequered history of the binary programme exemplifies this point. After about twenty years research and development in which the project only attracted substantial funding during the early 1970s, the Pentagon sought $5.8 million from the Congress in 1974 to build a production facility for the 155 mm projectile. The proposal was criticised in the Senate Appropriations Committee and defeated on the floor of the House of Representatives. Resubmitted in Fiscal Year 1976, the proposal was again defeated in the House by a margin of 219 votes to 185 (28 July 1975). Although the army wished to resubmit the proposal in subsequent years, it was blocked consistently by the Carter administration who feared that it might have an adverse impact upon its chemical arms talks with the Soviet Union.[94] Only in 1980, when American opinions had hardened in the wake of the invasion of Afghanistan, was Representative Richard Ichord (Democrat, Missouri) able to lead a successful Congressional initiative to approve $3.15 million to construct a binary plant at Pine Bluff, Arkansas. The incoming Reagan administration added $20 million to its FY 1981 Supplemental request to equip the plant. This was approved and the funds appropriated despite a narrow vote in the Senate. On 8 February 1982, President Reagan certified that the production of binary weapons was in the national interest, and the Department of Defense began to seek funding for binary production.

Over the next three years all such requests have been rebuffed. The Senate, which has a Republican majority, has usually voted in favour but only by narrow margins and twice in 1983 on the casting vote of the Vice-President. The House, which has a large Democratic majority, has decisively opposed funding and the Conference Committee has normally upheld its position. Only once (15 June 1983) has the House's majority against production fallen significantly (to a mere fourteen votes), when Representative Marvin Leath (Democrat, Texas) proposed an amendment to approve production but delay the final assembly of binary weapons for two and a half years (so allowing time for further negotiations). The conference in the wake of this vote authorised funding for binaries but proscribed their assembly before 1 October 1985, and required that assembly could only proceed thereafter if the President certified that it remained in the national interest.[95] Although the House endorsed this report in the aftermath of the shooting down of the Korean airliner, KAL 007, it later voted to instruct its conferees to delete any funding for binaries from the sums appropriated for 1984 (by 258 votes to 166). In 1984, the House again defeated a Pentagon request to procure components for binary production. Senator John G. Tower, chairman of the Senate Armed

Services Committee, reluctantly agreed not to promote the issue because 'in an election year, Congress is unlikely to take favourable action'.[96]

So controversial was the binary proposal that it was the only major weapon system deleted from the budget request for Fiscal Year 1984, even though the sum requested was $124.4 million out of a budget of $249.8 billion. Indeed, the retaliatory programme accounted for only 20 per cent of the proposed expenditure upon chemical warfare, which was projected to consume about $7 billion over the period 1984–8. The intense and sustained opposition to binaries cannot be explained by its likely costs, despite the fear of some critics that the programme could ultimately cost between $6 and $15 billion (an estimate firmly rejected by Pentagon spokesmen).[97] Nor can the opposition be explained by the depth of public protest, still less by the protests from the state most immediately concerned. When an environmental impact hearing was held in Pine Bluff, with adequate public notice, not a single person testified in opposition to the project.[98] Admittedly, Senator David Pryor and Representative Ed Bethune have been prominent opponents of binaries, but the other Congressmen from Arkansas have generally proffered their support, including Senator Dale Bumpers who has switched his vote since 1980 and Representative Beryl Anthony Jr whose district includes the Pine Bluff facility. Within Congress, nonetheless, the binary proposal has proved highly contentious, cutting across party and ideological lines (in the House, for example, opposition was led by the late Clement J. Zablocki, a liberal Democrat from Wisconsin, and by Bethune, a conservative Republican).

Critics have disputed the fundamental contention of the Department of Defense that the current arsenal is inadequate. They emphasise that large numbers of weapons are rated as serviceable, that deterioration is currently a highly localised problem, and that the army has been accused by the General Accounting Office of understating the serviceability of its stockpile.[99] Some have questioned the efficiency of binaries, claiming that many of the benefits have been exaggerated. They assert that these weapons, which have never been field-tested, will be less effective than unitary munitions since part of the payload will be wasted in the binary reaction and emitted as byproducts and/or as side-products. They argue, too, that the larger binary rounds could encumber American logistics; that any plane, carrying a Bigeye bomb, would be vulnerable to Soviet air defences (because of the altitude and mode of delivery required to optimise the density of agent over the target); and that the M687 projectile, the lead item in the programme, hardly redresses the principal deficiencies in the stockpile: indeed, critics seized upon Caspar Weinberger's admission that the shell requirement 'is not one of redressing a clear lack of military capability'.[100]

Several critics have added that whatever the merits of binary weaponry the breaking of America's moratorium on the production of chemical weapons would jeopardise other goals in foreign policy. They affirm that the United States has seized the high moral ground by its self-imposed moratorium, and that a reversal of policy could undermine any prospects of progress in the arms control negotiations. Among those who take this view are some of the most strident critics of the Soviet Union over the Yellow Rain allegations (like Representative Jim Leach, Republican Iowa) but who still believe that the United States should eschew binary rearmament.[101] Others fear that binary production could stimulate a proliferation of chemical weapons or even an arms race to exploit the recent advances in biotechnologies and in chemical or biological warfare.[102] Some fear, too, that an American commitment to a new generation of chemical weapons could impose fresh strains upon the transatlantic relationship, possibly risking West European support for the policies of theatre nuclear modernisation or economic burdening sharing within NATO. At the very least, argue these critics, the issue of forward deployment, that is, deploying binary weapons in Western Europe where they would contribute most effectively to deterrent or retaliatory doctrines, could provoke widespread opposition in Europe, even hazarding the displacement of the present stocks from West Germany.[103] Finally, it would seem that underlying these arguments, particularly on Capitol Hill, is a feeling of profound repugnance towards chemical weapons – a belief that these weapons, which could kill many more civilians than soldiers, are morally despicable, and that they should not be produced unless absolutely necessary.[104]

Some of these criticisms have more force than others. Complaining about the immorality of binary weapons while supporting the retention of a unitary stockpile, containing exactly the same nerve agents, is somewhat contrived. An aversion to chemical warfare is not the prerogative of binary critics – it is felt as deeply by the military as by civilians[105] – but the real issue is how to deter such warfare from occurring, pending the realisation of a verifiable ban on chemical weapons. Within this context, describing the present arsenal as adequate, largely on account of its size, hardly meets the Pentagon's concern about the credibility of the arsenal as a deterrent. Without binary modernisation, the United States will be left with a predominantly short-range inventory of weapons, containing a far from ideal mix of agent and munitions, a scant naval retaliatory capability, and an inability to deliver persistent agent beyond artillery range.[106]

Neither the M687 projectile nor the Bigeye bomb will correct these deficiencies in and of themselves. Of the items under evaluation, they are simply the closest to the point of production (the M687 having emerged from its development stage in 1976,[107] while the Bigeye, though still under development, is the only system which could be available before the 1990s to provide a persistent agent, deep strike capability). The doubts about the effectiveness of these weapons reflect the absence of field-testing and the Bigeye's mode of delivery. The US Army has professed immense confidence in the results of its simulant testing, completing over 2700 tests of the 155 mm shell. The concept appears perfectly feasible, but field-testing would have enabled the Pentagon, as it admits, to refine its munition effectiveness tables and to answer, in the words of a scientific review panel, 'serious questions on dissemination effectiveness and particularly on flashing characteristics'.[108] In these circumstances, the Administration might have sought a relaxation of the field-testing constraints from Congress, not merely to examine binary weapons but also to test the safety of existing munitions and some of the projected protective devices (such as the XM16 decontamination device, which is too large to be tested in a chamber, and the large area remote detector systems).

The Bigeye's mode of delivery has proved even more controversial. Originally it was intended to begin mixing the agents in the bomb prior to its release from the aircraft, but an experiment in October 1982 indicated that the bomb could explode if the mixing occurred at temperatures above 60° Fahrenheit. Subsequent tests have confirmed that the agents can be mixed successfully after release from the aircraft ('off station' mixing). The process requires the correct balance of time (fifteen to twenty seconds) and moderate temperature, so precluding the delivery of the bomb from low altitude. The bomb will either have to be dropped from 6000 feet, so exposing the aircraft to modern air defences, or, as Congressman Bethune argues, lofted upwards and over the target from a low level approach.[109] These constraints are certainly not ideal. Nevertheless, the Bigeye, which can be carried by tactical fighter aircraft (such as the F/A-18, A-4, A-6, AV-8, F-4, F-16 and F-111), permits its pilot, in approaching the target, to adopt more survivable tactics than the pilot who has to fly high, level, and slow to deliver VX from a TMU-28/B spray tank. As Dr Gold frankly concedes, 'The Bigeye is not a perfect solution, but it is the only solution we can have before the early nineties.'[110] Logistically, too, the Bigeye would be much easier to transport than the 2000 lb spray tank with its 4000 lb shipping container. Even the binary artillery round, which requires additional lift to transport its separate canister, will consume slightly less space than that required by unitary munitions (that is, if allowance is made for the space lost by the technical escort team and decontamination equipment which have to accompany the latter).[111]

Whether binary weapons, if produced, would precipitate a proliferation of chemical weapons or start an arms race are matters of conjecture. The causal link between vertical and horizontal proliferation, which has not occurred in the realm of nuclear weapons despite the confident predictions in the early 1960s, is not certain. As the Gulf War indicates, proliferation has already occurred without the stimulus of binary production. Direct emulation of American decisions may be of less relevance than the perceived merits of the weaponry, the military requirements of the states' concerned, and their production capabilities or access to supplies of chemical munitions. How the Soviet Union would respond to binaries is also far from clear. Ambassador Viktor L. Issraelyan has expressed apprehension about the binary programme, both privately and in the Committee on Disarmament (thereby, ironically, according the programme more credibility than its Western critics would admit).[112] But this apprehension, if genuine and widely shared, is only one of many factors which could effect the Soviet procurement process. Binary munitions do not represent any radical improvements in chemical weaponry, and the American programme, if fully developed, would produce a smaller, though more usable, stockpile of chemical weapons. At best the American programme may create a more credible, but still minimal, deterrent: it could blunt a Soviet CW threat but hardly imperils her military posture.

Undoubtedly the deployment of binaries could prove a contentious and divisive issue within the Alliance. In view of the difficulties already encountered over the deployment of Cruise and Pershing II missiles in Western Europe, the Reagan administration has prudently refrained from raising this issue prematurely. As early as March 1981, it informed all NATO countries that it would seek funding for the development and production of binaries, and no allied government opposed this national decision. Even if funding had been approved, the administration knew that several years would elapse before munitions could be filled and stocks accumulated.[113] Dr Gold argued, too, that investing in binaries would be worthwhile even without forward deployment, as they could be used in places other than Europe and they could be brought forward in time of crisis. The latter would not be easy, and other military assets would have to be delayed. Nevertheless, 'militarily significant quantities of weapons could be delivered with a small fraction of our lift capability . . . 60 C-141/B sorties could deliver 20,000 155 mm binary artillery shells and 1,000 Bigeye bombs in Europe'.[114] Such reasoning failed to convince Congressional critics who correctly perceived that the forward deployment of binaries would greatly enhance their credibility as a deterrent. Whether a deployment agreement could be reached is debatable. Despite the predictable opposition from some political parties and pressure groups, chemical warfare has hardly been the subject of intense public debate in Western Europe. As the only apparent consensus at governmental level is the commitment to continue the disarmament talks, any deployment approach from the United States would probably have to include another 'twin track' policy, that is, coupling the deployment of binaries with further arms control initiatives. Politically, though, it would seem unwise to press this issue until NATO has consolidated its deployment of the Cruise and Pershing II missiles.

After its experiences in the 97th and 98th Congresses, the immediate prospects of the binary programme appear somewhat bleak. Unless there is a radical change in the views or priorities of the 99th Congress (and these may be influenced by the Chemical Warfare Review Commission which has to report to Congress in April 1985),[115] NATO appears likely to be left dependent upon an ageing American retaliatory stockpile, with its array of tactical deficiencies, and an anti-chemical posture which has improved but is still beset by fundamental weaknesses. Maintaining and repairing the existing stocks will help. So, too, will the research and development programmes and the continued investment of resources in anti-chemical defence. Yet the inadequacies of NATO's posture seem likely to persist, compounded by a reluctance in Western Europe to discuss the issue of chemical warfare, to consider its implications for the Alliance as a whole and to devise a unified doctrine. Doubtless many still believe that the talks in Geneva will provide a panacea for this predicament.

8 The Geneva Negotiations: Problems and Prospects

Chemical warfare has always evoked profound feelings of repugnance. Ever since the emergence of sizeable chemical industries in the nineteenth century, international gatherings have sought to proscribe the military use of poisonous and asphyxiating weapons (the Brussels Convention of 1874 and the Hague Peace Conferences of 1899 and 1907). On 17 June 1925 twenty-eight states signed the Geneva Protocol, prohibiting the use in war of asphyxiating, poisonous or other gases and of all analogous liquids, materials or devices, as well as 'illogical' methods of warfare. Some one hundred states have since adhered to the Protocol, although several have qualified their ratifications, insisting that they only applied to their relations with other parties to the Protocol and would cease to be binding if an enemy state failed to respect the prohibitions of the Protocol. A standard of international law was thereby established, albeit one which has been breached on several occasions. The Protocol permitted the development, production, stockpiling and transfer of chemical weapons and contained no machinery to investigate alleged violations. It also enabled states to reserve the right to retaliate in kind and so was little more than a no first use agreement. Strenuous efforts have been made since 1968 to devise a more comprehensive agreement with mechanisms to detect violations and verify compliance.

Most nations agree that chemical weapons should be abolished. They have generally voted in support of resolutions expressing such sentiments in the General Assembly of the United Nations. They have also participated in various disarmament commissions, beginning with the Commission for Conventional Armaments in 1948.[1] Although these debates and commissions emphasised different aspects of disarmament, the main criticisms of chemical warfare were summarised in a report prepared for the United Nations in 1969. Chemical and biological weapons, it stated, were an additional drain on a nation's resources. If ever used in warfare, they would compound the risks of escalation to more dangerous weapons of mass destruction, with unpredictable effects upon society and the environment. The mere existence of chemical weapons would encourage proliferation among developing as well as developed nations, while their abolition would reduce international tension and contribute to more extensive measures of disarmament. Chemical and biological weapons could be abolished because they were inherently unpredictable in their effects on the battlefield and so 'their universal elimination would not detract from any nation's security'.[2] Among those promoting disarmament, the purported 'marginality' of chemical weapons (when compared with nuclear or conventional weapons, especially the new generation of precision-guided munitions) has been a fundamental assumption. As Jorma K. Miettinen asserted, 'there is no other area where the military risks would be smaller and the political gains larger than in disarmament of the chemical warfare machine'.[3]

During the 1950s and early 1960s chemical and biological warfare was discussed intermittently by the General Assembly, usually within the remit of various comprehensive disarmament proposals. It was also examined by the short-lived Ten-Nation Committee on Disarmament in 1960. At the twenty-first session of the General Assembly, in 1966, Hungary presented a draft resolution which dealt exclusively with chemical and bacteriological weapons. The Assembly eventually adopted an amended version, resolution 2162B(XX1), which called for the strict observance of the principles and objectives of the Geneva Protocol and invited all states to accede to the Protocol.[4] Two years later the Eighteen-Nation Committee on Disarmament (ENDC) discussed chemical and bacteriological warfare under the heading 'non-nuclear measures'. Having recommended that the Secretary-General appoint a group of experts to study the effects of chemical and biological warfare, the ENDC reviewed the report in 1969 and considered a British proposal to separate chemical and biological weapons and to seek a biological convention first.[5] In endorsing this approach, states did not assume that the prohibition of one category of weapons was less urgent than the other, but they accepted that an agreement banning biological weapons presented less intractable problems (especially after the unilateral renunciation of these weapons by the United States), and that a biological agreement should not be delayed in the quest for a chemical convention. By 1971 the disarmament committee – known as the Conference of the

Committee on Disarmament (CCD) – agreed to negotiate a convention which would prohibit the development, production and stockpiling of biological and toxin weapons.[6]

Following Soviet–American talks, separate but identical drafts of a BW convention were submitted by the Soviet Union, Bulgaria, Roumania, Czechoslovakia, Hungary, Mongolia, and Poland and by the United States. After considerable discussion in the CCD, a consensus was reached on a revised text which was duly adopted by the General Assembly in resolution 2826(XXVI). The brief Convention, containing a mere fifteen articles, was opened for signature on 10 April 1972 and entered into force on 26 March 1975. Dubbed by Miodrag Mihajlović, when presiding at the CCD on 11 April 1972, as 'the first international treaty providing for some measure of real disarmament',[7] the BW Convention has since incurred considerable criticism, particularly over its lack of verification procedures. Under the BW Convention, a suspicious party must first consult and co-operate with the other party to clarify any possible ambiguities; thereafter the former party, if still dissatisfied, can only bring the matter before the UN Security Council (Articles V and VI). Given the veto power of the permanent members of the Security Council, this virtually ensured that a complaint against any one of them would not be pressed successfully.[8]

Nevertheless, Article IX of the BW Convention commits all states-parties to negotiate 'in good faith' towards 'the recognised objective of effective prohibition of chemical weapons'. From 1971 onwards this issue has been discussed in the CCD and in the General Assembly as a separate topic. In these discussions the principal questions have included the scope of prohibition (that is, whether it should be comprehensive or initially of a partial nature); the activities and agents which should be subject to a prohibition; and the way in which compliance with a convention should be verified. These matters have proved extremely complicated, involving a multitude of political and technical difficulties. The complex connections between civil chemical industries and chemical war-making capabilities, the existence of 'dual-purpose' chemicals (toxic chemicals which are legitimately required as intermediaries in industrial manufacture), the use of harassing agents for the purposes of riot control and other such issues have ensured a plethora of proposals and papers, varying enormously in their content and permutations.

Defining the scope of the prohibition split the negotiating parties. Generally the East European states and the non-aligned countries favoured a comprehensive approach, banning not merely chemical

weapons but also their agents and means of delivery. Western states
saw numerous problems in this approach, including 'dual-purpose'
chemicals, delivery systems which could deliver conventional as well as
chemical munitions, the domestic use of herbicides and riot control
agents, and the task of verifying an agreement which was so sweeping
in content. They preferred a more gradual approach in which the ban
would be limited, initially, to those lethal chemical agents which could
be identified on the basis of specifically agreed criteria. Thereafter the
ban could be extended in a series of carefully defined steps to realise
the ultimate goal of a comprehensive prohibition.[9] Any agreed ban
would have to extend beyond the destruction of existing capabilities; it
would have to include the development, production and transfer of the
agents and weapons (research might seem a prerequisite too, but
monitoring small-scale research would be a daunting proposition and
some research would be required for anti-chemical protection).[10]

The parties to a convention would have to agree how the proscribed
activities and agents are to be delineated. Several criteria have been
advanced to meet this requirement, notably the purpose or intention
involved (a lethal chemical agent which has no peaceful use would fit
this criterion), quantity (that is, the production of quantities of agent in
excess of those required for peaceful purposes), and toxicity (with
limits established by reference to median lethality values). In advancing their gradualist approach in the early phase of the chemical talks,
Western delegations emphasised the link between scope and verification. They favoured restricting the scope of the convention to
proscriptions which could be verified. They were acutely concerned
about verification since they could not rely upon 'national technical
means' (as, for example, in the monitoring of the Strategic Arms
Limitation agreements) to observe compliance with a chemical
weapons convention. To supplement satellites and other national
intelligence-gathering activities, they insisted upon international
monitoring measures, especially on-site inspections, a highly contentious topic.[11]

The differences between the opposing blocs were exemplified in
their early proposals. In March 1972, the Soviet Union, its East
European allies and Mongolia presented a draft convention which was
closely modelled upon the Biological Weapons Convention. It proposed a comprehensive approach to the problem by applying the
'purpose' criterion to the scope of the prohibition (that is, banning all
chemical agents of types and in quantities which could not be justified
for peaceful purposes). It left issues of compliance to be settled by

consultation and co-operation between states who were a party to the convention or, if necessary by complaints to the Security Council.[12] Although some non-aligned members of the CCD approved some of the draft convention, the United States, supported by several Western members, felt that the draft was unacceptable, and that the detailed provisions on the scope of any CW ban and on its verification had to be discussed.

In subsequent negotiations there was a narrowing of the differences of opinion, at least on the less controversial issues (the scope of the ban and the adoption of the 'purpose' criterion, supplemented by toxicity measurements). Further draft conventions were submitted – by the Japanese in April 1974 (CCD/420) and by the British in August 1976 (CCD/512). The Japanese draft advocated a gradualist approach and the establishment of an international verification agency to observe the destruction of chemical agents or their diversion to peaceful uses, to consider reported violations, and to conduct on-site inspections. Yet the Japanese representatives in the CCD and the General Assembly emphasised that international inspections should not be conducted in an unduly intrusive manner[13] (Japan has no wish to compromise the secrets of its chemical industry). The British draft derived elements from the Japanese draft and from other proposals submitted to the CCD. It was reasonably comprehensive, including lethal and incapacitating agents, but left its position unclear on harassing and irritant agents such as CS. It followed the Japanese approach in favouring a strong international agency, which it dubbed a consultative committee, and stressed the relevance of confidence-building measures, already adopted one year earlier at Helsinki as an element in the European security agreement. The British draft envisaged states assuming obligations as soon as they signed a CW convention, namely the declaration of their CW agents, if any, and of their production facilities and an immediate cessation of production. It was thought that these declarations and the freeze on production would build confidence and enable states to ratify their signatures.[14] The British draft convention, though extensively discussed, was soon overtaken by the announcement that the first round of Soviet–American talks on chemical weapons was about to begin (16 August 1976) in Geneva, but outside the CCD.

The bilateral talks represented a somewhat belated fulfilment of the pledge given at the Moscow summit of 3 July 1974 by President Nixon and Secretary Brezhnev. They agreed to consider bringing forward a joint initiative on the prohibition of chemical weapons, a commitment reaffirmed by President Gerald Ford and Brezhnev at Vladivostok in November 1974. The first round of talks took place from 16 to 27 August 1976 and another eleven rounds were held before their adjournment in 1980. Charles C. Flowerree, the United States Representative to the Committee on Disarmament (1980–1), explained that these negotiations were based on 'a fact of life, although not always enthusiastically embraced by the non-aligned nations, that the *sine qua non* for progress on multilateral treaties in the field of arms control and disarmament is prior agreement by the United States and the Soviet Union on its major provisions'.[15] The bilateral talks overshadowed the endeavours of the CCD, diminishing its significance. Neither Britain nor Japan pressed their respective drafts as a basis for negotiation; neither wished to impede any possibility of progress in the bilateral meetings. Non-aligned members hardly welcomed this development, especially as the bilateral discussions failed to produce a prompt initiative by the superpowers.

To offset the criticism from the non-aligned countries and some Western states like Italy and The Netherlands, the Soviet Union and the United States issued an unusually informative report on their talks (CD/48). Presented during the tenth round of negotiations in Geneva, it indicated areas of agreement between the superpowers. These included the proscription of 'super-toxic lethal chemicals, other lethal or highly toxic chemicals or their precursors with the exception of chemicals intended for permitted purposes . . . as well as chemical munitions or other means of chemical warfare'. It was agreed, too, that states on ratifying a convention should declare their stockpiles of chemical weapons and their means of production, and that verification of their elimination within a specified period should be based on a combination of national and international measures, including a provision to request on-site investigations to examine suspected violations.[16] Both parties, in other words, had moved from their original positions in the early 1970s. Whether this represented 'substantial progress', as some commentators claimed,[17] is more debatable. In further negotiations, the United States failed to secure from the Soviets any amplification of the conditions under which they would permit international on-site inspections. The Soviet position, as Flowerree recalls, was 'rather rigid';[18] indeed, the stagnation of bilateral talks prevented the superpowers from resisting the pressure for a new international initiative from the non-aligned countries and several Western states (Australia, Belgium, Canada, France and Japan had joined the protests in 1979). By March 1980 the principle of an *Ad*

Hoc Working Group on Chemical Weapons was accepted within the expanded and reconstituted disarmament committee, the forty nation Committee on Disarmament (CD). In the summer of 1980, the bilateral talks were recessed and were not resumed in the wake of the American elections.

The difficulties encountered by the bilateral talks in 1980 reflected more than the lack of progress over the issues of verification and compliance. Just as the ratification process of SALT II was postponed in the wake of the Soviet invasion of Afghanistan, the bilateral talks foundered amidst the deteriorating international climate. These talks, like other arms control negotiations, could not be divorced from other issues in Soviet–American relations.[19] The achievements of the bilateral talks were reassessed by the incoming Reagan administration. Its spokesmen were far from impressed by the degree of progress. Morris Busby, the deputy US Representative to the CD, declared that

> major differences relating to the most fundamental and essential elements for a chemical weapons convention – verification and compliance – were not resolved. Although there was general agreement on some routine matters, little real progress was made in this area after early 1979, and the negotiations became dead-locked.[20]

Dr Gold was equally forthright:

> I guess you would have to really be an optimist to say that there was progress. We have had almost 4 years of bilateral negotiations with the Soviets from 1977 [SIC] to 1980 which really didn't get anywhere. They established a framework, but there was no significant motion on the substantive issue which is verification. Verification and compliance are the only real issues.[21]

While the administration's critics at home and abroad have urged a resumption of the talks,[22] the administration saw little purpose in further negotiation from a position of military weakness. So long as the 'large asymmetry in chemical warfare capabilities' persisted, the Soviets were thought to have little incentive to seek an arms control agreement.[23] 'The Soviets,' argued the Pentagon in written testimony, 'appear to have been interested in negotiations only to the extent that that process encouraged the United States to defer improvement of U.S. CW deterrent and retaliatory capabilities.'[24] The administration preferred to keep the discussions within a multilateral framework, which would meet the legitimate concerns of the non-aligned countries. It would not preclude the possibility of future informal discussions with the Soviet Union but would obviate the procedural problems involved in the bilateral talks. The confidential nature of those talks would be replaced by open discussions, in which issues like the 'Yellow Rain' allegations could be raised and the positions, attitudes, and sincerity of each side exposed to the world community. Some commentators feared that the Soviet Union had exploited the secrecy of the bilateral talks to convey an impression of themselves as generous and earnest in the negotiations, while knowing that the United States could not reveal the extent of their intransigence.[25]

The non-resumption of the bilateral talks enabled the *Ad Hoc* Working Group to seek an expanded remit. Originally accorded a relatively marginal role (it was only established for 1980 and was only later endowed with a chairman, Ambassador Okawa of Japan), its mandate was not to negotiate, but to define, through substantive examination, the issues which should be dealt with in the negotiations on a new chemical weapons convention. The Group was re-established on the same mandate on 12 February 1981 under the chairmanship of Curt Lidgard of Sweden. It held twenty-three meetings between 18 February and 17 August as well as additional informal consultations. In the early part of its work, the Working Group conducted a detailed examination of the issues to be dealt with in the negotiations and later considered the draft elements of a CW convention suggested by its chairman. This was the first discussion of the wordings of the articles of a future convention. They were described as 'elements' and not 'articles' to accommodate those delegations which had not been mandated by their governments to negotiate the text of a convention. The formulations were also conditional (using 'should' and not 'shall' throughout the text) and dissenting views were included where they had been raised (some delegations had not forwarded their views, while others merely considered the 'elements' as points for discussion). Nevertheless, the Group could report a convergence of views on many issues throughout 1980 and 1981. Important differences of opinion remained, but it felt able to request a more ambitious mandate for 1982.[26] The CD concurred; it required the Working Group 'to elaborate such a convention, taking into account all existing proposals and future initiatives with a view to enabling the Committee to achieve agreement at the earliest date'.[27]

Under the chairmanship of Ambassador Bogumil Sujka of Poland, the Working Group held forty-two meetings from 24 February to 15 September 1982, as well as a number of informal consultations. Following the practice introduced in the previous year, Ambassador Sujka held consultations with scientific experts on technical issues, like toxicity criteria and the methods of monitoring the destruction of chemical weapons. He also established nine open-ended Contact Groups to consider the various elements of a convention. These elements included the scope of a convention; definitions; declarations; the processes of destruction, diversion, dismantling and conversion; general provisions on verification; the preamble and final clauses of a convention; national implementation measures; national technical means of verification; and consultation, co-operation and the consultative committee. Each contact group had a co-ordinator who submitted its report for further discussion in the Working Group. The revised reports were attached *in extenso* to the report of the Working Group (CD/334). By its painstaking and meticulous endeavours, the Group has enabled the CD to move 'beyond the ritual posturing which has so often characterised the work of multilateral disarmament organizations.'[28]

The Working Group has profited, too, from its accumulation of expertise. It has received a profusion of working papers from the national delegations, covering such topics as the definition of precursors, the declaration and destruction of stocks and weapon facilities, and various aspects of verification. It has benefited from the presence of scientific experts in its technical discussions and from the use of informal Contact Groups (in 1983, these groups reviewed the issues of stockpiles; verification and compliance; definitions; and the prohibition of use – a highly contentious topic in the CD because of the legal implications involved in duplicating the provisions of the Geneva Protocol). Some members from the CD have attended workshops to become more acquainted with chemical weapon destruction facilities (Tooele, Utah, on 15–16 November 1983 and Munster, Lower Saxony, on 12–14 June 1984). Yet despite this sustained activity, and the energetic leadership of various chairmen, particularly Ambassador D. S. McPhail of Canada in 1983, progess has been slow. Apart from the difficulty of reaching a consensus among forty negotiating parties, including two ideologically opposed blocs and the group of twenty-one non-aligned nations, the topic has proved immensely complex. As the issues relate to fundamental questions of national security, and verification poses an unprecedented array of difficulties, a convention will not be readily accepted unless it addresses the full range of complexities and meets the concerns of both superpowers.[29]

In the early 1980s, Soviet–American relations deteriorated sharply over the issues of chemical and biological weapons. The Reagan administration protested vigorously over the alleged use of chemical and toxin weapons in Afghanistan and Indochina. In its reports to the United Nations and in a series of speeches before international fora, the United States condemned the Soviet Union and its allies for violating the Geneva Protocol. These violations, argued Eugene Rostow, then Director of the Arms Control and Disarmament Agency, 'have a negative impact on the entire arms control atmosphere'.[30] At the review meeting of the Conference on Security and Co-operation in Europe, Max Kampelman maintained that Soviet actions must affect 'our confidence in any agreement signed by the Soviet Union'.[31] Convinced of Soviet duplicity, the administration's spokesmen emphasised the importance of seeking more effective methods of verification and compliance. As Dr Gold explained, 'The evidence of the use of chemicals in Asia apparently has had an impact especially with respect to highlighting the importance of verification and compliance measures to arms control treaties. Soviet intransigence on verification is visible to our Allies and the nonaligned.'[32]

Compounding American concerns were their suspicions aroused over the Sverdlovsk incident. Late in 1979 reports began to circulate in the Western press that an epidemic had occurred in Sverdlovsk in the previous April, following an accidental release of anthrax from a suspected biological warfare facility in the city. The building in Compound 19 had attracted the attention of the United States intelligence community because of certain characteristics revealed in satellite photography (the venting system and animal pens, smokestacks, refrigeration facilities, the nearby revetments which could hold artillery shells, and the extremely tight security with sentries guarding the few paths leading through double barbed wire fences).[33] Although the exact origins of the alleged accident are still obscure, and some details are confusing (including the protracted nature of the epidemic and the willingness of the Soviets to let an American professor enter and re-enter Sverdlovsk during the epidemic), a large number of casualties and deaths are thought to have occurred (the estimates vary from twenty to 1000 fatalities,[34] with the number infected possibly in excess of 3000).[35] Initially the Soviet Union firmly denied the American allegations, but *Tass* later admitted that an outbreak of intestinal anthrax had erupted, caused by the black market sale of skins and meat from infected livestock. But a substantial sector of the American intelligence community claimed that it had evidence from 'secondhand' witnesses, indicating that the victims had probably suffered from pulmonary anthrax and had inhaled anthrax spores 'which could only have escaped from a military facility'.[36]

Commentators have debated extensively the plausibility of the Soviet and American explanations of the incident,[37] but the veracity of the claims and counter-claims was never the sole issue. The incident exposed the palpable inadequacies of the BW Convention, especially the lack of a formal complaints procedure when doubts about compliance had arisen and the absence of an investigatory process. When the United States presented its charges, the Soviet Union simply denied that there was 'any problem' requiring consultation and co-operation under Article V of the Convention. Of even more importance was the immense difficulty of interpreting the fragmentary evidence and of determining the truth. Without timely access to, and physical inspection of, the area of the alleged violation, conclusive evidence could not be ascertained. The Sverdlovsk incident, like the 'Yellow Rain' allegations, has reinforced the desire of the United States to base a Chemical Weapons treaty on more effective methods of verification.[38]

Unlike other arms control agreements, a Chemical Weapons Convention could not be monitored by national technical means (photoreconnaissance satellites, other photographic methods, radar, electronic surveillance, seismic instrumentation and air sampling, none of which operate on the territory of the party being monitored). Such methods may identify suspicious production facilities or possible storage sites or other movements and activities, involving chemical weapons, which could infringe a convention; but only on-site inspections, if unimpeded and promptly undertaken, could verify these suspicions. Effective verification would require a combination of national surveillance measures and international inspection procedures. An insistent American demand, this requirement has also been sought by states who lack any chemical warfare capability. These states include not only the allies of the United States but also many of the non-aligned countries who accept that on-site inspection is a prerequisite for an 'effective treaty'.[39]

The requirement is more easily stated than realised. Although there is a precedent in the International Atomic Energy Agency, which supervises nuclear power industries under the provisions of the Non-Proliferation Treaty, comparisons are hardly apposite. The

IAEA monitors a much smaller and more specialised industry; its remit is also restricted to civil and not military plants. As the chemical industries of the developed countries are large, diverse, and highly competitive, on-site inspection could raise legitimate fears about the protection of commercial and scientific secrets. As chemical weapons could be stored with other munitions or tested on the same proving grounds, on-site inspection could risk the disclosure of military secrets. These risks may seem more ominous when mutual confidence between the superpowers is low and more stringent degrees of verification are demanded.[40]

In any convention banning chemical weapons, verification would be required to monitor the destruction of chemical munitions as well as their production and filling facilities; the operations of any plant allowed to produce super-toxic lethal chemicals[41] for permitted purposes;[42] the non-production of chemical weapons; and the investigation of any suspected violations of the treaty. Various techniques have been proposed to implement these procedures with the aim of minimising, if not removing entirely, fears of intrusiveness and derogation of national sovereignty. It has been suggested that within thirty days of a convention entering into force states-parties should declare whether or not they possess any chemical weapons (specifying their type and quantity), production facilities, and any super-toxic lethal chemicals or key precursors[43] retained for protective purposes. Further information should include the locations of weapons stocks, production facilities and any permitted production facility, production rates of permitted or 'dual purpose' chemicals, and plans for the destruction of weapons and facilities. Once armed with this information, international inspectors under the auspices of a consultative committee could begin monitoring sites and facilities.

The mode of inspection has been vigorously debated. On 21 July 1982, the Soviet Union presented its 'Basic Provisions' on a CW Convention before the Committee on Disarmament. It proposed an agreed number of regular visits on a 'quota' basis as distinct from the 'continuous' monitoring favoured by the United States. Only on 2 April 1984 did the Soviet Union accept that the destruction of certain types of chemical weapons would have to be monitored by the continuous presence of inspection teams.[44] Indeed, systematic international on-site inspection, involving a routine presence without any element of suspicion, should build confidence in the regime established by the convention. The number of inspectors could be reduced by the on-site emplacement of chemical and physical instruments, capable of monitoring the destruction process. These devices would have to be operationally reliable, serviced by international inspectors, and protected by tamper-proof seals, containers and television cameras.[45]

The degree of intrusiveness could also be minimised in verifying the non-production of chemical weapons. The plants which produce key precursors for super-toxic agents could be monitored by random on-site inspections. Organised by the consultative committee, these inspections would involve an agreed number of visits, following an irregular pattern with limited advanced warning. The inspectors would seek to ensure that the quantities of chemicals produced and stock-piled at the facility met the declared quota, and that the plant had not been modified so that it could produce chemical warfare agents. They could correlate their data with information gleaned from satellite surveillance (of, say, any additional safety measures at a plant) and from the monitoring of effluent air and water by instruments some distance from the plant. In arranging such inspection to minimise industrial fears, the current national and international inspections of the highly competitive pharmaceutical industry could be taken as a model, *mutatis mutandis*.[46]

Monitoring 'dual purpose' chemicals poses much greater difficulties as they are produced in vast quantities at many sites in a host of countries. Among such chemicals are phosgene, hydrogen cyanide and cyanogen chloride and non-toxic chemicals, like ethylene and ethylene oxide, which could be precursors for mustard gas. Some of the inspection techniques used for verifying non-production could be applied to these bulk chemicals but, arguably, it may only be practical to require a declaration of 'all facilities producing these chemicals above a pre-arranged quantity together with their civil uses'.[47] Underpinning this provision, and all elements of a verification system, must be the safety net of verification by challenge. Separate from the routine inspection procedures, this regime would seek to deter states-parties from evading their obligations under the convention; to clarify ambiguous situations, settle disputes, and allay suspicions of non-compliance; and to provide advance notice of any breaches of the convention. To be implemented, this regime would require agreement upon the machinery for carrying out a challenge or an *ad hoc* on-site inspection; the criteria for effective verification; the basis for request-ing a challenge inspection; the rights and obligations of a challenged state; and the action to be taken in the event of a refusal.[48]

Ultimately the declaration of certain categories of information will be the key to any effective method of verification. It should enable on-site inspections to be directed in a relatively precise, cheap, and unintrusive manner. Once cross-checked with data derived from national intelligence means, the verification regime should enable clarifications to be sought without the disclosure of sources and methods of intelligence collection. Yet no system of verification can guarantee 100 per cent detection of every violation. Verification measures can only aim at a high probability of discovering any militarily significant breach of the treaty. By doing so they act as a deterrent; they compound the political risks and costs of treaty evasion and remind states that they are parties to a legally binding agreement, whose violation may cast doubt on their international commitments in other areas.[49] These judgements will vary from state to state, as will the assessment of a 'militarily significant' capability. In this context, however, Meselson and Perry Robinson argue persuasively 'that the effectiveness of verification measures is enhanced by a high level of chemical defense. Good defense greatly raises the scale of chemical warfare preparation needed to constitute a major military threat, making concealment more difficult and intrusive inspection less necessary'.[50]

Although verification has proved the most contentious issue in the Geneva talks, the scope of the convention is still far from settled.[51] Each state-party would undertake not to develop, otherwise acquire, stockpile, retain or transfer chemical weapons. The *Ad Hoc* Group has agreed that any treaty should include super-toxic lethal chemicals, other lethal chemicals and other harmful chemicals but, as late as February 1984, it had still not resolved whether herbicides and tear gases should be proscribed. It has to decide whether the prohibition on use should be extended to 'any armed conflict', as some states assert that international law pertaining to 'war' does not apply in 'wars of national liberation'. The Group has to resolve whether the chemicals contained in chemical weapons can be diverted to permitted purposes and to agree that the location of chemical weapon stocks should be included in the exchange of data. It has to agree timings on the declaration of destruction plans, the submission of progess reports, and the schedule of elimination.[52] It has still to determine how the process of destruction should be balanced between the CW powers during the period in which the stocks and facilities are to be eliminated. No state should be able to gain a military advantage over another because of the pace and priorities of its destruction activities.[53]

These shortcomings should not detract from the endeavours of the

Group in previous sessions. During 1983, while the Western allies pressed the Soviet Union to amplify its 'Basic Provisions' without much success,[54] several delegations (notably, Britain, France, The Netherlands and West Germany) sought to improve the CD's negotiating procedures and to promote solutions to the difficulties of verification.[55] On 10 February 1983, the United States presented its 'Detailed Views' on a Chemical Weapons Treaty. It stressed that each state-party would have a 'stringent obligation' to accept international on-site inspection from the consultative committee or from a fifteen member fact-finding panel.[56] The Soviet Union chose to respond, not in Geneva but in other venues, by reviving the idea of a chemical weapons-free zone in Europe. Previously mooted by the Palme Commission on Disarmament and Security Issues (June 1982),[57] this proposal was raised by East Germany in the United Nations General Assembly (November 1982) and by the Warsaw Pact (January 1983 and January and May 1984). Although some Western politicians and diplomats have supported the proposal,[58] others have drawn attention to its many shortcomings. In the first place, negotiating a regional ban could divert resources from the Geneva discussions on a comprehensive worldwide agreement. It would do so at a time when allegations were gaining credence, and would soon be confirmed (March, 1984), of the use of chemical weapons in the Gulf War. Secondly, verification of a regional ban would still require international on-site inspection in the regular and challenge modes (and as the Soviet proposal of January 1984 did not provide for verification, it seemed largely intended for the purposes of propaganda).[59] Thirdly, a chemical-free zone in peace is not analogous to a chemical-safe zone in war; chemical ammunition, deployed on the perimeter of a chemical weapons-free zone, could either be transported into the zone in war or, depending on the size of the zone, fired into it by missiles and aircraft.[60] The United States and its allies, as a consequence, were unlikely to endorse the concept.

On 17 January 1984, at the Stockholm conference on confidence-building and disarmament, Secretary of State George Shultz countered the Soviet proposal by announcing that the United States would present a draft treaty on a global ban of chemical weapons before the Conference on Disarmament (as the CD was now known). Lending impetus to this initiative was the Soviet declaration on 21 February 1984 of its willingness to accept the continuous presence of inspection teams at sites where certain types of chemical weapons were to be destroyed under a CW convention. While welcoming this statement, American representatives rightly perceived that it was not entirely clear on certain points (notably the distinction between types of weapons and the omission of any reference to inspection instruments), and that it avoided the destruction of production facilities and other important issues.[61] On 18 April 1984, Vice-President George Bush presented the draft US treaty before the Conference on Disarmament. The provisions of the draft treaty closely followed the 'Detailed Views' submitted by the United States in February 1983, but it also incorporated the views of many other delegations. It accepted that the institutional structure should consist of a consultative committee with its executive council and technical secretariat, and that international on-site inspection should be 'systematic' for some tasks and '*ad hoc*' for others. But in Article X it proposed that each member of the Fact-Finding Panel (reduced in composition to the United States, the Soviet Union and three other members – one Western, one Eastern and one non-aligned) should be able to request a 'special' on-site inspection of another party to the Convention, that is, of any of their military, government-owned or government-controlled facilities or locations. Within twenty-four hours of receiving the request, the technical secretariat would inform the party to be inspected and the latter would have to permit access within another twenty-four hours. As explained in Annex 11, H2, the 'specification of such locations and facilities should be a reasonable one', and Ambassador Fields confirmed that it would cover the private sector chemical industry as well as government-owned facilities.[62]

The draft treaty left scope for further negotiations. The Americans have emphasised that they would be willing to consider textual improvements from other delegations, but not a treaty which would be less strict in its verification procedures. If the treaty was the outcome of an internal struggle within the administration between those who wished to submit a draft convention and those who did not, as many commentators allege,[63] it at least represents a compromise and a renewed commitment to the disarmament process. It will also serve as a yardstick by which future negotiations can be assessed. The Soviet response was instructive. Having initially denounced the treaty as a 'propaganda trick' even before its terms were published, the Soviet delegation at Geneva agreed to study it while refusing to discuss its contents in detail. On 8 August 1984 the Soviets responded with a working paper on 'The organisation and functioning of the Consultative Committee'. They argued that decisions on 'matters of substance' by the Consultative Committee and its Executive Council should be on a basis of consensus (whereas under the American treaty if a consensus could not be reached within twenty-four hours, the majority view of those present and voting should prevail). In the absence of a consensus, the Soviets simply proposed that the differing opinions should be recorded in the report of the Consultative Committee or sent to the state concerned by the Executive Council. The Soviets also refused to specify any methods or time-frames for conducting on-site inspections. The Consultative Committee, they argued, should 'adopt, at its first session, the criteria that it will subsequently use to determine the modalities and time frames for on-site inspections'. In short Soviet concern about the non-intrusive character of such inspection contrasts dramatically with the American assumption that inspection is the *sine qua non* of any CW Convention: a task which should be entrusted to a Consultative Committee endowed with genuine and extensive powers.[64]

After the recent American initiatives, further progress will depend largely upon a considerable shift and amplification of the Soviet position. Whether this occurs will depend partly upon the state of relations between the superpowers and partly upon the priority which the Soviet Union accords to reaching an agreement. Discerning this priority from a Western perspective is highly speculative. Some commentators believe that the Soviet Union after its experience in the First World War, and its history of fighting wars on its own soil, has a 'clear self-interest' in negotiating a chemical warfare treaty,[65] or at least an incentive to do so since 'the utility of the weapon is dubious – for either side'.[66] Others are more cautious; they refuse to speculate on Soviet motives but highlight the 'progress' achieved in the bilateral talks from 1976–80 and urge a resumption of similar discussions to 'find out' more about Soviet attitudes.[67] Several spokesmen for the Reagan administration question these assumptions. They emphasise that the Soviet Union has always been negotiating from a position of strength in the chemical arms talks (even of increasing strength as the American capability has diminished due to the phasing out of obsolete delivery systems). They argue that the Soviets, though willing to accept 'a treaty similar to the current Biological Weapons Convention',[68] may simply wish to continue the negotiating process with the aim of diminishing interest in the modernisation of the American chemical deterrent. They regard Soviet initiatives, like Gromyko's speech before the special session of the UN General Assembly on 15 June 1982, as simply an attempt 'to try and head off our modernization program'.[69] Continued negotiations, moreover, fulfils the Soviet commitments under Article IX of the Biological Weapons Convention while underpinning their repeated declarations in favour of a chemical weapons treaty.

Had the Soviets proved more forthcoming at Geneva, such scepticism might not have commanded credibility. But their reluctance to amplify their 'Basic Provisions' proposal and their failure to respond constructively to the American draft treaty are hardly encouraging signs. Unless an abrupt change occurs in the Soviet negotiating position, the Reagan administration, in its second term, will doubtless revive the idea of promoting binary production as a bargaining chip in the talks. The administration has already advocated this proposal on the premise that the Soviets have little incentive to negotiate away a clear preponderant advantage in chemical weaponry. It has argued that funding the binary programme would provide the United States with additional leverage in the negotiations, as well as a means of bolstering the American chemical deterrent until an effective ban is concluded. Establishing a binary production base, asserts Dr Gold, 'will convey to the Soviet Union a strong signal that they cannot stonewall international efforts to achieve a verifiable chemical weapons ban and still prevent the United States from taking tangible steps to improve its deterrent posture'.[70]

Binaries are potentially useful as diplomatic instruments because some three years would elapse after the approval of funding before any munitions could be filled. By extrapolating from forecasts made by Pentagon spokesmen in April 1983, it would seem that the United States could not have an 'adequate stockpile' before the early 1990s.[71] Although the Fiscal Year 1984 Defense Authorizaton Act authorised production of binary munitions, it proscribed assembly before 1 October 1985 and permitted it thereafter only if the President certified that the assembly remained in the national interest. Should Congress ever approve funding for the binary weapons, another five negotiating sessions could at least be completed before production occurs. The Soviets, moreover, have evinced considerable concern about binary weapons in the Committee on Disarmament and in the conversation between Ambassador Viktor L. Issraelyan and Congressman Bethune.[72] The Soviets have emphasised this concern in their proposal for the schedule of destroying production facilities under a CW convention. Whereas the West favoured beginning the destruction of all such facilities within six months and completing destruction within ten years, the Soviets have insisted that destruction should only begin within six months of 'facilities producing binary weapons with completion of elimination within two years', while the destruction of all other weapon-producing facilities should begin within eight years and be completed within ten years.[73] If this Soviet concern is genuine, it could be exploited by American diplomats armed with the additional leverage of Congressional approval of binary funding.

The prospects of bargaining chip approach have been questioned by previous American administrations as well as by Congressional and scientific critics. They have feared that the production of binaries could be perceived as a change in America's commitment to arms control, and that it could spur further Soviet production efforts, so disrupting the progress which has been made at Geneva.[74] Predictions of imminent progress at Geneva have been a recurrent refrain over the past decade. Advanced in 1974 to block the production of binaries,[75] these predictions came to naught despite an international situation which was more favourable than currently for reaching an arms control agreement. Although there has been some progress during the course of the protracted negotiations, especially since the formation of the Working Group in Geneva, important differences remain particularly in the realm of verification. Technical difficulties, though real, cannot explain this failure entirely; the absence of political will has been as important.

The Soviet Union would undoubtedly denounce the modernisation of the American chemical deterrent, but, despite the rhetoric or any threats to respond in kind, she would still have to review her negotiating posture. Henceforth the failure to reach an agreement by a specific date would raise the spectre of a more effective American CW capability, able to retaliate in kind against rear area as well as front-line forces. Without the option of imposing a relatively one-sided degradation of performance (that is, by compelling NATO units particularly in rear areas to don their NBC protective gear, and operate encumbered, while the corresponding Warsaw Pact forces are not so handicapped), the battlefield utility of chemical weapons would be much reduced. In these circumstances banning chemical weapons, even at the expense of some intrusive measures of verification, might seem more attractive as a proposition; it would also redeem some international goodwill without forfeiting a clear military advantage.

Nevertheless, Congressional critics maintain that the production of binaries could prove counter-productive at Geneva. They fear that the United States, by abandoning its self-imposed moratorium, would lose 'the high moral ground' in the Geneva talks. The loss of moral authority would compound suspicions about the arms control policy of the Reagan administration, including the reluctance of the latter to resume the bilateral negotiations with the Soviet Union.[76] But these critics overlook the record of negotiating from the high moral ground over the last fifteen years – it has not been crowned with conspicuous success. Irrespective of whether the talks were conducted in bilateral or multilateral sessions, the self-imposed moratorium has hardly proved an asset of substance. It has neither prompted Soviet emulation[77] nor served as an inducement to reach an agreement.

Critics have also alleged that binaries would complicate the already highly detailed talks and provide another stumbling block to effective verification. As the precursors for binary weapon components can be produced in ordinary chemical factories without the need for special protective measures, these facilities would have to be included in the remit of any CW convention.[78] When these implications were recognised in the early 1970s, it was clear that they had to be accommodated within the proposed convention. As little confidence could be placed in verification measures which failed to constrain the potential technology, the Working Group has included binaries in its draft provisions. It has been able to do so because neither the precursors nor the agents nor the delivery systems are conceptually new.

More generally, the diplomatic utility of binaries may be questioned on account of the chequered history of bargaining chips in arms control negotiations. The record of bargaining with weapons is at best uneven; all too often, the weapons have been introduced only to attract more attention and pressure to retain them, and instead of being bargained away they are incorporated into a 'balanced' settlement. Critics have grounds for their suspicions, but to describe the introduction of binaries as 'obstructionism'[79] is possibly too severe. The fundamental aim of the Geneva talks would not be altered by employing a bargaining chip as additional leverage. Unlike the Strategic Arms Reduction Talks, these negotiations are not intended to reduce or limit particular weapons, still less to produce a balance of weapons between the various powers. A complete and verifiable ban on chemical weapons remains the objective, and, if attained, this would facilitate the prompt termination of the binary weapons programme.

Finally, there is the charge that employing binaries for diplomatic purposes may dilute public awareness of their military rationale. Certainly the public debates generated by NATO's 'twin track' approach over the Cruise and Pershing II missiles (that is, a commitment to deploy the missiles and to pursue arms control negotiations over this category of weapons) have set a none too encouraging precedent. There may also be reservations about the wisdom of giving the Soviet Union a rôle, however oblique, in the weapon procurement process of the United States. Even so, successive American administrations have committed themselves to seeking a verifiable ban as their overriding objective in the field of chemical weaponry. Their European allies are equally committed; they could hardly be expected to approve the forward deployment of these weapons – at some future time – unless every effort had been made to seek their prohibition. On the other hand, the potential impact of binary weapons as negotiating instruments should not be exaggerated. They neither guarantee success nor proffer leverage which is more than marginal. Introducing them at all merely reflects the failure of the policy based upon the self-imposed moratorium. Approving binary production would provide an incentive for the Soviet Union to negotiate seriously and to demonstrate that she really seeks a complete and verifiable ban on chemical weapons.

Estimates of whether a new Chemical Weapons Convention can be agreed in the near future vary enormously. Professor Meselson has been quoted as suggesting that a new treaty could be negotiated before 'the November election' (of 1984 presumably).[80] Congressman Bethune has tentatively forecast an agreement by the mid to late 1980s, while Ambassador Fields, writing in April 1983, doubted that there was 'any realistic prospect in the near future for achieving an effective ban'.[81] Should a treaty be negotiated, with or without the leverage of binary weapons, expectations must not be inflated about its potential benefits. The treaty may commit its adherents to eliminating 'the threat of chemical warfare' and to inhibiting the proliferation of chemical weapons (as some commentators have already suggested)[82] but neither of these consequences may accrue.

In the first place, the Convention like the Non-Proliferation Treaty may not be comprehensive in remit. States who possess or may wish to possess chemical weapons may decide either not to sign the treaty or not to ratify it. Secondly, the treaty will not be instantaneous in its effects. Several stages will have to be completed, including the declaration of stocks, production facilities and previous transfers of chemical weapons, to be followed by the destruction of stocks and facilities over a period of ten years. Throughout this period the superpowers will have to retain a credible deterrent to chemical attack as well as extensive measures of anti-chemical defence.[83] Thirdly, verification can never be 100 per cent successful. Despite the techniques of on-site inspection, stocks of bulk agents (which deteriorate less rapidly than filled munitions) or even small production facilities could be concealed effectively. Any loopholes or 'gray areas' in the Convention could be exploited by a state, like the Soviet Union, which takes a strictly literal interpretation of its commitments under international agreements.[84]

Ultimately compliance, and not verification, is the key issue, and the record of attempts to enforce treaty obligations by international sanctions or trade embargoes is hardly inspiring. Arguably the vaguest and least satisfactory aspect of the American draft convention is Article XIII, whereby 'Each party undertakes, to the extent it deems appropriate, to render assistance to any party to the Convention that the Security Council of the United Nations decides has been exposed to danger as a result of a violation of the Convention.'[85] Riddled with escape routes, the clause fairly reflects international realities, especially the significance of a treaty violation for another state's foreign policy (just as in 1936, when the British government chose to ignore its evidence of gas warfare in Abyssinia in preference for a policy of conciliating Italy). As Charles Flowerree observes, 'At bottom, all multilateral treaties relating to arms control and disarmament rely on the self-interest of the contracting parties and on the restraining effects of world opinion on would-be violators.'[86] Unfortunately these restraints, even if backed by international sanctions, have not always sufficed. When states have felt that their vital interests were at stake, some have accepted the political costs of violating international agreements and of incurring the opprobrium of 'world opinion'. Compliance, in short, remains a voluntary action and can neither be enforced easily nor taken for granted.

Notwithstanding these limitations, arms control advocates still maintain that a CW Convention could fulfil important objectives, particularly in the European context. They assume that chemical weapons would have only a marginal importance on the Central Front, and that the stigma attached to their usage would be enhanced by a new Convention. The creation of additional political and legal constraints, they assert, would inhibit the assimilation of chemical weapons by military forces[87] (in other words, lowering the expectation of chemical weapons being used could reduce the incentive for relevant training, doctrinal development, logistical planning and the overall priority of CW in military thinking). Also a CW Convention, despite lacking 100 per cent effective verification, should give some assurance that large-scale chemical warfare preparations can be detected. It would act thereby as a deterrent, reducing the possibility of massive surprise attacks with chemical weapons. These aims, though more plausible than grandiose claims of a treaty ridding the world of chemical weapons, contain an element of contradiction. Non-assimilation, like compliance, would be largely self-imposed and would doubtless vary in its effects from state to state. Should some countries discount the possibility of chemical warfare, this could impair their defensive as well as their offensive military planning, so undermining the assumption that clandestine operations, in violation of the treaty, would have to be large scale to be militarily significant (and so more easily detected).

Paradoxically, the risk of chemical warfare could even be enhanced by signing the Convention, that is, if nations are lulled into a false sense of security and let their chemical defences lapse. Research and development programmes will have to be preserved to minimise the possibilities of armed forces being surprised by new forms of chemical or biological attack in future battles. Improvements in NBC equipment and training will have to be sustained to raise the demands upon any would-be violator and to offset, at least partially, the consequences of non-compliance by adversaries. Finally, these defensive measures should be complemented throughout the ten years of a Convention by the retention of a credible deterrent to chemical attack.

9 Deterring Chemical Warfare

In 1967, NATO adopted the strategy of flexible response by which it proposed to deter any level of aggression by threatening to retaliate with appropriate levels of military force. Seeking to avoid undue reliance on nuclear weapons, and so enhance the credibility of its deterrent, NATO favoured responding to a conventional attack in kind. Committed to a forward defence of NATO territory, it would hope to hold any attack with conventional forces, while retaining the option of using nuclear weapons first, and hoping thereby to terminate the conflict on terms acceptable to the Alliance. NATO's policy on chemical weapons, including the retention of a chemical retaliatory capability, is incorporated within this strategy, specifically within MC 14-3 and its supporting document.[1] The chemical retaliatory capability is not assigned to NATO and could only be employed with the approval of the American President. It is retained to deter an attack with chemical weapons, or, in the event of an attack, could be used to undertake either a legal reprisal or retaliation. Yet the Allies, though agreed upon a no first use of chemical weapons, differ on how they should respond to a chemical attack. The lack of consensus, particularly about the rôle of retaliation in kind,[2] could be thrown into sharper relief if Congress ever approved the funding of the binary programme.

Apart from France, West Europeans have generally relied upon the threat of nuclear escalation to deter a major attack with chemical weapons. Denis Healey, when Britain's Secretary of State for Defence, argued that Britain must maintain adequate defences against chemical and biological attack but not a retaliatory capability 'because we have nuclear weapons, and obviously we might choose to retaliate in that way if that were the requirement'.[3] It has also been claimed that retaliation in kind would be less effective than nuclear attacks as it would be easier to protect military personnel against chemical agents. Nuclear weapons are more assimilated by NATO's forces than chemical munitions, and, unless chemical weapons were targeted upon

198

East European and Soviet homelands, their 'coercive impact' was 'likely to be rather small'. Once the Soviet Union has launched an attack, argues Uwe Nerlich, she is only likely to be constrained by 'the threat of a massive nuclear exchange between the two superpowers'.[4] This option, underlining the risks attached to the use of chemical weapons, need not comprise part of NATO's declaratory policy, but any move towards a negative declaratory policy, embracing a no first use of nuclear weapons, would be severely damaging to NATO in the realm of chemical warfare.

American defence spokesmen from successive administrations have flatly denied that the threat of nuclear escalation is a credible deterrent to chemical use. If plausible when the United States retained a clear nuclear superiority over the Soviet Union, the threat is much less credible now that the Soviet Union has attained parity in theatre nuclear and in strategic nuclear forces.[5] Moreover, threatening to retaliate with nuclear weapons against a chemical attack contradicts the desire to keep the barriers against the use of nuclear weapons as high as possible. American spokesmen assert, quite reasonably, that the nuclear threshold should not be lowered 'to counter threats which can be handled in other ways'.[6] While the possibility of escalation should never be renounced, adding elements of risk and uncertainty to Soviet calculations, it would seem imprudent to rely excessively upon the threat of nuclear escalation. It is too rigid in form,[7] and is hardly credible in the late 1980s. Should the Soviets start a war, their leadership would already have considered the likely military and political costs, including the possibility of nuclear retaliation. Having accepted this risk at the outset, they might consider that a one-sided use of chemical weapons could secure a military advantage at no additional risk.[8] In these circumstances, as General Bernard Rogers, SACEUR, has remarked, the nuclear threat is 'not an appropriate response'.[9]

The threat of conventional retaliation, coupled with a strong NBC protective posture, has also been considered as a possible deterrent to a minor chemical attack. Conventional retaliation, argues Robert Mikulak, could involve the removal of restrictions on attacking certain targets, or extending the conflict into new areas or even 'a surge of activity' with the bulk of the increased fire being directed against the units which were using chemical weapons or were trying to exploit their effects. This retaliation, he asserts, could be particularly effective against a 'minor chemical attack'.[10] So it might; but in view of Soviet doctrine, and the importance of a major war in Europe, a small-scale or highly localised attack is highly unlikely. Nor is the plausibility of NATO's proposed response enhanced by the numerical inferiority of her conventional forces. As this inferiority seems likely to persist for the foreseeable future, and is no longer mitigated by a decisive qualitative edge in weaponry, NATO will be obliged to employ all her conventional resources from the outset.[11] Indeed, as NATO seeks to redress the conventional imbalance by deploying precision-guided munitions and a whole spectrum of improved conventional weapons, chemical munitions may become even more attractive from a Soviet perspective. In a conventional battlefield they would serve as force multipliers, compounding the effects of their own conventional fire-power. By forcing NATO's troops into a protective posture, with all its attendant encumbrances, a chemical attack could degrade the effectiveness of NATO's forces and could negate, at least partially, some of the overall improvements which NATO had sought from deploying a new generation of conventional weapons.[12]

In procuring these weapons, NATO will be able to deploy some munitions whose properties are akin to those of chemical weapons. Scatterable mines, for example, should be highly effective in the rôle of area denial, restricting the mobility or channelling the movement of enemy forces. As these weapons will be considerably more difficult to protect against than mustard or nerve gas, they have been regarded as 'retaliatory options' which are more sensible militarily than retaliation in kind.[13] But if these munitions were already in use, and had failed to deter a chemical attack, their retaliatory threat would seem to be marginal. They would hold little promise of redressing the principal feature of chemical warfare, namely its capacity to alter radically the nature of combat. As described by the Stockholm International Peace Research Institute,

> The whole process of tactical manoeuvre, of using weapons and equipments and of supplying forward units would become considerably more complicated. A CB protective regimen would have to be enforced at all times, with troops either wearing respirators and protective clothing, or having them immediately at hand. Elaborate arrangements would be needed for the servicing of these equipments, for decontamination and for the resting of combat troops.[14]

The protective posture is both a critical component and a central problem in chemical deterrence. Effective NBC defences can save lives and reduce casualties; they may also contribute towards an attack with chemical weapons by threatening to blunt its tactical effects. Protection, though, is bought at a substantial price, namely a degradation of operational effectiveness which, in the view of Department of Defense officials, could range from 30 to 50 per cent. Improvements in equipment and training may reduce this factor but they cannot remove it entirely.[15] Sceptics question the basis of these calculations and suggest that the degradation could be much lower.[16] This could be true of highly trained professional forces like the British Army of the Rhine or RAF Germany. The degree of training of élite units, however, cannot be emulated by many of the conscript and reserve forces of NATO, for whom the degradation could be as bad, if not worse, than the American estimates. Some degradation will undoubtedly occur and it will affect some missions more severely than others. Reflected in human stress and operational compromise, it will encumber defending forces much more than their attacking adversaries (although the front-line units of the latter will be protected, they will have the crucial advantage of knowing where and when they can relax their anti-gas discipline).

Only the threat of retaliation in kind can reduce the possibility of an aggressor exploiting the imbalance caused by degradation. As Harold Brown, the former Secretary of Defense, explained, it would be a 'real deterrent balance', threatening to force the Soviets into a degraded mode of operations and thereby reducing their incentive to launch a chemical attack.[17] Defense spokesmen, under successive administrations, have underlined the centrality of this assumption. They have set aside any notion of deterrence based on punishment or on retaliation for its own sake, but have insisted upon the importance of denying the Soviets any tactical advantage.[18] Edwin Greiner, a former Acting Assistant Secretary for the Army, feared that unless the Soviets are 'threatened with retribution in kind, which could confuse them, delay them, or give them an additional dimension to worry about, they could very well take advantage of us'.[19]

To serve as an effective retaliatory deterrent, a chemical stockpile must be able to threaten the vital elements in an enemy's force structure. These include front-line, second and third echelon troops; command, control and communications centres; airfields; logistics facilities; and transportation nodes. The deterrent should be flexible, enabling commanders to choose from an array of retaliatory options. It should facilitate chemical strikes with the agent and weapon systems which are appropriate to particular targets and accord with the mission objectives. It should also be buttressed by sufficient munitions to ensure that an enemy cannot perceive any advantage from prolonging a chemical exchange.

America's chemical stockpile is simply inadequate to fulfil these requirements. Less than 10 per cent of the agent stock is in munitions which have some military utility. The vast majority of these are short range 155 mm and 8 inch artillery projectiles, which could only threaten front-line troops and their contamination would almost certainly fall on an ally's soil. Critically absent is any credible threat to impose long-term degradation upon rear area enemy targets, that is, by threatening them with persistent agent.[20] The United States possesses only a small number of aerial spray tanks which could deliver a persistent agent attack, and the flight requirements of aerial spraying would render their aircraft highly vulnerable to modern air defences.[21] Compounding these deficiencies are the problems of forward deployment. American chemical stocks are stored at eight major sites in the United States and at two overseas sites: Johnston Island and one in West Germany.[22] Some estimates suggest that only about 10 per cent of the American capability is prepositioned in West Germany.[23] Additional munitions would have to be transported during a conflict when there would be competing pressures for the limited space. The Department of Defense, in seeking funding for its modernisation programme, has sought to redress these shortcomings. It has sought to acquire weapons which are easier to store, handle and move and could provide in the Bigeye bomb a long-range persistent agent threat. Advocates of the programme maintain that deterrence, based upon retaliation in kind, can succeed, and that the abstention from chemical warfare in the Second World War is a powerful precedent.[24]

Critics dispute that there is any need to emphasise and enhance retaliation in kind as a component of chemical deterrence. They question the historical, strategic and tactical justifications for this approach, and argue that pursuing it would involve substantial political and opportunity costs for the Alliance. Their historical doubts are certainly persuasive. To derive precedents about battlefield retaliation in kind from the Second World War is misleading. Although mutual in-kind deterrence contributed to the non-use of chemical weapons from 1939 to 1945, it was never the sole factor. Moreover, as Perry Robinson argues, 'the main (though not the only) retaliatory threat both posed and perceived' was that of 'counter-city chemical air raids', a threat which is no longer credible with the advent of nuclear weapons.[25]

Somewhat less persuasive is the fear that enhancing America's chemical warfare capabilities would diminish the credibility of NATO's general deterrent. Creating a 'specific intra-war deterrent', it is argued, could reinforce Soviet perceptions of a diminished resolve by NATO to use nuclear weapons.[26] This argument runs counter to the whole trend of NATO thinking since the adoption of flexible response. With the onset of nuclear parity, NATO has heeded American pleas and urged its members to improve their conventional forces and to raise the nuclear threshold (or at least prevent it from falling further). The modernisation of America's chemical stockpile complements this concern, and American wishes are critical since neither the French nor the British nuclear deterrents are likely to be invoked following a chemical attack in Central Europe. Successive American administrations have made it abundantly clear that they do not regard nuclear escalation as an appropriate response to a chemical attack, although they have not foreclosed the possibility of escalation at a later stage in the war. As with improved conventional forces, a modernised chemical arsenal would not be a deterrent in and of itself; it would merely comprise part of a graduated and flexible range of options, which could be implemented without precipitate recourse to nuclear weapons.

Critics still doubt whether the existing capability to retaliate in kind needs to be improved. They believe that the existing stocks of nerve gas artillery ammunition could force enemy troops into a protective posture over a thirty day war or even longer. They maintain that this could degrade mission performance and slow the tempo of enemy operations, and that the threat would compound Soviet uncertainties about the likely outcome of initiating an attack with poison gas.[27] Yet others are not certain about how effective this threat would be if implemented. Its impact would hardly compare with the damage which might be inflicted by a surprise attack, since NATO would be retaliating against front-line forces whose anti-chemical defences were already on the alert. Soviet forces, though possibly vulnerable to surprise chemical attacks, are well-equipped in kit, drills and reconnaissance measures to withstand anticipated or repeated chemical attacks.[28] Retaliation in kind could pose indirect hazards, too. If dependent upon chemical artillery it could wreak substantial collateral damage, especially upon allied civilians downwind of the target. If air-delivered against targets in the Warsaw Pact's rear, retaliation could risk the possibility of escalation. In view of these risks, authorising chemical release could prove politically contentious within the Alliance and cause serious delays in NATO's decision-making.[29]

As a consequence, some question whether retaliation in kind could prove to be an effective operational response. If the degradation due to anti-chemical protection fulfils the expectations of some 'authoritative commentators', Perry Robinson maintains that 'retaliation in kind could do nothing to recover the loss'.[30]

Undoubtedly there are risks and imponderables attached to any policy of retaliation. Uncertainties abound in assessing the impact of a Soviet surprise attack and in evaluating the various modes of response, but these risks have to be placed in perspective. Collateral damage cannot be avoided if the Soviet forces launch chemical attacks on Central Europe. Any retaliation, even on minimal levels with the existing stocks of unitary munitions, would risk augmenting the tally of civilian casualties. Arguably, though, the NATO governments might consider that these risks were more acceptable than the risks associated with authorising tactical nuclear release. Should long-range retaliation be considered, the risks of escalation would have to be assessed in target selection (and hence the importance of peacetime planning on the rules of employment). If the Soviet Union had already attacked NATO's rear areas with chemical weapons, presumably assuming that this would not trigger a nuclear response, NATO might choose to respond in kind, and against the origin of the attack, on a similar assumption. NATO, in authorising retaliation in kind, would not be seeking to recover any 'loss' of degradation but to restore a degree of balance between the opposing forces by imposing similar degradation on the Pact's armies. By threatening to minimise the possibility of the Warsaw Pact exploiting any advantage gained by an initial surprise attack, NATO might reasonably hope to deter recourse to chemical warfare.

Nevertheless, some commentators insist that emphasising retaliation in kind greatly exaggerates the importance of poison gas. They accept that NATO has vulnerabilities which could be exploited in a surprise chemical attack, but claim that these are reducible through refinements in the design of masks, suits and detectors, through improved operational procedures, and 'through sustained attention to antichemical defence during training and exercising'.[31] They argue, too, that chemical weapons are of declining importance compared with developments in conventional arms (precision-guided munitions, high explosive anti-personnel weapons etc.) Investment in poison gas would seem to contradict current trends in NATO armament towards enhanced accuracy, greater kill probability, and reduced collateral damage. Any expenditure on binary weapons could divert scarce resources from more pressing requirements, such as strengthening conventional defences or modernising the theatre nuclear deterrent.[32]

Estimating the impact of chemical weapons upon the modern battlefield offers considerable scope for debate. Some commentators contend that they could be 'effective',[33] and that they could enable the Soviets to achieve a 'startling success'.[34] So wide is the gulf of opinion that it cannot be easily bridged without a mission-by-mission analysis of the advantages and disadvantages of chemical munitions – a requirement sought by advocates and critics of the binary programme.[35] It would be unwise, though, to impute Western assessments to the Soviet military. Chemical weapons would already appear to be integrated into Soviet operational planning, with crucial tasks identified as ones which could be facilitated with chemical strikes.[36] Such strikes may not be inevitable, but they are distinctly possible as NATO's vulnerabilities, though reducible in some respects, are still likely to persist, especially the limitations upon NBC training in some conscript and reserve forces and in the dependence upon civilian support.

The opportunity costs would have to be assessed in trying to enhance the chemical deterrent. Funds would not be spent on conventional weapons, all of which would certainly be needed during a war. Yet these costs are hardly excessive. Even the more pessimistic projections of the binary costs, ranging from $6 to $15 billion over a decade,[37] represents less than 1 per cent of the likely American defence budget over the same period. Although the Reagan administration may face more budgetary constraints in its second term, it has sustained an impressive volume of defence expenditure (including a request for $305 billions to Congress for Fiscal Year 1985).[38] Ultimately, despite the expression of concern from several European commentators, this is an American choice and will involve a very small proportion of her defence budget.

Irrespective of the strategic, doctrinal or economic arguments advanced in favour of binaries, political resistance could still be expected from Western Europe. This is unlikely to arise over the production of binary weapons, which is rightly perceived as an American concern, but may develop over the possibility of their forward deployment. In the wake of the controversy about the deployment of Cruise and Pershing II missiles, some European political leaders are likely to fear an adverse reaction from within their countries. Protest groups could exploit the perception of chemical weaponry as an odious legacy of the First World War and as a largely redundant capability, unused in the Second World War and now overshadowed by nuclear weapons. Should governments try to counter this impression, they could suffer from the legacy of previous attempts to stimulate interest in the threat from chemical warfare. As Hans Ruhle observes, the public, or at least that section of it interested in defence issues, would appear to have a 'threshold' of imaginable horrors, beyond which further unpalatable information has no effect.[39] Only in respect of its arms control dimension has chemical weaponry evoked much interest in Western Europe. Any re-emphasising of deterrence, therefore, may be presented as 'further evidence of the US preference for confrontation, while Europe prefers detente'.[40]

Complementing these instinctive reactions are more reasoned concerns. They might include fear lest any deployment decision antagonise the Soviets and undermine the prospects of the arms control negotiations; anxiety by the leaders of the prospective host country that the deployment could aggravate their political and security considerations; and more general alarm that the decision could be perceived both inside and outside NATO as an uncoupling of America's nuclear umbrella from Western Europe. Moreover, European leaders may feel that the cohesion of the Alliance should not be further strained until the furore over the Cruise and Pershing II deployments has diminished. Otherwise they might fear that the United States was risking political costs out of all proportion to the military gains.[41]

To suggest that these arguments could be raised does not mean that they inevitably will be. Much would depend upon the timing and circumstances of the debate, as well as the qualities of leadership and the degree of cohesion within the Alliance. European opinion is not monolithic; several commentators, including some senior military officers and specialists in Soviet studies, have argued that if NATO possessed 'effective and widespread means of retaliation in kind', coupled with the evident political will to use them, the Soviet Union could be deterred from initiating chemical warfare.[42] Should production funding ever be approved by the American Congress, the delay of some three years before any new munitions could be filled would be vital. It should provide ample time for further negotiations at Geneva and for the scheduled deployment of Cruise and Pershing II missiles to be completed or for the conclusion of any new negotiations over intermediate nuclear forces. In those circumstances the presentation of the issues, avoiding any semblance of panic while not trivialising the chemical threat,[43] could be as important as the arguments advanced (with the predictable emphasis upon the safety features of binaries and the importance of raising the nuclear threshold to enhance the credibility of the overall deterrent).

Whatever the tactics employed, the basic aims of chemical deterrence need not be compromised. Neither NATO nor the United States needs to match the chemical warfare capability of the Soviet Union. A more effective deterrent would not require parity on a round-for-round basis or even in types of chemical weapons. Nor would it require a larger agent stockpile (the current proposals of the US Joint Chiefs of Staff would seek to replace the present, largely ineffective, stockpile with a smaller but more military useful one). Nor is the concept designated to create a large number of casualties *per se*, although retaliation could inflict some casualties, and delay all recovery tasks including casualty care, if used to exploit the gaps in protective posture opened up by conventional attacks.[44] But the punitive effects of the threatened retaliation would be of less importance than the capacity 'to delay, disrupt and dilute Soviet combat power'.[45] By threatening to force the Soviets into their protective posture and to divert personnel from their primary tasks to largely defensive duties, NATO would be posing a serious counter to chemical attack and a more credible deterrent.

Ultimately the aim is to spare Europe or, ideally, anywhere else from the effects of chemical warfare. In trying to realise this objective disarmament and deterrence have been pursued, in various forms, and complemented by the maintenance of anti-chemical defences. Neither approach can now be set aside without adverse political repercussions nor are they necessarily contradictory (deterrence will remain necessary until a Convention can be agreed, and throughout the ten year period of the Convention). Their importance is underlined by the possibility of chemical warfare recurring. Although chemical weapons have only been used fitfully over the past seventy years, and have not won many battles (comparatively few weapons ever have in and of themselves), they could be employed effectively with other forms of weaponry, especially against ill-prepared and ill-equipped troops or troops heavily dependent upon civilian support. So long as the threat persists, the maintenance of a credible deterrent and extensive anti-chemical defences will be essential.

APPENDIX 1: SOME PROPERTIES OF CHEMICAL WARFARE AGENTS

US Army Code	Agents	Freezing point °C	Volatility 20°C, mg/m³	Casualty-producing dosages ICt 50 [a], mg-min/m³
	Lung irritants			
CL	Chlorine	−102	3 000 000	1 800
CG	Carbonyl chloride (phosgene)	−128	6 370 000	1 600
PS	Trichloronitromethane (chloropicrin)	−69	170 000	
DP	Trichloromethyl chloroformate (diphosgene)	−57	54 300	1 600
	Blood gases			
AC	Hydrogen cyanide	−14	891 000	Varies with concentration approx 2 000–5 000
CK	Cyanogen chloride	−7	2 600 000	7 000
	Vesicants			
HD	*Bis* (2-chloroethyl) sulphide (mustard)	14	610	200 (eye injury) 1000 (skin absorption)
	2-chlorovinyl dichloroarsine (lewisite)	−18	2 300	300 (eye injury)
HN-3	*Tris* (2-chloroethyl)amine (nitrogen mustard)	−4	100	200 (eye injury) 1000 (skin absorption)
HL	Mustard–lewisite mixture	−14	2 730	200 (eye injury) 1500–2000 (skin absorption)

Approx. lethal dosages LCt 50 [b]

Percutaneous, mg/man	Inhalation, mg-min/m³	Rate of action
n.a.	19 000	Rapid. Lethal on 30 mins exposure
n.a.	3 200	Delayed usually for 3 hrs or more for incapacitating or lethal effects
n.a.	20 000	Produces tears in seconds. Lethal concentrations are effective on 10 mins exposure.
n.a.	3 200	Delayed usually for 3 hrs or more for incapacitating or lethal effects.
n.a.	2 000 at 200 mg/m³ conc. / 4 500 at 150 mg/m³ conc.	Very rapid. Death within 15 mins. of receiving a lethal dosage.
n.a.	11 000	Produces tears in few secs; casualty effects 30 mins–1 hr; lethal effects within 15 mins.
4 500	1 500	Delayed – usually 4–6 hrs before first symptoms appear (sometimes up to 24 hrs)
n.a.	1 300	Blistering within 30 mins. Lethal concentrations are fatal in 10 mins.
n.a.	1 500	Most symptoms delayed 4–6 hrs but in some cases lacrymation, eye irritation and photophobia develop immediately.
above 10 000	1 500	Produces stinging and redness of skin within 30 mins; blistering delayed about 13 hrs.

NOTES

[a] ICt 50 is the approximate dosage which will produce casualties among about half the people exposed to the agent, if they lack any kind of protection: mg-min/m³

[b] LCt 50 is the approximate dosage which will kill about half the people exposed to the agent, if they are unprotected.

APPENDIX 1 – continued

US Army Code	Agents	Freezing point °C	Volatility 20°C, mg/m^3	Casualty-producing dosages ICt 50[a], $mg\text{-}min/m^3$
	Nerve agents			
GA	Ethyl NN-dimethyl-phosphoramidocyanidate (tabun)	−50	400	300
GB	Isopropyl methylphosphono-fluoridate (sarin)	−56	12 100	75
GD	1,2,2-trimethylpropyl methylphosphonofluoridate (soman)	−80	2 000	35
VX	O-ethyl S-2-diisopropylaminoethyl methylphosphonothiolate		10	5
	Some other casualty-producing agents			
	Saxitoxin (shellfish poison)	n.a.	n.a.	n.a.
	Botulinal toxin A	n.a.	n.a.	n.a.

NOTE This appendix is not meant to be a comprehensive list. Recent reports suggest that the Soviets may be developing a new liquid agent, possibly a thickened form of soman, with a view to permeating NATO's NBC suits, and new toxins, prepared as particulates, in the hope of passing through NATO's gas mask filters. D. Campbell 'Thatcher goes for Nerve Gas', *New Statesman* (11 January 1985), p. 9 and J. D. Douglass and H. Richard Lukens, 'The Expanding Arena of Chemical–Biological Warfare', p. 74.

| Approx. lethal dosages LCt 50 b | | Rate of action |
Percutaneous, mg/man	Inhalation, mg-min/m³	
1 000	400	Very rapid. Incapacitating effects 1–10 mins; lethal effects 10–15 mins.
1 700	100	Very rapid. Incapacitating effects 1–10 mins; lethal effects 2–15 mins.
1 000	70	Very rapid. Incapacitating effects 1–10 mins; lethal effects 1–15 mins.
15	36	Very rapid. Incapacitating effects 1–10 mins; lethal effects 4–24 hrs.
n.a.	5	Lethal effects may occur within 15 mins to 1 hr.
n.a.	0.02	Lethal effects in 12 to 24 hrs.

SOURCES M. Sartori, *The War Gases: Chemistry and Analysis* (London: Churchill, 1939); Department of the Army Technical Manual TM3–215 and Department of the Air Force Manual AFM 255–7; *Military Chemistry and Chemical Agents* (Washington DC, 1956); SIPRI, *The Problem of Chemical and Biological Warfare* vol. 1, pp. 86–7 and vol. II, pp. 42–3; Departments of the Army and Air Force TM3–200, *Guide to Chemical and Gas Warfare* (Washington DC, 1958); C. Wachtel, *Chemical Warfare* (New York: Chemical Publishing Co., 1941); A. M. Prentiss, *Chemicals at War* (New York: McGraw-Hill, 1937); United Nations General Assembly, *Report of the Secretary-General on Chemical and Bacteriological (Biological) Weapons and the Effects of their Possible Use*, A/7575 (1 July 1969) p. 66.

APPENDIX 2: PROPERTIES OF SOME HARASSING AND INCAPACITATING AGENTS

US Army Code	Agents	Freezing point °C	Volatility 20°C, mg/m³	Casualty-producing dosages ICt 50, mg-min/m³	Approx. lethal dosage Inhalation LCt 50, mg-min/m³
	Vomiting gases				
DA	Diphenylchloroarsine	44	7	15	15 000
DM	10-chloro-5, 10 dihydro-phenarsazine (adamsite)	195	<1	22 (for 1 minute exposure) 8 (for 60 minutes exposure)	30 000
DC	Diphenylcyanoarsine	30	3	25	10 000
PD	Phenyldichloroarsine	−16	404	16 as a vomiting gas 1800 as a blistering gas	2 600
	Tear Gases				
CN	Chloroacetophenone	55	105	80	11 000
CA	Bromobenzylcyanide (BBC)	25	130	30	4 000
CS	2-Chlorobenzalmalononitrile	95	10	10	25 000
	Incapacitating Agents				
BZ		190		110	n.a.

SOURCES M. Sartori, *The War Gases: Chemistry and Analysis* (1939); Dept. of the Army Technical Manual TM3-215 and Department of The Air Force Manual AFM 255–7, *Military Chemistry and Chemical Agents* (1956); SIPRI, *The Problem of Chemical and Biological Warfare*, vol. 1, pp. 86–7, vol. 2, p. 45; Departments of the Army and the Air Force TM3-200, *Guide to Chemical and Gas Warfare* (1958); *Report of the Enquiry into the Medical and Toxicological Aspects of CS* (Orthochlorobenzylidene Malononitrile) Cmnd 4775 (1970–1), xxi, p. 5.

APPENDIX 3: THE PERSISTENCY OF SELECTED CHEMICAL WARFARE AGENTS

Agent	Sunny, light breeze around 15°C	Weather conditions Windy and rainy, around 10°C	Calm, sunny, lying snow, around −10°C
Phosgene	few minutes	few minutes	$\frac{1}{4}$–1 hour
Hydrogen cyanide	few minutes	few minutes	1–4 hours
Cyanogen chloride	few minutes	few minutes	$\frac{1}{4}$–4 hours
Mustard gas	2–7 days	12–48 hours	2–8 weeks
Tabun	1–4 days	$\frac{1}{2}$–6 hours	1 day–2 weeks
Sarin	$\frac{1}{4}$–4 hours	$\frac{1}{4}$–1 hour	1–2 days
Soman	$2\frac{1}{2}$–5 days	3–36 hours	1–6 weeks
VX	3–21 days	1–12 hours	1–16 weeks

Sources United Nations General Assembly, *Report of The Secretary-General on Chemical and Bacteriological (Biological) Weapons and the Effects of Their Possible Use*, A/7575 (1 July 1969), p. 66; SIPRI, *The Problem of Chemical and Biological Warfare*, vol. 2, p. 130.

Notes and References

1 INTRODUCTION

1. J. B. S. Haldane, *Callinicus – A Defence of Chemical Warfare* (London: Kegan Paul, 1925) pp. 28–38.
2. H. Brown, Hearing before the Committee on Armed Services United States Senate, *Chemical Warfare*, 96th Congress, second session (4 September, 1980) p. 14.
3. Brig.-Gen. J. H. Rothschild, *Tomorrow's Weapons* (New York: McGraw-Hill, 1964) pp. 75–6.
4. S(tockholm) I(nternational) P(eace) R(esearch) I(nstitute), *The Problem of Chemical and Biological Warfare*, vol. 2, 'CB Weapons Today' (Stockholm: Almqvist & Wiksell, 1973) pp. 37–40, 64–72, 124–5; United Nations General Assembly, *Report of the Secretary-General on Chemical and Bacteriological (Biological) Weapons and the Effects of Their Possible Use*, A/7575 (1 July 1969) p. 8.
5. J. D. Douglass and H. Richard Lukens, 'The Expanding Arena of Chemical–Biological Warfare', *Strategic Review*, vol. 12, no. 4 (Fall, 1984), pp. 71–80.
6. J. Perry Robinson, 'Chemical Weapons', *CBW Chemical and Biological Warfare*, ed. by S. Rose (London: G. Harrap, 1968) p. 20.
7. *Report of the enquiry into the Medical and Toxicological Aspects of CS (Orthochlorobenzylidene Malononitrile)*, part ii, Cmnd 4775 (1971) pp. 16–17.
8. SIPRI, *The Problem of Chemical and Biological Warfare*, vol. 2, pp. 47–8.
9. Ibid., pp. 50–2; Brig.-Gen. J. H. Rothschild, *Tomorrow's Weapons*, pp. 36–8.
10. Department of the Army Technical Manual TM3-215 and Department of the Air Force Manual AFM 255-7, *Military Chemistry and Chemical Agents* (August 1956) pp. 26–9.
11. Ibid., pp. 22–6.
12. M. Meselson and J. Perry Robinson, 'Chemical Warfare and Chemical Disarmament', *Scientific American*, vol. 242, no. 4 (1980) p. 35; M. Meselson, statement included in Hearings before the Committee on Armed Services United States Senate, *Department of Defense Authorization for Appropriations for Fiscal Year 1983*, 97th Congress, second session (22 March 1982) p. 5062.

13. R. L. Wagner and T. S. Gold, 'Why We Can't Avoid Developing Chemical Weapons', *Defense 82* (July 1982) p. 7.
14. C. J. Dick, 'The Soviet Chemical and Biological Warfare Threat', *Journal of the Royal United Service Institute for Defence Studies*, vol. 126, no. 1 (March 1981) p. 48.
15. SIPRI, *The Problem of Chemical and Biological Warfare*, vol. 2, p. 140.
16. Brig. Gen. J. H. Rothschild, *Tomorrow's Weapons*, p. 69.
17. United Nations General Assembly, *Report of the Secretary-General* (1 July 1969) pp. 71–4, 80–1, 83–4.
18. Ibid., p. 86.
19. M. Meselson and J. Perry Robinson, 'Chemical Warfare and Chemical Disarmament', p. 38.
20. H. Brown, Hearings before the Committee on Armed Services United States Senate, *Department of Defense Authorization for Appropriations for Fiscal Year 1980*, 96th Congress, first session (25 January 1979) p. 97.
21. H. Kissinger, *Years of Upheaval* (Boston: Little, Brown, 1982) p. 134.

2 CHEMICAL WARFARE 1914–18

1. A. M. Prentiss, *Chemicals in War* (New York: McGraw-Hill, 1937) p. 656.
2. V. Lefebure, *The Riddle of the Rhine: Chemical Strategy in Peace and War* (London: Collins, 1921) pp. 109–10.
3. Thucydides, *History of the Peloponnesian War*, trans. by C. F. Smith, 4 vols (London: Heinemann, 1919) vol. 1, book 2, LXXVII, p. 401; and SIPRI, *The Problem of Chemical and Biological Warfare*, vol. 1, pp. 125–6.
4. W. D. Miles, 'I. Admiral Cochrane's Plans for Chemical Warfare; II The Chemical Shells of Lyon Playfair', *Armed Forces Chemical Journal*, vol. 11, no. 6 (1957) pp. 22–3, 40; and 'The Idea of Chemical Warfare in Modern Times', *Journal of the History of Ideas*, vol. 31 (April–June 1970) pp. 300–3; C. Lloyd, *Lord Cochrane Seaman – Radical – Liberator* (London: Longman, 1947) pp. 105 ff; and J. B. Poole, 'A Sword Undrawn: Chemical Warfare and the Victorian Age, Part 1', *The Army Quarterly and Defence Journal*, vol. 106, no. 4 (October 1976) pp. 463–9.
5. *The Reports to the Hague Conferences of 1899 and 1907*, ed. by J. B. Scott (Oxford: Oxford University Press, 1917) pp. 170, 176–7.
6. Maj-Gen. C. H. Foulkes, *'Gas!' The Story of the Special Brigade* (Edinburgh: Blackwood, 1934) p. 23.
7. J. Davidson Pratt, 'Historical Account of Offensive Chemical Warfare Research up to the Date of the Formation of the Chemical Advisory Committee in February 1916', P(ublic) R(ecord) O(ffice), MUN 5/385/1650/9.
8. U. Trumpener, 'The Road to Ypres: The Beginnings of Gas Warfare in World War I', *Journal of Modern History*, vol. 47 (September 1975), pp. 463–4.
9. Ibid., p. 462; and J. B. Poole, 'A Sword Undrawn: Chemical Warfare and the Victorian Age, Part II', *The Army Quarterly and Defence Journal*, vol. 107, no. 1 (January, 1977) p. 91.

10. W. S. Churchill, *The World Crisis 1915* (London: Thornton Butterworth, 1923) pp. 81–3; The Earl of Dundonald, *My Army Life* (London: Arnold, 1926) pp. 331–8.
11. C. H. Foulkes, *'Gas!' The Story of the Special Brigade*, p. 23.
12. U. Trumpener, 'The Road to Ypres', pp. 464–9; and SIPRI, *The Problem of Chemical and Biological Warfare*, vol. 1, pp. 131–2.
13. Major S. J. M. Auld, *Gas and Flame* (New York: Doran, 1918) pp. 21–5; U. Trumpener, 'The Road to Ypres', p. 473; Kronprinz Rupprecht von Bayern, *Mein Kriegstagebuch*, ed. by Eugen von Frauenholz, 3 vols. (Berlin, 1929) vol. 1, pp. 304–5.
14. Gen. E. von Falkenhayn, *General Headquarters 1914–1916 and its Critical Decisions* (London: Hutchinson, 1919) p. 84, 86–7. See also Brig-Gen. J. E. Edmonds and Capt. G. C. Wynne, *History of the Great War: Military Operations: France and Belgium, 1915*, vol. 1 (London: Macmillan, 1927) pp. 188–92.
15. J. E. Edmonds and G. C. Wynne, *History of the Great War*, vol. 1, pp. 176–92; C. R. M. F. Cruttwell, *A History of the Great War* (Oxford: Oxford University Press, 1934) p. 155; and 'An Account of German Cloud Gas Attacks on British Front in France', PRO, WO 32/5483.
16. E. von Falkenhayn, *General Headquarters 1914–1916*, p. 85. See also J. E. Edmonds and G. C. Wynne, *History of the Great War*, vol. 1, p. 183.
17. J. E. Edmonds and G. C. Wynne, *History of the Great War*, vol. 1, pp. 163–5.
18. 'An Account of German Cloud Gas Attacks on British Front in France', PRO, WO 32/5483.
19. J. E. Edmonds and G. C. Wynne, *History of the Great War*, vol. 1, pp. 215–20.
20. C. R. M. F. Cruttwell, *A History of the Great War*, pp. 157–8; V. Lefebure, *The Riddle of the Rhine*, pp. 33–4; and B. H. Liddell Hart, *A History of the War 1914–1918* (London: Faber & Faber, 1930), pp. 247–8.
21. The reports of Lieut. C. G. Douglas and Maj-Gen. H. S. M. Wilson, 25 and 29 May 1915, PRO, WO 142/99; and 'An Account of German Cloud Gas Attacks on British Front in France', PRO, WO 32/5483.
22. Sq. Ldr. E. D. Kingsley, 6 May 1915, Kingsley Mss, I(mperial) W(ar) M(useum), p. 27.
23. Sgt. E. W. Cotton, 24 May 1915, Cotton diary, IWM.
24. Sir J. French to Winifred Bennett, 27 April 1915, French Mss, IWM.
25. Lord Kitchener to Sir J. French, 24 April 1915, quoted in Maj-Gen. Foulkes, *'Gas!' The Story of the Special Brigade*, p. 19.
26. *The Times*, 29 April 1915, p. 9.
27. H. C. Peterson, *Propaganda for War* (New York: Kennikat Press, 1968), p. 63.
28. J. M. Read, *Atrocity Propaganda 1914–1919* (New Haven: Yale University Press, 1941), pp. 195–9. See also C. R. M. F. Cruttwell, *A History of the Great War*, pp. 153, 438.
29. Sir J. French to Lord Kitchener, 23 April 1914 quoted in Maj-Gen. C. H. Foulkes, *'Gas!' The Story of the Special Brigade*, p. 19.
30. Sir H. Wilson to his wife, n.d., quoted in Sir C. E. Callwell, *Field-Marshal*

Sir Henry Wilson, His Life and Diaries, 2 vols. (London: Cassell, 1927) vol. 1, p. 223.

31. R. Donald to Lloyd George, 6 May 1915, enclosing a letter from a colonel at the front, Lloyd George Mss, C/4/8/10. See also H. H. Asquith to the King, 27 and 29 April and 5 May 1915, PRO, CAB 37/127 and /128.

32. *The Times*, 6 May 1915, p. 9.

33. J. E. Edmonds, *History of the Great War*, vol. 2, p. 151–2; and Maj-Gen. C. H. Foulkes, 'Chemical Warfare in 1915', *Armed Forces Chemical Journal*, vol. 15, no. 6 (1961) p. 4.

34. Gen. E. Ludendorff, *My War Memories 1914–1918*, 2 vols. (London: Hutchinson, 1919) vol. 1, p. 141.

35. SIPRI, *The Problem of Chemical and Biological Warfare*, vol. 1, pp. 31–2; and N. Stone, *The Eastern Front 1914–1917* (London: Hodder & Stoughton, 1975) p. 112.

36. Sir J. French to the War Office, 16 June 1915, PRO, WO 32/5170.

37. Sir D. Haig, First Army Conference, 6 September 1915 and diary, 16 September 1915, Haig Mss, N(ational) L(ibrary of) S(cotland), vol. 174; J. E. Edmonds, *History of the Great War*, vol. 2, pp. 152–4.

38. *The Life of General Lord Rawlinson of Trent from his journals and letters*, ed. by Maj-Gen. Sir F. Maurice (London: Cassell, 1928) pp. 138–9.

39. J. E. Edmonds, *History of the Great War*, vol. 2, pp. 172–3, 178–80; E. von Falkenhayn, *General Headquarters 1914—1916*, p. 168; Maj-Gen. C. H. Foulkes, '*Gas!*', pp. 72–6; W. G. Macpherson *et al.*, *History of the Great War: Medical Services Diseases of War* (London: HMSO, 1923) vol. 2, p. 316.

40. 'Diary of Development of British Respirator', PRO, WO 32/5483. See also L. F. Haber, 'Gas Warfare 1915–1945. The Legend and the Facts'. (Stevenson Lecture, 1976) p. 7.

41. R. Harris and J. Paxman, *A Higher Form of Killing: The Secret Story of Gas and Germ Warfare* (London: Chatto & Windus, 1982) p. 17.

42. S. J. M. Auld, *Gas and Flame*, p. 63.

43. Lt-Gen. Sir G. F. N. Macready to the Chief of the French Military Mission, 17 January 1916, PRO, WO 142/99. See also 'An Account of German Cloud Gas Attacks on British Front in France', PRO, WO 32/5483; and Lt-Gen. C. Fergusson, 'Gas Attack on VI Corps', 22 December 1915, PRO, WO 142/99.

44. 'An Account of German Cloud Gas Attacks on British Front in France', PRO, WO 32/5483; A. T. Sloggett, 'Memorandum on Gas Poisoning in Warfare with notes on its Pathology and Treatment', 20 July 1916, PRO, WO 142/101; A. M. Prentiss, *Chemicals in War*, pp. 47–8, 154–7; and SIPRI, *The Problem of Chemical and Biological Warfare*, vol. 1, p. 43.

45. Report by a Vizefeldwebel, 8 April 1917, Hodgkin Mss, IWM.

46. This became the prevalent mode of British attack from 24 June 1916 to 19 March 1917 when 110 cloud attacks were made. C. H. Foulkes, 'Report on the Activity of the Special Brigade During the War', 19 December 1918, Foulkes Mss, Liddell Hart Centre for Military Archives, University of London, King's College, J-30. For a critical account of cylinder attacks see Gen. G. de S. Barrow to Adviser, GHQ, 18 August 1916, PRO, WO 158/270. See also Gen. E. Ludendorff, *My War Memories*, vol. 1, pp. 141–2 and C. H. Foulkes, '*Gas!*', pp. 176–8.

47. V. Lefebure, *The Riddle of the Rhine*, p. 38.
48. R. Hansilan, *Der chemische Krieg*, 3rd ed. (Berlin, 1937) pp. 20–3.
49. Capt. W. Miles, *History of the Great War: Military Operations: France and Belgium, 1916* (London: Macmillan, 1938) vol. 2, p. 203; and A. M. Prentiss, *Chemicals in War*, p. 656.
50. A. M. Prentiss, *Chemicals in War*, pp. 352–3.
51. Quoted in V. Lefebure, *The Riddle of the Rhine*, p. 58.
52. Capt. C. G. Douglas, 'Gas Shell Bombardment of Ypres 12/13 July 1917', 17 July 1917, PRO, WO 142/99.
53. W. G. Macpherson *et al.*, *History of the Great War*, vol. 2, pp. 294, 304–8.
54. Gen. E. Ludendorff, *My War Memories*, vol. 2, pp. 579, 597. See also Brig-Gen. H. Hartley, 'Chemical Warfare', n.d., PRO, WO 188/213.
55. Brig-Gen. Amos A. Fries and Maj. C. J. West, *Chemical Warfare* (New York: McGraw Hill, 1921) p. 388 and Maj-Gen. J. F. C. Fuller, *The Conduct of War 1789–1961* (London: Eyre Methuen, 1972) p. 174.
56. V. Lefebure, *The Riddle of the Rhine*, p. 77.
57. A. M. Prentiss, *Chemicals in War*, p. 683.
58. Ibid., pp. 658–9.
59. Ibid., p. 656.
60. Request from General I. Polivanoff, 16 February 1916, Kitchener Mss, PRO, 30/57/67; and A. M. Prentiss, *Chemicals in War*, p. 656.
61. J. K. Senior, 'The Manufacture of Mustard Gas in World War I', *Armed Forces Chemical Journal*, vol. 12, no. 5 (1958) pp. 16–17, 29.
62. Capt. H. M. Roberts, 'Report on the Manufacture of HS at HM Factory Avonmouth', December 1918, PRO, WO 142/225.
63. S. J. M. Auld, *Gas and Flame*, p. 25.
64. D. Winter, *Death's Men: Soldiers of the Great War* (London: Penguin, 1978) p. 126. See also Maj-Gen. C. H. Foulkes *'Gas!' The Story of the Special Brigade*, pp. 178, 184–5.
65. Brig. A. E. Hodgkin, diaries, 3 November 1916 and 8 February 1917, Hodgkin Mss, IWM.
66. A. E. Hodgkin, diaries, 24 January, 17 July and 5 October 1917, Hodgkin Mss, IWM.
67. S. J. M. Auld, *Gas and Flame*, pp. 59–60.
68. Ibid., p. 167; Sir D. Haig, diary, 1 May 1916, Haig Mss, NLS; and Lt-Col. C. G. Douglas, 'Note on the Total Casualties in the British Forces by Gas Warfare', 17 January 1919, Foulkes Mss, J-43.
69. A. E. Hodgkin, diary, 6 November 1917, Hodgkin Mss, IWM.
70. V. Lefebure, *The Riddle of the Rhine*, p. 124.
71. A. E. Hodgkin, diary, 14 April 1918, Hodgkin Mss, IWM.
72. W. G. Macpherson *et al.*, *History of the Great War*, vol. 2, pp. 288, 299.
73. J. F. C. Fuller, *The Conduct of War*, pp. 173–4. See also C. R. M. F. Cruttwell, *A History of the Great War*, pp. 431–3; L. F. Haber, 'Gas Warfare 1915–1945', p. 10; J. E. Edmonds and Lt-Col. R. Maxwell-Hyslop, *Military Operations France and Belgium 1918*, vol. 5 (London: HMSO, 1947) p. 606; SIPRI, *Problem of Chemical and Biological Warfare*, vol. 1, pp. 140–1.
74. Col. H. L. Gilchrist, *A Comparative Study of World War Casualties from Gas and other weapons* (Washington: US Government Printing Office, 1931) p. 47.

75. Lt-Col. C. G. Douglas, 'Note on the Total Casualties in the British Forces by Gas Warfare', 17 January 1919, Foulkes Mss, J-43.

76. A. M. Prentiss, *Chemicals in War*, p. 680.

77. Ibid., pp. 670–1. See also H. Hartley, 'Chemical Warfare', n.d., PRO, WO 188/213; J. B. S. Haldane, *Callinicus*, pp. 27–8; C. R. M. F. Cruttwell, *A History of the Great War*, pp. 153–4; J. F. C. Fuller, *The Conduct of War*, p. 174.

78. R. Harris and J. Paxman, *A Higher Form of Killing*, pp. 3, 34–6; and S. M. Hersh, *Chemical and Biological Warfare* (New York: Bobbs-Merrill, 1968) p. 5.

79. R. Hansilan, *Der chemische Krieg*, 2nd ed. (1927), p. 12; U. Trumpener, 'The Road to Ypres', p. 460.

80. 'Ministry of Pensions Figures showing the Number of Men Suffering from the After Effects of War Gases', 18 May 1926, PRO, WO 188/265; D. Winter, *Death's Men*, p. 252.

81. N. Stone, *The Eastern Front 1914–1917*, pp. 112, 228.

82. J. E. Edmonds and Lt-Col. R. Maxwell-Hyslop, *History of the Great War*, vol. 5, p. 606.

83. C. R. M. F. Cruttwell, *A History of the Great War*, p. 154.

84. Brig-Gen. H. Hartley, 'Chemical Warfare', n.d., PRO, WO 188/213.

3 THE FAILURE OF DISARMAMENT

1. Maj-Gen. Sir A. Lynden-Bell to Maj-Gen. C. H. Harington, 25 March 1919, enclosing 'Note by the General Staff on the Use of Gas', PRO, WO 32/5180.

2. W. S. Churchill to Maj-Gen. C. H. Harington, 28 March 1919, PRO, WO 32/5180.

3. *The Times*, 21 June 1922, p. 12. See also *Papers Relating to the F(oreign) R(elations of the) U(nited) S(tates)*, The Paris Peace Conference 1919, vol. 4 (Washington: US Government Printing Office, 1943) p. 362.

4. Ibid., vol. 4, pp. 561–2.

5. Maj. V. Lefebure, 'Chemical Warfare', *The Times*, 13 September 1921, p. 6; 'Chemical Disarmament', *The National Review*, vol. LXXVIII (Sept. 1921–Feb. 1922) pp. 51–9; 'Chemical Warfare: the possibility of its control', *Transactions of the Grotius Society*, vol. VII (1921) pp. 153–166.

6. 'Draft of the report of the Committee on Chemical Warfare Organisation', Foulkes Mss, J 18.

7. War Cabinet minutes, 16 October 1919, PRO, CAB 23/12 and Secretary of the C(ommittee of) I(mperial) D(efence), 'Chemical Warfare Policy', 5 March 1924, PRO, WO 188/144.

8. A. A. Fries and C. J. West, *Chemical Warfare*, pp. 23, 53–73; and L. P. Brophy and G. J. B. Fisher, *The Chemical Warfare Service: Organizing for War* (Washington: Office of the Chief of Military History, Dept. of the Army, 1959) pp. 3–5.

9. F. J. Brown, *Chemical Warfare: A Study in Restraints* (Princeton: Princeton University Press, 1968) p. 159.

10. Gen. P. C. March, *The Nation at War* (New York: Doubleday, 1932) pp. 333–5.
11. F. J. Brown, *Chemical Warfare*, pp. 73–82.
12. Maj-Gen. C. H. Harington to Churchill, 8 May 1919; Sir A. Lynden-Bell to Harington, 10 May 1919; and W. S. Churchill, minute, 12 May 1919, PRO, WO 32/5185 and WO 32/5184.
13. Sir E. Montagu to Lord Chelmsford, 14 May 1919, Foulkes Mss, J 62.
14. Lord Fisher, 'Gas Warfare', 17 May 1920, PRO, CAB 24/106.
15. Extract from the minutes of the League of Nations committee, 1 June 1920, PRO, WO 32/5185. See also E. M. Spiers, 'Gas and the North-West Frontier', *The Journal of Strategic Studies*, vol. 6, no. 4 (December, 1983) pp. 94–112.
16. 'A Summary of Important Notes and Papers in connection with the Policy of gas warfare in order of dates from 1899' and 'Second Report of the Secretary of the Chemical Warfare Committee', 31 March 1922, p. 7, PRO, WO 188/212 and WO 33/1014.
17. 'First Report of the Secretary of the Chemical Warfare Committee', 31 March 1921, pp. 8 and 21, PRO, WO 33/987B.
18. *The New York Times*, 6 June 1921, p. 1.
19. L. P. Brophy and G. J. B. Fisher, *The Chemical Warfare Service*, pp. 21–2. See also F. J. Brown, *Chemical Warfare*, pp. 87–93, 124–5.
20. *The Times*, 8 September 1921, p. 12.
21. *The Times*, 1 September 1921, p. 9; and J. B. S. Haldane, *Callinicus*.
22. E. M. Spiers, 'Gas and the North-West Frontier', pp. 99–102.
23. Capt. S. J. M. Auld, 'Chemical Warfare', *The Royal Engineers Journal* (February, 1921) pp. 58–9.
24. Col. N. P. McCleland, 'Notes on the Use of Gas in Open Warfare', September 1925 and Comptroller, Chemical Warfare Research, 'Use of Gas in Open Warfare', 15 February 1926, PRO, WO 188/143.
25. Brig. C. H. Foulkes, 'Lecture at Delhi on 16 January 1920 to the Viceroy, Commander-in-Chief and members of the Supreme Council', Foulkes Mss, J63. See also B. H. Liddell Hart, *Paris or the Future of War* (London: Kegan Paul, 1925) pp. 50–5, and *The Remaking of Modern Armies* (London: John Murray, 1927) pp. 80–7; S. J. M. Auld, 'Chemical Warfare', pp. 60–71; Col. J. F. C. Fuller, *The Reformation of War* (London: Hutchinson, 1923) pp. 108–11, 121–35, 154–5; A. A. Fries and C. J. West, *Chemical Warfare*, pp. 435–9.
26. Gen. J. J. Pershing to Sen. W. E. Borah, 10 December 1926, Pershing Mss, Library of Congress, Box 81; and Sir H. Wilson, memoranda on gas warfare, 16 April 1920 and June 1920, PRO, WO 32/5185.
27. *The New York Times*, 8 January 1922, p. 17.
28. *Conference on the Limitation of Armament, Washington November 12, 1921–February 6, 1922* (Washington, 1922) pp. 730, 732, 734, 736. See also the notes in the Pershing Mss, Box 81.
29. A. J. Balfour to Lloyd George, 6 January 1922, PRO, WO 188/144.
30. *Conference on the Limitation of Armament*, p. 748.
31. *FRUS*, 1922, vol. 1, p. 269.
32. F. J. Brown, *Chemical Warfare*, pp. 93–5; Sir R. Horne, 'Gas Warfare', 22 June 1922, and CID, 'Chemical Warfare Policy', 5 March 1924, PRO,

WO 188/144. See also First Report of the Secretary of the Chemical Warfare Committee, 31 March 1921, PRO, WO 33/987B.

33. Gen. F. R. L. Cavan, 'Chemical Warfare Policy', 23 February 1924, PRO, CAB 4/11. See also B. H. Liddell Hart, 'Germany and Gas Tactics', *The Times*, 12 November 1924, p. 15.

34. League of Nations, 'Report of the Temporary Mixed Commission for the Reduction of Armaments', 30 July 1924, A.16 1924. IX, p. 30.

35. League of Nations, *Proceedings of the Conference for the Supervision of the International Trade in Arms and Ammunition and on Implements of War. Held at Geneva, May 4th to June 17th, 1925*. Verbatim report of First Meeting of the General Committee (7 May 1925), Document A. 13. 1925. IX, p. 155.

36. Ibid., Verbatim report of the Seventeenth Meeting (5 June 1925), p. 307 and of the Fourteenth Meeting of the Military, Naval and Air Technical Committee, 26 May 1925, Part II, pp. 532–41.

37. *The New York Times*, 6 June 1925, p. 1; and League of Nations, *Proceedings of the Conference*, Verbatim Report of the Seventeenth Meeting (5 June 1925) p. 314.

38. League of Nations, *Proceedings of the Conference*, pp. 77–84.

39. United States Senate, *Congressional Record*, 69th Congress, 2nd Session, 1926 (LCVIII) p. 152.

40. Ibid., p. 144.

41. *The Times*, 1 May 1929, p. 16.

42. *A Brief History of the Chemical Defence Experimental Establishment, Porton* (March 1961) pp. 17–18. See also R. Harris and J. Paxman, *A Higher Form of Killing*, pp. 46–7.

43. Minutes of 215 and 217 Meetings of the CID, 22 July and 11 November 1926, PRO, CAB 2/4.

44. Minutes of 221 Meeting of the CID, 25 February 1927, PRO, CAB 2/5.

45. Compare R. Harris and J. Paxman, *A Higher Form of Killing*, p. 44 with E. M. Spiers, 'Gas and the North-West Frontier', pp. 94–112.

46. Tenth, Fourteenth and Seventeenth Reports of the C(hemical) W(arfare) (later Defence) and) R(esearch) D(epartment), 31 March 1930, 31 March 1934 and 31 March 1937, PRO, WO 33/1231, 33/1359 and 33/1484.

47. 'Policy with regard to the possible use of gas as a retaliatory measure in war', 23 June 1936, PRO, CAB 4/24.

48. *House of Lords*, Fifth Ser., vol. 71 (11 July 1928) cols. 980–2; See also Seventh report of the CWRD, 31 March 1927, PRO, WO 33/1153.

49. *Parl. Deb.*, Fifth Ser., vol. 229 (9 July 1929) col. 683.

50. G. Woker, 'Chemical and Bacteriological Warfare', in Inter-Parliamentary Union, *What Would be the Character of A New War?* (London: Gollancz, 1933) pp. 368–72; and H. G. Wells, *The Shape of Things to Come* (London: Hutchinson, 1935), p. 132.

51. P. Noel-Baker, *Disarmament* (London: Hogarth Press, 1926) p. 47; H. G. Wells, *The Shape of Things to Come* p. 133; B. Russell, *Which Way to Peace?* (London: M. Joseph, 1936) p. 31. Compare with J. Kendall, *Breathe Freely! The Truth about Poison Gas* (London: G. Bell, 1938) pp. 15, 73.

52. *House of Lords*, Fifth Ser., vol. 71 (11 July 1928) col. 972. See also G. Woker, 'Chemical and Bacteriological Warfare', p. 363 and J. Kendall, *Breathe Freely*, pp. 15–16.
53. G. Woker, 'Chemical and Bacteriological Warfare', p. 356; Viscount Cecil, *The Great Experiment* (London: J. Cape, 1941) pp. 183–4.
54. V. Lefebure, 'Chemical Warfare: The Possibility of Its Control', pp. 156–64; P. Noel-Baker, *Disarmament*, pp. 281–5; and *The Times*, 7 December 1928, p. 10.
55. *Parl. Deb.*, Fifth Ser., vol. 262 (1 March 1932) col. 921. On the disarmament movement, see J. J. Underwood, 'The Roots and Reality of British Disarmament Policy 1932–1934', unpublished PhD thesis (Leeds University, 1977) pp. 3–28.
56. P. Noel-Baker, *The First World Disarmament Conference 1932–33* (Oxford: Pergamon Press, 1979) pp. 69–71, 74–8, 81–2; Sir J. Simon, speech, 8 February 1932, PRO, FO 411/15, no. 6; H. Hoover, 'Disarmament plan', 22 June 1932, *FRUS* (1932) vol. 1, pp. 179–82.
57. H. S. Gibson to W. R. Castle, 10 May 1932, *FRUS* (1932) vol. 1, pp. 120–1.
58. H. L. Stimson to H. R. Wilson, 21 September 1932, *FRUS* (1932) vol. 1, p. 333.
59. *Documents on British Foreign Policy*, Second Series, vol IV (London: HMSO, 1950) pp. 558–65. For the draft convention, see PRO, CAB 24/239, CP 74(33).
60. H. L. Stimson to H. R. Wilson, 12 November 1932, *FRUS* (1932) vol. 1, p. 377.
61. Minutes of 384th meeting of the Army Council, 30 July 1935 and Air Ministry letter, 30 August 1935, PRO, WO 32/4315 and WO 32/3663; T. H. O'Brien, *Civil Defence* (London: HMSO, 1955), pp. 51–2, 58.
62. League of Nations, Series of Publications 1936, C.201.M.126., 1936, VII, especially appendices 3 and 6–9.
63. *Il Gironale d'Italia*, 9 April 1936, p. 1. See also letter from the Italian Government to the Council and Members of the League, 30 April 1936, C.208.M.130., 1936, VII.
64. *The Times*, 20 April 1936, p. 8.
65. League of Nations, *Official Journal* (April 1936), 91 session of the Council, 10th meeting, 20 April 1936, p. 380.
66. Seventeenth report of the CDRD, 31 March 1937, PRO, WO 33/1484. See also Minutes of 221 Meeting of the CID, 25 February 1927; Ninth report of the CWRD, 31 March 1929; and 'Offensive Gas Warfare Methods', Enclosure 45A, 7 September 1936, PRO, CAB 2/5; WO 33/1204; WO 32/3663. See also H. Ochsner, *History of German Chemical Warfare in World War II Part I the Military Aspect* (Historical Office of the Chief of the Chemical Corps, 1949) p. 15.
67. Enclosure 45A, and the Nineteenth report of the CDRD, 31 December 1938, PRO, WO 32/3663 and WO 33/1634.
68. Ibid., and League of Nations, *Official Journal*, 102 and 103 sessions, 19 September and 30 November 1938, pp. 863–65 and 878–81.
69. Eighth and Nineteenth reports of CWRD, and CDRD, 31 March 1928 and 31 December 1938, PRO, WO 33/174 and WO 33/1634.

70. T. H. O'Brien, *Civil Defence.*, pp. 58–9, 67–71, 76–82, 100–1, 230–3.
71. Seventeenth and Nineteenth reports of the CDRD, 31 March 1937 and 31 December 1938, PRO, WO 33/1484 and 33/1634.
72. Minutes of the 280 meeting of the CID, 10 July 1936 and A. Duff Cooper to Sir C. Deverell, 26 November 1936, PRO, CAB 2/6 and WO 32/3663. See also Col. Henry Pownall, diary, 9 July 1936, *The Diaries of Lieutenant-General Sir Henry Pownall*, ed. B. Bond (London: Leo Cooper, 1972) vol. 1, p. 115.
73. Minutes 5 and 6, and Sir C. Deverell, 'Development of Gas Weapons and Apparatus for Offensive Purposes', 3 November 1936, PRO, WO 32/3663; and P. Harris, 'British Preparations for Offensive Chemical Warfare 1935–39', *Journal of the Royal United Services Institute for Defence Studies*, vol. 125, no. 2 (June 1980) p. 58.
74. Enclosure 62A, 13 April 1937; Minutes 64, 73 and 121, 7 May and 9 July 1937, 2 November 1938; Enclosure 91A, 7 January 1938, PRO, WO 32/3663.
75. Although phosgene was considered as a useful charging for aircraft bombs. 'Memorandum on the value of Phosgene as a charging in Air Force and Army Weapons', CDRD report, 11 December 1939, PRO, AIR 2/8658.
76. 114 meeting of the T(reasury) I(nter) S(ervice) C(ommittee), 16 December 1937, PRO, T 161/1321.
77. 115 meeting of the TISC, 21 December 1937, PRO, T 161/1321.
78. 'The Manufacture of Toxic Gas for Use in War', CID Paper 1465–B, 26 July, 1938, PRO, CAB 4/28.
79. 175 and 201 meetings of the TISC, 21 October 1938 and 6 February 1939, PRO, T 161/1327 and T 161/1330. See also 'Memorandum on the Position in the Event of an Early Gas Blitz', 19 February 1941, Weir Mss, Churchill College, Cambridge, 20/16.
80. Anglo-French conversations on chemical warfare 1939', PRO, WO 193/740.
81. Seventeenth report of the CDRD, 31 March 1937, PRO, WO 33/1484. See also Brown, *Chemical Warfare*, pp. 149–56.
82. H. L. Stimson, memorandum, 25 May 1932, *FRUS* (1932) vol. 1, p. 182.
83. 'The Manufacture of Toxic gas for Use in War', CID Paper 1465–B, 26 July 1938, PRO, CAB 4/28.
84. A. Chayes, 'An Inquiry into the Workings of Arms Control Agreements', *Harvard Law Review*, vol. 85, no. 5 (March 1972) p. 907; and J. P. Perry Robinson, 'Chemical Arms Control and the Assimilation of Chemical Weapons', *International Journal*, vol. XXXVI, no. 3 (Summer 1981) p. 520.

4 AVOIDING CHEMICAL WARFARE 1939–45

1. SIPRI, *The Problem of Chemical and Biological Warfare*, vol. 1, pp. 294–335.
2. 'Notification by the British Government to the German Government on

the Outbreak of War Relative to the Geneva Protocol', PRO, WO 193/711 and *The Times*, 2 September 1939, p. 9.

3. 'Review of the Effects of the Offensive Use of Chemical Warfare in a War Such as is Envisaged in the European Appreciation, 1939', p. 4, PRO, WO 193/713. *A Brief History of . . . Porton*, p. 23.

4. 'Interrogation of German Air Ministry (OKL) Technical Personnel Luftwaffe Lager, near Kiel', B(ritish) I(ntelligence) O(bjectives) S(ub-Committee), Report No. 9, pp. 96, 101, 105 and 109.

5. 'Interrogation of Certain German Personalities Connected with Chemical Warfare', BIOS, Report No. 542, pp. 22–3.

6. F. J. Brown, *Chemical Warfare*, pp. 238–41; and SIPRI, *The Problem of Chemical and Biological Warfare*, vol. 1, p. 303.

7. 'Interrogation of German CW Personnel at Heidelberg and Frankfurt', BIOS, Report No. 41, pp. 9 and 11.

8. H. Ochsner, *History of German Chemical Warfare: Pt. I*, p. 15.

9. Col. V. Pozdnyakov, 'The Chemical Arm', *The Soviet Army*, ed. B. H. Liddell Hart (London: Weidenfeld & Nicolson, 1956) pp. 384–90.

10. SIPRI, *The Problem of Chemical and Biological Warfare*, vol. 1, pp. 290–1; 'Chemical Warfare–Paris Area', C(ombined) I(ntelligence) O(bjectives) S(ub-Committee) II/1.

11. 'The manufacture of CW materials by the Japanese', BIOS/JAP/PR/395, pp. 2–3.

12. 'Report on Scientific Intelligence Survey in Japan, September and October 1945', BIOS/JAP/PR/745, pp. 3–4; 'Development of Chemical Warfare Training in the Japanese Air Force', BIOS/JAP/PR/186, pp. 1–2.

13. 'Japanese Chemical Warfare Training Offensive and Defensive', BIOS/JAP/PR/685, p. 18; 'Intelligence Report on Japanese Chemical Warfare, vol. 1 "General Organization Policies and Intentions Tactics" ', BIOS/JAP/PR/1338, p. 17.

14. BIOS/JAP/PR/685, p. 113; BIOS/JAP/PR/745, p. 43; BIOS/JAP/PR/1338, pp. 5, 21; Brig-Gen. J. H. Rothschild, *Tomorrow's Weapons*, p. 92.

15. BOS/JAP/PR/685, p. 114.

16. H. Ochsner, *History of German Chemical Warfare*, pp. 17–18; BIOS/JAP/PR/1338, p. 7; BIOS, Report No. 41, p. 6; 'Examination of Various German Scientists', BIOS, Report No. 44, p. 1.

17. General Staff Committee on Chemical Warfare, Proceedings of 6th meeting, 4 April 1940, PRO, WO 106/1627.

18. C(hiefs) O(f) S(taff), 'Chemical Warfare Policy', 25 April 1940, PRO, WO 193/713.

19. 'The Use of Gas in Home Defence. Memorandum by CIGS', 15 June 1940, PRO, WO 193/732.

20. Maj-Gen. K. M. Loch to Maj-Gen. R. H. Dewing, 16 June 1940, PRO, WO 193/732.

21. Brig. K. N. Crawford, 'Memorandum on the Use of Gas in the Defence of the United Kingdom', 21 June 1940, PRO, WO 193/732.

22. Churchill to Maj-Gen. Ismay, 30 June 1940, PRO, WO 193/732. See also M. Gilbert, *Finest Hour Winston S. Churchill 1939–1941* (London: Heinemann, 1983) pp. 617–8.

23. Gen. Sir J. Dill to Maj-Gen. Ismay, 2 July 1940, PRO, WO 193/732.
24. Churchill to Maj-Gen. Ismay, 14 July 1940, Churchill Mss, 20/13, quoted in M. Gilbert, *Finest Hour*, p. 665.
25. Churchill, minute, 31 August 1940, PRO, PREM 3/88/3.
26. Churchill, minutes, 28 September and 6 October 1940, PRO, PREM 3/88/3.
27. Churchill, marginalia on minute of Sir E. Bridges, 20 November 1940, PRO, PREM 3/88/3.
28. Minutes of the first meeting of the RAF Committee on Chemical Warfare, 14 September 1940; and 'Requirements of Phosgene Filled Bombs and Phosgene Gas Capacity for the Royal Air Force', 25 December 1940, PRO, AIR 2/5117.
29. 'Chemical Warfare', Annex 1, p. 3 and COS (40) 345th meeting, 11 October 1940, PRO, WO 193/711 and CAB 79/7.
30. Correspondence between Director of Plans and Air Officer Commanding-in-Chief, Bomber Command, 19 and 23 January 1941; and 'Contamination of Beaches by Gas Bombing as an Anti Invasion Measure,' 1 November 1941, PRO, AIR 2/5117 and AIR 2/5200.
31. R. Harris and J. Paxman, *A Higher Form of Killing*, p. 115.
32. Gas stocks reports, PRO, PREM 3/88/3.
33. COS (41) 437th meeting, 28 December 1941, PRO, CAB 79/16.
34. 'Chemical Warfare', Annex 1, pp. 4–5, PRO, WO 193/711; 'Memorandum on the Position in the Event of an Early Gas Blitz', 10 February 1941, Weir Mss, 20/16.
35. *A Brief History of . . . Porton*, pp. 23–5.
36. Gas stocks reports, PRO, PREM 3/88/3.
37. COS, meeting, 9 December 1940, PRO, WO 193/725.
38. War Office to Commander in Chief Middle East, 12 December 1940; Lt-Gen. Sir A. Wavell to CIGS, 30 December 1940; COS, meeting, 1 January 1941; War Office to Lt-Gen. Wavell, 4 January 1941, PRO, WO 193/725.
39. W. S. Churchill, *The Second World War*, vol. IV (London: Cassell, 1951), p. 180 and pp. 294–5. See also 8th meeting of Defence Committee, 18 March 1942, PRO, CAB 69/4, DO(42) and COS (42) 94th meeting, 24 March 1942, PRO, CAB 79/19.
40. Minutes of 11 meeting of Defence Committee, 17 April 1942, and COS 'Chemical Warfare. Report', 13 April 1942, PRO, WO 193/711 and PREM 3/88/2.
41. *A Brief History of . . . Porton*, p. 26.
42. COS (42) 101st meeting, 31 March 1942, PRO, CAB 79/20. For an excellent account of British intelligence fears of chemical warfare, see F. H. Hinsley, *British Intelligence in the Second World War: Its Influence on Strategy and Operations*, vol. II (London: HMSO, 1981) pp. 116–23 and Appendix 6.
43. Quoted in COS, 'Chemical Warfare Policy-Association of Commonwealth Governments', 22 February 1944, PRO, PREM 3/89.
44. *The Public Papers and Addresses of Franklin D. Roosevelt*, compiled by S. I. Rosenman (New York: Harpers, 1950) 1942 vol. 'Humanity on the Defensive', p. 258.

45. L. P. Brophy and G. J. B. Fisher, *The Chemical Warfare Service*, pp. 54–7.
46. Ibid., pp. 64–5; and COS, 'Chemical Warfare Policy', PRO, PREM 3/89.
47. L. P. Brophy and G. J. B. Fisher, *The Chemical Warfare Service*, pp. 65–9.
48. Ibid., pp. 70–8.
49. R. Harris and J. Paxman, *A Higher Form of Killing*, pp. 116–17.
50. Records of the United States J(oint) C(hiefs of) S(taff), JCS 825/4, 29 September 1944 and 825/6, 13 June 1945, R.G. 218, National Archives, Washington DC.
51. F. H. Hinsley, *British Intelligence in the Second World War*, pp. 119–20.
52. Ibid., pp. 120–1.
53. COS, report (43)198(0), 19 April 1943, PRO, CAB 121/100 quoted in F. H. Hinsley, *British Intelligence in the Second World War*, p. 121.
54. *The Times*, 22 April 1943, p. 4. See also J. Stalin to Churchill, 19 April 1943 and the report of British gas stocks totalling 32 023 tons by 27 March 1943, PRO, PREM 3/88/3.
55. *The Public Papers and Addresses of Franklin D. Roosevelt*, 1943 'The Tide Turns', pp. 242–3.
56. COS, to Gen. D. D. Eisenhower, 8 September 1943, PRO, PREM 3/88/3.
57. *The Times*, 15 May 1942, p. 3.
58. *The Times*, 23 April, 1943, p. 3.
59. BIOS Report No. 542, p. 23.
60. H. Ochsner, *History of German Chemical Warfare*, p. 22; and 'Examination of Various German Scientists', BIOS Report No. 44, pp. 2–3.
61. A. Hitler, *Mein Kampf* (London: Hutchinson, 1969), p. 183.
62. BIOS Report No. 542, pp 24–5. See also H. Ochsner, *History of German Chemical Warfare*, p. 13; and BIOS Report No. 41, p. 6.
63. H. Ochsner, *History of German Chemical Warfare*, pp. 18, 21–2.
64. Ibid., pp. 22–3; and F. J. Brown, *Chemical Warfare*, p. 244.
65. BIOS Report No. 542, pp. 22–23; and A. Speer, *Inside The Third Reich* (London: Weidenfeld & Nicolson, 1970) p. 413.
66. 'Chemical Warfare Installations in the Munsterlager Area', CIOS, Report No. 31/86, Appendix II, p. 7.
67. B. Tannor, 'C ml C Intelligence in European Theater', *Chemical Corps Journal*, vol. 1, no. 3 (1947) p. 43; SIPRI, *The Problem of Chemical and Biological Warfare*, Vol. 1, p. 304.
68. The International Military Tribunal, *Trial of the Major War Criminals* (Nuremberg, 1948) vol. XVI, p. 527. See also A. Speer, *Inside the Third Reich*, pp. 413–14; and BIOS Report No. 542, p. 25.
69. V. Pozdnyakov, 'The Chemical Arm', pp. 390–1; and CIOS Report No. 31/86, Appendix IV, p. 31.
70. Churchill to Stalin, 9 April 1942, PRO, PREM 3/88/3.
71. Joint Plannning Staff, 'Chemical Warfare in Connection with Crossbow', 5 July 1944 and Chiefs of Staff to Churchill, 5 July 1944, PRO, PREM 3/89.
72. Churchill to H. Morrison, 4 July 1944, PRO, PREM 3/89.
73. Churchill to General Ismay for COS Committee, 6 July 1944, PRO, PREM 3/89.

74. Minutes of 227 meeting of COS Committee, 8 July 1944, PRO, WO 193/712.
75. R. Harris and J. Paxman, *A Higher Form of Killing*, p. 88. See also Lord Hankey to Churchill, 6 December 1941, PRO, PREM 3/65.
76. E. Brown to Churchill, 9 March 1944, PRO, PREM 3/65.
77. 'Military Considerations Affecting the Initiation of Chemical and Other Special Forms of Warfare', PRO, PREM 3/89.
78. Ibid.
79. Ibid.
80. Ibid.
81. Gen. Ismay to Churchill, 28 July 1944, PRO, PREM 3/89.
82. Churchill to Ismay, 29 July 1944, PRO, PREM 3/89.
83. Admiral W. D. Leahy to C. Hull, 22 September 1944, JCS, 176/10.
84. Joint Intelligence Subcommittee, 'The Use of Chemical Warfare by the Germans', 29 January, 19 and 28 February, 28 March, and 23 April 1945, PRO, PREM 3/89.
85. COS meeting, 19 June 1945, PRO, WO 193/724.
86. D. Birdsell, 'United States Army Chemical Warfare Service Logistics Overseas, World War II' (Pennsylvania: University of Pennsylvania, PhD dissertation, 1962), p 489; and F. J. Brown, *Chemical Warfare*, pp. 262–5.
87. 'Chemical Warfare Interim Report', 29 November 1943, PRO, WO 106/4594A.
88. Admiral W. D. Leahy, *I Was There* (London: Gollancz, 1950) p. 512.
89. F. J. Brown, *Chemical Warfare*, pp. 267–9. See also D. E. Lilienthal, *The Journals of David E. Lilienthal*, 2 vols (New York: Harper & Row, 1964) vol. 2, p. 199; H. Riegelman, *Caves of Biak* (New York: Dial Press, 1955) p. 153.
90. JCS 825/5, 5 March 1945.
91. JCS 825/6, 13 June 1945.
92. JCS 825/8, 6 July 1945. See also J. E. van Courtland Moon, 'Chemical Weapons and Deterrence: The World War II Experience', *International Security*, vol. 8, no. 4 (Spring 1984) pp. 24–5.
93. JCS 825/7, 13 June 1945.
94. BIOS/JAP/PR/1338, pp. 8–9; 'Japanese Chemical Warfare Policies and Intentions', BIOS/JAP/PR/724, p. 5; BIOS/JAP/PR/745, p. CW-22-4; BIOS/JAP/PR/685, p. 114.
95. BIOS/JAP/PR/724, pp. 1–4.
96. BIOS/JAP/PR/745, pp. CW-22-3–CW-22-4.
97. BIOS/JAP/PR/1338, pp. 9–11.

5 GAS AND THIRD WORLD CONFLICTS

1. SIPRI, *The Problem of Chemical and Biological Warfare*, Vol. 1, p. 142.
2. Ibid., vol. 1, pp. 162–210; G. Lewy, *America in Vietnam* (New York: Oxford University Press, 1978) pp. 248–66; J. B. Neilands *et al.*, *Harvest of Death: Chemical Warfare in Vietnam and Cambodia* (New York: Free

Press, 1972); W. A. Buckingham, *Operation Ranch Hand: The Air Force and Herbicides in Southeast Asia 1961–1971* (Washington DC: Office of Air Force History, 1982).

3. D. Mack Smith, *Mussolini* (London: Weidenfeld & Nicolson, 1981) pp. 157, 171; K. Holmloe, *Desert Encounter* (London: Harrap, 1936) pp. 239, 261; E. Salerno, *Genocidio in Libia* (Milan, 1979) pp. 50–63.

4. A. Sbacchi, 'Legacy of Bitterness: Poison Gas and Atrocities in the Italo-Ethiopian War 1935–36', *Geneva-Arica*, vol. XIII, no. 2 (1974) p. 31; B. Mussolini, directive, 30 December 1934, *Opera Omnia di Benito Mussolini*, hereafter referred to as OO, ed. by E. and D. Susmel (Florence, 1978) vol. 27, p. 142.

5. League of Nations, Series of Publications 1936, C.201.M.126. 1936. VII, appendix 8.

6. D. Mack Smith, *Mussolini's Roman Empire* (London: Penguin, 1977) p. 60.

7. A. Sbacchi, 'Legacy of Bitterness', pp. 33–5; Maj. P. Murphy, 'Gas in the Italo-Abyssinian Campaign', *Chemical Warfare Bulletin*, vol. 23, no. 1 (January 1937) p. 1; D. K. Clark, *Effectiveness of Toxic Chemicals in the Italo-Ethiopian War*, Tactics Division Staff Paper ORO-SP-87 (Bethesda: Johns Hopkins University, Operations Research Office, 1959) p. 16.

8. D. K. Clark, *Effectiveness of Toxic Chemicals*, p. 16; League of Nations, *Official Journal* (April 1936) p. 371.

9. D. K. Clark, *Effectiveness of Toxic Chemicals*, pp. 16–17; A. J. Barker, *The Civilizing Mission* (New York: Dial Press, 1968) p. 242; G. Martelli, *Italy Against the World* (London: Chatto & Windus, 1937) p. 234.

10. M. Durand, *Crazy Campaign: A Personal Narrative of the Italo-Abyssinian War* (London: Routledge, 1936) p. 18.

11. B. Mussolini to Marshal P. Badoglio, 28 December 1935, OO, vol. 27 p. 306; A. Sbacchi, 'Legacy of Bitterness', pp. 36–9.

12. League of Nations, *Official Journal* (April, 1936) p. 371.

13. J. F. C. Fuller, *The First of the League Wars* (London: Eyre & Spottiswoode, 1936) pp. 38–9; D. K. Clark, *Effectiveness of Toxic Chemicals*, p. 18.

14. G. L. Steer, *Caesar in Abyssinia* (London: Hodder & Stoughton, 1936) p. 8.

15. D. Mack Smith, *Mussolini*, pp. 199–200; B. Mussolini, *My Autobiography* (London: Hutchinson, rev. ed., 1939) p. 337.

16. League of Nations, *Official Journal* (June, 1936) 92nd session of the Council; Annex 1597, C 208.M.130. 1936. VII; Count Ciano to the Secretary-General, League of Nations, *Official Journal* (July 1936) p. 778.

17. A. Sbacchi, 'Legacy of Bitterness', pp. 37–41; G. Martelli, *Italy Against the World*, pp. 256–7; M. Durand, *Crazy Campaign*, pp. 50–1.

18. D. K. Clark, *Effectiveness of Toxic Chemicals*, p. 5.

19. League of Nations, *Official Journal* (July 1936) p. 778; A. J. Barker, *The Civilizing Mission*, pp. 165–72.

20. G. L. Steer, *Caesar in Abyssinia*, pp. 8, 234; H. Matthews, *Eyewitness in Abyssinia* (London: Secker & Warburg, 1937) p. 62; P. Knightley, *The First Casualty* (London: Deutsch, 1975) pp. 173–85.

21. P. Murphy, 'Gas in the Italo-Abyssinian Campaign', p. 4.
22. G. L. Steer, *Caesar in Abyssinia*, pp. 234, 286–7.
23. M. Durand, *Crazy Campaign*, p. 304. See also J. W. S. Macfie, *An Ethiopian Diary. A Record of the British Ambulance Service in Ethiopia* (London: Hodder & Stoughton, 1936) p. 117; and League of Nations, *Official Journal* (April, 1936) p. 371.
24. H. Matthews, *Eyewitness in Abyssinia*, pp. 257–8.
25. Ibid., pp. 258–67.
26. G. L. Steer, *Caesar in Abyssinia*, p. 298.
27. Ibid., p. 276. See also A. J. Barker, *The Civilizing Mission*, pp. 252–60.
28. League of Nations, *Official Journal* (April, 1936) p. 371.
29. J. W. S. Macfie, *An Ethiopian Diary*, p. 78; *John Melly of Ethiopia*, ed. by K. Nelson and A. Sullivan (London: Faber & Faber, 1937) p. 240.
30. Sir S. Barton, telegram no. 174, 10 April 1936, PRO, FO 371/20154.
31. League of Nations, *Official Journal*, Special Supplement No. 151, Records of the Sixteenth Assembly, 30 June 1936, p. 23.
32. B. Mussolini to Marshal R. Graziani, 8 June 1936, OO, vol. 28, p. 265.
33. A. Adamthwaite, *France and the Coming of the Second World War 1936–1939* (London: Frank Cass, 1977) pp. 32–6.
34. *Daily Mail*, 29 April 1936, p. 12. See also D. Waley, *British Public Opinion and the Abyssinian War 1935–6* (London: Maurice Temple Smith, 1975) pp. 73–6.
35. Committee of Imperial Defence, 'The Use of Gas by Italy in the War with Abyssinia', Memorandum by the Chiefs of Staff Sub-Committee, 1 April 1936, PRO, CAB 4/24.
36. CAB 27(36), 6 April 1936, PRO, CAB 23/83.
37. CAB 30(36), 22 April 1936, PRO, CAB 23/84.
38. League of Nations, *Official Journal* (April 1936), pp. 379–87.
39. *Parl. Deb.*, Fifth Ser., vol. 311 (29 April 1936) col. 915.
40. Hsu Long-hsuen and Chang Ming-kai, *History of the Sino-Japanese War (1937–1945)* (Taiwan, 1972) pp. 168–71; Ministry of Information of the Republic of China, *China After Five Years of War* (London: Gollancz, 1943) p. 49; E. Snow, *Scorched Earth* (London: Gollancz, 1941) p. 48.
41. BIOS/JAP/PR 1338, pp. 17–18.
42. 'Japan's Use of Gas', *China Newsweek* (6 February 1943) PRO, WO 208/3044.
43. League of Nations, *Official Journal* (May–June 1938) 101st session of the Council, second meeting (10 May 1938) and Annex 1702, C.166.M.93, 1938. VII, pp. 307 and 381.
44. League of Nations, *Official Journal* (May–June 1938) 101st session of the Council, eighth meeting (14 May 1938) p. 378.
45. League of Nations, *Official Journal* (August–September 1938) 'Communications Received Concerning the Use of Poison Gas', C.251.M.149. 1938, VII, pp. 665–8.
46. League of Nations, *Official Journal* (November 1938) 103rd session of the Council, second meeting (30 September 1938) p. 881.
47. *Parl. Deb.*, fifth ser., vol. 336 (16 May 1938) col. 57.
48. Shuhsi Hsu, *The War Conduct of the Japanese* (Shanghai, 1938); C. J. Argyle, *Japan at War 1937–45* (London: A. Barker, 1976) p. 123.

49. 'Comments of CDR5 on CX. 37431/111/61022 of 28.1.42', 9 February 1942; 'An Appraisal of General Ho Ying Chin's Report on the Use of Gas by the Japanese', 14 July 1942; 'Jap Use of Gas in Changteh Battle', 17 May 1944; 'Use of Gas by the Japanese', 27 February 1945, PRO, WO 208/3044; 'Situation Report', 14 September 1938, *US Military Intelligence Reports. China 1911–1941*, ed. P. Kesaris (Frederick, Maryland: University Publications of America, 1983) reel X, 0758, p. 14.

50. Gen. Sir H. Alexander to Sir A. Wavell, 6 April 1942, PRO, WO 208/3044.

51. BIOS/JAP/PR/1338, pp. 8–9; BIOS/JAP/PR/724, p. 5; BIOS/JAP/PR/685, p. 114.

52. 'Further Information on the Use of Gas by Japanese Troops in China', C.283.M.171. 1938. VII (6 September 1938) League of Nations Archive R 3611; *The New York Times* (31 August 1938), p. 4; 'Alleged Use of Gas by Japanese Troops near Ichang', 6 November 1941; British Army Staff Washington to War Office, 29 June 1944, PRO, WO 208/3044 and WO 106/4594A.

53. BIOS/JAP/PR/1338, p. 8.

54. 'Japan's Use of Gas', PRO, WO 208/3044.

55. Wangshihchieh Pasfco to Ambassador Koo, 4 June 1942, PRO, WO 208/3044.

56. 'Intelligence Report on Japanese Chemical Warfare Vol. III "The Manufacture of CW Materials by the Japanese" ', BIOS/JAP/PR/395, p. 10.

57. 'Comments of C.D.R.5 on CX. 37431/11/61022 of 28.1.42', 9 February 1942; 'Alleged use of Gas by Japanese Troops near Ichang', 6 November 1941; 'Japan's Use of Gas', PRO, WO 208/3044.

58. BIOS/JAP/PR/1338, pp. 90–1.

59. 'Collection of Combat Examples of the Use of Smoke and Others (TN war gases)', June 1943, PRO, WO 208/2578.

60. 'Appendix A to letter no. 4832/GS1(t)', 9 May 1943, PRO, WO 208/3044; BIOS/JAP/PR/685, p. 114.

61. BIOS/JAP/PR/395, pp. 8–13.

62. E. Snow, *Scorched Earth*, p. 173.

63. F. Utley, *China At War* (London: Faber & Faber, 1939) pp. 110, 170.

64. 'Appendix A to letter no. 4832/GS1(t)', 9 April 1943; and 'A study of the use of poison gas by the enemy in the Changteh Battle', 2 May 1944, PRO, WO 208/3044.

65. Foreign Office telegram, no. 288, 20 March 1942, PRO, WO 208/3044.

66. *The Public Papers and Addresses of Franklin D. Roosevelt*, 1942 vol., p. 258; and 1943 vol., pp. 242–3.

67. 'A Study of the Use of Poison Gas by the Enemy in the Changteh Battle', 2 May 1944, PRO, WO 208/3044; BIOS/JAP/PR/1338, p. 8.

68. BIOS/JAP/PR/724, pp. 1–4; BIOS/JAP/PR/1338, p. 7.

69. British Army Staff Washington to War Office, 29 June 1944; Military Attaché Chungking to War Office, 5 July 1944; COS(44)226th meeting, 7 July 1944, PRO, WO 106/4594A; WO 208/3044; CAB 79/77.

70. 'Use of Gas by the Japanese', 27 February 1945, PRO, WO 208/3044.

71. Ibid.; BIOS/JAP/PR/395, pp. 6–13.

72. 'Japan's Use of Gas', 6 February 1943, PRO, WO 208/3044.
73. *The New York Times*, 31 August 1938, p. 4; J. Belden, 'Alleged Use of Gas by Japanese Troops near Ichang', 6 November 1941, PRO, WO 208/3044.
74. SIPRI, *The Problem of Chemical and Biological Warfare*, vol. 1, pp. 159–61, 336–41; D. A. Schmidt, *Yemen: the Unknown War* (London: Bodley Head, 1968) pp. 257–73.
75. US Department of State, *Chemical Warfare in South East Asia and Afghanistan, Report to the Congress from Secretary of State Alexander M. Haig, Jr.*, 22 March, 1982, Special Report No. 98, hereafter referred to as the *Haig Report*, pp. 11, 15, 21.
76. US Department of State, *Reports of the Use of Chemical Weapons in Afghanistan, Laos and Kampuchea* (August 1980) and *Update to the Compendium on the Reports of the Use of Chemical Weapons* (March 1981).
77. S. Seagrave, *Yellow Rain* (London: Abacus, 1981) p. 189; 'Moscow's Poison War: Mounting Evidence of Battlefield Atrocities', *Backgrounder*, no. 165 (5 February 1982) p. 3.
78. R. R. Burt, Hearings before the Subcommittees on International Security and Scientific Affairs and on Asian and Pacific Affairs of the Committee on Foreign Affairs House of Representatives, *Foreign Policy and Arms Control Implications of Chemical Weapons*, 97th Congress, second session (30 March 1982) p. 26.
79. L. R. Ember, 'Yellow Rain', *Chemical and Engineering News*, 9 January 1984, p. 11.
80. C. J. Mirocha, Hearings . . . *Foreign Policy and Arms Control Implications of Chemical Weapons*, p. 51; and *Haig report*, p. 23.
81. *Haig report*, pp. 8–17; and US Department of State, *Chemical Warfare in Southeast Asia and Afghanistan: An Update. Report from Secretary of State George P. Shultz, November 1982*, Special Report No. 104, hereafter referred to as the *Shultz report*, p. 8.
82. *Shultz report*, pp. 4–8; *Note verbale dated 4 August 1983 from the Acting Permanent Representative of the United States of America to the United Nations addressed to the Secretary-General*, A/38/326, 5 August 1983; US Department of State, *Chemical Weapons Use in Southeast Asia and Afghanistan*, Current policy No. 553 (21 February 1984) p. 2; and 'The United States Initiative to Ban Chemical Weapons', *Press Book* (18 April 1984).
83. *Haig report*, pp. 13–14.
84. Hon. W. J. Stoessel, Hearing before the Committee on Foreign Relations United States Senate, *Situation in Afghanistan*, 97th Congress, second session (8 March 1982) p. 10.
85. *Haig report*, pp. 14–17.
86. *The Daily Telegraph*, 9 November 1982, p. 19; and *The Washington Post*, 9 September 1982, p. A21.
87. G. B. Carter, 'Is Biotechnology Feeding the Russians?' *New Scientist* (23 April 1981) p. 216.
88. *Haig report*, p. 30.
89. R. R. Burt, Hearings . . ., Appendix 1, p. 194; *Haig report*, p. 17.

90. L. R. Ember, 'Yellow Rain', p. 26; S. Watson and D. Cullen, Hearings . . . *Foreign Policy and Arms Control Implications of Chemical Weapons*, pp. 40, 59–63, 67–9.

91. S. Watson and D. Cullen, ibid; R. L. Bartley and W. P. Kucewicz, ' "Yellow Rain" and the Future of Arms Agreements', *Foreign Affairs*, vol. 61, no. 4 (Spring 1983) p. 810.

92. S. J. D. Schwartzstein, statement included in Hearing before the Subcommittee on Arms Control, Oceans, International Operations and Environment of the Committee on Foreign Relations United States Senate, *Yellow Rain: The Arms Control Implications*, 98th Congress, first session (24 February 1983) p. 109. See also *Haig report*, p. 17.

93. *Letter dated 20 May 1982 from the Permanent Representative of the Union of Soviet Socialist Republics to the United Nations addressed to the Secretary General*, A/37/233; for critiques of the elephant grass theory see 'The Soviet Elephant Grass Theory', *Science*, vol. 217 (2 July 1982) p. 32; and *Chemical and Bacteriological (Biological) Weapons Report of the Secretary-General*, 1 December 1982, A/37/259, hereafter referred to as the *2nd UN Report*, p. 19.

94. *Haig report*, p. 17.

95. Dr S. Watson, Hearings . . ., pp. 113–14; *Haig report*, p. 17.

96. R. R. Burt, Hearings . . ., Appendix 1, p. 191.

97. *The New York Times*, 14 September 1981, p. A8.

98. *The New York Times*, 15 September 1981, p. A6.

99. N. Wade, 'Toxin Warfare Charges May be Premature', *Science*, vol. 214 (2 October 1981) p. 34; R. L. Bartley and W. P. Kucewicz, 'Yellow Rain', p. 812.

100. R. R. Burt, Hearing before the Subcommittee on Arms Control, Oceans, International Operations and Environment of the Committee on Foreign Relations United States Senate, '*Yellow Rain*', 97th Congress, first session (10 November 1981), pp. 15–16.

101. M. Meselson, ibid., pp. 29–31.

102. N. Wade, 'Toxin Warfare Charges', p. 34; D. Cullen, Hearings . . ., p. 70.

103. *The New York Times*, 24 November 1981, p. C1.

104. *The New York Times*, 3 March 1982, p. A27.

105. Dr Jane Hamilton-Merritt, 'The Poisoning of the H'Mong', *Bangkok Post*, 7 March 1982, pp. 21, 24–5; and Dr A. R. Townsend, responses to questions in Hearing . . . *Yellow Rain: The Arms Control Implications*, pp. 106–7.

106. *Chemical and Bacteriological (Biological) Weapons Report of the Secretary-General*, 20 November 1981, A/36/613 pp. 34–5.

107. *Second UN Report*, p. 25.

108. Ibid., p. 47.

109. Ibid., p. 50.

110. *The New York Times*, 18 December 1981, p. A31.

111. *Letter dated 23 June 1982 from the Permanent Representative of Canada to the United Nations addressed to the Secretary-General*, 25 June 1982, A/37/308, pp. 11–12. Human Stachybotryotoxicosis can occur by the handling (skin contact and/or inhalation) of contaminated fodder. See

H. B. Schiefer, 'The Possible Use of Chemical Warfare Agents in Southeast Asia', *Conflict Quarterly* (Winter 1983) pp. 32–41.

112. 'Adelman UN Remarks on CBW', *United States Information Service*, 9 December 1982. See also R. L. Bartley and W. P. Kucewicz, 'Yellow Rain', pp. 816–17.

113. M. Meselson *et al.*, 'Origin of Yellow Rain', *Science*, vol. 222 (28 October 1983) p. 366; L. R. Ember, 'Yellow Rain', pp. 12, 17; S. Budiansky, 'Softening of US Charges', *Nature*, vol. 308 (1 March 1984) p. 5; J. W. Nowicke and M. Meselson, 'Yellow Rain – A Palynological Analysis', *Nature*, vol. 309 (17 May 1984) pp. 205–6.

114. M. Meselson *et al.*, 'Origin of Yellow Rain', pp. 366, 368; L. R. Ember, 'Yellow Rain', pp. 21–2; E. Marshall, 'Yellow Rain: Filling in the Gaps', *Science*, vol. 217 (2 July 1982) pp. 31–2.

115. M. Meselson *et al.*, 'Origin of Yellow Rain', pp. 366, 368; L. R. Ember, 'Yellow Rain', pp. 22–6.

116. *The Washington Post*, 2 June 1983, p. A11.

117. S. Murphy, A. Hay, S. Rose, *No Fire No Thunder* (London: Pluto Press, 1984) pp. 53–4.

118. *The New York Times*, 2 June 1983, p. 16.

119. G. Evans, *The Yellow Rainmakers: Are Chemical Weapons Being Used in Southeast Asia?* (London: Verso, 1983) pp. 47–69, 76, 175.

120. S. Watson, Hearings . . ., p. 66.

121. E. Marshall, 'Yellow Rain', pp. 32–3.

122. M. Richardson, 'Chemical Warfare: The Case Against the Soviet Union', *Pacific Defence Reporter* (September 1982), p. 55.

123. E. Marshall, 'The Apology of Yellow Rain', *Science*, vol. 221 (15 July 1983) p. 242.

124. The State Department also argued that the levels of toxin would have killed the bees, but this misinterpreted Meselson's theory which argued that the pollen was excreted before the toxin was added to it. *The New York Times*, 2 June 1983, p. 16.

125. C. J. Mirocha *et al.*, Letter on chemical warfare, *The New York Times*, 13 June 1983, p. A14.

126. 'An Epidemiological Investigation of Alleged CW/BW Incidents in S.E. Asia', *Letter dated 25 August 1982 from the Permanent Mission of Canada to the United Nations addressed to the Secretary-General*, Conference room paper 1/Add.11.

127. *Haig report*, p. 7.

128. L. R. Ember, 'Yellow Rain', p. 30. However, some deaths associated with 'toxic attacks' in 1983 occurred from eating contaminated animal products after an attack. US Department of State, *Chemical Weapons Use* (21 February 1984) p. 2.

129. *Letter dated 23 June 1982*, p. 11.

130. Testimony of S. Watson, Xeu Vang Vangyi and R. R. Burt, Hearings . . . *Foreign Policy and Arms Control Implications of Chemical Weapons*, pp. 25, 72, 199.

131. Asian Lawyers Legal Inquiry Committee, *Alleged Violations of Human Rights in Kampuchea and Laos* (June 1982) p. 6.

132. *NATO Review*, No. 3, June 1984, p. 29; *The House of Commons*, Sixth

ser., Vol. 33, 2 December 1982, col. 256; *Die Welt*, 25 November 1981 and a Thai report that French scientists had found 7 toxin specimens, *The Wall Street Journal*, 24 January 1983, p. 30. Professor A. Heyndrickx, University of Ghent, also believes that mycotoxins have been used as chemical munitions but his methods of laboratory analysis have been controversial. R. Stevenson, 'Yellow rain: now the analysts battle it out', *Chemistry in Britain*, Vol. 20, no. 7 (July 1984), pp. 593–5.

133. Ambassador J. F. Leonard and Rear Admiral T. D. Davies, Hearings . . . *Yellow Rain: The Arms Control Implications*, pp. 96–7.

134. *The Wall Street Journal*, 14 December 1982, p. 34.

135. L. Eagleburger, statement in Hearings . . . *Foreign Policy and Arms Control Implications of Chemical Weapons*, p. 3. As late as September 1982, a Gallup opinion poll revealed that 57 per cent of the American public was still unaware of the Yellow Rain charges, and that the largest section of opinion, 42 per cent, believed that the US government should only respond diplomatically even if the charges were true, *The Wall Street Journal*, 15 September 1982, p. 30.

136. *Report of the Specialists Appointed by the Secretary-General to investigate allegations by the Islamic Republic of Iran concerning the use of chemical weapons*, 26 March 1984, S/16433, pp. 8–10, 12.

137. N. C. Livingstone and J. D. Douglass, *CBW: The Poor Man's Atomic Bomb* (Institute for Foreign Policy Analysis, Cambridge Mass., 1984); and G. K. Vachon, 'Chemical Weapons and the Third World', *Survival*, vol. 26, no. 2 (March/April 1984), pp. 79–81.

138. F. C. Iklé, 'After Detection – What?' *Foreign Affairs*, vol. 39, no. 2 (January 1961) pp. 208–220; R. L. Bartley and W. P. Kucewicz, 'Yellow Rain', pp. 823–6.

6 THE SOVIET CHEMICAL WARFARE POSTURE

1. C. W. Weinberger, *Annual Report to Congress Fiscal Year 1983* (Washington: US Govt. Printing Office, 1982) pp. 111–43.

2. Gen. G. S. Brown, Hearings before the Committee on Armed Services United States Senate, *The Defense Posture of the United States for FY 1978*, 95th Congress, first session (25 January 1977) p. 452; Hon. P. A. Pierre and Lt-Gen. D. R. Keith, joint statement in *Hearings on Military Posture and H.R. 1872 (H.R. 4040) and H.R.2575 (S429) and H.R.3406*, 96th Congress, first session (23 February 1979), p. 132; Brig-Gen. G. G. Watson, statement in Hearings before a subcommittee of the Committee on Appropriations House of Representatives, *Department of Defense Appropriations for 1984*, 98th Congress, first session (12 April 1983) p. 456.

3. Gen. G. S. Brown, Hearings . . . p. 453.

4. A. M. Prentiss, *Chemicals in War*, p. 653.

5. SIPRI, *The Problem of Chemical and Biological Warfare*, vol. 1, p. 309; and F. J. Brown, *Chemical Warfare*, pp. 234–5.

6. US D(epartment) o(f) D(efense), *Continuing Development of Chemical Weapon Capabilities in the USSR* (October, 1983) p. 12; Written answer in Hearings before the Committee on Armed Services United States Senate, *Department of Defense Authorization for Appropriations for Fiscal Year 1983*, hereafter referred to as *Written answer*, 97th Congress, second session (15 March 1982) p. 4820.

7. J. Erickson, 'The Soviet Union's Growing Arsenal of Chemical Warfare', *Strategic Review*, vol. 7, no. 4 (Fall, 1979) p. 65; C. J. Dick, 'Soviet Chemical Warfare Capabilities', *International Defense Review*, vol. 14, no. 1 (1981) p. 32.

8. C. J. Dick, ibid., p. 32; Lt-Col. G. M. Lovelace, 'Chemical Warfare', *NATO's Fifteen Nations* (Dec. 1981–Jan. 1982) p. 54; Dr T. S. Gold, statement in Hearings before a Subcommittee of the Committee on Appropriations House of Representatives, *Department of Defense Appropriations for 1983*, 97th Congress, second session (23 June 1982) p. 263; *Written answer*, p. 4831. Yet the recent DoD report still gives the size of the force as 80 000 men, US DoD, *Continuing Development*, p. 17.

9. *Written answer*, p. 4824; C. N. Donnelly, 'Winning the NBC War. Soviet Army Theory and Practice', *International Defense Review*, vol. 14, no. 8 (1981) p. 991.

10. *Written answer*, p. 4831; C. J. Dick, 'Soviet Chemical Warfare Capabilities', pp. 32–3.

11. *Written answer*, p. 4831.

12. Ibid., pp. 4831–2; N. Polmar and N. Friedman, 'Their Missions and Tactics', *US Naval Institute Proceedings*, vol. 108, no. 10 (October 1982) p. 42.

13. J. Erickson, 'The Soviet Union's Growing Arsenal', p. 66; and C. J. Dick, 'Soviet Chemical Warfare Capabilities', p. 33.

14. Maj. S. Z. Kovacs, 'Soviet Chemical Troops: An Analysis of Articles in *Military Herald*' (Garmish, Germany, 1979) p. 19.

15. C. J. Dick, 'Soviet Chemical Warfare Capabilities', p. 33; and FM 30–40, *Handbook on Soviet Ground Forces* (1975) pp. 6–109.

16. Ibid.; and J. Erickson, 'The Soviet Union's Growing Arsenal', p. 67.

17. FM 30–40, *Handbook on Soviet Ground Forces* pp. 6–108–6–109; K. G. Benz, 'NBC Defense–An Overview, Part 1: Protection Equipment', *International Defense Review*, vol. 16, no. 12 (December 1983) p. 1790.

18. K. G. Benz, 'NBC Defense Part 1', p. 1789; C. J. Dick, 'Soviet Chemical Warfare Capabilities', p. 34; Lt-Col. G. M. Lovelace, 'Chemical Warfare', p. 55.

19. C. N. Donnelly, 'Winning the NBC War', pp. 992–3; A. M. Hoeber, *The Chemistry of Defeat: Asymmetries in US and Soviet Chemical Warfare Postures* (Institute for Foreign Policy Analysis, Cambridge, Mass., 1981) pp. 38–9.

20. Dr J. P. Wade, Hearings before the Subcommittee of the Committee on Appropriations House of Representatives, *Department of Defense Appropriations for 1982*, 97th Congress, first session (15 September 1981) p. 796.

21. C. J. Dick, 'Soviet Chemical Warfare Capabilities', p. 34; A. Hoeber and J. D. Douglass, 'The Neglected Threat of Chemical Warfare', *International Security*, vol. 3, no. 1 (Summer, 1978) p. 61.

22. J. Erickson, 'The Soviet Union's Growing Arsenal', p. 69.
23. Ibid.; FM 30–40, *Handbook on Soviet Ground Forces*, pp. 6-104–6-109; C. J. Dick, 'Soviet Chemical Warfare Capabilities', p. 35.
24. Brig-Gen. G. G. Watson, Hearings . . . (12 April 1983) p. 483.
25. A. Hoeber and J. D. Douglass, 'Neglected Threat of Chemical Warfare', p. 61; Lt-Col. G. M. Lovelace, 'Chemical Warfare', p. 55.
26. L. Gouré, *War Survival in Soviet Strategy USSR Civil Defense* (Centre for Advanced International Studies, University of Miami, 1976) pp. 75, 167; D. M. Kyle, 'Chemical Warfare', *Armed Forces Journal International*, vol. 119 (November 1981) p. 62.
27. J. Erickson, 'The Soviet Union's Growing Arsenal', p. 66; J. P. Wade, Hearings . . . (15 September 1981) p. 806.
28. Maj-Gen. N. J. Fulwyler, Hearings before the Committee on Appropriations House of Representatives, *Department of Defense Appropriations for 1982*, 97th Congress, first session (15 September 1981) p. 786; A. Hoeber, *Chemistry of Defeat*, p. 42.
29. Maj. S. Z. Kovacs, 'Soviet Chemical Troops', p. 14; J. Erickson, 'The Soviet Union's Growing Arsenal', pp. 69–70; and J. P. Wade, Hearings . . . (15 September 1981) p. 806.
30. J. Erickson, 'The Soviet Union's Growing Arsenal', p. 70; C. N. Donnelly, 'Winning the NBC War', p. 991; C. J. Dick, 'Soviet Chemical Warfare Capabilities', p. 33.
31. US DoD., *Continuing Development*, p. 17; US DoD., *Soviet Military Power 1984* (Washington: US Govt. Printing Office, 1984), hereafter referred to as *Soviet Military Power 1984*, p. 72.
32. C. J. Dick, 'Soviet Chemical Warfare Capabilities', p. 33; C. N. Donnelly, 'Winning the NBC War', p. 991.
33. *The New York Times*, 15 February 1974, p. 4.
34. Lt-Col. R. S. Malooley, 'Gas is Not a Dirty Word in Soviet Army', *Army Magazine* (September 1974) p. 22; A. Hoeber, *Chemistry of Defeat*, p. 40; Hon. E. A. Miller and Lt-Gen. H. H. Cooksey, statement in Hearings before the Committee on Armed Services United States Senate, *FY 78 Authorization for Military Procurement, Research and Development, and Active Duty, Selected Reserve and Civilian Personnel Strengths*, 95th Congress, first session (2 March 1977) pp. 5269–70; Maj-Gen. N. J. Fulwyler, Hearing . . . (15 September 1981) p. 786.
35. Quoted by T. S. Gold, Statement . . . (23 June 1982) p. 264.
36. J. M. Deutch, statement in Hearings . . . *Department of Defense Authorization for Appropriations for Fiscal Year 1983* (22 March 1982) p. 5067.
37. M. Meselson, 'Comments on the Defense Science Board (DSB) Chemical Warfare Panel Report' in . . . *Department of Defense Authorization for Appropriations for Fiscal Year 1983* (22 March 1982) p. 5061.
38. Ibid. See also the joint letter of S. M. Meyer and M. Meselson, *The New York Times*, 12 November 1980, p. A30.
39. J. P. Perry Robinson, 'Chemical and Biological Warfare: An Analysis of Recent Reports Concerning the Soviet Union and Vietnam', *ADIU Occasional Paper No. 1* (Science Policy Research Unit, University of Sussex, 1980) pp. 19–22; and 'The Changing Status of Chemical and Biological Warfare: Recent Technical, Military and Political Develop-

ments', *World Armaments and Disarmament: SIPRI Yearbook 1982* (London: Taylor & Francis, 1982) pp. 331–5; Russell Committee Against Chemical Weapons, *The Threat of Chemical Weapons* (Spokesman pamphlet 78, Nottingham, 1982) p. 14; L. R. Ember, 'Chemical Weapons: Build up or Disarm?' *Chemical and Engineering News* (15 December 1980) pp. 22–7.

40. J. P. Perry Robinson, 'Chemical Warfare Capabilities of the Warsaw and North Atlantic Treaty Organizations: An Overview From Open Sources', SIPRI, *Chemical Weapons: Destruction and Conversion* (London: Taylor & Francis, 1981) p. 10; C. J. Dick, 'Soviet Chemical Warfare Capabilities', p. 31.

41. T. S. Gold, statement in Hearings . . . *Department of Defense Authorization for Appropriations for Fiscal Year 1983* (15 March 1982) p. 4749; A. M. Hoeber, *Chemistry of Defeat*, p. 43.

42. J. P. Wade, Hearings . . . (15 September 1981) pp. 806–7.

43. T. S. Gold, statement in Hearings . . . *Department of Defense Appropriations for 1983*, p. 264. See also US DoD, *Continuing Development*, p. 12.

44. N. R. Augustine, *Hearings on Military Posture and HR.3689 (HR.6674)* before the Committee on Armed Services House of Representatives, 94th Congress, first session (7 March 1975) p. 4191.

45. US DoD *Continuing Development*, pp. 8–11.

46. H. Ruhle, 'Chemische Waffen and Europaische Sicherheit 1980–90', *Europäische Wehrkunde*, vol. 27, no. 1 (January 1978) p. 6; J. P. Perry Robinson, 'Chemical Warfare Capabilities of the Warsaw and North Atlantic Treaty Organisations: An Overview from Open Sources,' pp. 27–8.

47. J. P. Wade, Hearing . . . (15 September 1981) p. 807; *Soviet Military Power 1984*, p. 73.

48. US DoD *Continuing Development*, pp. 12, 14–16; *House of Commons*, Sixth ser., vol. 37 (24 February 1983) col. 516.

49. US DoD *Continuing Development*, p. 2; J. S. Finan, 'Soviet Interest in a Possible Tactical Use of Chemical Weapons', *Canadian Defence Quarterly*, vol. 4, no. 2 (1974) p. 11; 'Chemische Waffen in Warschauer Pakt', *Soldat und Technik*, no. 9 (1970) p. 478; P. Ganas, 'Nouveaux Développements en Guerre Chimique et Biologique', *Forces Aériennes Françaises*, vol. 24 (1969) pp. 449–75.

50. Lt-Col. G. M. Lovelace, 'Chemical Warfare', pp. 54–5.

51. J. P. Wade, Hearing . . . (15 September 1981) p. 806; J. R. Schlesinger, Hearing before the Committee on Appropriations House of Representatives, *Department of Defense Appropriations for 1976*, 94th Congress, first session (26 February 1975) p. 190; H. Brown, Hearing . . . *Chemical Warfare*, pp. 13–14; T. S. Gold, statement in . . . *Department of Defense Appropriations for 1983*, p. 264.

52. A. M. Hoeber, *Chemistry of Defeat* pp. 42–3; Lt-Col. G. M. Lovelace, 'Chemical Warfare', p. 54.

53. Jean-Baptiste Margeride, 'Le Problème de la Guerre Chimique', *Stratégigue*, no. 3 (1982) p. 122; *Statement on the Defence Estimates 1984*, Cmnd. 9227–1, p. 40; *House of Commons*, Sixth ser., vol. 41 (19 April 1983), col. 85; H. Ruhle, 'Chemische Waffen', p. 6.

54. C. N. Donnelly, 'Winning the NBC War', p. 990.
55. R. M. Kidder, 'Chemical Weapons at NATO's backdoor', *The Christian Science Monitor*, 13 December 1979, p. 1; and J. Erickson, 'The Soviet Union's Growing Arsenal', p. 65.
56. T. S. Gold, statement in . . . *Department of Defense Appropriations for 1983*, p. 264.
57. H. Brown, Hearing . . . *Chemical Warfare*, p. 27; US DoD, *Continuing Development*, p. 3; A. M. Hoeber and J. D. Douglass, 'Neglected Threat of Chemical Warfare', p. 63; T. S. Gold, statement in . . . *Department of Defense Appropriations for 1983*, p. 263.
58. US DoD *Continuing Development*, p. 3.
59. FM 30–40, *Handbook on Soviet Ground Forces*, p. 6–83.
60. C. J. Dick, 'Soviet Chemical Warfare Capabilities', pp. 35–6; and 'The Soviet Chemical and Biological Warfare Threat', *J(ournal of the) R(oyal) U(nited) S(ervices) I(nstitute for Defence Studies)*, vol. 126, no. 1 (March 1981) p. 48; J. S. Finan, 'Soviet Interest in a Possible Tactical Use of Chemical Weapons', p. 13; Lt-Col. G. Eifried, 'Russian CW: Our Achilles Heel, Europe', *Army* (December, 1979) p. 25.
61. C. J. Dick, 'Soviet Chemical and Biological Warfare Threat', p. 48.
62. US DoD, *Continuing Development*, pp. 3–4; Lt-Col. G. Eifried, 'Russian CW', p. 25; Lt-Col. D. M. O. Miller, Col. W. V. Kennedy, J. Jordan and D. Richardson, *The Balance of Military Power* (London: Salamander, 1981) p. 67.
63. H. Brown, *Annual Report to Congress Fiscal Year 1981* (Washington: US Government Printing Office, 1980) p. 92.
64. Maj. C. J. Davidson, 'Situation Report on Chemical Weapons', *JRUSI*, vol. 125, no. 2 (June 1980) p. 63.
65. US DoD, *Continuing Development*, p. 5.
66. SIPRI, *The Problem of Chemical and Biological Warfare*, vol. 2, p. 140.
67. Rear Admiral W. R. Smedberg, Hearings . . . *Department of Defense Authorization for Appropriations for Fiscal Year 1983* (15 March 1982) pp. 4773, 4775.
68. *Congressional Record*, 16 September 1980, S 12,647; M. Meselson and S. M. Meyer, letter in *The New York Times*, 12 November 1980, p. A30.
69. P. A. Pierre and Lt-Gen. D. R. Keith, Hearings . . . (23 February 1979) p. 132; *Written answer*, p. 4827.
70. H. Brown, Hearings before the Committee on Armed Services United States Senate, *Department of Defense Authorization for Appropriations for Fiscal Year 1981*, 96th Congress, second session (31 January 1980) p. 49.
71. US DoD, *Continuing Development*, pp. 12, 14–16.
72. J. M. Weinstein and H. G. Gole, 'Chemical Weapons Rearmament and the Security of Europe: Can Support be Mustered?' (Strategic Studies Institute, US Army War College, Carlisle Barracks, Pennsylvania, 20 January 1983) p. 22.
73. J. P. Perry Robinson, 'Recent Developments in the Field of Chemical Warfare', *RUSI and Brassey's Defence Yearbook 1983* (London: Brassey's, 1983) pp. 171–2.

74. R. L. Wagner and T. S. Gold, 'Why We Can't Avoid Developing Chemical Weapons', *Defense 82* (July, 1982) p. 4.
75. Lt-Gen. D. R. Keith, *Hearings on Military Posture and H.R.10929 and H.R.1872 (H.R.4040)* before the Committee on Armed Services House of Representatives, 96th Congress, first session (27 March 1979) p. 2201; Maj-Gen. N. J. Fulwyler, Hearing . . . (15 September 1981) p. 786.
76. FM 30–40 *Handbook on Soviet Ground Forces*, pp. 6–111.
77. C. J. Dick, 'Soviet Chemical Warfare Capabilities', p. 35.
78. *Soviet Military Power 1984* p. 70; H. Brown, *Department of Defense Annual Report, Fiscal Year 1979* (Washington: US Govt. Printing Office, 1978), p. 157; Lt-Col. G. Eifried, 'Russian CW', p. 25.
79. Although Sovietologists disagree over whether authority to use chemical weapons has already been given, they agree that it would be given to divisional, as distinct from Army, commanders. C. J. Dick, 'The Soviet Chemical and Biological Warfare Threat', pp. 49, 51; A. M. Hoeber, *Chemistry of Defeat*, p. 49.
80. J. M. Weinstein and H. G. Gole, 'Chemical Weapons Rearmament', pp. 10–11; W. M. Carpenter (ed.), *Evaluation of Chemical Warfare Policy Alternatives 1980–1990* (Stanford Research Institute, 1977) pp. 15–16.
81. V. Ye. Savkin, *The Basic Principles of Operational Art and Tactics* (1972) translated by US Air Force, p. 165.
82. A. M. Hoeber, *Chemistry of Defeat*, p. 47; W. M. Carpenter, *Evaluation of Chemical Warfare Policy*, p. 15; J. M. Weinstein and H. G. Gole, *Chemical Weapons Rearmament*, p. 11.
83. R. L. Wagner and T. S. Gold, 'Why We Can't Avoid Developing Chemical Weapons', p. 4.
84. Brig-Gen. G. G. Watson, Hearings . . . (12 April 1983) p. 480; Sgt. Bagley, Hearings . . . *Department of Defense Authorization for Appropriations for Fiscal Year 1983* (15 March 1982) p. 4797.
85. Lt-Col. G. Eifried, 'Russian CW', p. 26.
86. J. Erickson, 'The Soviet Union's Growing Arsenal', p. 70; A. M. Hoeber, *Chemistry of Defeat*, pp. 47–8; A. M. Hoeber and J. D. Douglass, 'Neglected Threat of Chemical Warfare', p. 65.
87. Marshal V. D. Sokolovskiy, *Soviet Military Strategy*, ed. by H. F. Scott (London: Macdonald & Janes, 1975) 3rd ed., p. 68.
88. Ibid., p. 243.
89. V. Ye. Savkin, *Basic Principles of Operational Art and Tactics*, pp. 107, 230, 235–6.
90. Brig. Gen. W. E. Klein, Hearings before the sub-committee on Strategic and Theater Nuclear Forces Committee on Armed Services United States Senate, *Department of Defense Authorization for Appropriations for Fiscal Year 1984*, 98th Congress, first session (7 April 1983), p. 2752.
91. Hon. E. A. Miller and Lt-Gen. H. H. Cooksey, Hearings . . . (2 March 1977) pp. 5269–70.

7 NATO'S PREPARATIONS FOR CHEMICAL WARFARE

1. *The Stars and Stripes*, 18 March 1980, p. 2.

2. Gen. C. W. Abrams, *Hearings on Military Posture and H. R. 12564* before the Committee on Armed Services House of Representatives, 93rd Congress, second session (14 February 1974) p. 292; *The New York Times*, 15 February 1974, p. 4.

3. For a review of the evidence over the alleged killing of sheep by the Army's testing of VX at the Dugway Proving Ground, Utah, see J. D. Douglass, 'Chemical Weapons: An Imbalance of Terror', *Strategic Review*, vol. 10, no. 3 (Summer, 1982) pp. 40–2.

4. *The New York Times*, 26 November 1969, pp. 1, 16.

5. R. L. Wagner, Hearings before the Committee on Appropriations United States Senate, *Binary Chemical Weapons*, 97th Congress, second session (6 May 1982) p. 130; Gen. G. S. Brown, Hearings before the Committee on Appropriations House of Representatives, *Department of Defense Appropriations for 1976*, 94th Congress, first session (26 February 1975), p. 190; B. Roberts, *US Chemical Warfare Readiness Program* (Congressional Research Service, Issue Brief No., 1B82125, Washington, 1982) p. 8.

6. Lt-Col. D. M. Parker, 'Facing the NBC Environment', *Military Review*, vol. 54, no. 5 (May 1974) pp. 25–6; W. M. Carpenter, *Evaluation of Chemical Warfare Policy*, pp. 41–2.

7. Lt-Col. D. M. Parker, 'Facing the NBC Environment', p. 26; W. Lepkowski, 'Chemical Warfare: One of the Dilemmas of the Arms Race', *Chemical and Engineering News* (2 January 1978), p. 17; A. M. Hoeber, *Chemistry of Defeat*, pp. 55–7.

8. R. Godson (ed.), *Intelligence Requirements for the 1980s: analysis and estimates* (Washington DC: National Strategy Information Center, 1980), pp. 124–5.

9. *The New York Times*, 26 November 1969, p. 16 and 26 June 1973, p. 18; R. L. Wagner, Hearings . . . *Binary Chemical Weapons*, p. 130.

10. Maj-Gen. N. J. Fulwyler, statement in *Hearings on Military Posture and H.R.5968 Department of Defense Authorization for Appropriations for Fiscal Year 1983* before the Committee on Armed Services House of Representatives, 97th Congress, second session (18 March 1982) p. 838; N. R. Augustine and Maj-Gen. H. H. Cooksey, joint statement in Hearings . . . *Military Posture and HR 3689 (HR 6674)*, pp. 4147–8; Lt-Gen. D. R. Keith, Hearings . . . (27 March 1979) pp. 2202–3.

11. E. Ulsamer, 'Airpower – NATO's foremost deterrent', *Air Force Magazine* (April, 1978) p. 25.

12. J. M. Lenorovitz, 'USAF Improving Defenses Against Chemical Threat', *Aviation Week and Space Technology* (19 May 1980) pp. 109–110; Maj. S. C. Hall, 'Air Base Survivability in Europe. Can USAFE survive and fight?' *Air University Review*, vol. XXXIII, no. 6 (September–October 1982) pp. 36–46; Dr T. S. Gold, statement in . . . *Department of Defense Appropriations for 1983*, p. 308.

13. Maj. J. F. Brosnan, 'A Case for Marine Corps Chemical Warfare Readiness', *United States Naval Institute Proceedings*, vol. 105, no. 11 (November 1979) p. 108. H. Brown, Hearings before the Committee on Armed Services United States Senate, *Department of Defense Authorization for Appropriations. Fiscal Year 1980*, 96th Congress, first session (25 January 1979) p. 97.

14. T. S. Gold, statement in ... *Department of Defense Appropriations for 1983*, pp. 307–8; Admiral W. R. Smedberg, Hearings before the Committee on Armed Services United States Senate, *Department of Defense Authorization for Appropriations for Fiscal Year 1983*, 97th Congress, second session (15 March 1982) pp. 4773–5, 4804–5.
15. N. R. Augustine and Maj-Gen. H. H. Cooksey, joint statement ... *Military Posture and HR3689 (HR6674)*, pp. 4147–8; Gen. G. S. Brown, statement before the Committee on Armed Services United States Senate, *FY77 Authorization for Military Procurement. Research and Development and Active Duty, Selected Reserve and Civilian Personnel Strengths*, 94th Congress, second session (29 January 1976) p. 434; Col. G. G. Watson, *Hearings on Military Posture and H.R.10929* before the Research and Development subcommittee of the Committee on Armed Services House of Representatives, 95th Congress, second session (2 March 1978) p. 697.
16. Gen. B. W. Rogers, Hearings before the Committee on Appropriations United States Senate, *Department of Defense Appropriations for 1980*, 96th Congress, first session (7 March 1979), pp. 840–1; Lt-Gen. D. R. Keith, Hearings ... (27 March 1979) p. 2203; J. M. Weinstein and H. G. Gole, 'Chemical Weapons Rearmament', p. 16; Maj-Gen. N. J. Fulwyler, statement in Hearings ... *Military Posture and H.R.5968*, p. 838.
17. T. S. Gold, statement in Hearings before a subcommittee of the Committee on Appropriations House of Representatives, *Department of Defense Appropriations for 1984*, 98th Congress, first session (12 April 1983), p. 452 and statement in ... *Department of Defense Appropriations for 1983*, p. 268.
18. T. S. Gold, 'US Chemical Warfare Policy and Program', *NATO's Sixteen Nations*, vol. 28, no. 1 (February–March 1983) p. 70.
19. D. M. Kyle, 'Chemical Warfare', p. 62; T. S. Gold, Hearings before the Committee on Armed Services United States Senate, *Department of Defense Authorization for Appropriations for Fiscal Year 1984*, 98th Congress, first session (7 April 1983) p. 2797.
20. *Northern European Security Issues: Report of a Staff Study Mission to five NATO Countries and Sweden November 29–December 14, 1982 to the Committee on Foreign Affairs U.S. House of Representatives*, 97th Congress, second session (1983) p. 12.
21. NATO, *NATO Standardization Agreement (STANAG): NBC Defence Equipment Operations Guidelines*, unclassified (19 September 1977) p. 2.
22. K. G. Benz, 'NBC Defense – An Overview, Part 2: Detection and Decontamination', *International Defense Review*, vol. 17, no. 2 (1984) p. 160; B. L. Harris, 'Chemical Warfare – A Primer', *CHEMTECH*, vol. 12 (January, 1982) p. 34; 'British Equipment for NBC Defence', *Defence Materiel* (March/April 1981) p. 36.
23. K. G. Benz, 'NBC Defense Part 2', p. 160; Brig-Gen. G. G. Watson, Hearings ... (12 April 1983) p. 473.
24. 'British equipment for NBC defence', p. 36.
25. K. G. Benz, 'NBC Defense Part 2', pp. 160–1; T. J. Gander, 'Some Recent Trends in NBC Defence Equipment', *Jane's Defence Weekly*, vol.

4 (4 February 1984) pp. 153–4; J. L. Ditzian, 'Designing for the NBC Environment', *National Defense* (May 1984) pp. 36–8.

26. T. J. Gander, 'Some Recent Trends', p. 156; K. G. Benz 'NBC Defense – An Overview, Part 1: Protection Equipment', *International Defense Review*, vol. 16, no. 12 (December 1983) p. 1788; 'British equipment for NBC defence', pp. 37, 39.

27. M. Meselson and J. Perry Robinson, 'Chemical Warfare and Chemical Disarmament', p. 37.

28. T. J. Gander, 'Some Recent Trends', p. 157; K. G. Benz, 'NBC Defense Part 1', p. 1790.

29. Brig-Gen. L. B. Lennon, 'Defense Planning for Chemical Warfare', *Chemical Weapons and Chemical Arms Control*, ed. by M. Meselson (New York: Carnegie Endowment for International Peace, 1978) p. 9; T. S. Gold answers to Congressman C. W. Bill Young, Hearings . . . *Department of Defense Appropriations for 1984*, pp. 514–5.

30. Assembly of Western European Union, 'Nuclear Biological and Chemical Protection. Report submitted on behalf of the Committee on Defence Questions and Armaments by Mr Banks, Rapporteur', document 838 (29 April 1980) pp. 33, 35.

31. B. Fritz, 'The AMF 30 Modular NBC Shelter', *International Defense Review*, vol. 15, no. 11 (November 1982) pp. 1590–2. Written answer to Congressman Bill Chappell, Hearings . . . *Department of Defense Appropriations for 1983*, p. 316.

32. Assembly of Western European Union, *Nuclear Biological and Chemical Protection*, pp. 32, 34.

33. T. S. Gold, statement in Hearings . . . *Department of Defense Appropriations for 1983*, p. 308.

34. Admiral B. W. Compton, T. S. Gold and Air Force answer in ibid., pp. 306, 315–7.

35. Ibid., pp. 310–11, 317–19; T. S. Gold, Hearings . . . *Department of Defense Appropriations for 1984*, p. 485.

36. Lt-Gen. D. R. Keith, *Hearings on Military Posture and H.R.10929* before the Committee on Armed Services House of Representatives, 95th Congress, second session (2 March 1978) p. 705.

37. B. Fritz, 'A New NBC Clothing Concept from France', *International Defense Review*, vol. 15, no. 11 (November, 1982) p. 1587.

38. H. Stelzmüller, 'NBC Defense a German viewpoint', *International Defense Review*, vol. 15, no. 11 (November, 1982) pp. 1574–5.

39. 'British Equipment for NBC Defence', p. 44; Col. A. G. Vicary and Wing Commander J. Wilson, 'Nuclear Biological and Chemical Defence', *JRUSI*, vol. 126, no. 4 (December, 1981) p. 11.

40. H. Stelzmüller, 'NBC Defense', p. 1575; Assembly of Western European Union, *Nuclear Biological and Chemical Protection*, pp. 29, 31.

41. H. Stelzmüller, 'NBC Defense', pp. 1573, 1576–7; T. J. Gander, 'Deco-contain: Advanced NBC Decontamination', *Jane's Defence Weekly*, vol. 4 (4 February 1984) p. 167.

42. T. S. Gold, statement in Hearings . . . *Department of Defense Appropriations for 1983*, p. 308.

43. Ibid., p. 310; T. J. Gander, 'Some Recent Trends in NBC Defence Equipment', p. 157.
44. P. Dirnhuber and D. M. Green, 'Effectiveness of Pyridostigmine in Reversing Neuromuscular Blockade Produced by Soman', *Journal of Pharmacy and Pharmacology*, vol. 30 (1978) pp. 419–25.
45. 'British equipment for NBC defence', p. 45; M. Meselson and J. Perry Robinson, 'Chemical Warfare and Chemical Disarmament', p. 38.
46. T. S. Gold and Sgt. Endicott, Hearings ... *Department of Defense Appropriations for 1984*, pp. 447–8, 484–6.
47. Maj-Gen. N. J. Fulwyler, *Hearings on Military Posture and H.R.5968*, p. 846.
48. Lt-Col. G. Eifried, 'Russian CW', pp. 26–7.
49. Brig-Gen. G. G. Watson and Lt-Col. P. R. L. Anderson, 'An Urgent Need: Stockpiling Modern Chemical Munitions', *Military Review*, vol. 54, no. 1 (January 1984) p. 62.
50. Maj-Gen. N. J. Fulwyler, *Hearings on Military Posture and H.R.5968*, p. 847; R. L. Wagner, statement in Hearings before the Committee on Armed Services United States Senate, *Department of Defense Authorization for Appropriations for Fiscal Year 1983*, 97th Congress, second session (15 March 1982) p. 4787.
51. Lt-Gen. K. Burke, Hearings before the Committee on Armed Services United States Senate, *Department of Defense Authorization for Appropriations for Fiscal Year 1983*, 97th Congress, second session (15 March 1982) pp. 4764–5, 4794–6; T. S. Gold, *Department of Defense Authorization and Oversight Hearings on H.R.2287 (H.R.2969)* before the Committee on Armed Services House of Representatives, 98th Congress, first session (18 April 1983) p. 1564; Brig-Gen. T. A. Baker, Hearings before a Subcommittee of the Committee on Appropriations House of Representatives, *Department of Defense Appropriations for 1984*, 98th Congress, first session (12 April 1983) p. 476.
52. Col. G. G. Watson, Hearings ... (2 March 1978), p. 696; Brig-Gen. L. B. Lennon, 'Defense Planning for Chemical Warfare', p. 10.
53. R. L. Wagner, Hearings ... *Department of Defense Authorization for Appropriations for Fiscal Year 1983*, p. 4787.
54. Assembly of Western European Union, *Nuclear Biological and Chemical Protection*, p. 30.
55. S. R. Bowman, *US Chemical Warfare Program* (Congressional Research Service, Library of Congress, issue brief no. 1B 82125, 1983) p. 9; H. Brown, Hearings before the Committee on Armed Services United States Senate, *Department of Defense Authorization for Appropriations for Fiscal Year 1981*, 96th Congress, second session (5 June 1980), p. 2662.
56. *Congressional Record-Senate* (16 September 1980) S 12634.
57. H. Brown and Gen. B. W. Rogers, Hearings before the Committee on Armed Services United States Senate, *Department of Defense Authorization for Appropriations for Fiscal Year 1980*, 96th Congress, first session, (25 January and 8 February 1979) pp. 97, 675.
58. Maj-Gen. N. J. Fulwyler, Hearings before the Committee on Armed Services United States Senate, *Department of Defense Authorization for Appropriations for Fiscal Year 1983*, 97th Congress, second session (15 March 1982) p. 4800.

59. Lt-Col. G. Eifried, 'Russian CW', p. 28; Brig-Gen. L. B. Lennon, 'Defense Planning for Chemical Warfare', p. 11.

60. K. G. Benz, (NBC Defense Part 2', p. 164; Maj. N. V. Raymond, 'Is USAFE Ready for Chemical Warfare?' *Air Force Magazine* (November 1979) p. 103.

61. S. R. Bowman, *US Chemical Warfare Program*, p. 9.

62. R. L. Wagner, Hearings . . . *Binary Chemical Weapons*, p. 73.

63. R. D. M. Furlong, 'The Strategic Situation in Northern Europe improvements vital for NATO', *International Defense Review*, vol. 12, no. 6 (1979) p. 909; SIPRI, *The Problem of Chemical and Biological Warfare*, vol. 2, pp. 226–7.

64. Lt-Col. G. Eifried, 'Russian CW', p. 28; Col. A. G. Vicary and Wing Commander J. Wilson, 'Nuclear Biological and Chemical Defence', p. 12.

65. M. Meselson and J. Perry Robinson, 'Chemical Warfare and Chemical Disarmament', p. 40.

66. Assembly of Western European Union *Nuclear biological and chemical protection*, pp. 36–44.

67. A. Hay, S. Murphy, S. Rose and J. Perry Robinson, 'Chemical Warfare in the Eighties', *Journal of the Medical Association for Prevention of War* (Autumn, 1982) p. 353.

68. *Colorado Springs Gazette – Telegraph*, 22 November 1979, p. 7; and Assembly of Western European Union, *Nuclear Biological and Chemical Protection*, pp. 37, 42, 44.

69. *Congressional Record – Senate* (13 July 1983) p. S9789.

70. J. Perry Robinson, Hearings . . . *Binary Chemical Weapons*, pp. 43, 49.

71. *The Daily Telegraph*, 22 November 1984, p. 5.

72. The Federal Ministry of Defence, *White Paper 1983*, p. 152. See also U. Nerlich, 'Chemical Warfare Policy Alternatives: Defense and Negotiations Options', *NATO's Strategic Options Arms Control and Defense*, ed. by D. S. Yost (New York: Pergammon Press, 1981) p. 206.

73. R. L. Wagner and T. S. Gold, 'Why We Can't Avoid Developing Chemical Weapons', p. 6.

74. Col. G. G. Watson, Hearings . . . (2 March 1978) p. 699.

75. *Congressional Record-House* (10 September 1980), p. H8709; Maj-Gen. H. H. Cooksey, Hearings before the Committee on Appropriations United States Senate, *Department of Defense Appropriations for 1976*, 94th Congress, first session (12 May 1975), p. 490.

76. Lt-Col. G. Eifried, 'Russian CW', p. 25; *New York Times*, 24 May 1981, VI, p. 37; *Written Answer*, p. 4761; J. Perry Robinson, 'Chemical Weapons and Europe', *Survival*, vol. XXIV, no. 1 (January/February 1982) p. 11.

77. T. S. Gold and Brig-Gen. G. G. Watson, statements in Hearings . . . *Department of Defense Appropriations for 1984*, pp. 448–9, 459–60.

78. Ibid., p. 449.

79. Maj-Gen. N. J. Fulwyler, Hearings . . . *Department of Defense Authorization for Appropriations for Fiscal Year 1983*, p. 4801.

80. *Congressional Record-Senate* (8 November 1983) p. S15 634; Dr Dee, Hearings . . . *Binary Chemical Weapons*, pp. 137–9.

81. *Congressional Record – Senate* (13 July 1983) p. S9784, S9801; (8

November 1983) p. S15 636; M. Meselson, Hearings . . . *Binary Chemical Weapons*, p. 36.

82. T. S. Gold, Hearings . . . *Binary Chemical Weapons*, p. 103.

83. T. S. Gold, statement in Hearings . . . *Department of Defense Appropriations for 1984*, pp. 449–50.

84. R. L. Wagner, Hearings . . . *Department of Defense Authorization for Appropriations for Fiscal Year 1983*, p. 4787; *Written Answer*, p. 4832.

85. T. S. Gold, Hearings . . . *Department of Defense Appropriations for 1983*, pp. 300–2, 322–4.

86. T. S. Gold, statements in Hearings . . . *Department of Defense Appropriations for 1984*, p. 453; and *Binary Chemical Weapons*, p. 110.

87. T. S. Gold, statement in Hearings . . . *Department of Defense Appropriations for 1983*, p. 268.

88. 'The Quiet Comeback of Chemical Warfare', *Chemical Week*, vol. 129, no. 8 (19 August 1981) pp. 53–6.

89. T. S. Gold and Maj-Gen. N. J. Fulwyler, Hearings . . . *Department of Defense Appropriations for 1983*, pp. 284–5.

90. Sen. C. Levin, Hearings . . . *Chemical Warfare*, p. 41.

91. T. S. Gold, statement in Hearings . . . *Department of Defense Appropriations for 1983*, p. 269; R. L. Wagner and T. S. Gold, 'Why We Can't Avoid Developing Chemical Weapons', p. 9; *Los Angeles Times* (10 March 1982) p. 9.

92. W. M. Carpenter, 'Evaluation of Chemical Warfare Policy', p. 27.

93. M. Meselson, Hearings . . . *Department of Defense Authorization for Appropriations for Fiscal Year 1983*, pp. 5057–8; J. D. Douglass, 'Chemical Weapons', p. 45.

94. P. A. Pierre, Hearing before the Research and Development Subcommittee of the Committee on Armed Services House of Representatives, *Department of Defense Authorization for Appropriations Fiscal Year 1979*, 95th Congress, second session (2 March 1978) p. 704; *The Washington Star* (30 January 1979) p. A-4.

95. *Department of Defense Authorization Act 1984*, 12 September 1983, Committee on Armed Services, House of Representatives, 98th Congress, first session, Report No. 98–352, p. 86.

96. *The Washington Post* (25 May 1984), p. A1.

97. *Congressional Record – Senate* (16 September 1980) p. S12 639 and (8 November 1983) p. S15 638; *Written Answer*, p. 4837; T. S. Gold, statement in Hearings . . . *Department of Defense Appropriations for 1984*, pp. 454–5.

98. *Congressional Record – House* (22 July 1982) p. H4495; (10 September 1980) H8708.

99. US Comptroller General, Report to the Committee on Foreign Affairs House of Representatives of the United States, *Chemical Warfare: Many Unanswered Questions*, GAO/1PE-83-6 (29 April 1983) p. 30. *Congressional Record – Senate* (16 September 1980) pp. S12 638–9; (13 July 1983) p. S9784; (8 November 1983) p. S15 636; M. Meselson, Hearings . . . *Binary Chemical Weapons*, pp. 35–6.

100. C. W. Weinberger, answer to Senator Sam Nunn, Hearings before the Committee on Armed Services United States Senate, *Department of*

Defense Authorization for Appropriations for Fiscal Year 1984, 98th Congress, first session (1 February 1983) p. 121; *Congressional Record – Senate* (13 July 1983) pp. S9790 and 9804. See also M. Meselson and J. Perry Robinson, Hearings . . . *Binary Chemical Weapons*, pp. 31, 37, 44–5, 51; *Congressional Record – House* (15 June 1983) p. H4003.

101. *Congressional Record – House* (22 July 1982) pp. H4475–6; *Congressional Record – Senate* (16 September 1980) p. S12 644 and (13 July 1983) pp. S9785 and S9789; J. F. Leonard, statement . . . *Binary Chemical Weapons*, p. 6.

102. J. Perry Robinson, statement . . . *Binary Chemical Weapons*, pp. 47, 60; 'Old Fears, New Weapons: Brewing a Chemical Arms Race', *The Defense Monitor*, vol. IX, no. 10 (1980) p. 7.

103. G. Hart, letter to the *Wall Street Journal* (4 February 1982) p. 31; *Congressional Record – Senate* (16 September 1980) p. S12 644 (13 July 1983) p. S9787 (8 November 1983) p. S15 638; J. F. Leonard, M. Meselson and J. Perry Robinson, statements . . . *Binary Chemical Weapons*, pp. 7, 38, 43.

104. *Congressional Record – House* (10 September 1980) p. H8710; *Congressional Record – Senate* (13 July 1983) p. S9785 (8 November 1983) p. S15 628; *The New York Times*, 13 July 1983, p. A18.

105. T. S. Gold, statement . . . *Department of Defense Appropriations for 1984*, p. 446.

106. *Written answer*, p. 4838.

107. T. S. Gold, Hearings . . . *Department of Defense Appropriations for 1984*, p. 507.

108. M. Meselson, statement and Hearings . . . *Binary Chemical Weapons*, pp. 37, 66–7.

109. *Congressional Record – House* (15 June 1983), p. H4003.

110. T. S. Gold, Hearings . . . *Department of Defense Appropriations for 1984*, p. 489; see also pp. 467–9, 492 and answers by Admiral J. J. Barth, pp. 502–3, Gen. J. Tietge, Hearings . . . *Binary Chemical Weapons*, pp. 132–3.

111. The DoD calculates that each C-141/B sortie could carry either 60 Bigeye bombs or 8 TMU-28/B spray tanks or 608 155 mm binary shells or 504 155 mm unitary shells. *Written Answer*, pp. 4820–1.

112. L. G. Fields to J. W. Warner, 7 April 1983, *Congressional Record – Senate* (13 July 1983) p. S9803.

113. R. R. Burt, Hearings . . . *Binary Chemical Weapons*, p. 81; *Written Answer* p. 4834.

114. *Written Answer*, p. 4835; T. S. Gold, Hearings . . . *Department of Defense Appropriations for 1984*, p. 474.

115. *DoD Authorization Act 1985*, 26 September 1984, Committee on Armed Services House of Representatives, 98th Congress, second session, Report 98-1080, pp. 141–2.

8 THE GENEVA NEGOTIATIONS: PROBLEMS AND PROSPECTS

1. *The United Nations and Disarmament 1945–1970* (New York: United Nations, 1970) pp. 349–58.
2. United Nations General Assembly, *Report of the Sec-General on Chemical and Bacteriological (Biological) Weapons'* (1 July 1969), p. 115.
3. J. K. Miettinen, 'Chemical Warfare and Arms Control Crisis and Concern', *Bulletin of Peace Proposals*, vol. 14, no. 3 (1983) p. 251; see also M. Meselson, Hearings . . . *Department of Defense Authorization for Appropriations for Fiscal Year 1983*, p. 5065; J. P. Perry Robinson, Hearings before the Subcommittee on National Security Policy and Scientific Developments of the Committee on Foreign Affairs House of Representatives, *US Chemical Warfare Policy*, 93rd Congress, second session (14 May 1974) p. 319; Rear Adm. T. Davies, Hearings before the Committee on Armed Services United States Senate, *Department of Defense Authorization for Appropriations for Fiscal Year 1984*, 98th Congress, first session (7 April 1983) p. 2770.
4. *The United Nations and Disarmament 1945–70*, pp. 355–7.
5. 'Draft Convention for the Prohibition of Biological Methods of Warfare with Associated Draft Security Council Resolution tabled by the United Kingdom in the Conference of the Eighteen-Nation Committee on Disarmament in Geneva on 10 July, 1969', Cmnd. 4113 (1968–9) liv.
6. *United Nations Disarmament Yearbook* (New York: United Nations 1978) vol. 3, p. 234.
7. Ibid.; N. A. Sims, *Approaches to Disarmament* (London: Quaker Peace & Service, 1979) pp. 63–4.
8. F. Barnaby, 'CBW–an unresolved horror', *The Bulletin of Atomic Scientists* vol. 36, no. 6 (June 1980) pp. 8–9.
9. *United Nations Disarmament Yearbook* (New York: United Nations, 1976) vol. 1, pp. 169–70.
10. V. J. Adams, 'The Abolition of Chemical Weapons', *Arms Control and Disarmament*, vol. 4, no. 2 (September, 1983) p. 149.
11. *United Nations Disarmament Yearbook*, vol. 1, p. 170.
12. 'Draft Convention on the prohibition of the development, production and stockpiling of chemical weapons and on their destruction, dated 28 March, by Bulgaria, the Byelorussian Soviet Socialist Republic, Czechoslovakia, Hungary, Mongolia, Poland, Romania, the Ukranian Soviet Socialist Republic and the Union of Soviet Socialist Republics', document CCD/361 (1972), Cmnd. 5344 (1972–3) vii, pp. 135–9.
13. 'Draft Convention by Japan on the Prohibition of the Development, Production and Stockpiling of Chemical Weapons and on their Destruction', document CCD/420 (1974), Cmnd. 6512 (1975–6) x, pp. 163–9; *United Nations Disarmament Yearbook*, vol. 1, p. 175.
14. 'Draft Convention by the United Kingdom on the Prohibition of the Development, Production and stockpiling of Chemical Weapons and on their destruction', document CCD/512 (1974), Cmnd. 7269 (1977–8) ix, pp. 186–91; N. A. Sims, 'Britain, Chemical Weapons and Disarmament', *ADIU Report*, vol. 2, no. 3 (July–August 1980) p. 2.

15. C. C. Flowerree, 'Chemical Weapons: A Case Study in Verification', *Arms Control Today*, vol. 13, no. 3 (April, 1983) p. 7.
16. 'USSR–United States Joint Report on Progress in the Bilateral Negotiations on the Prohibition of Chemical Weapons', document CD/48 (7 August 1979).
17. M. Meselson and J. Perry Robinson, 'Chemical Warfare and Chemical Disarmament', p. 43; J. Perry Robinson, Hearings ... *Binary Chemical Weapons*, p. 48.
18. C. C. Flowerree, 'Chemical Weapons', p. 7.
19. G. K. Vachon, 'Chemical Weapons and the Third World', p. 82.
20. M. D. Busby, Hearings ... *Binary Chemical Weapons*, p. 91.
21. T. Gold, Hearings before the Subcommittee on Strategic and Theater Nuclear Forces Committee on Armed Services United States Senate, *Department of Defense Authorization for Appropriations for Fiscal Year 1984*, 98th Congress, first session (7 April 1983) p. 2739.
22. Rear Adm. T. Davies, ibid., p. 2776; J. Perry Robinson and M. Meselson, Hearings ... *Binary Chemical Weapons*, pp. 48 and 59.
23. T. Gold, Hearings ... *Department of Defense Appropriations for 1984*, p. 501.
24. *Written Answer*, p. 4843.
25. S. R. Bowman, *US Chemical Warfare Program*, p. 5.
26. *The United Nations Disarmament Yearbook* (New York: United Nations, 1982) vol. 6, pp. 211, 215–23; 'Report of the *Ad Hoc* Working Group on Chemical Weapons to the Committee on Disarmament', document CD/220 (17 August 1981).
27. 156th plenary meeting of the Committee on Disarmament, 18 February 1982, Report of the Committee on Disarmament, *Official Records of the General Assembly: Thirty-Seventh Session, Supplement No. 27* (A/37/27).
28. V. J. Adams, 'The Abolition of Chemical Weapons', p. 154.
29. D. Summerhayes, 'Chemical Weapons: postures, plans and prospects for control', *ADIU Report*, vol. 5, no. 6 (November/December 1983) pp. 2–3.
30. J. Aita, 'US Urges Stronger Effort on Chemical Weapons Ban', *United States Information Service*, 5 November 1982.
31. M. Kampelman, 'US Seeks Ban on Chemical Warfare', *United States Information Service*, 16 February 1982.
32. T. Gold, Hearings ... *Department of Defense Authorization for Appropriations for Fiscal Year 1984*, p. 2736.
33. L. H. Gelb, 'Keeping an Eye on Russia', *New York Times Magazine* (29 November 1981) p. 33.
34. Ibid., pp. 31, 64; M. Popovskiy, Hearings before the Subcommittee on Oversight of the Permanent Select Committee on Intelligence House of Representatives, *The Sverdlovsk Incident: Soviet Compliance with the Biological Weapons Convention?* 96th Congress, second session (29 May 1980) p. 5.
35. *Soviet Military Power 1984*, p. 73.
36. Ibid.; Lt-Gen. E. T. Tighe, Hearings ... *Chemical Warfare*, p. 23; L. H. Gelb, 'Keeping an Eye on Russia', pp. 59–60.

37. Z. Medvedev, 'The Great Russian Germ War Fiasco', *The New Scientist*, vol. 87 (31 July 1980) pp. 360–1; P. Towle, 'The Soviet Union and the Biological Weapons Convention', and J. P. Perry Robinson, 'Discussion of "The Soviet Union and the Biological Weapons Convention"', and a Guide to Sources on the Sverdlovsk Incident', *Arms Control*, vol. 3, no. 3 (December 1982), pp. 31–56.

38. M. Kampelman, 'US Seeks Ban on Chemical Warfare'; V. J. Adams, 'The Abolition of Chemical Weapons', p. 156.

39. T. Gold, Hearings . . . *Department of Defense Appropriations for 1984*, p. 475; *Written Answer*, pp. 4818–9; N. A. Sims, 'Britain, Chemical Weapons and Disarmament', p. 3.

40. N. A. Sims, ibid.; J. P. Perry Robinson, 'The Negotiations on Chemical-Warfare Arms Control', *Arms Control*, vol. 1, no. 1 (May, 1980) p. 46.

41. At Geneva, toxicity criteria have been used to distinguish between 'super-toxic lethal chemical' which has a median lethal dose less than or equal to 0.5 mg/kg (subcutaneous administration) or 2000 mg-min/m³ (by inhalation), 'other lethal chemical' which has a median lethal dose greater than 0.5 mg/kg (subcutaneous administration) or 2000 mg-min/m³ (by inhalation) and less than or equal to 10 mg/kg (subcutaneous administration) or 20 000 mg-min/m³ (by inhalation), and 'other harmful chemical' which has a median lethal dose greater than 10 mg/kg (subcutaneous administration) or 20 000 mg-min/m³ (by inhalation), 'Report of the *Ad Hoc* Working Group on Chemical Weapons to the Committee on Disarmament', document CD/416 (22 August 1983), Annex 1, p. 4.

42. Permitted purposes are defined as 'non-hostile purposes, that is, industrial, agricultural, research, medical, law enforcement, other peaceful or protective purposes; and military purposes which are not related to the use of chemical weapons'. Ibid, Annex 1, p. 3.

43. Although an agreed definition of key precursors is still being sought, they are basically chemicals which are of vital importance in producing a CW agent.

44. CD/CW/WP.78 (2 April 1984). See also Soviet Union, 'Basic Provisions of a Convention on the Prohibition of the Development, Production and Stockpiling of Chemical Weapons and their Destruction', CD/294 (21 July 1982).

45. The Ministry of Foreign Affairs of Finland, *Technical Evaluation of Selected Scientific Methods for the Verification of Chemical Disarmament* (Helsinki, 1984) pp. 71–2; Federal Republic of Germany, 'Verification of the Destruction of Chemical Weapons', document CD/518 (17 July 1984).

46. The Ministry of Foreign Affairs of Finland, *Technical Evaluation of Selected Scientific Methods*, 73–4; United Kingdom of Great Britain and Northern Ireland, 'Verification of Non-Production of Chemical Weapons', document CD/514 (10 July 1984).

47. United Kingdom of Great Britain and Northern Ireland, 'Verification of Non-Production of Chemical Weapons', document CD/353 (8 March 1983).

48. United Kingdom, 'Chemical Weapons Convention: Verification and

Compliance – the Challenge Element', document CD/431 (10 February 1984).

49. R. Mikulak, 'Preventing Chemical Warfare', *Chemical Weapons and Chemical Arms Control*, ed. by M. Meselson, pp. 77, 79.

50. M. Meselson and J. Perry Robinson, 'Chemical Warfare and Chemical Disarmament', p. 43.

51. For a list of these differences as late as February 1984, see 'Chairman's suggestion for a Working Structure for the Negotiations on a Chemical Weapons Convention', document CD/CW/WP.67 (28 February 1984).

52. CD/CW/WP.67 (28 February 1984).

53. Ambassador Louis G. Fields Jr., statement to the Conference on Disarmament, 5 July 1984, p. 5.

54. T. S. Gold, Hearings before the Committee on Armed Services House of Representatives, *Department of Defense Authorization and Oversight Hearings on HR 2,287 (HR 2,969) Department of Defense Authorization of Appropriations for Fiscal Year 1984 and Oversight of Previously Authorized Programs*, 98th Congress, first session (18 April 1983) p. 1567.

55. N. A. Sims, 'Chemical Weapons – Control or Chaos?', *Faraday Discussion Paper No. 1* (The Council for Arms Control, 1984) p. 6.

56. CD/343. See also CD/387 and CD/353.

57. *Common Security. A programme for disarmament: The Report of the Independent Commission on Disarmament and Security Issues* (London: Pan Books, 1982) pp. 150–1, 177–8.

58. Ambassador J. F. Leonard, Hearings . . . *Binary Chemical Weapons*, pp. 6, 9.

59. *The Times*, 12 January 1984, p. 4.

60. S. J. Lundin, 'A Chemical Weapons Free Zone in Europe? An Analysis', *Chemical Weapons and Arms Control Views from Europe* (Rome: Centro di Studi Strategici, 1983) pp. 22–31.

61. *Fiscal Year 1985 Arms Control Impact Statements*, Committee on Foreign Relations United States Senate, 98th Congress, second session (March 1984) p. 186; Ambassador L. G. Fields, statement to the Conference on Disarmament (12 July 1984) p. 5.

62. CD/500 (18 April 1984). See also the speeches of Vice-President G. Bush, 18 April 1984, *United States Information Service*, and Ambassador L. G. Fields, Conference on Disarmament, 12 and 19 July 1984.

63. *The Washington Post*, 5 April 1984, p. A35; *Science*, vol. 224 (20 April 1984) p. 264; *The Wall Street Journal*, 6 April 1984, p. 2.

64. Gen. F. Amadei and E. Jacchia, 'Of Interdiction of Chemical Warfare', *Chemical Weapons and Arms Control Views from Europe*, p. 9; V. J. Adams, 'The Abolition of Chemical Weapons', p. 150; CD/532 (8 August 1984).

65. G. Lyons, 'Invisible Wars', *Harpers*, vol. 263, no. 1579 (December, 1981) p. 52.

66. Rear Admiral T. Davies, Hearings . . . *Department of Defense Authorization for Appropriations for Fiscal Year 1984*, p. 2770.

67. J. P. Perry Robinson and M. Meselson, Hearings . . . *Binary Chemical Weapons*, pp. 48, 59.

68. A. Hoeber, Hearings on Military Posture and H.R. 5968, *Department of Defense Authorization for Appropriations for Fiscal Year 1983* before the Committee on Armed Services House of Representatives, 97th Congress, second session (18 March 1982) p. 827.

69. M. MacDonald, Hearings on *Department of Defense Appropriations for 1983* before a Subcommittee of the Committee on Appropriations House of Representatives, 97th Congress, second session (23 June 1982) p. 277.

70. T. Gold, Hearings . . . *Department of Defense Authorization for Appropriations for Fiscal Year 1984*, p. 2738; Ambassador L. G. Fields to Sen. J. W. Warner, 6 April 1983, ibid., p. 2782.

71. T. Gold, Hearings . . . *on HR 2,287 (HR 2,969), Department of Defense Authorization of Appropriations for Fiscal Year 1984 and Oversight of Previously Authorized Programs*, p. 1565.

72. *Congressional Record*, 13 July 1983, S 9803; and Ambassador L. G. Fields to Senator J. W. Warner, 6 April 1983, Hearings . . . *Department of Defense Authorization for Appropriations for Fiscal Year 1984*, p. 2783.

73. CD/CW/WP. 67 (28 February 1984).

74. F. C. Ikle, Hearings before the Special Subcommittee on Arms Control and Disarmament of the Committee on Armed Services, House of Representatives, *Review of Arms Control and Disarmament Activities*, 93rd Congress, second session (8 May 1974) p. 9; H. Brown, Hearings . . . *Chemical Warfare*, pp. 5, 10 and 20.

75. *Congressional Record*, 11 June 1974, S 18 733.

76. *Congressional Record*, 22 July 1982, H 4475; 16 September 1980, S 12 644; 13 July 1983, S 9785.

77. Brig-Gen. G. G. Watson, Hearings before the Committee on Armed Services United States Senate, *Department of Defense Authorization for Appropriations for Fiscal Year 1984*, 98th Congress, first session (7 April 1983) p. 2790.

78. J. Lundin, 'The Scope and Control of Chemical Disarmament Treaties Particularly With Regard to Binary Chemical Weapons', *Co-operation and Conflict*, vol. 8, no. 3/4 (1973) pp. 145–53.

79. J. Perry Robinson, *The United States Binary Nerve Gas Programme: National and International Implications* (ISIO monographs, first series, no. 10, 1975) p. 31.

80. *Science*, vol. 224 (20 April 1984) p. 263.

81. Congressman E. Bethune and Ambassador L. G. Fields to Senator J. W. Warner, 6 April 1983, Hearings . . . *Department of Defense Authorization for Appropriations for Fiscal Year 1984*, pp. 2772, 2782.

82. T. Gold, Hearings . . . *Department of Defense Appropriations for 1984*, p. 455; and V. J. Adams, 'The Abolition of Chemical Weapons', p. 148.

83. H. Brown, Hearings . . . *Chemical Warfare*, p. 4; J. P. Wade, Hearings . . . *Department of Defense Appropriations for 1982*, p. 810.

84. L. Gelb, 'Keeping an Eye on Russia', p. 172; Commander J. J. Tritten, 'Their Broken Promises', *United States Naval Institute Proceedings*, vol. 110, no. 8 (August 1984) p. 60.

85. CD/500, p. 11.

86. C. C. Flowerree, 'Chemical Weapons', p. 2.

87. R. Mikulak, 'Preventing Chemical Warfare'; and J. Perry Robinson in

'General discussion', *Chemical Weapons and Chemical Arms Control*, pp. 76 and 86.

9 DETERRING CHEMICAL WARFARE

1. T. Gold and Maj-Gen. N. J. Fulwyler, Hearings ... *Department of Defense Appropriations for 1983*, pp. 276–7.
2. J. Perry Robinson, Hearings ... *Binary Chemical Weapons*, pp. 42–9; J. F. Calvert, 'Chemical Weapons: Problems and Policy Formulation' (Pennsylvania: Strategic Studies Institute, US Army War College, Carlisle Barracks, 1981) p. 10; Bagwax, 'Chemical Weapons: Time for a Fresh Look', *British Army Review*, no. 67 (April, 1981) pp. 11–12.
3. 'Select Committee on Science and Technology Minutes of Evidence, 18 July 1968', Cmnd. 139–xxi (1967–8) xiv, p. 459. See also *Parl Deb.*, Fifth ser., vol. 801 (8 May 1970) p. 389.
4. U. Nerlich, 'Chemical Warfare Policy Alternatives', pp. 210–11.
5. H. Brown, Hearings ... *Chemical Warfare*, pp. 4, 15; T. Gold, Hearings ... *Department of Defense Appropriations for 1984*, p. 475; Brig. Gen. G. G. Watson and Lt-Col. J. P. L. Anderson, 'An Urgent Need', p. 63.
6. R. L. Wagner, Hearings ... *Department of Defense Authorization for Appropriations for Fiscal Year 1983*, p. 4787; A. M. Hoeber, Hearings on Military Posture and H. R. 5968, *Department of Defense Authorization for Appropriations for Fiscal Year 1983* before the Committee on Armed Services House of Representatives, 97th Congress, second session (18 March 1982) p. 827.
7. Lt-Col. G. M. Lovelace, 'Chemical Warfare', p. 56.
8. A. M. Hoeber, *The Chemistry of Defeat*, pp. 64–5; Col. C. H. Bay, 'The Other Gas Crisis – Chemical Weapons: Part II', *Parameters*, vol. 9 no. 4 (1979) p. 68.
9. *The Stars and Stripes* (18 March 1980), p. 2.
10. R. Mikulak, 'Preventing Chemical Warfare', pp. 73–4.
11. H. Ruhle, 'Chemische Waffen und Europaische Sicherheit 1980–90', *Europaische Wehrhunde*, vol. 27, no. 1 (January 1978) p. 8; A. M. Hoeber, *The Chemistry of Defeat*, p. 64.
12. T. Gold, Hearings ... *Department of Defense Authorization for Appropriations for Fiscal Year 1983*, p. 4752–3 and Hearings ... *Department of Defense Appropriations for Fiscal Year 1984*, pp. 474–5.
13. J. Perry Robinson, Hearings before the Subcommittee on National Security Policy and Scientific Developments of the Committee on Foreign Affairs House of Representatives, *US Chemical Warfare Policy*, 93rd Congress, second session (2 May 1974) p. 66.
14. SIPRI, *The Problem of Chemical and Biological Warfare*, vol. 2, p. 150; Col. C. H. Bay, 'Chemical Warfare and the Military Balance', *Parameters*, vol. 7, no. 2 (1977) p. 47.
15. R. L. Wagner and Maj-Gen. N. J. Fulwyler, Hearings ... *Department of Defense Authorization for Appropriations for Fiscal Year 1983*, pp. 4746, 4787 and 4801.

16. M. Meselson and J. Perry Robinson, 'Chemical Warfare and Chemical Disarmament', p. 40; J. P. Perry Robinson, 'Chemical Weapons and Europe', *Survival*, vol. XXIV, no. 1 (January/February 1982) p. 13.

17. H. Brown, Hearings before a subcommittee of the Committee on Appropriations, House of Representatives, *Department of Defense Appropriations for 1981*, 96th Congress, second session (4 February 1980) p. 508.

18. J. Schlesinger, Hearings before a subcommittee of the Committee on Appropriations House of Representatives, *Department of Defense Appropriations for 1976*, 94th Congress, first session (26 February 1975) p. 118; T. Gold, Hearings . . . *Department of Defense Appropriations for 1984*, p. 475.

19. E. Greiner, Hearings before the Committee on Armed Services, United States Senate, *FY Authorization for Military Procurement, Research and Development, and Active Duty, Selected Reserve and Civilian Personnel Strengths*, 95th Congress, first session (22 March 1977) p. 4020.

20. R. L. Wagner, Hearings . . . *Department of Defense Authorization for Appropriations for Fiscal Year 1983*, p. 4787.

21. Ibid.; T. Gold, Hearings . . . *Department of Defense Appropriations for 1983*, pp. 266–7; Col. J. E. Leonard, 'Chemical Warfare – An Urgent Need For a Credible Deterrent' (Pennsylvania: US Army War College, Carlisle Barracks, 1982) p. 35.

22. Department of Defense answer, Hearings . . . *Department of Defense Appropriations for 1983*, pp. 320–1.

23. *Congressional Record*, 13 July 1983, p. S 9789.

24. Brig-Gen. G. G. Watson and Lt-Col. P. R. L. Anderson, 'An Urgent Need', p. 65; R. L. Wagner, Hearings . . . *Department of Defense Authorization for Appropriations for Fiscal Year 1983*, pp. 4789–90.

25. J. Perry Robinson, 'Chemical Weapons and Europe', p. 12.

26. Ibid., p. 13; and J. Perry Robinson, 'The Changing Status of Chemical and Biological Warfare: Recent Technical, Military and Political Developments', p. 337.

27. M. Meselson, Hearings . . . *Binary Chemical Weapons*, p. 35; J. Perry Robinson, 'Chemical Weapons and Europe', p. 13.

28. C. N. Donnelly, 'Winning the NBC War', p. 993.

29. U. Nerlich, 'Chemical Warfare Policy Alternatives', p. 210.

30. J. Perry Robinson, 'Chemical Weapons and Europe', p. 13.

31. Ibid.; M. Meselson, Hearings . . . *Department of Defense Authorization for Appropriations for Fiscal Year 1983*, p. 5065.

32. H. Feigl, 'Communication', *Chemical Weapons and Chemical Arms Control*, pp. 102–3; U. Nerlich, 'Chemical Warfare Policy Alternatives', p. 212; J. M. Weinstein and H. G. Gole, p. 31; J. Perry Robinson, 'Chemical Weapons and Europe', p. 16.

33. W. Lepkowski, 'Chemical Warfare', p. 17.

34. Brig-Gen. G. G. Watson and Lt-Col. P. R. L. Anderson, 'An Urgent Need', p. 59.

35. A. M. Hoeber, *The Chemistry of Defeat*, pp. 56–7 and M. Meselson, Hearings . . . *Department of Defense Authorization for Appropriations for Fiscal Year 1983*, p. 5065.

36. J. Erickson, 'The Soviet Union's Growing Arsenal', p. 70; R. Burt, 'Deterrence and the Alliance – What Role for Chemical Weapons?' *Evaluation of Chemical Warfare Policy Alternatives*, p. 62.
37. J. Perry Robinson, statement in Hearings . . . *Binary Chemical Weapons*, p. 41.
38. *Congressional Quarterly*, vol. 42, no. 5 (4 February 1984) p. 187.
39. H. Ruhle, 'Chemische Waffen', p. 5.
40. J. M. Weinstein and H. G. Gole, 'Chemical Weapons Rearmament', p. 33.
41. Ibid., pp. 32–4, 48; H. Feigl, 'Communication', p. 102.
42. C. N. Donnelly, 'Winning the NBC War', p. 996; C. J. Dick, 'Soviet Chemical Warfare Capabilities', p. 38; H. Ruhle, 'Chemische Waffen', p. 10; Sq. Ldr. A. F. Graveley, 'Defence or Deterrence', pp. 18–20; Gen. Sir M. Farndale reported in *The Daily Telegraph*, 22 September 1984, p. 5.
43. H. Ruhle, 'Chemische Waffen', p. 10.
44. *Written answer*, pp. 4840–1.
45. Maj-Gen. N. J. Fulwyler, Hearings on Military Posture and H.R.5968 *Department of Defense Authorization for Appropriations for FY 1983*, p. 839.

Select Bibliography

As material for this book has been drawn from a wide variety of sources, only some items will be listed here. For references to *Parliamentary Debates*, to the *Congressional Record*, to the *Official Journal* of the League of Nations and to articles or speeches reported in newspapers, readers should consult the Notes section. They may also wish to consult the more comprehensive bibliographies in the SIPRI volumes, in *CBW An Introduction and Bibliography*, edited by J. P. Perry Robinson (Center for the Study of Armament and Disarmament, Los Angeles: California State University, 1974) and in *Arms Control and Disarmament a Bibliography*, edited by R. D. Burns (Santa Barbara: ABC-Clio, 1977).

1 Primary Sources

Official papers consulted in the preparation of this book included those of the Admiralty, War Office, Air Ministry, Cabinet, Committee of Imperial Defence, the Prime Minister, Chiefs of Staff Committee and the Foreign Office in the Public Record Office. The other manuscript collections consulted were:

Churchill College, Cambridge
Weir, Viscount, papers

House of Lords
Lloyd George, David, papers

Imperial War Museum
British Intelligence Objectives Subcommittee Reports
Combined Intelligence Objectives Subcommittee Reports
Cotton, E. W., diaries
French, Field Marshal Sir John, papers
Hodgkin, Brig. A. E., diaries
Kingsley, Sq. Ldr. E. D., papers

United Nations Library, Geneva
League of Nations Archive

Library of Congress, Washington DC
Pershing, Gen. John J., papers
Leahy, Admiral William D., papers

Liddell Hart Centre for Military Archives, King's College, University of London
Foulkes, Brig. Charles H.

National Archives, Washington DC
RG 218 Records of the United States Joint Chiefs of Staff
National Library of Scotland
Haig, Earl, papers
Public Record Office
Kitchener, Lord, papers

2 Documents and Printed Primary Sources

Conference on the Limitation of Armament, Washington. 12 November
   1921–6 February 1922 (Washington DC: US G(overnment) P(rinting)
   O(ffice), 1922).
Documents on British Foreign Policy 1919–1939 (London: HMSO).
Documents on the Laws of War, ed. by Roberts, A. and Guelff, R. (Oxford:
   Oxford University Press, 1982).
League of Nations. *Report on the Temporary Mixed Commission for the
   Reduction of Armaments.* 30 July 1924, A.16.1924.IX.
League of Nations. *Proceedings of the Conference for the Supervision of the
   International Trade in Arms and Ammunition and on Implements of War.*
   Held at Geneva, 4 May to 17 June 1925. A.13.1925.IX.
Papers Relating to the Foreign Relations of the United States (Washington DC:
   USGPO, annual).
Rosenman, S. I. (compiler). *The Public Papers and Addresses of Franklin D.
   Roosevelt.* 1942 Volume 'Humanity on the Defensive', 1943 Volume 'The
   Tide Turns'. Harpers, New York, 1950.
Scott, J. B. (ed.). *The Reports to the Hague Conferences 1899 and 1907.*
   Oxford University Press, Oxford, 1917.
Susmel, E. and D. (eds.). *Opera Omnia di Benito Mussolini.* Florence, 1951–
U.S. Arms Control and Disarmament Agency. *Arms Control and Disarma-
   ment Agreements. Texts and History of Negotiations.* Washington D.C.,
   1977.
U.S. Military Intelligence Reports. China 1911–1941 ed. by P. Kesaris.
   University Publications of America, Frederick, Maryland. 1983.

3 Official Reports and Publications

Assembly of Western European Union. *Nuclear, biological and chemical
   protection. Report submitted on behalf of the Committee on Defence
   Questions and Armaments by Mr Banks, Rapporteur.* Document 838. 29
   April 1980.
Common Security. *A programme for disarmament. The Report of the
   Independent Commission on Disarmament and Security Issues.* Pan Books,
   London, 1982.
Federal Minister of Defence. *White Paper 1983. The Security of the Federal
   Republic of Germany.* Bonn, 1983.

Letter dated 23 June 1982 from the Permanent Representative of Canada to the United Nations addressed to the Secretary-General transmitting a 'Study of the Possible Use of Chemical Warfare Agents in Southeast Asia' by H. B. Schiefer. A/37/308.

Letters dated 25 August and 7 September 1982 from the Permanent Mission of Canada to the United Nations addressed to the Secretariat transmitting reports entitled respectively 'An epidemiological investigation of alleged CW/BW agents in SE Asia' and 'Report on possible use of CW agents in southeast Asia'. Conference room paper 1/Add.11.

Letter dated 20 May 1982 from the Permanent Representative of the Union of Soviet Socialist Republics to the United Nations addressed to the Secretary-General. A/37/233.

Ministry of Defence. *Medical Manual of Defence Against Chemical Agents* (London: HMSO, 1972).

Ministry of Foreign Affairs of Finland. *Technical Evaluation of Selected Scientific Methods for Verification of Chemical Disarmament* (Helsinki, 1984).

Note verbale dated 4 August 1983 from the Acting Permanent Representative of the United States of America to the United Nations addressed to the Secretary-General. A/38/326.

Report of the Enquiry into the Medical and Toxicological aspects of CS (Orthochlorobenzylidene Malononitrile), Cmnd 4775, 1970–1, xxi.

Statement on the Defence Estimates 1984, Cmnd 9227–1, 1984.

United States Department of Defense. *Continuing Development of Chemical Weapon Capabilities in the USSR* (Washington DC: USGPO, October, 1983).

United States Department of Defense. *Soviet Military Power 1984* (Washington DC: USGPO, 1984).

United States Department of State. *Chemical Warfare in South East Asia and Afghanistan. Report to the Congress from Secretary of State Alexander M. Haig Jr.* 22 March 1982, Special Report 98.

United States Department of State. *Chemical Warfare in South East Asia and Afghanistan: An Update Report from Secretary of State George P. Shultz.* November 1982, Special Report No. 104.

United States Department of State. *Chemical Weapons Use in Southeast Asia and Afghanistan.* Current Policy No. 553, 21 February 1984.

United States Department of State. *Reports of the Use of Chemical Weapons in Afghanistan, Laos and Kampuchea.* August, 1980.

United States Department of State. *Update to the Compendium on the Reports of the Use of Chemical Weapons.* March, 1981.

United Nations General Assembly. *Chemical and Bacteriological (Biological) Weapons Report of the Secretary-General.* A/37/259, 20 November 1981.

United Nations General Assembly. *Chemical and Bacteriological (Biological) Weapons Report of the Secretary-General.* A/37/259, 1 December 1982.

United Nations General Assembly. *Report of the Secretary-General on Chemical and Bacteriological (Biological) Weapons and the Effects of their Possible Use.* A/7575, 1 July 1969.

United Nations Security Council. *Report of the Specialists Appointed by the Secretary-General to Investigate Allegations by the Islamic Republic of Iran Concerning the Use of Chemical Weapons.* S/16433, 26 March 1984.

World Health Organisation. *Health Aspects of Chemical and Biological Weapons: Report of a WHO Group of Consultants* (Geneva, 1970).

4 United States Department of the Army

'Chemical Warfare – An Urgent Need for a Credible Deterrent', by Col. J. E. Leonard (Pennsylvania: US Army War College, Carlisle Barracks, 19 April 1982).
'Chemical Weapons: Problems and Policy Formulation', by J. F. Calvert (Pennsylvania: Strategic Studies Institute, US Army War College, Carlisle Barracks, 20 December 1981).
'Chemical Weapons Rearmament and the Security of Europe: Can Support be Mustered', by J. M. Weinstein and H. G. Gole (Pennsylvania: Strategic Studies Institute, US Army War College, Carlisle Barracks, 20 January 1983).
Guide to Chemical and Gas Warfare. TM3-200. Departments of the Army and Air Force, 1958.
Handbook on Soviet Ground Forces. FM 30-40. Department of the Army, 30 June 1975.
'Lethal Chemical Warfare: Option or Myth', by R. J. Baird (Pennsylvania: Army War College, Carlisle Barracks, 18 October 1974).
Military Chemistry and Chemical Agents. TM3-215. Department of the Army and AFM 255-7. Department of the Air Force, August 1956.
Operations. FM 100–5, 20 August 1982.
'Soviet Chemical Troops: An Analysis of Articles in *Military Herald*', by Maj. S. Z. Kovacs (Garmish, 1979).
'The Other Gas Crisis: Chemical Weapons', by Col. C. H. Bay (Pennsylvania: Strategic Studies Institute, US Army War College, Carlisle Barracks, 30 June 1979).

5 Congressional Hearings

This section will only refer to special sessions devoted to aspects of chemical and biological warfare. For the hearings on the annual submissions of the Department of Defense readers should consult the Notes.

House of Representatives
Committee on Foreign Affairs. *Chemical-Biological Warfare: US Policies and International Effects.* Hearings before the Subcommittee on National Security Policy and Scientific Developments. 91st Congress, first session. 18, 20 November, 2, 9, 18, 19 December 1969.
Committee on Foreign Affairs. *US Chemical Warfare Policy.* Hearings before the Subcommittee on National Security Policy and Scientific Developments. 93rd Congress, second session. 1, 2, 7, 9, 14 May 1974.
Committee on Foreign Affairs. *Strategic Implications of Chemical and Biological Warfare.* Hearing before the Subcommittee on International

Security and Scientific Affairs and on Asian and Pacific Affairs. 96th Congress, second session. 24 April 1980.

Committee on Foreign Affairs. *Use of Chemical Agents in Southeast Asia Since the Vietnam War.* Hearing before the Subcommittee on Asian and Pacific Affairs. 96th Congress, first session. 12 December 1979.

Committee on Foreign Affairs. *Foreign Policy and Arms Control Implications of Chemical Weapons.* Hearings before the Subcommittees on International Security Affairs and Scientific Affairs and on Asian and Pacific Affairs. 97th Congress, second session. 30 March and 13 July 1982.

Permanent Select Committee on Intelligence. *Soviet Biological Warfare Activities.* A Report of the Subcommittee on Oversight. 96th Congress, second session. June 1980.

Permanent Select Committee on Intelligence. *The Sverdlovsk Incident: Soviet Compliance with the Biological Weapons Convention?* Hearing before the Subcommittee on Oversight. 96th Congress, second sesson. 29 May 1980.

Senate

Committee on Appropriations. *Binary Chemical Weapons.* 97th Congress, second session. 5 and 6 May 1982.

Committee on Armed Services. *Chemical Warfare.* 96th Congress, second session. 4 September 1980.

Committee on Foreign Relations. *Yellow Rain.* Hearing before the Subcommittee on Arms Control, Oceans, International Operations and Environment. 97th Congress, first session. 10 November 1981.

Committee on Foreign Relations. *Situation in Afghanistan.* 97th Congress, second session. 8 March 1982.

Committee on Foreign Relations. *Yellow Rain: The Arms Control Implications.* Hearing before the Subcommittee on Arms Control, Oceans, International Operations and Environment. 98th Congress, first session. 24 February 1983.

6 Miscellaneous Reports

American Chemical Society. *Chemical Weapons and US Public Policy: A Report of the Committee on Chemistry and Public Affairs* (Washington DC, 1977).

Asian Lawyers Legal Inquiry Committee. *Alleged Violations of Human Rights in Kampuchea and Laos.* June, 1982.

Bowman, S. R. *US Chemical Warfare Program.* Congressional Research Service. Library of Congress. Issue brief no. 1B82125, 1983.

Carpenter, W. M. (ed.) *Evaluation of Chemical Warfare Policy Alternatives 1980–1990* (Stanford Research Institute, 1977).

Comptroller-General of US General Accounting Office. Report to the Committee on Foreign Affairs House of Representatives of the United States. *Chemical Warfare: Many Unanswered Questions.* GAO/1PE–83–6, 29 April 1983.

Copson, R. W. *Yellow Rain and Related Issues: Implications for the United States.* Congressional Research Service. Library of Congress. Issue brief no. 1B82025, 10 August 1982.

Gilchrist, Col. H. L. *A Comparative Study of World War Casualties from Gas and other weapons* (Washington DC: USGPO, 1931).

McCullough, J. M. *Chemical and Biological Warfare: Issues and Developments During 1974.* Congressional Research Service. Library of Congress. Report no. 75-13-SP, 2 January 1975.

Midwest Research Institute. *Studies on the Technical Arms Control Aspects of Chemical and Biological Warfare.* 4 vols (Kansas City, Missouri, 1972).

Roberts, B. *US Chemical Warfare Readiness Program.* Congressional Research Service. Library of Congress. Issue brief no. 1B82125, 20 December 1982.

7 Books and Monographs

A Brief History of the Chemical Defence Experimental Establishment, Porton. March 1981.

Auld, Maj. S. J. M. *Gas and Flame* (New York: Doran, 1918).

Barker, A. J. *The Civilizing Mission* (New York: The Dial Press, 1968).

Bonds, R. (ed.) *The Soviet War Machine* (London: Purnell, 1977).

Brophy, L. P. and Fisher, G. J. B. *The Chemical Warfare Service: Organizing for War. United States Army in World War II: The Technical Services* (Washington DC: USGPO, 1959).

Brophy, L. P., Miles, W. D. and Cochrane, R. C. *The Chemical Warfare Service From Laboratory to Field. United States Army in World War II: The Technical Services* (Washington DC: USGPO, 1959).

Brown, F. J. *Chemical Warfare: A Study in Restraints* (Princeton: Princeton University Press, 1968).

Buckingham, W. A. *Operation Ranch Hand. The Air Force and Herbicides in Southeast Asia 1961–1971* (Washington DC: Office of Air Force History, 1982).

Chemical Weapons and Arms Control Views from Europe (Rome: Centro Di Studi Strategici, 1983).

Clark, D. K. *Effectiveness of Chemical Weapons in WW1* (Bethesda, Maryland: Operations Research Office, Johns Hopkins University, 1959).

Clark, D. K. *Effectiveness of Toxic Chemicals in the Italo-Ethiopian War* (Bethesda, Maryland: Operations Research Office, Johns Hopkins University, 1959).

Clark, R. *We All Fall Down; The Prospect of Biological and Chemical Warfare* (London: Allen Lane, 1968).

Cookson, J. and Nottingham, J. *A Survey of Chemical and Biological Warfare* (London: Sheed & Ward, 1969).

Durand, M. *Crazy Campaign: A Personal Narrative of the Italo-Abyssinian War* (London: Routledge, 1936).

Edmonds, Brig-Gen. J. E. *et al. History of the Great War: Military Operations* (London: Macmillan, 1928–47).

Evans, Grant. *The Yellow Rainmakers: Are Chemical Weapons Being Used in Southeast Asia?* (London: Verso, 1983).

Falkenhayn, Gen. E. von. *General Headquarters 1914–1916 and its Critical Decisions* (London: Hutchinson, 1919).

Foss, C. (ed.) *Jane's Armour and Artillery 1983–84* (London: Janes, 1983).

Foulkes, Maj-Gen. C. H. *'Gas!' The Story of the Special Brigade* (Edinburgh: Blackwood, 1934).

Fries, Brig-Gen. A. A. and West, Maj. C. J. *Chemical Warfare* (New York: McGraw Hill, 1921).

Fuller, Maj-Gen. J. F. C. *The Reformation of War* (London: Hutchinson, 1923).

Fuller, Maj-Gen. J. F. C. *The First of the League Wars* (London: Eyre & Spottiswoode, 1936).

Fuller, Maj-Gen. J. F. C. *The Conduct of War 1789–1961* (London: Eyre Methuen, 1972).

Gilbert, M. *Finest Hour Winston S. Churchill 1939–1941* (London: Heinemann, 1983).

Godson, R. (ed.) *Intelligence Requirements for the 1980's: Analysis and Estimates* (Washington DC: National Strategy Information Center, 1980).

Gouré, L. *War Survival in Soviet Strategy USSR Civil Defence* (University of Miami: Center for Advanced International Studies, 1976).

Haldane, J. B. S. *Callinicus – A Defence of Chemical Warfare* (London: Kegan Paul, 1925).

Hansilan, R. *Der Chemische Krieg.* 3rd ed. (Berlin, 1937).

Harris, R. and Paxman, J. *A Higher Form of Killing: The Secret Story of Gas and Germ Warfare* (London: Chatto & Windus, 1982).

Hersh, S. M. *Chemical and Biological Warfare* (New York: Bobbs-Merrill, 1968).

Hessel, F. A. *Chemistry in Warfare* (New York: Hastings House, 1940).

Hinsley, F. H. *British Intelligence in the Second World War: Its Influence on Strategy and Operations*, vol. 2 (London: HMSO, 1981).

Hoeber, A. M. *The Chemistry of Defeat: Asymmetries in US and Soviet Chemical Warfare Postures* (Cambridge, Mass: Institute for Foreign Policy Analysis, 1981).

Inter-Parliamentary Union. *What Would be the Character of a New War?* (London: Gollancz, 1933).

Kendall, J. *Breathe Freely! The Truth about Poison Gas* (London: G. Bell, 1938).

Kleber, B. and Birdsell, D. *The Chemical Warfare Service: Chemicals in combat. United States Army in World War II: The Technical Services* (Washington DC: USGPO, 1966).

Leahy, Adm. W. D. *I Was There* (London: Gollancz, 1950).

Lefebure, Maj. V. *The Riddle of the Rhine: Chemical Strategy in Peace and War* (London: Collins, 1921).

Lewy, G. *America in Vietnam* (New York: Oxford University Press, 1978).

Liddell Hart, B. H. *Paris or the Future of War* (London: Kegan Paul, 1925).

Liddell Hart, B. H. *The Remaking of Modern Armies* (London: John Murray, 1927).

Liddell Hart, B. H. *A History of the War 1914–1918* (London: Faber & Faber, 1930).

Liddell Hart, B. H. (ed.) *The Soviet Army* (London: Weidenfeld & Nicolson, 1956).

Liepman, H. *Death from the Skies: A Study of Gas and Microbial Warfare* (London: Secker & Warburg, 1937).

Lilienthal, D. E. *The Journals of David E. Lilienthal* 2 vols. (New York: Harper & Row, 1964).

Livingstone, N. A. and Douglass, J. D. *CBW: The Poor Man's Atomic Bomb* (Cambridge, Mass: Institute for Foreign Policy Analysis, 1984).

Long-hsuen, Hsu and Ming-kai, Chang. *History of the Sino-Japanese War (1937–1945)* (Taiwan, 1972).

Ludendorff, Gen. E. *My War Memories 1914–1918.* 2 vols. (London: Hutchinson, 1919).

Macfie, J. W. S. *An Ethiopian Diary. A Record of the British Ambulance Service in Ethiopia* (London: Hodder & Stoughton, 1936).

Macpherson, W. G. *et al. History of the Great War: Medical Services Diseases of War*, vol. 2 (London: HMSO, 1923).

March, Gen. P. C. *The Nation at War* (New York: Doubleday, 1932).

Martelli, G. *Italy Against the World* (London: Chatto & Windus, 1937).

Matthews, H. *Eyewitness in Abyssinia* (London: Secker & Warburg, 1937).

Meselson, M. (ed.) *Chemical Weapons and Chemical Arms Control* (New York: Carnegie Endowment for International Peace, 1978).

Miller, D. M. O., Kennedy, Col. W. V., Jordan, J. and Richardson, D. *The Balance of Military Power* (London: Salamander, 1981).

Murphy, S., Hay, A. and Rose, S. *No Fire No Thunder* (London: Pluto Press, 1984).

Neilands, J. B. *et al. Harvest of Death: Chemical Warfare in Vietnam and Cambodia* (New York: Free Press, 1972).

Nelson, K. and Sullivan, A. (ed.) *John Melly of Ethiopia* (London: Faber & Faber, 1937).

Noel-Baker, P. *Disarmament* (London: Hogarth Press, 1926).

Noel-Baker, P. *The First World Disarmament Conference 1932–33* (Oxford: Pergamon Press, 1979).

O'Brien, T. *Civil Defence* (London: HMSO, 1955).

Ochsner, H. *History of German Chemical Warfare in World War II: Part 1, The Military Aspect* (Historical Office of the Chief of the Chemical Corps, 1949).

Peterson, H. C. *Propaganda for War* (New York: Kennikat Press, 1968).

Petty, R. T. (ed.) *Jane's Weapon Systems 1983–84* (London: Janes, 1983).

Prentiss, A. M. *Chemicals in War: A Treatise on Chemical Warfare* (New York: McGraw-Hill, 1937).

Read, J. M. *Atrocity Propaganda 1914–1919* (New Haven: Yale University Press, 1941).

Riegelman, H. *Caves of Biak* (New York: Dial Press, 1955).

Robinson, J. P. P. *The United States Binary Nerve Gas Programme: National and International Implications.* ISIO monographs. First series, no. 10, 1975.

Rose, S. (ed.) *CBW Chemical and Biological Warfare* (London: Harrap, 1968).

Rothschild, Brig-Gen. J. H. *Tomorrow's Weapons* (New York: McGraw-Hill, 1964).

Russell Committee Against Chemical Weapons. *The Threat of Chemical Weapons* (Nottingham: Russell Press, 1982).

Salerno, E. *Genocidio in Libia* (Milan, 1979).

Sartori, M. *The War Gases: Chemistry and Analysis* (London: Churchill, 1939).

Savkin, V. Ye. *The Basic Principles of Operational Art and Tactics*, translated by the US Air Force (Washington DC: USGPO, 1972).

Schmidt, D. A. *Yemen: The Unknown War* (London: The Bodley Head, 1968).

Scott, H. F. (ed.) *Soviet Military Strategy* (London: Macdonald & Janes, 1975).

Seagrave, S. *Yellow Rain* (London: Sphere Books, 1981).

Sims, N. A. *Approaches to Disarmament* (London: Quaker Peace & Service, 1979).

Smith, D. Mack. *Mussolini's Roman Empire* (London: Penguin, 1977).

Smith, D. Mack. *Mussolini* (London: Weidenfeld & Nicolson, 1981).

Snow, E. *Scorched Earth* (London: Gollancz, 1941).

Speer, A. *Inside The Third Reich* (London: Weidenfeld & Nicolson, 1970).

Steer, G. L. *Caesar in Abyssinia* (London: Hodder & Stoughton, 1936).

Stockholm International Peace Research Institute. *The Problem of Chemical and Biological Warfare*, Volume 1 The Use of CB Weapons. 1971. Volume 2. CB Weapons Today. 1973. volume 3. CBW and the Laws of War. 1973. Volume 4. CB Disarmament Negotiations, 1920–70. 1971. Volume 5. The Prevention of CBW. 1971. Volume 6. Technical Aspects of Early Warning and Verification. 1975.

Stockholm International Peace Research Institute. *Chemical Disarmament: Some Problems of Verification* (Stockholm, 1973).

Stockholm International Peace Research Institute. *Delayed Toxic Effects of Chemical Warfare Agents* (Stockholm: Almqvist & Wiksell, 1975).

Stockholm International Peace Research Institute. *Chemical Weapons: Destruction and Conversion* (London: Taylor & Francis, 1980).

Stockholm International Peace Research Institute. *World Armaments and Disarmament: SIPRI Yearbook 1982* (London: Taylor & Francis, 1982).

Storella, M. C. *Poisoning Arms Control: The Soviet Union and Chemical/Biological Weapons* (Cambridge, Mass: Institute for Foreign Policy Analysis, 1984).

United Nations. *The United Nations and Disarmament 1945–1970* (New York: United Nations, 1970).

United Nations. *The United Nations Disarmament Yearbook*. 6 vols. (New York: United Nations, 1976–82).

Utley, F. *China at War* (London: Faber & Faber, 1939).

Wachtel, C. *Chemical Warfare* (New York: Chemical Publishing, 1941).

Waitt, Brig-Gen. A. H. *Gas Warfare: The Chemical Weapon Its Use and Protection Against It* (New York: Duell, Sloan & Pearce, 1942).

Winter, D. *Death's Men: Soldiers of the Great War* (London: Penguin, 1978).

Yost, D. S. (ed.) *NATO's Strategic Options Arms Control and Defense* (New York: Pergamon Press, 1981).

8 Articles and Lectures

Adams, V. J. 'The Abolition of Chemical Weapons', *Arms Control and Disarmament*, vol. 4, no. 2, September, 1983.

Auld, Capt. S. J. M. 'Chemical Warfare', *The Royal Engineers Journal*, February, 1921.

Bagwax. 'Chemical Weapons: Time for a Fresh Look', *British Army Review*, no. 67, April, 1981.

Bambini, Maj. A. P. 'Chemical Warfare', *Military Review*, vol. LXI, no. 4, April, 1981.

Barnaby, F. 'CBW – An Unresolved Horror', *The Bulletin of Atomic Scientists*, vol. 36, no. 6, June, 1980.

Bartley, R. L. and Kucewicz, W. P. '"Yellow Rain" and the Future of Arms Agreements', *Foreign Affairs*, vol. 61, no. 4, Spring 1983.

Bay, A. 'Chemical Warfare: Perspectives and Potentials', *Strategy and Tactics*, July–August, 1980.

Bay, Col. C. H. 'Chemical Warfare and the Military Balance', *Parameters*, vol. 7, no. 2, 1977.

Bay, Col. C. H. 'The Other Gas Crisis – Chemical Weapons', *Parameters*, vol. 9, no. 3, September, 1979; and no. 4, December, 1979.

Bay, G. A. 'Defense Against Chemical Attack', *Armor*, vol. 87, part 3, May–June, 1982.

Benz, K. G. 'NBC Defense – An Overview, Part 1: Protection Equipment', *International Defense Review*, vol. 16, no. 12, December, 1983.

Benz, K. G. 'NBC Defense – An Overview, Part 2: Detection and Decontamination', *International Defense Review*, vol. 17, no. 2, February, 1984.

'British equipment for NBC defence', *Defence Materiel*, March–April, 1981.

Brosnan, Maj. J. F. 'A Case for Marine Corps Chemical Warfare Readiness', *United States Naval Institute Proceedings*, vol. 105, no. 11, November, 1979.

Buckingham, W. A. 'Operation Ranch Hand: Herbicides in Southeast Asia', *Air University Review*, vol. XXXIII, no. 5, July–August, 1983.

Budiansky, S. 'Softening of US Charges', *Nature*, vol. 308, 1 March 1984.

Carlton D. and Sims, N. A. 'The CS Gas Controversy: Great Britain and the Geneva Protocol of 1925', *Survival*, vol. 13, 1971.

Carter, G. B. 'Is Biotechnology Feeding the Russians?', *New Scientist*, 23 April 1981.

Chayes, A. 'An Inquiry into the Workings of Arms Control Agreements', *Harvard Law Review*, vol. 85, no. 5, March, 1972.

'Chemische Waffen in Warschauer Pakt', *Soldat und Technik*, no. 9, 1970.

Clarke, K. and Turnbull, J. H. 'The Chemical Battlefield, Part One: The Soviet Threat', *Defence*, vol. XV, no. 3, March, 1984.

Clarke, K. and Turnbull, J. H. 'The Chemical Battlefield, Part Two: Equipment for Protection', *Defence*, vol. XV, no. 7, July, 1984.

Clarke, K. and Turnbull, J. H. 'The Chemical Battlefield, Part Three: Equipment for Protection', *Defence*, vol. XV, no. 9, September, 1984.

Coggins, Rear Adm. C. H. 'Is Russia Outstripping us in Weapons of Mass Destruction?', *Armed Forces Chemical Journal*, vol. 17, no. 3, 1963.

Davidson, Maj. C. J. 'Situation Report on Chemical Weapons', *Journal of the Royal United Services Institute for Defence Studies*, vol. 125, no. 2, June, 1980.

Dick, C. J. 'Soviet Chemical Warfare Capabilities', *International Defense Review*, vol. 14, no. 1, 1981.

Dick, C. J. 'The Soviet Chemical and Biological Warfare Threat', *Journal of Royal United Services Institute for Defence Studies*, vol. 126, no. 1, March, 1981.

Dirnhuber, P. and Green, D. M. 'Effectiveness of Pyridostigmine in Reversing Neuromuscular Blockade Produced by Soman', *Journal of Pharmacy and Pharmacology*, vol. 30, 1978.

Ditzian, J. L. 'Designing for the NBC Environment', *National Defense*, May, 1984.

Dodd, N. L. 'Chemical Warfare and the Defence Precautions Available Against Them', *Defence Materiel*, vol. 1, part 3, 1976.

Dodd, N. L. 'Chemical Defense Equipment', *Military Review*, vol. LVII, no. 11, November 1977.

Dodson, C. A. 'The Case for CBR', *Army*, vol. 12, no. 1, 1961.

Donnelly, C. N. 'Winning the NBC War. Soviet Army Theory and Practice', *International Defense Review*, vol. 14, no. 8, 1981.

Douglass, J. D. 'Chemical Weapons: An Imbalance of Terror', *Strategic Review*, vol. 10, no. 3, Summer, 1982.

Eifried, Lt-Col. G. 'Russian CW Our Achilles Heel, Europe', *Army*, vol. 29, December, 1979.

Ember, L. R. 'Chemical Weapons: Build up or Disarm?', *Chemical and Engineering News*, 15 December 1980.

Ember, L. R. 'Yellow Rain', *Chemical and Engineering News*, 9 January 1984.

Erickson, J. 'Soviet Military Capabilities', *Current History*, vol. 71, no. 420, October, 1976.

Erickson, J. 'The Soviet Union's Growing Arsenal of Chemical Warfare', *Strategic Review*, vol. 7, no. 4, Fall, 1979.

Ewing, R. H. 'The Legality of Chemical Warfare', *American Law Review*, vol. 61, January–February, 1927.

Finan, J. S. 'Soviet Interest in and Possible Tactical Use of Chemical Weapons', *Canadian Defence Quarterly*, vol. 4, no. 2, 1974.

Flowerree, C. C. 'Chemical Weapons: A Case Study in Verification', *Arms Control Today*, vol. 13, no. 3, April, 1983.

Flowerree, C. C. 'The Politics of Arms Control Treaties: A Case Study', *Journal of International Affairs*, vol. 37, no. 2, Winter, 1983–4.

Foulkes, Maj-Gen. C. H. 'Chemical Warfare in 1915', *Armed Forces Chemical Journal*, vol. 15, no. 6, 1961.

Fritz, B. 'A New NBC Clothing Concept from France', *International Defense Review*, vol. 15, no. 11, November, 1982.

Fritz, B. 'The AMF 30 Modular NBC Shelter', *International Defense Review*, vol. 15, no. 11, November, 1982.

Ganas, P. 'Nouveaux Développements en Guerre Chimique et Biologique', *Forces Aériennes Françaises*, vol. 24, 1969.

Gander, T. J. 'Decocontain: Advanced NBC Protection', *Jane's Defence Weekly*, vol. 4, 4 February 1984.

Gander, T. J. 'Some Recent Trends in NBC Defence Equipment', *Jane's Defence Weekly*, vol. 4, 4 February 1984.

Gibbs, Lt. L. D. 'CBR: What are we waiting for?', *Infantry*, vol. 68, no. 4, July–August, 1978.

Gold, T. S. 'US Chemical Warfare Policy and Program', *NATO's Sixteen Nations*, vol. 28, no. 1, February–March, 1983.

Graveley, Sq. Ldr. A. F. 'The Voices of Experience: Learning for the Future from the Chemical War of 1915–1918', *The Army Quarterly and Defence Journal*, vol. 110, no. 4, October, 1980.

Graveley, Sq. Ldr. A. F. 'Defence or Deterrence? The Case for Chemical Weapons', *Journal of the Royal United Services Institute for Defence Studies*, vol. 126, no. 4, December, 1981.

Gundel, H. 'The Case for CB Weapons', *Ordnance*, vol. 47, January–February, 1963.

Haber, L. F. 'Gas Warfare 1915–1945. The Legend and the Facts', Stevenson Lecture, 1976.

Hall, Maj. S. C. 'Air Base Survivability in Europe', *Air University Review*, vol. XXXIII, no. 6, September–October, 1982.

Harris, B. L. 'Chemical Warfare – A Primer', *CHEMTECH*, vol. 12, January, 1982.

Harris, B. L. 'Skin-Penetrating Incapacitants: A Credible Deterrent?', *Military Review*, vol. LXII, no. 3, March, 1982.

Harris, P. 'British Preparations for Offensive Chemical Warfare 1935–39', *Journal of the Royal United Services Institute for Defence Studies*, vol. 125, no. 2, June, 1980.

Hay, A., Murphy, S., Rose, S. and Perry Robinson, J. P. 'Chemical Warfare in the Eighties', *Journal of the Medical Association for Prevention of War*, Autumn, 1982.

Henry, Maj. B. C. 'It's Time to face the Reality of Chemical Warfare', *Marine Corps Gazette*, March, 1979.

Hoeber, A. M. and Douglass, J. D. 'The Neglected Threat of Chemical Warfare', *International Security*, vol. 3, no. 1, Summer, 1978.

Iklé, F. C. 'After Detection – What?', *Foreign Affairs*, vol. 39, no. 2, January, 1961.

Kalven, J. '"Yellow Rain": the public evidence', *The Bulletin of Atomic Scientists*, vol. 38, no. 5, May, 1982.

Kyle, D. M. 'Chemical Warfare', *Armed Forces Journal International*, vol. 119, November, 1981.

Lefebure, Maj. V. 'Chemical Warfare: The Possibility of Its Control', *Transactions of the Grotius Society*, vol. VII, 1921.

Lefebure, Maj. V. 'Chemical Disarmament', *The National Review*, vol. LXXVIII, September 1921–February 1922.

Lenorovitz, J. M. 'USAF Improving Defenses Against Chemical Threat', *Aviation Week and Space Technology*, 19 May 1980.

Lepkowski, W. 'Chemical Warfare: One of the Dilemmas of the Arms Race', *Chemical and Engineering News*, 2 January 1978.

Lovelace, Lt-Col. G. M. 'Chemical Warfare', *NATO's Fifteen Nations*, vol. 26, no. 6, December 1981–January 1982.

Lundin, J. 'The Scope and Control of Chemical Disarmament Treaties Particularly With Regard to Binary Chemical Weapons', *Co-operation and Conflict*, vol. 8. nos. 3/4, 1973.

Malooley, Lt-Col. R. S. 'Gas is Not a Dirty Word in the Soviet Army', *Army*, vol. 24, September, 1974.

Margeride, J-Baptiste. 'Le Problème De La Guerre Chimique', *Stratégique*, no. 2, 1982; and no. 3, 1983.

Marriot, J. 'Chemical & Biological Warfare', *International Defense Review*, vol. 1, 1969.

Marriot, J. 'Chemical Warfare', *Defence*, September, 1972.

Marriot, J. 'Chemical Warfare', *NATO's Fifteen Nations*, vol. 22, no. 3, 1977.

Marshall, E. 'Yellow Rain: Filling in the Gaps', *Science*, vol. 217, 2 July 1982.

Marshall, E. 'The Apology of Yellow Rain', *Science*, vol. 221, 15 July 1983.

Medvedev, Z. 'The Great Russian Germ War Fiasco', *The New Scientist*, 31 July 1980.

Meselson, M. and Perry Robinson, J. P. 'Chemical Warfare and Chemical Disarmament', *Scientific American*, vol. 242, no. 4, April, 1980.

Meselson, M. *et al*. 'Origin of Yellow Rain', *Science*, vol. 222, 28 October 1983.

Miettinen, J. K. 'Chemical Warfare and Arms Control Crisis and Concern', *Bulletin of Peace Proposals*, vol. 114, no. 3, 1983.

Miles, W. D. 'I: Admiral Cochrane's Plans for Chemical Warfare; II: The Chemical Shells of Lyon Playfair', *Armed Forces Chemical Journal*, vol. 11, no. 6, 1957.

Miles, W. D. 'The Idea of Chemical Warfare in Modern Times', *Journal of the History of Ideas*, vol. 31, April–June, 1970.

Moon, J. E. van Courtland. 'Chemical Weapons and Deterrence: The World War II Experience', *International Security*, vol. 8, no. 4, Spring, 1984.

'Moscow's Poison War: Mounting Evidence of Battlefield Atrocities', *Backgrounder*, no. 165, 5 February 1982.

Murphy, Maj. P. 'Gas in the Italo–Abyssinian campaign', *Chemical Warfare Bulletin*, vol. 23, no. 1, January, 1937.

Nerlich, U. 'Die Bedeutung chemischer Kampfmittel für die Verteidigungskonzeption 1980–90 aus der Sicht der Bundesrepublik Deutschland', *Europäische Wehrkunde*, vol. 26, no. 7, July, 1977.

Norwicke, J. W. and Meselson, M. 'Yellow Rain – A Palynological Analysis', *Nature*, vol. 309, 18 May 1984.

'Old Fears, New Weapons: Brewing A Chemical Arms Race', *The Defense Monitor*, vol. IX, no. 10, 1980.

Oulton, Sq. Ldr. P. D. 'Is There a Case for Chemical and Biological Warfare?', *British Army Review*, no. 4, 1973.

Parker, Lt-Col. D. M. 'Facing the NBC Environment', *Military Review*, vol. 54, no. 5, May, 1974.

Paxman, J. 'Poison Gas: A Higher Form of Killing', *The Listener*, vol. 103, 5 June 1980.

Polmar, N. and Friedman, N. 'Their Missions and Tactics', *United States Naval Institute Proceedings*, vol. 108, no. 10, October, 1982.

Poole, J. B. 'A Sword Undrawn: Chemical Warfare and the Victorian Age, Part I', *The Army Quarterly and Defence Journal*, vol. 106, no. 4, October, 1976; and Part II, vol. 107, no. 1, January, 1977.

Raymond, Maj. N. V. 'Is USAFE Ready for Chemical Warfare', *Air Force Magazine*, November, 1979.

Richardson, M. 'Chemical Warfare: The Case Against the Soviet Union', *Pacific Defence Reporter*, September 1982.

Robinson, J. P. P. 'Chemical Warfare', *Science Journal*, vol. 3, no. 4, April, 1967.

Robinson, J. P. P. 'The Special Case of Chemical and Biological Weapons', *The Bulletin of Atomic Scientists*, vol. 31, no. 5, May, 1975.

Robinson, J. P. P. 'Chemical and Biological Warfare: Analysis of Recent Reports Concerning The Soviet Union and Vietnam', *Armament and Disarmament Information Unit (ADIU) Occasional Paper*, no. 1, March, 1980.

Robinson, J. P. P. 'The Negotiations on Chemical Warfare Arms Control', *Arms Control*, vol. 1, no. 1, May, 1980.

Robinson, J. P. P. 'Chemical Arms Control and the Assimilation of Chemical Weapons', *International Journal*, vol. XXXVI, no. 3, Summer, 1981.

Robinson, J. P. P. 'Chemical Weapons and Europe', *Survival*, vol. 24, January–February, 1982.

Robinson, J. P. P. 'Discussion of "The Soviet Union and the Biological Weapons Convention", and a Guide to Sources on the Sverdlovsk Incident', *Arms Control*, vol. 3, no. 3, December, 1982.

Robinson, J. P. P. 'Recent Developments in the Field of Chemical Warfare', *Royal United Services Institute and Brassey's Defence Yearbook 1983* (London: Brassey's, 1983).

Rosser-Owen, D. 'NBC Warfare and Anti-NBC Protection', *Armada International*, no. 1, 1984.

Ruhle, H. 'Chemische Waffen und europäische Sicherheit 1980–1990', *Europäische Wehrkunde*, vol. 27, no. 1, January, 1978.

Sbacchi, A. 'Legacy of Bitterness: Poison Gas and Atrocities in the Italo-Ethiopian War 1935–36', *Geneva–Africa*, vol. XIII, no. 2, 1974.

Scammell, J. M. 'The Outlawry of Poison Gases in Warfare', *Current History*, vol. 30, June, 1929.

Schiefer, H. B. 'The Possible Use of Chemical Warfare Agents in Southeast Asia', *Conflict Quarterly*, Winter, 1983.

Senior, J. K. 'The Manufacture of Mustard Gas in World War I', *Armed Forces Chemical Journal*, vol. 12, no. 5, 1958.

Sims, N. A. 'Britain, Chemical Weapons and Disarmament', *ADIU Report*, vol. 2, no. 3, July–August, 1980.

Sims, N. A. 'Mycotoxins and Arms Control', *ADIU Report*, vol. 3, no. 6, November–December, 1981.

Sims, N. A. 'Chemical Weapons – Control or Chaos?', *Faraday Discussion Paper No. 1*, The Council for Arms Control, 1984.

'Soviet Military Power: Questions and Answers', *The Defense Monitor*, vol. XI, no. 1, 1982.

Spiers, E. M. 'Gas and the North-West Frontier', *The Journal of Strategic Studies*, vol. 6, no. 4, December, 1983.

Stelzmüller, H. 'NBC Defense a German Viewpoint', *International Defense Review*, vol. 15, no. 11, November, 1982.

Stevenson, R. 'Chemical Warfare: A History of Horror', *Chemistry in Britain*, vol. 19, no. 4, April, 1983.

Stewart, Lt-Col. J. A. 'REME in a Chemical War', *Journal of The Royal Electrical and Mechanical Engineers*, no. 4, 1979.

Stubbs, M. 'CBR and the Army Reorganization', *Armed Forces Chemical Journal*, vol. 17, no. 3, 1963.

Summerhayes, D. 'Chemical Weapons: Postures, Plans and Prospects for Control', *ADIU Report*, vol. 5, no. 6, November–December, 1983.

Tannor, B. 'C ml C Intelligence in European theater', *Chemical Corps Journal*, vol. 1, no. 3, 1947.

'The quiet comeback of chemical warfare', *Chemical Week*, vol. 129, no. 8, 19 August 1981.

Tower, J. 'The Politics of Chemical Deterrence', *The Washington Quarterly*, Spring, 1982.

Towle, P. 'The Soviet Union and the Biological Weapons Convention', *Arms Control*, vol. 3, no. 3, December, 1982.

Tritten, Commander J. J. 'Their Broken Promises', *United States Naval Institute Proceedings*, vol. 110, no. 8, August, 1984.

Trumpener, U. 'The Road to Ypres: The Beginnings of Gas Warfare in World War I', *Journal of Modern History*, vol. 47, September, 1975.

Ulsamer, E. 'Airpower – NATO's Foremost Deterrent', *Air Force Magazine*, April, 1978.

Vachon, G. K. 'Chemical Disarmament – A Regional Initiative', *Millenium*, vol. 8, no. 2, 1979.

Vachon, G. K. 'Chemical Weapons and the Third World', *Survival*, vol. 26, no. 2, March–April, 1984.

Vicary, Col. A. G. and Wilson, Wing Commander, J., 'Nuclear Biological and Chemical Defence', *Journal of the Royal United Services Institute for Defence Studies*, vol. 126, no. 4, December, 1981.

Vinet, E. 'La Guerre des Gaz et les travaux des services chimiques françaises', *Chimie & Industrie*, vol. 12, nos. 11–12, December, 1919.

Wade, N. 'Toxin Warfare Charges May Be Premature', *Science*, vol. 214, 2 October 1981.

Wade, N. 'Yellow Rain and the Cloud of Chemical War', *Science*, vol. 214, 27 November 1981.

Wagner, R. L. and Gold, T. S. 'Why We Can't Avoid Developing Chemical Weapons', *Defense 82*, July, 1982.

Watson, Brig-Gen. G. G. and Anderson, Lt-Col. P. R. L. 'An Urgent Need: Stockpiling Modern Chemical Munitions', *Military Review*, vol. 54, no. 1, January, 1984.

Index